GERTRUD JARON LEWIS

By Women, for Women, about Women
The Sister-Books of Fourteenth-Century Germany

The late medieval Sister-Books are works authored by women. This first-ever comprehensive study of these writings is based both on the published texts and on all known manuscripts. The Sister-Books, some composed in Latin, others in Middle High German, were written by Dominican nuns in the German-speaking countries during the first half of the fourteenth century.

This study discusses the authors, their relationship to their intended audience of monastic women, their particular style of writing, and the special genre of this unique literary corpus. The Sister-Books depict women 'in the world' in complex social situations and present nuns in their various relationships to the clergy and to each other. These women understand monastic life as an opportunity for sanctification and spiritual growth through spiritual and ascetic exercises. In speaking of visions, heavenly voices, and other miracles, the authors also participate in the theological discussions of their time. The humanity of Christ and an *imitatio Christi,* the Trinity and the Eucharist, are all issues of great concern to them.

The rhetorical approach to these women's writings is here successfully combined with a feminist perspective that proves indispensable for getting to the core of the texts. The hagiographic cast of these narratives cannot diminish the particularity and the authenticity of the images of late medieval women that they reveal.

The special fascination of the Sister-Books lies in the voice of women themselves writing about women and speaking their problems, joys, and suffering, specifically to other women. This study will be welcomed by readers interested in women's studies, medieval literature, social history, and the history of piety.

Texts of eight of the nine Sister-Books (comprising some 473 pages) are provided on microfiche.

GERTRUD JARON LEWIS is a professor of German. Her research and publications have long been devoted to medieval German women authors. She discovered a previously unknown manuscript of the Adelhausen Sister-Book. She translated with Jack Lewis Gertrud von Helfta's *Spiritual Exercises* into English, and is the author of the important *Bibliographie zur deutschen Frauenmystik des Mittelalters.*

BX 4220.G2 LEW

STUDIES AND TEXTS 125

By Women, for Women, about Women

The Sister-Books of Fourteenth-Century Germany

GERTRUD JARON LEWIS

PONTIFICAL INSTITUTE OF MEDIAEVAL STUDIES

ACKNOWLEDGMENTS

Research for the volume was made possible through generous grants provided by the Social Sciences and Humanities Research Council of Canada. This book has been published with the help of a grant from the Canadian Federation for the Humanities, using funds provided by the Social Sciences and Humanities Research Council of Canada.

CANADIAN CATALOGUING IN PUBLICATION DATA

Lewis, Gertrud Jaron
By women, for women, about women :
the Sister-Books of fourteenth-century Germany

(Studies and texts, ISSN 0082–5238 ; 125)
Includes bibliographical references and index.
ISBN 0–88844–125–8

1. Christian literature, German –
Women authors – History and criticism.
2. Christian literature, Latin (Medieval and modern) –
Women authors – History and criticism.
3. Christian literature, Latin (Medieval and modern) –
Germany – History and criticism.
4. German literature – Middle High German, 1050–1500 –
History and criticism.
5. Nuns in literature. 6. Nuns as authors.
7. Dominican sisters – Germany – History.

I. Pontifical Institute of Mediaeval Studies. II. Title.
III. Series: Studies and texts
(Pontifical Institute of Mediaeval Studies) ; 125

PT179.L48 1996   830.9′9287′09023   C95–933274-X

Printed by
Edwards Brothers Incorporated, Michigan, USA

Pontifical Institute of Mediaeval Studies
59 Queen's Park Crescent East
Toronto, Ontario, Canada M5S 2C4

To the memory of

JACK LEWIS
1929–1993

Contents

Texts reproduced on microfiche

FICHE 1   *see endpapers*

[Adelhausen Sister-Book.] 1880. "Die Chronik der Anna von Munzingen. Nach der ältesten Abschrift mit Einleitung und Beilagen." Ed. J. König. *Freiburger Diözesan Archiv* 13:129–236 [153–189].

[Engeltal Sister-Book.] 1871. *Der Nonne von Engeltal Büchlein von der Genaden Uberlast.* Litterarischer Verein in Stuttgart. Ed. Karl Schröder. Tübingen [Pp. 1–44].

[Gotteszell Sister-Book.] 1893. "Aufzeichnungen über das mystische Leben der Nonnen von Kirchberg bei Sulz Predigerordens während des XIV. und XV. Jahrhunderts." Ed. F.W.E. Roth. *Alemannia* 21:123–148.

[Kirchberg Sister-Book.] 1893. "Aufzeichnungen über das mystische Leben der Nonnen von Kirchberg bei Sulz Predigerordens während des XIV. und XV. Jahrhunderts." Ed. F.W.E.Roth. *Alemannia* 21:103–123 [104–123].

[Oetenbach Sister-Book.] 1889. "Die Stiftung des Klosters Oetenbach und das Leben der seligen Schwestern daselbst, aus der Nürnberger Handschrift." Ed. H. Zeller-Werdmüller and Jakob Bächtold. *Zürcher Taschenbuch* n.s. 12:213–276 [217–276].

FICHE 2   *see endpapers*

[Töss Sister-Book.] 1906. *Das Leben der Schwestern zu Töss beschrieben von Elsbet Stagel, samt der Vorrede des Johannes Meyer und dem Leben der Prinzessin Elisabet von Ungarn.* Ed. Ferdinand Vetter. Deutsche Texte des Mittelalters 6. Berlin: Weidmann [Pp. 12–95].

[Unterlinden Sister-Book.] 1930. "Les *vitae sororum d'Unterlinden.* Edition critique du manuscrit 508 de la Bibliothèque de Colmar." Ed. Jeanne Ancelet-Hustache. *Archives d'Histoire Doctrinale et Littéraire du Moyen Age* 5:317–517 [335–509].

[Weiler Sister-Book.] 1916. "Mystisches Leben in dem Dominikanerinnenkloster Weiler bei Eßlingen im 13. und 14. Jahrhundert." Ed. Karl Bihlmeyer. *Württembergische Vierteljahreshefte für Landesgeschichte,* n.s. 25:61–93 [68–85].

Illustrations

Abbreviations

A	The Adelhausen Sister-Book
AfdA	*Anzeiger für deutsches Altertum und deutsche Literatur*
CF	Christian Fathers Series
CS	Cistercian Studies Series
D	The Diessenhofen Sister-Book
DictTheol.	*Dictionary of Theology,* ed. Karl Rahner et al.
DSp.	*Dictionnaire de spiritualité ascétique et mystique, doctrine et histoire*
DTC	*Dictionnaire de théologie catholique*
DVJS	*Deutsche Vierteljahrsschrift für Literaturwissenschaft und Geistesgeschichte*
E	The Engeltal Sister-Book
EDR	*Encyclopedic Dictionary of Religion*
FDA	*Freiburger Diözesan-Archiv*
G	The Gotteszell Sister-Book
GAG	Göppinger Arbeiten zur Germanistik
K	The Kirchberg Sister-Book
LexMA	*Lexikon des Mittelalters*
LThK	*Lexikon für Theologie und Kirche*
MHG	Middle High German
NCE	*New Catholic Encyclopedia*
NEB	*New Encyclopedia Britannica*
O	The Oetenbach Sister-Book
OGE	*Ons geestelijk erf*
PL	*Patrologiae cursus completus, series latina,* ed. J.P. Migne
PMLA	*Publications of the Modern Language Association of America*
QFGD	Quellen und Forschungen zur Geschichte des Dominikanerordens in Deutschland
RB	*The Rule of St. Benedict 1980*
STh	*Summa Theologiae* (Thomas Aquinas)
T	The Töss Sister-Book
U	The Unterlinden Sister-Book
Verflex.	*Die deutsche Literatur des Mittelalters-Verfasserlexikon*
W	The Weiler Sister-Book
WbM	*Wörterbuch der Mystik,* ed. Peter Dinzelbacher
ZfdA	*Zeitschrift für deutsches Altertum und deutsche Literatur*
ZfdPh	*Zeitschrift für deutsche Philologie*

Women have a say in this book. The Sister-Books, a collection of texts written by female authors in Dominican communities of fourteenth-century Germany, provide further proof (if proof is needed) that medieval women did raise their voices and did so directly through their own literary medium. The authors of these books deliberately and confidently entrusted their thoughts to what one of them calls "the monument of letters." Yet the task of making "the mute women" of the Middle Ages speak, a task central to much historical study, is no less relevant to the authors of these *Nonnenbücher* or *Schwesternbücher*; for even after they had spoken out, they were silenced by centuries of virtual neglect.

With the exception of a handful of academic writers, the larger interested audience in English-speaking countries has remained unaware of the late medieval Sister-Books. The texts (in Latin and Middle High German) have been all but inaccessible, and translations (with the exception of a few excerpts) have not been available. Indeed, until not too long ago (roughly the 1970s), these works have been the object of scholarly prejudice and misinterpretation.

This study aims to draw greater attention to the Sister-Books and to help clarify some misconceptions concerning them. I have made an attempt to integrate, as far as it is relevant, the research of other scholars, to many of whom I am deeply indebted. My main intention, however, is to lead the reader directly to the texts. This has often meant extensive quotation from the Sister-Books themselves. All translations are mine, and I have tried to stay as close to the original as possible, even risking at times a certain stylistic awkwardness. But although translation inevitably loses much of the charm and freshness of the Middle High German, it seems a risk worth taking in order to familiarize the reader with these writings. It is by no means my intention to present the Sister-Books as accomplished literary masterpieces just because they were written by women. Nevertheless, this study of late medieval women's writings should provide new perspectives on the history of ideas. Furthermore, I hope to encourage others to work on critical editions so that accessible English translations can then be produced.

Throughout this study I have treated the Sister-Books as works of literature, not, as has been the case in the past, solely as historical document, or cultural reportage, or theological treatises. Still, we ought to remember that they did not come about in a vacuum. The Sister-Books are literary works which are nevertheless embedded in historical fact, in the life of actual monastic communities in southern German-speaking countries at a critical period of the late Middle Ages. The texts portray women and aspects of their lives; they also show their theological concerns and their spiritual aspiration. The texts are a reflection of historical realities we can no longer grasp in all their detail; but their literary expression allows us to discern something of the images of a lived reality. These works are also steeped in the tradition of medieval legend. The authors deliberately cater to the readers' expectations, often interpolating the miracle stories and visions to which a medieval audience had become accustomed.

The chapters of this book attempt to bring out the complex issues underlying this *corpus*. Introductory historical background notes point to its *Sitz im Leben*. Chapter 1 deals with the specifics of the nine different texts, their individual authors, and their places of origin. Chapter 2 provides a textual analysis that reveals the authors' familiarity with the guiding rules of rhetoric, and that establishes the Sister-Books as a genre of their own. A survey of the reception of the Sister-Books through the centuries yields a typical pattern of how women's writings have often been received. This third chapter amply shows why a feminist approach to these texts is essential: in many cases scholars, up to the last quarter of the twentieth century, did not take the authors of the Sister-Books seriously.

The *karismata* and visions of the Sister-Books have traditionally been the source of the critics' deepest scorn. Rhetorical methodology enables us to look behind the legendary patterns. And a survey of the kinds of charisms and visions (and visionary contents) helps us gain an insight into the scope of these women's world.

Chapter 5 discusses these women's manifold spiritual and theological concerns revealing that the issues raised do not differ much from those common to contemporary intellectual and theological questions and values. However, their approach to understanding the divine mystery complements in many instances the book knowledge of the "learned masters." The following chapter, therefore, discusses the relationship between the men of the Order of Preachers and these Dominican women, presenting the much debated *cura monialium* issue as seen from the women's point of view.

Below the hagiographic veneer, as it were, the Sister-Books permit the reader a number of socio-cultural insights into the lives of women both in the world and the cloister. These texts are among the rare sources of first-hand descriptions of women by women themselves. Especially the cloistered life is described in some detail by those who spent their life living it. One aspect of their monastic life seems among the most important to these Dominican women: the ideal of learnedness is upheld throughout these books. The final chapter, therefore, looks at the nuns' intellectual striving as depicted in the Sister-Books.

The study finishes with a short epilogue (instead of a conclusion) on the image of women. It is an attempt to bring together the many facets of such an image that a close reading of the texts has yielded. And while our findings cannot be applied to *the* medieval woman, the Sister-Books offer some examples of self-confident, intelligent, saintly women. These images of strong women have for a long time been suppressed in our secular and church history. Many more need to be uncovered. Perhaps this study can play a small role in the continuing process of rehabilitating our forebears in history.

Any study in the medieval period is likely to cross the boundaries of several disciplines. As a student of literature I have also had to deal with art, history, monasticism, theology, among other subjects, in order to do justice to these texts. And I could not have done it alone. It is impossible to name all those to whom I am indebted. Many colleagues have contributed indirectly through stimulating discussions during annual meetings of medievalists at Kalamazoo. My thanks also to numerous librarians and archivists in European monasteries and municipal and university libraries who kindly gave me access to manuscript material (see Appendix). I am also grateful to the Library of the Pontifical Institute of Mediaeval Studies in Toronto and to Laurentian University's Interlibrary Loan Services. I can single out only a few friends and family members who offered to read some earlier version of my manuscript (or parts thereof) and helped generously with scrutinizing my translations and writing, preventing me from committing major blunders (in monastic vocabulary, for example), helping to bring new and relevant publications to my attention, and more. Special thanks to Jane Enkin, Elisabeth Gössmann, Gisela Hoffmann, Margarete Klar, Jack Lewis, Justin Lewis, Suzanne Noffke OP, Marilyn Orr, Josef Schmidt, Debra L. Stoudt, and most of all to Mary Norton from whose careful editorial advice I greatly benefitted. Needless to say, however, full responsibility for the end result lies with me alone.

Finally, my deep gratitude goes to The Social Sciences and Humanities Research Council of Canada for funding a study trip to Europe to locate and study the manuscripts and for granting a two-year relief from teaching in cooperation with Laurentian University. Without the extra time provided by this generous grant, this book would still have been only a note in my file of "things to be done."

Nine different texts, composed during the first half of the fourteenth century, make up the body of literature known as the Sister-Books. *Nonnenbücher* or *Schwesternbücher* is the term conventionally used for these writings in German literary history. Traditionally each one of these texts has been identified by the place name of the individual monastery's site or by the monastery's name. Each text deals with one particular community of the so-called Second Order within the Order of Preachers, that is, the cloistered women of the Dominican Order. The term 'monastery' is used in this study in its conventional meaning for a cloistered women's religious community; 'convent' (Latin *conventus*, that is, 'assembly') was the usual name given to the friars' communities within the Order of Preachers that St. Dominic founded and that came to be called the Dominicans.[1] As is the case in the texts themselves, the terms 'nuns' and 'sisters' are here used interchangeably.

The nine monasteries in question are Adelhausen, Diessenhofen, Engeltal, Gotteszell, Kirchberg, Oetenbach, Töss, Unterlinden, and Weiler.[2] These women's communities belonged to the Dominican province of Teutonia, which encompassed almost all of the Christianized German-speaking area during the thirteenth century, including Alsace, Switzerland, Swabia, and Bavaria (see map). The province was split in 1303 into Teutonia and Saxony.[3]

During the thirteenth century, the number of monasteries for Dominican women in this part of the world increased dramatically. In central Europe, by the late twelfth century, lay people experienced a re-

---

1. The name "Dominicans," popularly interpreted as *Domini canes*, that is, "the hounds of the Lord," came into use only in the fifteenth century. I will, nevertheless, make use of it in this study of fourteenth-century texts.

2. A larger repertory of similar texts from other monasteries may either be lost or waiting to be discovered in private collections (Ringler 1980a, 3) or in uncatalogued monastic libraries. Both Muschg (1935, 212) and Gieraths (1956, 37) mention a missing text from the monastery of Altenhohenau (Bavaria); and the nuns in the Dominican monastery in Regensburg, Heilig Kreuz, found it necessary to destroy their own old chronicle during the nineteenth century for fear that it might be seized by enemy invaders (*750 Jahre* 1983, 31).

3. This sketch is based mainly on Grundmann (1935); the more recent historical studies consulted include Elm (1980a; 1980b); Frank (1984); Herlihy (1990); Hinnebusch (1973); Leff (1976); Lerner (1972); Southern (1970); Vicaire (1964).

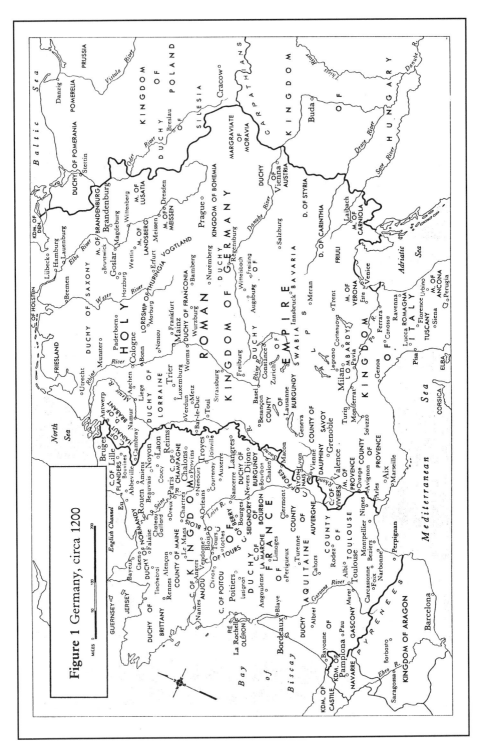

Figure 1 Germany, circa 1200

newed appreciation for religious ideals. Traditionally the monastic way of life had been understood as the only possible means of fully realizing the gospel challenge, and spiritually motivated women and men sought entrance into the monastic orders in unprecedented numbers. Women had, of course, chosen to enter religious communities before that time and for a variety of spiritual reasons. But some women had also sought refuge in monasteries as a way of refusing to accept the forms of life traditionally available to them. Women's monasteries had long been regarded as liberating women from the constraints of marriage as well as from societal restrictions on their education and learning. The situation had now changed considerably. By the year 1200, there was an imbalance in the western European population. The religious fervor of the time drew many men to the priesthood; and a large number of men also died in frequent wars. One result of this imbalance was a marked increase in the number of women wanting to become monas-tics, since marriage was, in many cases, no longer a viable choice. Soon the communities available to women were overcrowded and unable to accept further postulants. The existing monastic orders quickly reached saturation and showed growing reluctance to establish any more monasteries for women.[4]

Thus a large number of unmarried or widowed women decided to form spiritual communities of their own. Such a choice was highly un-conventional, indeed almost unknown. Eventually the women began to gather in groups of like-minded female companions, and later came to be known as beguines. Many of these women seem to have deliberately chosen this life as an "attractive alternative ... to traditional cloistered life," understanding their activities as "a life of service to others in the midst of the world."[5]

Usually members of the upper social echelon, the beguines deliber-ately fended for themselves, in order to remain independent, and made a living by whatever means they were able. The beguines were typically occupied with baking bread, brewing beer, spinning, weaving, taking care of the poor and sick, thus fulfilling the works of mercy [Mt. 25]. By helping with burials, they added the seventh act of mercy [Tb. 1:20],

---

4. On women seeking refuge, see Bell (1985, 55); cf. also Dinzelbacher's *Rol-lenverweigerung* (1988b, 38). On the paucity of marriageable men, see Bolton (1976, 147). I have intentionally refrained from referring to *die Frauenfrage* ("the question of women"), as many scholars still do. The term goes back to the late nineteenth century historians and reveals often a clearly patronizing attitude.

5. Bynum (1987b, 126); Freed (1972, 324).

which also became a money-making enterprise. In 1216, Pope Honorius III gave these women permission to live together in poverty and chastity – although without binding vows – so that they could pursue their religious ideals. Precisely because they were not separated in cloistered communities but worked in "the world" and stayed in touch with family and friends, the intensely spiritual beguines exerted a positive influence on the laity.[6]

However, the fact that the beguines had chosen to live a monastic life while living in the world, and the fact that many of them pursued their theological interests, often made such unaffiliated communities of "irregular religious women" – in spite of the initial papal approval – highly suspect, both in the eyes of the clergy and of ordinary parishioners.[7] The popular Franciscan preacher Berthold von Regensburg (†1272) and the influential Dominican General Humbert of Romans (†1277), among others, railed against the "arrogance" of lay people who "dared" to acquire some theological knowledge of their own.[8] Thus, although they remained loyal to the Church, the beguines had found themselves endangered to an extent scarcely imaginable to us; for the beguines expanded during a period that also saw the rise of many suspect sectarian movements and the far-reaching tentacles of the Inquisi-

---

6. Scholars seem to agree that the members of this thirteenth- and fourteenth-century poverty movement were mainly the rich who had become voluntarily poor. See Neumann (1960, 105ff.), McDonnell (1969, 96ff.), Bolton (1976, 146), Shahar (1981, 62), Degler-Spengler (1984, 82), Bynum (1987b, 124f.), Langer (1987, 28). Only Thiele (1988, 12) still holds the view that the beguines were poor before they joined the movement. On the beguines' work, see Wehrli-Johns (1985, 15); Neumann (1960, 98). For the papal decision, see Degler-Spengler (1984, 82f.). For the beguines' influence on the laity, see Löhr (1930, 91).

Like the twentieth century women's movement it sometimes resembles, the beguines also attracted negative reaction because they represented a new direction taken by women (Elm 1980a, 46). It is in my view anachronistic, however, to see the medieval beguine movement as a deliberate "female counterculture," as some feminist interpreters have argued; see for example, Rebekka Habermas, "Die Beginen – eine 'andere' Konzeption von Weiblichkeit?" in: *Die ungeschriebene Geschichte: Historische Frauenforschung* (Wien: Frauenverlag, 1984), pp.199–207. On the other hand, Shahar (1981, 61) speaks more appropriately of the unambiguously religious characteristics of the beguine movement.

7. See Herlihy (1990, 67). The term "beguine" eventually became synonymous with heretic (Elm 1980a, 46). Some beguinages (MHG: *samnunge*) remained independent and were successful; indeed, some of the Belgian ones have survived to the present day (Elm 1980a, 42).

8. Oediger (1953, 52).

tion.[9] In this unfavorable social climate, many beguines realized they needed protection and, as a consequence, eagerly sought affiliation with a monastic order. This was the case for the nine monasteries featured in the Sister-Books whose authors in most cases specifically trace the beginning of their communities to a beguinage that eventually sought incorporation into the order of St. Dominic.[10]

Their unconventional approach to the apostolic way of life (living "the gospel ... without compromises"[11]), made the early thirteenth-century mendicant orders (the Dominicans, the Franciscans, the Carmelites, the Augustinians, and the later medieval *Fratres saccati*) seem the perfect answer to the Church's immediate needs. As confessors and stimulating preachers, especially the learned friars of the Order of Preachers were soon much in demand among the populace in general. From the mid-thirteenth century on, a great number of already existing women's communities requested official affiliation with and eventually incorporation into the Order of Preachers as well as other orders.[12]

These early Dominican communities lived according to the Rule of St. Augustine. More flexible than the widely-observed traditional Rule of St. Benedict, the Rule of St. Augustine was confirmed for the new order by Pope Gregory IX in 1232. Originally consisting of a letter "of spiritual advice to some religious women about the daily problems of

9. The Roman Curia laid the foundation for the Inquisition in Verona in 1184. In 1231, Pope Gregory IX put the Order of Preachers in charge of the Inquisition in Germany. An intense persecution followed lasting from 1231–1233. The Order of St. Francis joined forces with the Dominicans in 1236 (Leff 1967, 36). The public burning of heretics became so common in thirteenth-century Germany that Berthold von Regensburg assumed that the audiences he preached to had all witnessed such events. See Hauck (1911, 397).

10. This is not the place for a comprehensive discussion of the beguines. Besides Grundmann (1931, 1935), Greven (1912); Phillips (1941); McDonnell (1954, repr. 1969); Neumann (1960) have dealt with the beguines, mainly of Northern France, Belgium, and the Rhine country. See Leff (1967); Lerner (1972) on the heretical movements. For a Marxist view, see Bernd Rüdiger, "Zur Reflexion der Frauenfrage in der deutschen Mystik des 13. und 14. Jahrhunderts," in: *Untersuchungen zur gesellschaftlichen Stellung der Frau im Feudalismus*, Magdeburger Beiträge zur Stadtgeschichte 3, (Magdeburg, 1981), pp. 13–46.

11. Schillebeeckx (1983, 236).

12. The affiliation of a great number of thirteenth-century beguines with the mendicant orders as tertiaries or *conversae,* that is, as lay people who follow certain monastic rules, is not relevant in the context of the Sister-Books and therefore excluded from this discussion.

living together"[13] and written by St. Augustine to the nuns of Hippo in North Africa in 423, this "Rule" (Epistola CCXI) had, in fact, been adopted by many religious groups from the early twelfth century on, when the popes refused to sanction any new orders.[14] The Dominican women who were the authors of the Sister-Books refer to this "primitive constitution" as the Rule of San Sisto since it had first been given to the nuns of San Sisto in Rome.[15] This "Rule" was later, in 1259, thoroughly revised by Humbert of Romans who created a new constitution specifically for Dominican women. Having undergone only minor changes, Humbert's constitution remained in effect for the cloistered nuns of the Second Order of St. Dominic until after the Second Vatican Council; a new constitution was adopted in 1971.[16]

Since an especially large number of women had sought incorporation into the Order of Preachers in the province of Teutonia, more than anywhere else, the number of Dominican women's communities around 1300 in Teutonia alone had risen to sixty-five, with eighty to one hundred women each. These Dominican women's communities, most of which started out in great material poverty, soon flourished, reaching a spiritual high point by the end of the thirteenth century, at the time when the friars' morale was in many instances in decline. The First Order of St. Dominic had reached its peak when most of the Dominican women's communities had asked for incorporation into the order (during the 1240s). By 1300, the wave of founding new monasteries within the mendicant orders had generally ceased. Their characteristic mendicant and itinerant life had left the friars more open to corruption than the cloistered nuns. On the other hand, the monastic spirit among women, as revealed in the Sister-Books, remained strong until the mid-fourteenth century.[17]

13. Southern (1970, 241f.); see also Wilms (1920, 28–30).

14. Galbraith (1925, 1, 11, 21).

15. Denifle (1886a, 641) maintains that St. Dominic himself had earlier adapted the Rule of St. Augustine for the women of San Sisto in Rome, who had been under his personal guidance, but Vicaire (1964, 428–435) is much more cautious, pointing out the many uncertainties regarding this Rule, its origin, and its adaptation during and after St. Dominic's time.

16. Monssen (1964, 47–58). See *Book of Constitutions* (1987).

17. This brief summary relies on studies by Elm (1980b) and Frank (1984, esp. 174–197), unless otherwise mentioned. In addition, see Leff (1976) for a useful discussion of the changes in the Church and the society of the Middle Ages.

Grundmann (1935, 220) explains that the large number of women incorporated into the order in southwest Germany was influenced by a collision of the ideas of

But the following years saw change, in some cases as a reaction against male-imposed rules. In Töss, for instance, life in the monastery had increasingly become secularized. Not only had the community at large acquired great riches, individual nuns were administering their private possessions. They had changed their originally austere cells or dormitories to comfortable living quarters; they hired private servants; and many of them regularly left the formerly strict enclosure for personal reasons. Many other women's monasteries experienced a general neglect of monastic obligations. Indeed, after the mid-fourteenth century the entire Order of Preachers was apparently ripe for internal reform.[18]

Such a deterioration is perhaps not surprising. Demanding ideals that intended to combine community life with apostolic mission in the world at large, required much individual and collective energy and charism. But the slow decay of these ideals at this time was not only peculiar to the new mendicant orders. Monastic life itself – including that of the traditional orders – was in a severe crisis. The difficulties of the religious communities in turn reflected the upheavals in Church and society during the fourteenth and fifteenth centuries. The papacy was in turmoil; there were political conflicts all over the German lands; and the Black Death raged over the countryside from about 1348 to 1352, decimating the population in some areas by thirty to forty per cent.[19] The decline of the monastic orders during the late Middle Ages, then, should be understood not in isolation but as one phenomenon within the totality of change, in the intellectual, political, and economic realm.

---

the new mendicant orders prevalent in the south with those of the beguine movement most strongly represented in the north. By contrast, there were only forty-nine friars' convents in that same province; during the same period, in all other Dominican provinces together, there were seventy-six women's communities (Decker 1935, 111). Of these thirteenth-century monasteries only four survive today with an uninterrupted history: Heilig Kreuz in Regensburg (Bavaria), the oldest Dominican women's monastery established in Germany; Lienz; Schwyz (Switzerland); and Spires. Walz (1967, 28) notes that ironically it was during the period of rapid decline in the Dominican men's monasteries (roughly between 1300 and 1366) that the so-called "Dominican mysticism," usually associated with Eckhart, Tauler, and Suso, flourished.

18. Däniker-Gysin (1958, 23); Löhr (1924, 2–6).

19. The Order of Preachers in Teutonia alone lost 124,000 men and women (Muschg 1935, 158). The monasteries, thus shrunk in size and needing new members, reduced their conditions for acceptance. As a consequence, the level of their intellectual and spiritual life declined (Hinnebusch 1973, 324).

A movement to revive the monastic ideal began – at least among the Order of Preachers – under the inspiration and strong influence of the Dominican Catherine of Siena (†1380) and her long-time confessor, Raymund of Capua (later to be General of the Order of Preachers) in Bologna.[20] This monastic reform, lasting throughout the fifteenth century, was characterized notably by a new interest in history and increased emphasis on education. For the Dominican nuns, this reform movement spread from Schönensteinbach, a Cistercian monastery destroyed by war in 1375 that was subsequently reestablished as a Dominican community in 1397 by the Dominican reformer Konrad von Preußen (†1426). Schönensteinbach's influence was felt throughout the southern German monasteries and beyond, as other communities struggled to reinvigorate the monastic ideal.[21]

Reform meant a return to the ascetic life laid down by monastic constitution. Within the Order of Preachers reform entailed a renewed commitment to the original mandate of studying and preaching – a mandate that, in the women's monasteries, encouraged a deep interest in learning and writing. And since good library holdings had been a part of the Dominican tradition, literature played a decisive role in concerted efforts to revitalize Dominican community life for both women and men. Thus the Order of Preachers came to be very influential in disseminating manuscripts. During the fifteenth century activities in the scriptoria increased, especially among the women who concentrated on building up their monastic libraries. Indeed, the pre-Reformation monastic renewal in Germany became crucial for the preservation of many vernacular texts. For the Dominican women in the so-called reform monasteries believed in circulating reform literature. And the Sister-Books describing the early Dominican women became, among other manuscripts, an important part of this reformist reading.[22]

Moreover, the Dominican friar Johannes Meyer (1422–1485) was, as a confessor in women's monasteries, much involved in the reform movement; he also played an influential role in publicizing the nuns'

---

20. This short discussion concentrates on the Dominicans even though almost all the religious orders participated in the fifteenth-century monastic reform movement. For a helpful survey of the monastic reform, with special emphasis on the women's communities in the Alsace, see Barthelmé (1931).

21. Müller (1971, 20).

22. For the importance of literature in the Dominican reform, see Williams-Krapp (1986a, 356ff.; 1993); Rapp (1985, 350). See also Heusinger (1959, 138).

literary works. Meyer was the order's first historian, "an untiring compiler and note taker ... but not a critical talent," whose most important work, the five-part *Buch der Reformacio Predigerordens* of 1468, deals with the reform monastery of Schönensteinbach.[23] Meyer considered the Sister-Books particularly important to the programme of monastic renewal within the Second Order of St. Dominic.

Unfortunately, his reformist zeal also led him to edit and to alter some of the texts. Although his historical facts appear generally to be correct, his pronouncements on the early Dominican women and especially some of his textual editing must be treated with caution. A case in point: many of the manuscripts of the Sister-Books copied during the period of reform have been transmitted to us in shortened versions; Meyer's 1482 moralistic rewriting of the Adelhausen book (codex [F] 107 and 108) from which he excerpted didactic passages omits much of the narrative.

But these attitudes are not untypical. Fifteenth-century scribes or editors were concerned primarily with asceticism, virtues, and prayer. When copying the Sister-Books, they were often not interested in and thus ignored the foundation histories of the individual monasteries. Fortunately, some of these chronicles were preserved in monastery archives, and modern editors might be able to reinstate them into the relevant texts (see, for example, Ruth Meyer's critical edition of the Diessenhofen Sister-Book, 1995). Nevertheless, in spite of such editorial flaws, the reform movement within the Order of Preachers proved crucial to the survival of many religious vernacular texts of the Middle Ages. And specifically, it must be credited with the preservation of the nine Sister-Books that are the focus of this study.

---

23. Loe (1918, 2, 12); Verflex. 6:480. For Johannes Meyer's life and work, see Albert (1898) and Fechter (Verflex. 6:474–489).

A comprehensive study of the nine texts that comprise this body of literature has never been done. Because the Sister-Books as a whole have not yet been critically edited, a solid text basis has been missing. As a way to alleviate this problem, I have made use of all the available manuscripts. This research has convinced me that the Sister-Books originally consisted both of a chronicle and a series of entries about individual sisters. My conclusions must be considered tentative, though, until reliably edited critical texts of each book are available.

This chapter deals individually with some specifics of each Sister-Book, discussing the place and time of origin, the author, and the manuscript tradition of each text. The nine books are dealt with in a roughly chronological order; exact dates for the composition of most texts cannot be established.

1. ADELHAUSEN

The beginning of the Adelhausen monastery goes back to a group of beguines in the Freiburg area who, in 1234, left their parish jurisdiction in order to live a communal life. According to the Adelhausen text (*A* 153), a beguinage was the basis for this first Dominican-oriented community in Freiburg. The Adelhausen women adopted the Rule of St. Augustine, following the example of the Strasbourg Dominican women's monastery St. "Marx" (originally St. Markus), founded in 1225. These data are confirmed by Johannes Meyer's later historical account of the monastery of Adelhausen.[1] The Adelhausen beguinage had, from the beginning, been influenced by itinerant friars preachers. These Dominicans had "eagerly advised" Countess Kunigunde von Sulz "to join this gathering so that they could become a monastery" (*A* 153). Apparently the noble widow's assets were needed for the fledgling community to survive. This Countess, as a nun of Adelhausen, later went to the papal court to ask for official incorporation of the community into the Order of Preachers (*A* 154), a request granted by

---

1. The abbreviation *A* refers to the printed text of the Adelhausen Sister-Book (ed. by J. König; see Bibliography, p. 292), and is followed by the page number; line numbers are added only after lengthy quotations. Meyer's history of the Adelhausen monastery is found in manuscript [F] 107, which is partially printed by König in various footnotes and appendices: in this case, see König (1880, 134f. n.6).

Pope Innocent IV in 1245. The community counted seventy members at that time "who together served God in great poverty," Johannes Meyer explains. However, once established, the Adelhausen monastery attracted many women of high nobility, whose rich dowry accounted for the fact that the Adelhausen nuns became quite wealthy during the following decades.[2]

The Adelhausen community, like all the monasteries we are here concerned with, had its spiritual high point in the thirteenth and early fourteenth centuries. Having then experienced a decline, the community successfully undertook an internal reform in 1465, aided by Dominican nuns from Colmar and by Johannes Meyer. Adelhausen was among the few surviving cloistered monasteries of St. Dominic's Second Order existing well into the eighteenth century. The monastery eventually assumed the function of a teaching institute but was dissolved in 1867.[3]

The Adelhausen Sister-Book, composed during the second decade of the fourteenth century, is transmitted to us in four different manuscripts, two of them more or less complete versions. There is no critical edition. J. König's 1880 diplomatic edition (that is, the publication of one unaltered manuscript, in this case [F] 98 printed "true to the original") needs to be supplemented with the chronicle contained in the Einsiedeln manuscript and further compared with other Adelhausen manuscripts. The work was originally composed in Latin but the earliest manuscript is extant only in a Middle High German translation, dated at roughly 1345–1350.[4]

The Adelhausen book (including the unpublished manuscript material) consists of an introductory chronicle which is followed by a series of over thirty entries on individual sisters of the community.[5] These passages vary

2. A fifteenth century copy of the papal bull (dated Lyon, July 15, 1245) confirming Adelhausen's incorporation into the Order of Preachers is preserved in codex [F] 107, Freiburg Stadtarchiv. A cadastral register (the Adelhausen "*Urbar*" written by Anna von Munzingen, codex [F] B 16), extant from the year 1327, shows respectable land holdings. See Meyer in: König (1880, 135, n.6).

3. On Adelhausen's history, see König (1880, 144) and Wilms (1928, 48). For the modern history of the nine monasteries, I have relied on the usual dictionaries, such as Cottineau, *Dictionnaire d'histoire et de géographie ecclésiastique*, NCE, and LThK.

4. So-called diplomatic editions, like that of König, were very fashionable among late nineteenth century scholars (see the contemporary critique by Philipp Strauch, *AfdA* 7(1881) 96). Blank (1962, 61) suggests this translation date.

5. Here as elsewhere, the count depends on the definition of a full entry. In the Adelhausen text, two names appear twice: Anna Turnerin's entry is on page 69, but her name is mentioned again on page 186; and there are two entries for Berchte von Oberried (a problem that Martin Buber [1909, 80], for instance, tried to solve by referring to Berchte the Older and Berchte the Younger).

in length from a few lines to several paragraphs. The average entry typically contains the description of one or two stereotypical "special graces" in the life of a sister whose name could often be easily exchanged with another sister. One *vita*-like account in the Adelhausen text concerning Else von der Neustatt (*A* 177–183) probably constitutes, judging by its difference in style and content, a previously written, self-contained piece that the author integrated into her work.

A self-identification by the Adelhausen author is found in the Freiburg manuscript, inserted between sermons that the copyist attached to the Adelhausen text. It reads:

> I, Sister Anna von Munzingen, who wrote this book, ask that all those who read it or hear it read faithfully remember me in God and ask him that I become a perfect human being and that my life come to a good end; and that those, who after my death read it or hear it read, ask God, if I am in any travail, that I may come to the eternal joy straightaway. In this, may the Father, and the Son, and the Holy Spirit help me and you. Amen (*A* 192. 24–31).

This colophon is the only place in the entire work where the author speaks in the first person. A further identification, this time made by the scribe, is found at the end of the text: "When Sister Anna von Munzingen wrote the book, in which all of this is written, one counted the year 1318 after God's birth" (*A* 189). Anna von Munzingen was a member of a respected aristocratic family of Freiburg. She is listed as the sixth prioress of the Adelhausen community and documented for the years 1316, 1317, and 1327.[6]

---

6. On Anna von Munzingen, see König (1880, 148); Blank, Verflex. 1:365f. A note must be inserted concerning the names of the women in the Sister-Books. The "von" meaning either "of" or "from," as in the name of Anna von Munzingen, will be left untranslated throughout this study in order to keep its ambiguity; that is, it either refers to noble descent as it often does in these cases or else to the place of origin of a person. It will be up to critical editions to identify, as far as possible (as some editors have already done in a few cases), the families of the sisters named in these nine texts. Moreover, as is still the case in some areas of Germany today, names of female members of a family often have a MHG feminine ending (*–in*) attached to their last name. For example, one reads both the forms of the modernized Elisabeth Kempf and Kempfin, Elsbeth Stagel and Stagelin or even Stäglin. I have preserved the feminine forms, whenever found in the MHG texts. And finally, the spelling of proper names, even of family or place names, varies considerably within a text and even more among the various manuscripts. For example, Berchte (probably the contemporary Bertha) appears also as Behte and Bechte. In a few cases, where one has a choice, I have opted for the simpler version for convenience's sake, such as Töss instead of Töß.

2. UNTERLINDEN

The Dominican monastery of Unterlinden was situated in the city of Colmar in the Alsace, less than fifty kilometers (about one day's journey on horseback) west of Adelhausen. According to codex [C] 576(1929), Unterlinden was founded by two noble widows of Colmar who, encouraged by the preachers of Strasbourg, came together with their children to live communally. They soon attracted other women. At first living in a place called Unterlinden ("Under the linden trees") that belonged to one of the women, then moving to *Uf Mülin* in 1232, they returned to Unterlinden in 1252 because the city offered more protection during recurring local wars. In the spiritual care of the friars after 1234, the community was canonically incorporated into the Order of Preachers in 1245 (the papal bull is dated 1246).[7]

The Unterlinden community existed until the French Revolution. It was re-founded in Colmar in 1899, but moved to Orbey-Tannach, France, in 1926. What was left of the old Unterlinden buildings (its church and the upstairs choir, and part of the monastery's beautiful original cloister) was turned into the Colmar municipal museum.[8]

The Unterlinden Sister-Book was composed, partially from previously written material, around 1320 by Sister Katharina von Unterlinden. Scarcely anything is known about this author except for a few clues she provides. Her self-identification *Ego soror Katharina*, "I, Sister Katharina, nourished from childhood in this same monastery, have accomplished this work" (*U* 480) begins the colophon. And earlier in the book she states: "In my old age, I composed the first text of this work on wax tablets with my own hands and joined it together with my faltering eyes" (*U* 335). Sister Katharina's exact name is a matter of dispute. She might be identical with a prioress Katharina who died either in 1330 or 1345, but the only certain evidence of her existence,

---

7. The Colmar manuscript [C] 576 (1929), critically edited by Wittmer (1946), contains the Unterlinden obituary and a short history; see esp. pp. 25–27, 4–6. For distances covered on horseback, see Tuchman (1978, 56).

8. The cloister still shows the large stone plates under which the sisters were buried for many centuries. While most of the exhibits now housed in the Unterlinden museum are from the fifteenth century (such as Martin Schongauer and the Isenheim Altar), there are some samples of late medieval coloured glass windows and early stone sculptures of saints, that is, art objects that could have been part of the daily life of the Unterlinden nuns. The museum also contains the reconstruction of a seventeenth century wine cellar with a colossal wine press (*trotte*) that helps us understand the *trotte*-image in medieval prose (for instance, *A* 155).

Figure 2 Unterlinden, the monastery cloister

besides the Sister-Book, is her correspondence with the controversial preacher, the Dominican Venturino de Bergamo (1304–1346).[9]

The Unterlinden text has been preserved in its Latin form in one manuscript in Colmar, written in Unterlinden itself after 1485, and in one fragmented version (the Paris manuscript). It is on these two codices that Jeanne Ancelet-Hustache based her 1930 critical edition of the Latin Unterlinden text. Since then, a late fifteenth century MHG version of the *Vitae Sororum* by Elisabeth Kempfin, prioress of Unterlinden (1469–1485), was found. Kempfin's adaptation includes a chronicle, *dz buoch von der stifftung*, as an essential first component of this work for which she utilized a "manuscript from this same monastery," presumably the document contained in codex [C] 576. This foundation history reads like an extension of the first eight chapters in Katharina von Unterlinden's text. Both authors seem to have based their history on the same chronicle existing in their monastery, except that Katharina is content with "picking only some flowers" from this document (*U* 336), while Elisabeth, some 150 years later, finds it necessary to integrate the contents of the old manuscript into her translation of Katharina's *Vitae Sororum*. Katharina's chronicle is followed by some forty entries of differing lengths (up to as much as 3400 words for a single entry) on individual sisters of the Unterlinden community. The stemma of the Unterlinden text was convincingly established by Karl-Ernst Geith.[10]

In spite of occasional repetitions, all the entries in the Unterlinden text are of some substance and show individuating features; that is, they are generally not interchangeable (as could be argued for entries in other Sister-Books. As Hester Reed Gehring noted, the Unterlinden as well as the Töss Sister-Books are structured in such a way that relatively long entries on three major figures are grouped in the middle of the work, "like a medieval triptych."[11]

9. Wax tablets, often ivory plates covered with wax, were in general use for writing and in schools up to the fifteenth century (Wattenbach 1958, 78 and 81). On Katharina's identity, see Dinzelbacher, Verflex. 4:1073; Ancelet-Hustache (1930, 323); Geith (1984, 33); LThK 10:668. As far as is known at this time, the author's name was Katharina von Gueberschwihr. Variants are von Gebersweiler, Gebilswilr, Guebwiller, Geweswiler (and the frequently used but definitely faulty form von Gebweiler). In line with recent scholars, for instance, Dinzelbacher, Verflex 4:1073–1075 and Glente (1988a, 176), I am using the less controversial name Katharina von Unterlinden when referring to the author of the Unterlinden text.

10. On Kempfin, see Geith, Verflex 4:1115–1117, and Geith (1980/81). For the stemma Geith (1986) also made use of an early printed version prepared by Matthias Thanner in 1624, preserved in an edition by Bernardus Pez 1725.

11. Gehring (1957, 15).

3. GOTTESZELL

Situated just outside of Schwäbisch-Gmünd, Württemberg, the remnants of the original Gotteszell monastery still feature the old cloister. According to Hieronymus Wilms' index of Dominican women's monasteries, the Gotteszell community started as early as 1227. Other historians date the beginning to 1240. In that year, two widows made the monastery foundation possible because one of them had a considerable dowry.[12]

The Gotteszell women, who followed the Rule of St. Augustine, were incorporated into the Order of Preachers by Innocent IV in 1246. As of 1280, the nuns are documented as the *"sanctimoniales in Cella Dei,"* that is, the cell of God or "Gotteszell." After a decline during the fifteenth century, the community was reformed with the help of sisters from the Nürnberg Katharinenkloster in 1478. The Gotteszell monastery later thrived and continued as a fully self-supporting monastic community until its property was badly damaged during the Thirty Years War (1618–1648). Gotteszell was forcefully expropriated by the state in 1808; its buildings were turned into a penal institution.[13]

The Gotteszell Sister-Book had until the late 1970s been mistaken for a part of the Kirchberg text. Then Hans Peter Müller (1977/78) and Siegfried Ringler (1980a) argued convincingly that what seemingly constituted a second half of the Kirchberg Sister-Book represented a different and autonomous work. Among other criteria, the peculiar tradition of the manuscripts, the contents of the entries, as well as geographical and historical hints in the text, were decisive. The final proof is that the Library Catalogue of the Engeltal monastery of the year 1447 lists this text separately.[14] In identifying Gotteszell as the origin of this

12. Concerning the history of Gotteszell, Wilms (1928, 44) also cites a source according to which the Gotteszell nuns were later, in 1289, reprimanded by the Provincial Hermann von Minden, for having trespassed the rule of enclosure. Kolb (1977, 96 and 115) insists that the later foundation date is accurate. Historical data for this monastery are scarce.

13. The papal bull, dated March 13, 1246, is still extant (Graf 1984, 195). For the early history, see Wilms (1928, 44) and Kolb (1977, 101); see Erzberger (1902, 267–269) for more recent developments. See Schneider (1975, 211) concerning the monastic reform.

14. Roth published the Kirchberg and Gotteszell texts together as one piece, exactly as it appeared in the manuscript he used. Going by stylistic criteria alone, he himself already noticed the discrepancy between the two parts but simply assumed that the Kirchberg book had been composed by two authors (1893, 104).

The library catalogue of Engeltal is kept in the Nürnberg *Staatsarchiv, Nürnberger Salbücher*, Nr. 45a (Ringler 1980a, 52). It contains two separate listings of

particular text, Klaus Graf bases his argument mainly on three histori-cally certifiable family names of sisters in this work, especially on the name Margaretha von Rosenstein who is documented as a nun of the Gotteszell monastery around 1330. Other text references, such as the location of a lepers' hospital in the nearby town Schwäbisch Gmünd (*G* 135) and a historical reference to the day the monastery buildings burnt down (*G* 138, 146) (although such fires were not infrequent), corroborate the finding.[15]

The Gotteszell text has been transmitted in two mid-fifteenth century manuscripts. The MHG text consists of about one dozen entries (300–400 words each) on individual sisters of this community. These entries are preceded by a lengthy and previously written *vita*-like piece on Adelheit von Hiltegarthausen.

The sparse manuscript tradition of this work presumably accounts for the fact that so far, of the Gotteszell text, no chronicle has been found. Nor is any name of an author or editor known; internal evi-dence speaks of the writer as a member of the Gotteszell community. Her impersonal, dry style resembles that of the Unterlinden text in some respects so that a relatively early date of composition may be assumed. Graf estimates that the Gotteszell text was composed "not before 1320/30."[16]

---

codices, one referring to "A little book of a monastery that is situated in Ulm in Swabia", the other naming "A little book about the blessed community of Kirch-berg" (Ringler 1980a, 96). Ringler argues that these two separate codices, that have since been lost, were presumably copied together into one manuscript; this manu-script (or a copy thereof) then served as a source for the two fifteenth-century manuscripts extant today. This may explain why we find the Gotteszell text attached to the Kirchberg text in both cases – in the Mainz manuscript even with-out a real break, thus causing the editor's confusion.

Ringler (1980a, 96) gave this second text the distinctly "preliminary, abbreviat-ed" title *"Ulmer Schwesternbuch"* because of a reference to the city of Ulm at the end of the book. Later research by Graf (1984), following a suggestion by Müller (1977/78, 47f.), convincingly points to the Dominican women's monastery of Got-teszell. As Graf (1984, 195) argues, the mere mentioning of Ulm at the end of the book does not mean the close proximity of this city; furthermore, other than Got-teszell there was no Dominican women's monastery in or near Ulm that existed for any length of time. Williams-Krapp speculates that the name of the city of Ulm could simply have been a scribe's misunderstanding (quoted by Graf 1984, 195).

15. For identifying the monastery as Gotteszell, see Graf (1984, 193–195) and Müller (1977/78, 47f.).

16. On style and early dating, see Ringler, (1980a, 107); Graf (1984, 195, n.26).

4. ENGELTAL

According to the Engeltal Sister-Book (*E* 1) and according to historical documents, the Dominican monastery of Engeltal in Franconia was based on a beguine community. It was built on a site donated by Ulrich von Königstein auf Reicheneck in 1240 and incorporated into the Order of Preachers in 1248. During the early fourteenth century, Engeltal developed into a much renowned centre of spirituality and learning. The two best known personalities of the Engeltal monastery are the writers Christine Ebner (1277–1356) and Adelheid Langmann (1306–1375). In 1339, Ludwig der Bayer placed Engeltal under the protection of the Nürnberg magistrate. Engeltal succumbed to the consequences of the Protestant Reformation in 1565 after a reform attempt, made by the Dominican women of Nürnberg's Katharinenkloster in 1513, had failed.[17]

The Engeltal Sister-Book was written after 1328 and is generally dated to circa 1340. Only two manuscripts of the Engeltal text have survived. The work is often referred to as "The Nun of Engeltal's Little Book of the Overwhelming Burden of Graces," *Der Nonne von Engeltal Büchlein von der Gnaden Überlast*. This title was taken by its first editor Karl Schröder (1871) from the introduction of the text (*E* 1). The manuscripts, as was the scribes' habit, remained untitled.[18]

The Engeltal text consists of a chronicle, comprising roughly one sixth of the entire text, and of accounts of individual sisters of the Engeltal community. Close to fifty women (as well as some lay brothers and chaplains) are identified by name; the author refers to the nuns as *frawe*, a term typically used for ladies of nobility. Most entries consist only of a few lines. There is one *vita*-like account of Alheit von Trochau, presumably the historically documented Adelheid von Trok-

---

17. See Grundmann (1935, 223–228) for a history of Engeltal based on archival material. Voit (1958, 1,3 and 5, 76) lists the preserved documents pertaining to the incorporation. As for the noble founder of Engeltal, worldly patrons were usually essential because of the high cost of starting a women's monastery; cloistered women were usually not able to provide fully for themselves. Dinzelbacher, LexMA 3:1922f. and Knapp (1987, 43) explain that Ludwig der Bayer was made German king in 1314 and later emperor (1328–1347); his battles with both the popes and the House of Habsburg dominated much of the history of the time; the mendicant orders seem to have generally been on his side. On the monastery's reform, see Graber (1957, 3); Wilms (1928, 71); Schneider (1975, 211).

18. The recurring term "the little book" (MHG *büechelin*), a diminutive form that the authors or editors use to identify their writing, must be understood both as an expression of humility and a term of endearment.

kau, and a lengthy entry on Diemut Ebnerin von Nürnberg. Other previously written pieces may be the entries on Anna von Weitersdorf, and Elsbeth Meierin von Nürnberg.[19]

A post scriptum in the Nürnberg codex, which the editor dates to at least fifty years after the completion of the copy of the manuscript, claims that Christine Ebner was the author: "Kristein Ebnerin made a little book about the divine graces granted by our Lord to the sisters in her monastery ... ." Moreover, Ringler's close study of the Vienna *codex scotensis* resulted in locating a self-identification of the author: *"ich cristin ebnerin"* ([W] fol. 118r), thus confirming that she is, indeed, the main author responsible for the Engeltal text.[20]

Christine Ebner, the daughter of a Nürnberg city aristocrat, entered the Engeltal community at the age of twelve. As a visionary, she eventually became widely respected and was consulted by famous people of her time, such as Kaiser Karl IV in 1350. Her spiritual friendship with the secular itinerant priest Heinrich von Nördlingen (†1379) resulted in their correspondence, documented from 1338 on. Christine Ebner also worked for almost forty years on her autobiographical "Life and Revelations" and is considered an early representative of Franconian literature. While Christine Ebner's grave is not known, an epitaph in her honor in the Nürnberg St. Sebaldus church gives December 27, 1356 as a possible but unconfirmed date of her death.[21]

5. KIRCHBERG

The foundation of the monastery of Kirchberg in Sulz on the Neckar, Württemberg, was financially backed by Count Burkhard III von Hohenberg. The extant document of a land purchase of 1237 lists as buyers *sanctae et devotae feminae* whose first identifiable prioress was Williburg von Hohenberg, a sister of Count Burkhard. This community

---

19. Voit (1958, 34) identifies Alheit von Trochau.

20. For the dating, see Schröder (1871, 47). For Christine Ebner's identity as the author of the Engeltal Sister-Book, see Ringler (1980a, 88), Ringler, Verflex. 2: 297–302, Ringler (1988).

21. Heinrich von Nördlingen also visited Christine Ebner in Engeltal after 1351 and put her in touch with like-minded thinkers and writers of her time (Volpert 1971, 149, 156), such as Margarethe Ebner in Maria Medingen. Heinrich von Nördlingen also introduced Christine Ebner to the late-thirteenth-century work of the mystic Mechthild von Magdeburg, *Das fließende Licht der Gottheit* (Grabmann 1910/11, 41). Ebner's Revelations is about to be critically edited by Ursula Peters; see also Kramer (1991, 191f.).

of women was incorporated into the Order of Preachers by Pope Innocent IV in Lyon in 1245. Parallelling similar stories in other Sister-Books, a 1699 Swabian history by Franciscus Petrus refers to a trip by two Kirchberg nuns to the papal curia in 1245 from which they supposedly brought back relics and ornaments.[22]

The Kirchberg community experienced an early high point during the thirteenth century. Ten years after its small beginning, it counted thirty sisters and by 1268 eighty members belonged to the monastery. But later, Kirchberg declined. During the late fifteenth and early sixteenth centuries, the Kirchberg community is described as one of the most ill-reputed monasteries in the Province of Teutonia. An internal reform of the Kirchberg monastery was eventually successful during the sixteenth century.[23]

The Kirchberg monastery was officially closed in the early 1800s. During this process, its entire library was lost. One copy of the monastery's own Sister-Book (today in Stuttgart) was rescued by the last nun to leave the premises in 1855. Today the remaining buildings are still referred to as "Kloster Kirchberg." Some headstones going back to the thirteenth century are preserved. Kirchberg serves today as an ecumenical retreat house.[24]

The MHG Kirchberg Sister-Book was published in 1893 by F.W.E. Roth based on the Mainz manuscript only. Aiming at a "diplomatic edition," Roth deliberately made no attempt to alter anything he found in his single source. As of today, five full or partial manuscripts are known to be extant. Ringler's comparison of the Mainz and Vienna Kirchberg manuscripts turned up over seventy mistakes in Roth's printed text. Still, quotations are from Roth's edition (that is, pages *K* 104–123), as it is the only MHG version in print. The manuscripts, however, as well as Ringler's corrections are taken into account.[25]

On the basis of a *vita* of Sister Irmegard von Kirchberg composed by the same writer who authored the Sister-Book, Müller and Ringler

22. Krauss (1894, 292) was able to show that the name Kirchberg (that is, "church mountain") does not originate with the foundation of the monastery but can be traced back to the eleventh century. On Williburg von Hohenberg, see Müller (1977/78, 46); Krauss (1894, 294, 299). Müller (1977/78, 46) quotes Petrus, *Suevia ecclesiastica, sev clericalia collegia tum secularia tum regulara* (Augsburg and Dillingen, 1699), pp. 459ff.

23. Krauss (1894, 297, 313, 318f.); Wilms (1928, 44f.).

24. Müller (1977/78, 43); Krauss (1894, 326); *Sulzer Bilderbogen* (1990).

25. Roth (1893, 104); Ringler (1980a, 98–104).

were able to identify Elisabeth von Kirchberg as the author responsible for the Kirchberg text. Her self-identification appears in a fifteenth-century Berlin manuscript of the Irmegard–*vita*: "I ask all those who read this or hear it read that they, for the love of God, remember me. I am called Sister Elisabeth by God's grace, whom God has taken from the Jews."[26]

The little that is known about Sister Elisabeth's life is gathered from her own occasional remarks in the Irmegard–*vita* and from some scribal notes in the Stuttgart codex. Apparently of Jewish parentage, she had come, at the early age of four, to the Kirchberg community where she eventually became good friends with the much older Sister Irmegard. It seems Elisabeth von Kirchberg personally knew and is a contemporary of the sisters she writes about in the Sister-Book. But Elisabeth von Kirchberg, too, integrated previously written material into her work. In this case, it is the lengthy entry on Mechthilt von Waldeck (*K* 118–123) which was, no doubt, meant to constitute the culminating point of the Kirchberg text. This particular piece lists the year 1305 for Mechthilt's death and thus provides the *terminus post quem* for the book. However, most interpreters agree that the work was composed some time after the Adelhausen and Engeltal books. Müller thinks the Kirchberg text could have been written any time between 1305 and 1340.

6. TÖSS

The community of Töss had its origin in a beguinage in Winterthur. The secular founder and patron of the Töss monastery was Count Hartmann IV von Kyburg. Like the Adelhausen monastery, Töss followed the example of St. Marx in Strasbourg by adopting the Rule of St. Augustine; it became the first women's community to do so in this particular area of Switzerland. The Töss monastery was officially incorporated into the Order of Preachers by Innocent IV in 1245; but even prior to this date, the nuns had for several years been spiritually cared for by the friars of Zürich.[27]

---

26. Ringler (1980a, 93 and 106f.) and Müller (1977/78, 53) identified her on the basis of a fifteenth-century Berlin manuscript ([B] mgq 730, fol. 205v–231v) of the *vita* of Sister Irmegard of the monastery of Kirchberg. The name appears on fol. 230b.

27. Henggeler (1934, 30) writes that, according to oral tradition, this *samnunge* of beguines began as early as 1200. Däniker-Gysin (1958, 12–14) explains that the contribution of a co-foundress of Töss, Eufemia von Herten, who is mentioned in a 1343 document written in Töss itself, has not been sufficiently corroborated by

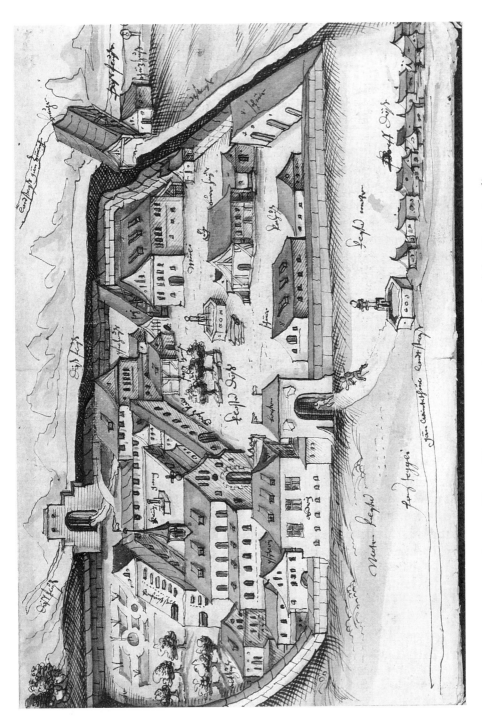

Figure 3 *Kloster Döss*, a seventeenth-century sketch by Hanns Jeggli

The Töss community flourished both spiritually and economically throughout the thirteenth and fourteenth centuries, normally housing between sixty and one hundred women at any given time. During the fifteenth century, like so many other monasteries, the community experienced a moral decline, but unlike most of them it refused the internal reform offered to them under the auspices of the Schönensteinbach monastery. Following the Protestant Reformation, the Töss monastery was dissolved by the state in 1525. Today nothing is left of the Monastery of St. Maria in Töss. Its site has been occupied by the large *Maschinenfabrik Winterthur-Töß* for over one hundred years.[28]

The manuscript tradition of the Töss text is comparatively well established. Currently four manuscripts (besides several fragments) of a presumably complete version of the text are known. One manuscript, contained in codex Cent. V 10a in the Nürnberg municipal library, is the only illuminated manuscript of any of the Sister-Books. Ferdinand Vetter's text edition (1906), *Das Leben der Schwestern zu Töß beschrieben von Elsbet Stagel*, which is based on the St. Gallen manuscript (and which integrates editorial work by Karl Bihlmeyer), must be appreciated for what it accomplished at the time of publication. Nevertheless, neither its text nor its critical apparatus are adequate any longer. As the only text in print, it is used here as a basis, but again, the text is compared with the other manuscripts for crucial passages.[29]

---

any other historical sources. Archival documents show that the monastery was built by permission of Bishop Heinrich von der Tanne of Constance in 1233 who, in 1240, also offered the women protection. For the history of Töss, see also Sulzer (1903, 6–8); Pfister (1964, 286); Grundmann (1935, 232ff.).

28. Henggeler (1934, 30) speaks about the great amount of land acquired by the Töss monastery, especially during the fourteenth century. For the early history, see also Wilms (1928, 38) and Heer (1947, 6).

29. For this study, I restrict myself to that portion of the Töss text that comes close to what might be considered the fourteenth-century version of this Sister-Book. The fifteenth-century additions by Johannes Meyer (as found in [N]) which Vetter included in his text, such as Meyer's own Preface, the *vitae* of both Elsbet Stagel and of the mother of Heinrich Suso, and Meyer's concluding remarks (Vetter 1906, 1–11, 95–98, 121f.) are not considered. Nor can Elsbet Stagel be automatically identified as the author of what Vetter calls the "Prologue by Elsbet Stagel" (1906, 12–16). My textual interpretation also excludes the lengthy *vita* of Elisabeth of Hungary (Vetter 1906, 98–120) which was attached to the Töss Sister-Book, but whose present form is so saturated with extraneous elements that it might jeopardize an attempted balanced view of the Töss book (see also Grubmüller 1969, who established the manuscript tradition). It seems preferable to

The Töss text consists of a chronicle and about forty entries of differing length dealing with individual sisters of the Töss community. The longer pieces are the chapters on Jüzi Schulthasin, Sophie von Klingnau, Elisabeth Bechlin, Mechthild von Stanz, together possibly with those on Adelheit von Frauenberg, and Elsbet von Cellikon. All of these may constitute previously written self-contained pieces that the editors or compilers incorporated. The first twenty-eight entries on choir sisters are followed by accounts of seven lay sisters; two further entries were apparently attached later. It is assumed that this division was made – and somewhat artificially compressed into the symbolic number of thirty-three chapters – by Johannes Meyer for his 1454 edition of this Sister-Book. Together with the Unterlinden work, the Töss text represents the most voluminous among the nine books with around 40,000 words.[30]

The conventional but outdated assumption that Elsbet Stagel was the only author of the Töss text is largely based on Johannes Meyer's assertions. His introductory "life" of Elsbet Stagel, where he writes that "Elysabeth Staglin von Zürich ... put together, wrote and composed" the book (T 2), stresses her close connection with Heinrich Suso (or Seuse), the fourteenth century Dominican mystic, under whose influence Stagel grew both intellectually and spiritually. Johannes Meyer apparently wanted to attribute more authority to the Töss text by implying that, while written by a woman, it was composed under Suso's tutelage.

Elsbet Stagel, the daughter of a Zürich senator, entered the Töss community as a child of six and died about 1360. Highly educated, she became known as a writer, scribe, and translator, but was perhaps made most famous for her spiritual friendship and literary cooperation with Heinrich Suso. Within the Töss text, however, the name of Elsbet Stagel is only mentioned in one entry: "The blessed Sister Elsbet Staglin who wrote all this" (T 93). The context implies that she either wrote this particular passage (and identifies herself, as is not unusual, with an objective third person pronoun) or that she composed an earlier part thereof (and is credited with having done so by a later editor). Other

---

proceed this way until a conclusive critical edition is at our disposal. I am not arguing here for a "genuine" versus a less genuine text of the "original" Töss Sister-Book, but I am proposing an identifiable basis for the interpretation.

30. Grubmüller (1969, 201) believes on the ground of text comparisons that the prologue, the Bechlin–*vita* and a few inserts stem from the pen of one individual.

sisters, such as Willi von Konstanz (*T* 48), are also mentioned in the Töss Sister-Book as having been writers or scribes. As is the case with most texts in this *corpus*, one cannot speak of a single author responsible for the entire work. It may well have been, as Klaus Grubmüller suggests, a collective of sisters of the Töss community, who authored some entries, compiled written accounts, and integrated oral reports, completing their task in circa 1340.[31]

7. OETENBACH

The Oetenbach community was started in an empty, dilapidated house in the city of Zürich by Gertraut von Hilzingen and two other women in 1231, one of them, Mechthild von Woloshofen, surviving long enough to witness the community's move to their fourth and final homestead (*O* 219f.). The author of the Oetenbach Sister-Book proudly underlines the fact that the women accomplished everything by themselves implying that this community never had a secular founder or patron (*O* 232f.). Living off alms at first, the sisters were then joined by a group of Zürich beguines who had supported themselves by the work of their own hands (*O* 221). This merger helped establish the women's independence. Shortly thereafter, the growing community needed larger living quarters. Their first choice, "on the Sihlfeld," proved unfortunate because the buildings were located on a flood plain (*O* 221).

Supposedly following someone's dream vision, they built a wooden monastery in 1221 just outside of Zürich near the Oetenbach (that is, "Otto's brook"). The community, consisting of sixty-four members at that time (*O* 222), adopted the Rule of St. Augustine. Following their petition, the Oetenbach sisters were confirmed by Pope Gregory IX in 1239 and fully incorporated into the Order of Preachers by Innocent IV in 1245. The women had been in close touch with the Zürich friars since the start of their communal life.[32]

Oetenbach's economic situation began to improve when "the reputation of their blessed life spread far into the world," the lengthy chronicle of the Oetenbach Sister-Book explains (*O* 232): "Noble lords" from

31. On Stagel and Suso, see Krebs (1953, 256f.); Grabmann (1926, 479). Concerning the authorship of Töss entries, Grubmüller (1969, 199–201) assumes, for instance, that Willi von Konstanz could have composed a number of other entries in the Töss text. Regarding the date of the Töss text, see also Strauch, *AfdA* 31 (1907) 22.

32. I am relying on Halter (1956, 11 and 19ff.) for the data other than the ones given in the Oetenbach Sister-Book itself.

Figure 4 Kloster Oetenbach, detail from an engraving of the city of Zürich by Jos. Murer, 1576

far and wide sent their daughters to this community, consequently also providing much needed support. When by 1285 the number of community members had doubled again, the community made a final, much debated move back into the city of Zürich (O 234) whose walls provided better protection. The colourful description of this move explains among other details that the sisters "dug out of their cemetery the bones of the blessed sisters and took them along, as hard as this was on them" (O 235).[33]

Their new monastery, the so-called Neu-Oetenbach, existed until 1525. The last remnants of the buildings of this largest of the medieval monasteries in the Zürich area were removed only in the twentieth century to make room for a city street.[34]

Only a single manuscript, dating from the mid-fifteenth century, has been located of the Oetenbach Sister-Book. It was made available in print in H. Zeller-Werdmüller's and Jakob Bächtold's 1889 diplomatic edition. Some editorial comments are provided, but the editors' intention was not to interfere with the manuscript except to add punctuation marks. The Oetenbach text, composed in Middle High German, shows traces of a Zürich dialect; its orthography is generally that of a Nürnberg scribe. The Oetenbach text can be dated to some time after 1340; this *terminus post quem* is the year Sister Elsbeth von Beggenhofen died (O 270).[35]

No doubt due to its efficient fourteenth-century editor, the final version of this Sister-Book is a well-structured piece of writing.[36] Three

33. In 1310, by order of the Provincial Egino von Stoffen, the Dominican women's communities were cut back to a maximum of sixty members (Wilms 1920, 96). Halter's historical studies (1956, 39) corroborate the Oetenbach chronicle.

34. For a detailed description of the Oetenbach monastery complex and its church, see Konrad Escher, "Das ehemalige Kloster Oetenbach. Geschichte und Baugeschichte." In: *Die Kunstdenkmäler des Kantons Zürich IB* (Basel: Birkhäuser, 1939), pp. 270–275. See also Pfister (1964, 283).

35. For the dialect, see Zeller-Werdmüller and Bächtold (1889, 215, 217). A scribe's orthography is one way of identifying the area where a manuscript was copied, since no spelling rules were in existence until long after printing had been invented.

Elsbeth von Beggenhofen is documented in archival material; she entered the Oetenbach community in 1281 and died on June 21, 1340 (Pfister 1964, 283f.).

36. I do not see any reason to concur with Blank's (1962, 70) assumption that the author or editor of the chronicle must be someone outside of the monastery because of the third person plural used throughout when talking about the sisters.

long entries, presumably previously composed accounts, on Ita von Hohenfels, Ita von Hutwil, and Elsbeth von Beggenhofen dominate the text; they are matched by three shorter pieces on Jüzi Goldsteinin, Adelheit Schwarzin, and Hilta von Opfikon. Four of these six women identified by name are historically documented for the thirteenth century. The Oetenbach text distinguishes itself among the other Sister-Books by a detailed and vivid account of the monastery's history in a lengthy initial chronicle whose basic accuracy has been confirmed by archival sources.[37]

No name of any author or editor has been transmitted. A first-person singular is encountered only once, in the prologue to the chronicle (O 218). The Oetenbach text (with around 14,000 words) is the shortest one in this literary *corpus*.

8. DIESSENHOFEN[38]

The Diessenhofen community was started by beguines from nearby Winterthur who had moved to Diessenhofen and then, by permission of Bishop Heinrich von der Tanne in Constance, moved again, in 1242, to a permanent site just outside of Diessenhofen. Since this area was called "valley of St. Catherine" (Katharinental), the women chose St. Catherine as their patron. The community, living according to the Rule of St. Augustine, is historically documented for 1242. The monastery was incorporated into the Order of Preachers by Pope Innocent IV in 1245. It was presumably Albert the Great who consecrated the new monastery church in 1269. By 1280, the Diessenhofen community had grown from an original forty sisters to over one hundred and fifty. It is documented that Meister Eckhart visited the monastery in 1324. There is no historical source, however, to corroborate the legend that

---

It is much more likely that the writer who bases some of her chronicle on what "they talked about over fifty years later" (O 228) speaks of the earliest members of her community as "they".

37. For the identification of the names, see Muschg (1935, 114); for an over-all evaluation of the book, see Dinzelbacher, Verflex. 7:170.

38. The Diessenhofen Sister-Book is also referred to as the Katharinental Sister-Book. My choice of name follows the new edition of the *Verfasserlexikon*. The monastery's official title was "St. Katharinental near Diessenhofen." The critical edition by Ruth Meyer, "St. Katharinentaler Schwesternbuch," is used as the text basis for this study. Exceptionally, references to this text do not refer to a page but to the number of an entry, as is the usual practice for the Diessenhofen Sister-Book.

Bruder Klaus von der Flüe prevented the monastery from burning to the ground in 1460.[39]

The Diessenhofen monastery was one of only a few Swiss monasteries that outlasted the Protestant Reformation more or less intact. After a decline during the seventeenth century, the Diessenhofen community flourished again under Prioress Josepha Dominika von Rottenberg during the early eighteenth century. Having survived the political oppression of the early nineteenth century, Diessenhofen was finally dissolved in 1869. It was at that time that most of its numerous art works were scattered. Some remaining buildings, dating from the eighteenth century, are used today as a senior citizens' home.[40]

Various versions of the Diessenhofen Sister-Book have been transmitted in a number of manuscripts. The Nürnberg, St. Gallen, and Frauenfeld codices contain a chronicle that presumably goes back to the early fourteenth-century. The remainder consists of sixty rather uneven entries on sisters of the Diessenhofen community.[41]

No author of the Diessenhofen text is known by name. The work was obviously compiled by a writer or editor who not only composed a number of entries of her own but also integrated already existing passages plus three lengthy *vita*-like entries on Elsbeth von Stoffeln, Elsbeth Hainburgin, and Anne von Ramswag. The core of the text was composed some time between 1318 and circa 1343, as stated in Ruth Meyer's 1995 critical edition of the Diessenhofen text.[42]

9. WEILER

The Weiler community (near Esslingen, Neckar) was founded in 1230 as the first monastery of the Order of Preachers in the diocese of Constance. Preserved archival documents establish the acquisition of a

---

39. For historical background studies, see Pfister (1964, 291); Müller (1971, 11); Frei-Kundert (1929, 141, 3). The documents pertaining to Katharinental's incorporation are extant, dated July 12, 1245, see Müller (1971, 17f.). Regarding Eckhart's visit, any time between 1314 and 1320, see Däniker-Gysin (1958, 21) and Borst (1978, 298) who moreover suggests that Suso, while not mentioned in the text, may also have been in Katharinental between 1339 and 1346.

40. For the later history of Diessenhofen, see Wilms (1928, 37); Muschg (1935, 229); Göpfert (1978, 143).

41. Dates are suggested by Borst (1978, 290); Grubmüller, Verflex.2:94. Meyer (1995, 42) speaks of a basic text of 58 entries to which others were added later.

42. Meyer (1995, 38) singles out D 33, 40, and 41 as pre-written texts; see also Kunze (1952, 46f.) For dating the text, see Meyer (1995, 37).

parcel of land by some Esslingen beguines in Weiler at that time. Documents attest as well to the confirmation of this community in 1236 by Pope Gregory IX and the sisters' incorporation into the Order of Preachers by Pope Innocent IV on September 9, 1245. The desperate economic situation of the Weiler community during its early existence and well into the fourteenth century coincided with its spiritual flourishing, as portrayed in the Weiler text. At one point during the fourteenth century the number of sisters at Weiler rose to above 130 until an order of the provincial in 1362 restricted the community to seventy members.[43]

Internal reform in 1478 temporarily halted the community's spiritual decline during the fifteenth century. However, as a consequence of the Reformation, the Weiler monastery was dissolved in 1592, after the last "stiff-necked" nuns (*halsstarrig*), as a contemporary document refers to them, had finally left the premises. The remaining monastery buildings were ravaged during the Thirty Years' War and finally completely destroyed in 1796. Today there are no remnants of the Weiler monastery; the acreage on which the monastery had been erected was used as a horse stud farm (*Das Gestüt Weil*) between 1817 and 1932.[44]

Three manuscripts of the Weiler text have been preserved, two dating back to the late fifteenth century and one to around 1500, located today in Nürnberg, München, and Graz respectively. The Weiler text consists of some twenty-seven entries on individual sisters. The first six entries are relatively substantial, that is, up to 700 words, while all the remaining are short (some as few as sixty words). A short section (*W* 84f.) deals with the community as a whole. No chronicle has been preserved. The reader's attention is drawn at one point (*W* 80) to a local war, presumably a reference to a battle fought between the town of Esslingen and Count Eberhard von Württemberg, which may have affected the monastery.[45] The Weiler text ends with a reference to "this jubilee year" (*W* 85), thus dating itself to the year 1350.

---

43. The historical data concerning Weiler are based on Bihlmeyer (1916, 61–64); Wilms (1928, 41); Uhrle (1968, 171, 21, and 31ff.). For a historical survey of the *numerus clausus* and Hermann von Minden's role in this complex issue, see Löhr (1925, 162). In practice, the maximum number of members per community depended on the economic viability of each monastery, see Langer (1987, 25).

44. For Weiler's historical development, see Wilms (1928, 41); Bihlmeyer (1916, 64); LThK 10:992. Information regarding the current use of the Weiler buildings kindly provided by the Stadtarchiv, Stadt Esslingen am Neckar, Letter of 15 September 1989.

45. Bihlmeyer (1916, 80, n. 93); Uhrle (1968, 39).

The author or editor of the Weiler Sister-Book remains unknown. An "I"-narrator of the prologue switches to "we" for the rest of the text, the author thus identifying herself with the Weiler community (*W* 69, 74, 76). The author, or one of several authors, says of herself that she helped out in the sick room (*W* 72) and that she personally experienced the priorate of Gisela von Grüningen. This prioress is documented for the year 1315[46] and held the office "for a long time" (*W* 77).

Judging by language and content, the second part of the book (*W* 82ff.) was composed by a different sister of the Weiler monastery. She not only wrote an addition to the existing entries but also felt that editorial work was needed on some of the similes her predecessors had used.[47]

The Weiler book was published by Bihlmeyer who based his 1916 edition on codex [M] while showing the most important variants of manuscripts [N] and [Gr] in his critical apparatus.

46. Bihlmeyer (1916, 86).

47. The later author, for instance, adds a tale (*W* 83f.) about "a noble devout lady" who asked "our Lord" to show her the four worthiest sisters of the Weiler monastery. Using this ploy, she then proceeds to clarify some similes of the preceding text: the first entry on Sister Wila describes her as "by God compared to the bees" (*W* 72), an allusion to the topos of the "mystical bee"; the second one elaborates that "Sister Wila was likened to the bees sucking in ... the sweetness of graces but outwardly being pricked with the stings of an austere life" (*W* 83f.). Similarly, in the earlier entry, Sister Mechtilt Büglin "was by God compared to a morning star" (*W* 77); the later explanation reads: "Sister Mechtilt Büglin could be compared to the morning star for that is how radiant her life was in all this country" (*W* 83). A third case, that of Elisabeth von Esslingen (*W* 69 and 83) follows the same pattern; the name change to Effingen was undoubtedly caused by a later scribe misreading the long s. The addition regarding a fourth sister, however, has no earlier parallel (*W* 84); it may go back to an entry that was lost.

ONE BODY OF LITERATURE

Even though the Sister-Books differ from fictional writing in as much as they are, like other hagiographic works, based on the lives of actual women in an historically identifiable place and time, they are here treated as written documents and hence as pieces of literature. In the following chapter, our concern lies with the characteristics of these narrative texts composed by authors who were fully aware of their creative task.

1 The Authors and Authenticity

The term "author" in the Sister-Books often simultaneously signifies initiator, author, compiler, editor, narrator. In many cases, one might imagine a team of sisters in the monastery (concerned with documenting the monastery's history and the community's saintliness) sharing the editorial task.[1] The reader occasionally senses an author's strong guiding hand at work in the narration, such as "I here begin to write" (*W* 68), "And that I wrote this little book" (*G* 148). On the other hand, the author's personality typically hides behind her preeminent role as a writer – an attitude characteristic both of monastic humility and of medieval authors, for whom individuality plays only a minor role.

What seems to be of great importance to all the authors is a close identification with their community. Whether it is the "I"- or the "we"-narrator at work, references to "our prioress," "our monastery," "our homestead," and "our orchard" abound. In the Gotteszell Sister-Book, the author acts directly as the sisters' spokesperson, when she says: "the community was confident that ..." (*G* 136). The Diessenhofen author marks a certain point in time with "When I entered this monastery" (*D* 31). And even with the formulaic opening of many entries, "We also had a saintly sister" (*O* 229, *W* 70), an author sees herself as one of the community whose story she is about to preserve in writing.[2]

---

1. As an example, Sister Irmegard in Kirchberg presumably helped Sister Elisabeth with compiling material for the book, Müller (1977/78, 54) suggests.

2. The authors use *ein heilige swester*, "a saintly sister," throughout. A catalogue of canonized members of the Dominican Order (Raymund Devas, *The Dominican Saints*, 1901) does not list any of the names mentioned in the Sister-Books.

The general high esteem for the written word is evident in Christine Ebner's praise for Engeltal's Chaplain Ulschalk: "He became such a saintly man that songs were sung about him" (*E* 3). And Elisabeth von Kirchberg states that, while the entire community witnessed something worth recording, *das sah wir alle* (*K* 108), she is the one who feels moved to set it down in writing because, as the author of the Gotteszell book explains, some things simply should not be hidden in silence, *Es ist aber das nicht zu versweigen* (*G* 146). And it is this urge to write, rather than being made to write, that is characteristic for the authors of the Sister-Books.

Nevertheless, as one might expect of any medieval work, the topos of obedience can also be found, especially in a monastic context. The Gotteszell author writes of Adelheid: "When she was still alive, it was so usual for us that God would do great things with her that no attention was paid to writing it down, except that now obedience has forced us to do so" (*G* 134). Similarly Christine Ebner states: "Now I would like to write something about the overwhelming burden of graces. But unfortunately I have a lowly mind and do not know letters, except that I am obliged by obedience to these things" (*E* 1). The topos of the *Schreibbefehl*, writing by command, needs not be taken literally; but if we do, such phrases might refer to obeying the respective prioress to whom the sisters are bound by their monastic vow of obedience.[3]

The humility formula, also contained in this Engeltal quotation, reads more explicitly in the Unterlinden Sister-Book:

What I have learned [of Herburg von Herkenheim] is so magnificent that I had to entrust it above all to the monument of letters with – God is my witness – a truthful pen, but only in simple words, as it conforms to my lowly mind. I have diligently examined ... everything that is to be included in this book. I have heard it from credible sisters whose testimony is most believable .... This I have said now so that, after having removed all doubts, these most truthful assurances will be believed. But now I will have to return to the sequence of the tale I undertook and from which I have digressed a little (*U* 388. 31–389.12; cf. *U* 394).

This conscious digression reveals full awareness of the author's task.

---

3. The phrase repeatedly used in the Unterlinden text that the narrator reveals something *per ordinem* means she writes "in a sequence, in an orderly fashion" (for instance, *U* 415, 455, 462, 464, 468); it need not imply writing by obedience, as understood by Peters (1988b, 131).

Katharina von Unterlinden here combines a humility formula, an authenticity claim, her expressed admiration for her subject, her deliberate choice of style, and finally her great respect of letters. In medieval religious works, Julius Schwietering explains, the humility formula is no longer a *captatio benevolentiae* directed to the audience but rather a gesture to God, which the medieval audience expected of all authors. Aware of the large discrepancy between their intended praise of God and their own weakness in this endeavor, they expressed a real sense of humility.[4]

As is typical for legendary material, the authors of the Sister-Books, eager to claim authenticity, pay close attention to sources (*Wahrheitsbeteuerung*). Such "factuality, textually derived, is important in hagiographic discourse," Edith Wyschogrod explains, "because a sense of historical veracity is necessary to generate moral practices in the text's addressees."[5] The Sister-Books' authors, therefore, in an attempt to render their accounts credible, feel they must meticulously identify the origin of their stories. They credit either the community as a whole (*K* 113, 122; *E* 22; *T* 35), or one or several sisters whom they represent as eye witnesses (*K* 105, 108; *G* 125; *T* 28, 41; *E* 31, 39; *D* 12, 40). The Unterlinden author claims, sisters "have assured me under testimony of truth how they quite secretly perceived all this with their own ears" when these God-pleasing nuns who received "revelations from above and many divine consolations" were still alive (*U* 389). Older sisters, authors claim, have given personal testimony (*A* 179; *D* 41); and some state that they approached a sister on her deathbed to ask for relevant information as to which "special graces" she might have received during her lifetime (*U* 345; *T* 33, 55; *W* 76).[6]

The author sometimes also functions as her own witness to a tale she tells (*D* 40; *W* 71). Especially noteworthy is the Engeltal author's own vision used for the authentication of a story: "I will tell you of Else von Regensburg. One Pentecost Day I, Christine Ebnerin, stood

---

4. For the humility topos, see Schwietering (1954, 1283f.); and Lutz (1984, 79). Women writers at that period, Gössmann (1987, 14 and 1988b, 190) points out, often commute the formula of the weak female into precisely its opposite [based on 1Co. 1:27]; that is, that God specifically "chose what is weak by human reckoning."

5. For the truth claim in legends, see Günter (1910, 175–178); Blank (1962, 105). See also Wyschogrod (1990, 30).

6. Additional references given in parentheses throughout are similar text passages that corroborate a point made; they are in no way meant to be exhaustive.

next to her. There I saw during the *Veni Creator* that the Holy Spirit, in the shape of a dove, came on her head and that a fiery wheel hovered above her" (*E* 42; cf. [W] 118r). A source can also be identified as hearsay: "A virtuous sister, blessed Gepe von Tettingen [of Töss], also told us that the blessed Sister Mechthilt von Konstanz told her that she saw this same Sister Elsbet one night" (*T* 92f.). Other testimonies are supposed to come from a confessor who permits himself to speak of a person's saintliness after her death (*U* 386, 412; *O* 244), or else from a servant (*E* 22). A community's saintliness can even be authenticated from outside the cloister walls. A watchman of Winterthur is said to have witnessed miraculous lights above the monastery, confirming *wunderlichen ding*, "miraculous happenings," taking place inside (*T* 59; cf. *K* 117; *E* 37).

At times an author notes that material previously composed in the community by the older sisters "before us" is integrated into the text (*T* 16; *U* 433; *D* 40). On other occasions, the author claims that she refrains from telling something because she does not know enough and hence feels inadequate to write about it (*K* 110, 118; *E* 5) – an effective device for heightening her credibility.

2. Language[7]

Unsuspecting readers of the Sister-Books are easily taken aback by the naiveté of a language saturated with legendary commonplaces and strained by the apparent credulity of the authors. In our attempt to properly understand what lies behind this often unattractive façade, Ringler's decisive insights prove most helpful. His study demonstrates that the authors of the Sister-Books intentionally chose a legendary mode as a style peculiarly appropriate for their work. Ringler explains that "it is no longer adequate to assume that the legendary style we find in this literature reflects the ineptness of authors addicted to miracles;

---

7. This sub-chapter concentrates only on a few selected points. Readers are generally referred to the still valid monograph by Gehring (1957) with a detailed analysis of the Sister-Books' language based on six of the nine texts. Gehring distinguishes between the language of silence (1957, 25ff.) and figurative language (pp. 51ff.); and the language of visions and mysticism (pp. 127–340). While Gehring's introduction adopts some of the long-standing prejudices against the Sister-Books, and while she never questions her approach to these texts as works of mysticism, her work (including the glossary) is still indispensable. In addition, Lüers' 1926 language study, while primarily concerned with Mechthild von Magdeburg, is in many respects also relevant for the Sister-Books.

rather their literary expression, which consciously follows legendary patterns, must be taken seriously as such."[8]

All of the texts use a simple style (Gehring's terms are "unpretentiousness and transparent simplicity"), the so-called *sermo humilis*. This "humble style" was recommended by the Church and is found in many religious prose works of the Middle Ages, both in Latin and the vernacular. Although simple, it is not a naive style but rather a highly developed special narrative form. Thus the Unterlinden author repeatedly stresses that she tells her story "simply" (*U* 367) or "in a brief and simple way," *simplicibus uerbis expressi* (*U* 413, 439). She writes, nevertheless, as Walter Muschg points out, in "a thoroughly literary Latin betraying a high level of education." In the vernacular texts, this simple style reflects the mode of oral story-telling – a source on which much of the material was based. Typically, therefore, paratactic structures as well as sentences starting with 'then,' 'there,' and 'and' are also characteristic.[9]

Moreover, the authors of the Sister-Books deliberately make use of legendary clichés by adapting pre-fabricated formulations to their own immediate needs. That is, while the literary commonplace must not be understood verbatim, it is by no means empty of a concrete meaning. For in spite of their legendary character, these books are still an authentic way of communicating worthwhile ideas and observations. However, just as it is impossible to "translate" a good metaphor by explicitly spelling out its literal sense, any attempt to dissolve a legendary cliché must necessarily fall short because its complex meaning could not be captured. If an author writes, for instance, (as happens in

---

8. Ringler (1980a, 11, 91) based this insight on a comparison between Christine Ebner's Revelations (written in a language "of critical self-reflection and ecstatic emotions") and the language this same author used in the Engeltal Sister-Book ("serene" and seemingly reflecting "a world of pious naiveté and charm").

9. Concerning the simple style, see Gehring (1957, 23); for the use of the *sermo humilis* in the Church, see Gurevich (1990, 13); Lutz (1984, 79), and for Katharina's Latin, see Muschg (1943, 15). Ringler (1975, 265) speaks of a special narrative form in the Sister-Books. For orality, see Albert B. Lord, "Characteristics of Orality." *Oral Tradition* 2 (1987), 54–72. For the use of parataxis, see Erich Auerbach, *Mimesis: Dargestellte Wirklichkeit in der abendländischen Literatur*, 1st ed. 1946, 5th ed. (Bern and München: Francke, 1971), pp. 159f.; he interprets parataxis under certain circumstances as a special "weapon of rhetorical skill." Such deliberate simplicity, as found in the Sister-Books, is easily misinterpreted, see for instance Wehrli (1980, 660) who speaks of *"eine schlichte, oft auch hilflos chronikalische Manier."*

a number of cases) of a sister who was seen levitating above the ground, this image may have meant to the contemporary audience that she was spiritually more advanced than her sisters in the community; or that she had no consideration for material things and hence defied gravity; or that she was lifted up closer to God through grace thus symbolically expressed; or that she, at the moment described, underwent an intense religious experience; or some of these meanings together plus the possibility that there may, indeed, have been some such occurrence.[10]

Besides many other typical formulations, the topos of ineffability, both on the part of the narrator (*K* 107) and put into a visionary's mouth (*E* 25) is not infrequent in the Sister-Books. Because of its stereotypical use, it is intriguing when an author occasionally varies the formula. The Oetenbach text, for example, states that an experience could not be "forced" into words (*O* 244); and a sister says laconically that not only was what she had seen ineffable but, moreover, "she imagined that nobody would understand it," anyway (*O* 252).

Among other rhetorical devices, anaphora and *repetitio* (or else *conduplicatio*) are most frequently present in this particular story-telling mode, since they are connected with orally transmitted tales as a mnemonic device. The example from the Oetenbach text illustrates how the repetition of the word "joy" effectively emphasizes Ita von Hohenfels's search for happiness:

> She turned her mind only to how she would find joy in the world. And no matter how much joy and recreation she had, she was never satisfied and always searched for better and more joy. For she imagined that this was not the proper joy, and yet she did not otherwise know how to search for joy. And when her lord, the Knight von Hohenfels, died and she became a widow, her heart had many a thought how to lead her life so that she could find joy ... (*O* 237.20–238.1; cf. *A* 167f.).

Ita's search ends when a spiritual experience renders "all worldly joy ... indifferent to her" (*O* 238).

Characteristic for the religious vocabulary of that time are words referring to sweetness in connection with taste and smell and in a figur-

---

10. For the meaning of a commonplace, see also Dinzelbacher (1982b, 64). Benz (1969, 218), among many others, maintains, "it is impossible to relegate all the testimonies concerning levitation into the realm of legends."

ative meaning, such as "divine sweetness" (*W* 72),[11] as well as many terms relating to flowing, such as being "inundated" or "overflowing" with grace. The authors also show a preference for paired adjectives and superlatives. Indicative of the style of their period are, moreover, their many hyperboles, and some allegorical references, number symbolism (*O* 220), and alliteration, such as the angels *sungen ein so suzzen sank* (*E* 35). Many similes as well, notably the world "like dung" (*T* 54) or "bitter as vermouth" (*T* 62) are conventional, as are some light (*E* 19), fire (*T* 41), seal (*K* 106), and mirror images (*K* 111), and occasional bridal references (*U* 358; *K* 118f.). The traditional image for the monastery as a "garden of delights," *[h]ortus deliciarum* or *wurtzgarten* (*U* 346; *T* 12) is also utilized.

Biblical references are found on every page, as one would expect of authors imbued with scripture readings during their liturgy, at work and at meal time. Grete Lüers traces especially metaphors of the seal, of drunkenness, of embracing, and of the "liquified soul" to the Song of Songs. This poem's strong influence is also responsible for a number of expressions that are simultaneously reminiscent of courtly poetry; that is, phrases like, *das ir hercz verwundet was von gotlicher mynn und begird* (*K* 107) [Sg. 4:9]. The typical *Minnesang* phrase, *Ich pin dein, so pist du mein,* "I am yours hence you are mine," (*K* 122), eliminating the subject-object-distinction between two lovers, also alludes to the Canticle [Sg. 2:5 and 16]. Innovative composites with *minne,* such as "love-sick," are found especially in the Töss Sister-Book.[12]

Finally, the verb *dunken* ("to seem, appear") and the formulations "as if" and "as it were," (*Vnd wz ir wie, quasi, ut sibi uidebatur*) play an important role in the Sister-Books, suggesting an attempt in objectivity. They are used both for the narrator's own view and for supposed hallucinatory experiences attributed to sisters (*K* 107; *D* 25; *T* 19; *U* 359).[13]

While as modern readers of these texts, we still need to make a conscious effort to overcome our aversion to clichés, the point has been made that the medieval audience may have found the repeated use of

---

11. Concerning "sweet," see Gehring (1957, 280–292); Langer (1982, 67); see also the bibliographical data on the use of "sweet" compiled by Dinzelbacher (1990, 23 n.36). The Töss text has an oxymoron playing on a sister's name: "the exceedingly sweet Sister Beli von Sure" – *sur* meaning "sour" (*T* 41).

12. Lüers (1926, 87 and 27–29); see also Blank (1962, 157)

13. On visions in the Sister-Books that typically start with "she imagined" (*do dynkt si*) as "imaginative" visions, see Langer (1987, 122).

allegories and other such devices, including legendary patterns, as inter-
esting and witty as we find them boring.[14] We are, therefore, especially pleased when confronted with what appear to be fresh, albeit
stark images, like the one in the Töss text: Jüzi Schulthasin understood
that "as impossible as it would be for one human being to stab another
one in his eye and break it out without him knowing it, it was one
thousand times more impossible for God not to know everything" (T
74). Images like that may help shatter the impression, gained from a
cursory glance at these works, of an overly saccharin tone.

3. Intention

In line with the rhetorical conventions of the time, some authors of the
Sister-Books specifically state that their texts were written in honor of
God and for the improvement of the audience. Elisabeth von Kirchberg's opening line reads: "For the eternal praise of our Lord Jesus
Christ and for the great betterment of all those who read this or hear
it read, I will write a little" (K 104). The Weiler author uses the formulaic ending: "God be praised for all his grace. Amen" (W 85).

The Sister-Books instruct by telling stories and by presenting nuns
as role models in their openness to divine grace. Katharina von Unterlinden writes, "exempli gratia enarrabo" (U 367), and the entry on Richi
in the Töss text concludes with a voice heard by another sister: "If you
lived like Richi von Schalchen, oh how greatly you would profit then"
(T 84). "To lead a moral life one does not need a theory about how one
should live, but a flesh and blood existent," Wyschogrod explains in a
similar context.[15]

Usually the accounts of an extraordinary happening or the "life" of
a special sister stand on their own, leaving the moral implication to the
readers and listeners. Only rarely are there any direct exhortations like
the one in the Oetenbach text: "From this [tale] of the saintly severe
life of this blessed sister ..., we should improve" (O 247). While the
authors' didactic purpose is apparent throughout, and while they clearly
wish to reaffirm the values of their audience, they are not overly
preachy or pedantic.[16] The work is written, the Töss author suggests,

---

14. Werner Schütz, *Geschichte der christlichen Predigt* (Berlin, New York: de
Gruyter, 1972), p. 59.

15. Wyschogrod (1990, 3 and 9); see also Dinzelbacher (1988a, 15).

16. Wyschogrod (1990, 10): "The [hagiographic] tale is not intended to elicit
replication but to inspire a new catena of moral events appropriate for the addres-
see's life."

to rekindle the audience's religious fervor. Describing herself in conversation with Elisabet Bechlin, she explains: "In many places now, divine love starts to become extinguished in human hearts"; it is, therefore, good to talk about exemplary lives (*T* 87).

The explicit intention of improving the reading and listening audience, however, does not *eo ipso* imply, as has, at times, been charged, a general decline in the community's morale at the time of writing. For history shows that the Dominican women's monasteries generally remained in good shape, both spiritually and economically, at least until the years of the Black Death (1348–1352). Instead, typical for the Sister-Books is the topos *laudatio temporis acti*, that is, the notion that times past always look more praiseworthy than the present. And although these texts were to edify a fourteenth century audience which by then lived in relatively comfortable surroundings in comparison with their forebears, the authors simultaneously insist that "much could also be written about our contemporaries" (*T* 14). The Weiler narrator specifically explains: "One would also like to write about the living sisters who are still with us and among us. But they do not want to grant permission that something be written about them while they are still alive" (*W* 85). The sisters' humility, then, forbids them to speak about their own virtues so that the authors can only point to the saintliness of the current community as a whole.[17]

The texts, then, are also written, the authors explain, to preserve noteworthy events of the lives of sisters in their communities (*U* 420; *W* 68) and to commemorate the monasteries' glorious past. The Diessenhofen preface reads: "I have written this book of the blessed sisters who have departed from our community, the monastery of Diessenhofen," so that we will not "forget it all"; and "as insignificant as" the book is, "I have still put it together with much trouble for the improvement of those who hear it" (*D* "Vorrede").

4. The Audience
The Sister-Books are composed for the benefit of the audience, *ad utilitatem legencium* (*U* 351). Often the authors directly confront their readers or listeners: "so that you may better be aware of God's great mira-

---

17. Following Johannes Meyer's fifteenth-century perspective, interpreters have often understood the Sister-Books as a *Reformschrift* , that is, an exhortation to return to "severe asceticism"; see Gehring (1957, 9); Blank (1962, 89; Langer (1987, 54). For the opposite view, see Ringler (1980a, 109). Regarding the women's monasteries during the early fourteenth century, see Dinzelbacher, Verflex 7:172.

cles" (*D* 41). In pursuing their didactic purpose, however, the narrators never talk down to the women they write for. Rather they count themselves among those who need betterment (*O* 247; *U* 346).

This equal footing with their audience is, in fact, a decisive characteristic of the Sister-Books. Going one step beyond the usual assumption of medieval religious authors who generally presuppose an identical value system with their audience, these authors directly address a specific audience of like-minded women located in their immediate and wider vicinity. They envision their work being read in the refectory and the workroom of their own and neighboring communities.[18]

This close relationship with the audience accounts for the lively contact the authors establish. Frequent interjections, much more typical for an oral presentation than for a written work, enliven the narration, encouraging the audience to pay close attention, such as, "You should know" and "Note this!" (*K* 105); "*Nec mirum!*" (*U* 358); and "I will now reveal to you" (*E* 17). Asides, too, seem to draw the audience into the authors' confidence: "If only we lazy and indolent ones had such humility" (*U* 352). Obviously the authors feeling so close to their audience were able to calculate in advance the specific reaction a topos or key term would elicit among their readers or listeners. They do not only appeal to reason and understanding but also evoke emotions and stimulate the imagination; in short, they elicit a total response.[19]

Notably, the authors also expect the audience's creative participation, as Katharina von Unterlinden explains:

> You should further know that I have shortened this [tale] (painting the surface as if picking some flowers for pleasure), thereby giving to the women-readers an opportunity to put their knowledgeable hands on this unformed material at some time in order to perfect this glorious work (*U* 336. 10–14).

Likening her splendid work to a *florilegium* (that is, a collection of different text passages, immensely popular in the later Middle Ages), the

---

18. Haas (1988, 365) speaks of "Literatur aus dem Kloster fürs Kloster." See also Haas (1987b, 156); Ohlenroth (1992, 424). The Gotteszell and Töss authors (*G* 147; *T* 16) each use a masculine pronoun referring to the intended audience. Although its use is grammatically dictated through the context, there is a possibility that the authors also aimed at a wider audience.

19. This "facet of the living audience" is something the Sister-Book has in common with homilies, see Murphy (1971, xx).

author invites her audience to cooperate so that her task will be accomplished. The "perfection" of her work, of course, does not simply mean that more material be added to the text, as some of her sisters obviously understood her to say (which may account for later additions to these texts), but rather that the purpose of her writing be fulfilled by the audience. The listener and reader are generally called upon not to judge the work but to validate it.[20]

Accordingly, the Gotteszell text contains a note, written presumably by a later scribe, explaining how the book was received by its first audience:

> After this little book had been composed and was publicly read to the community for the sake of betterment, a very blessed sister saw in her sleep four eyes telling her that they wanted to illuminate and guarantee this little book that it had been written in all things according to truth ... (G 147. 36–40).

She then explains that the eyes were "the four heavenly animals that Saint John had seen" [Rv. 4:6]. The author thus legitimizes her literary work through a vision or a dream, as is often the case in medieval religious prose. The passage simultaneously reveals the audience's satisfied reaction to the work.

The Sister-Books overcome the boundaries normally found between author and audience. In these works, women talk directly to women in a manner that not only presupposes full understanding but also expects full cooperation in that the text, such as the meaning behind the legendary clichés, is not only easily deciphered by an audience trained to do so, but also eagerly anticipated. The relationship can even be understood as a reciprocal one, because the author, on her part, relies on and gains strength from the community that affirms and so completely supports her work.[21]

20. The general notion that a work remains unfinished until received by the reading audience is stressed again for modern literature, see Walter Rees, *Literarische Rezeption*, Metzler 194 (Stuttgart: Metzler, 1980), p. 56.

21. On the audience's reaction, see also Haas (1983, 41). Hans Robert Jauß prefers Gadamer's term of "a melting of horizons" (*Horizontverschmelzung*) for the text-audience relationship; the audience, he states, is always both active and receptive; see "Rezeptionsästhetik–Zwischenbilanz: Der Leser als Instanz einer neuen Geschichte der Literatur," *Poetica 7* (1975) 325–343, esp. 333, 338.

5. The Structure
a. A Two-Part Division: Chronicle and Exempla

The Sister-Books' foundation story (*buoch der stifftung; liber fundacionis*) typically begins with the introduction of a few women, referred to as "beguines" and as "widows," who assembled to live a communal religious life. The chronicle then follows a recognizable traditional pattern.

After the original members had attracted a number of like-minded women, they decided to move to a larger building. While considering this relocation, miracles of various sorts led them to a certain location. The Töss author, for instance, speaks of "several beautiful blissful lights shining on the site" and a voice being heard there (*T* 13), while the Diessenhofen text is more elaborate:

> Now you shall know that the site on which this monastery is built used to be a miserable backwoods area not fit for anyone. But ... our Lord ... adorned this site with special miracles. Several people who passed by on the street at night and those who travelled up and down the Rhine, saw beautiful candles and large lights burning there. And occasionally, one saw beautiful lambs running around that nobody knew about except that they, by God's grace, were seen by honest people several times (*D* "Gründungsgeschichte").

The Oetenbach author relates that a villager's dream vision had led them to one of the many locations where they had lived: "a man in the village of Zollikon, a village not far from the city of Zürich, dreamed of a site called *Fundenwert* ["worth finding"] which is now called Old-Oetenbach." And he also saw "that very many birds alighted there; and then they all lifted up again and flew away" (*O* 221). The author explains that this dream foretold a new location for the Oetenbach women where they did not stay for long. The Kirchberg chronicler explains they were forced to change building sites when their corner stone kept moving away from them. After three moves, the stone located itself on land that was eventually donated to them for the construction of a monastery (ms. [S] cod.hist.330, f.15). (In most cases, the building ground was donated by noble families of the area.)[22]

Second, all chronicles relate, in a more or less elaborate way (most detailed in the Oetenbach text),[23] how the women, after having built

---

22. For the legendary motif of the moving stones, see Günter (1910, 56, 64).

23. On the Oetenbach text as an example of medieval history writing, see Kunze (1952, 96f.).

their homestead, took it upon themselves, usually by walking to the papal court on foot, to ask the pope for incorporation of their community into the Order of Preachers. Some texts give the precise and historically verifiable date during the 1240s of this major accomplishment. The Engeltal text, for instance, relates how the newly elected prioress, Diemut von Gailenhusen, undertook this trip:

> She stood up on her feet and walked with a sister and a lay brother to Rome. There was a friar preacher at the papal court. And when he perceived their seriousness and their saintliness, he conveyed to the pope their desire, more than they themselves could have done. And the pope confirmed their privileges and [issued] their bull (*E* 7.12–17).

While the Engeltal author takes Rome as the generic term for the papal court, Anna von Munzingen reports more correctly that the Adelhausen representative went to Lyon where, because of the thirteenth general council, the pope resided in 1245: "This same countess," that is, the founding widow, Kunigunde von Sulz, "travelled to the Council of Lyon where the Emperor Friedrich was banned. There she acquired [our incorporation into] the order" (*A* 154). Such long journeys, as the ones mentioned here, were no mean feat for women at a time when the roads were notoriously dangerous.

Third, in their poor but saintly life, these early Dominican communities were reaffirmed in their religious fervor by miraculous signs. The authors often employ standard monastic tales as a proof that God's blessing rested on the new monasteries.

Following the chronicle, the second part of the Sister-Books consists of the *exempla*. The authors present tales about exceptional individual sisters, some of whom may have lived as early as the beginning of the thirteenth century. Their stories deal with both the special virtues of selected sisters and with various signs of divine grace they are said to have received.[24]

In some entries, such as in the Töss text, an internal structure is discernible in the second part of the book, dividing most passages

---

24. In its broadest meaning and as used in the Middle Ages, *exemplum, bispel,* is an "illustrative story" with edifying and didactic intent; that is, the *exemplum* always refers to the tale itself, not to the character represented, see Bremond and Le Goff and Schmitt (1982, 27ff). *Exempla,* such as miracle stories, were widely employed in sermons and legendary writings as a teaching device. See also Haas (1987a, 292).

between "real life" asceticism and "special graces," *sunder gnad* – a pattern frequently encountered in medieval hagiography. In general, the individual entries range from independent pieces of several pages to very short paragraphs. The accounts may contain glimpses of a family background, scenes from the monastic life, and special graces granted to an individual, and they may deal in a sober tone with the ascetic life of a sister. Other entries comprise only a few sentences and consist of nothing but a cliché miracle more or less arbitrarily attached to a certain name or even entries without any name, starting with "We also had a sister." What matters in these tales is their *exemplum* character. Hence, no attempt is made in this interpretation to decide where the boundaries between historical accuracy (if any) and legendary material might lie. Obviously there are degrees of historicity.

The *exempla* of the Sister-Books also provide some information, more or less between the lines, about the community life of these women, about their attitude to the clergy, about their view of the world outside the cloister, about their spiritual and theological interests, and more. Since it has been shaped into a narrative, such information cannot *eo ipso* be taken as hard fact. Nevertheless, the reader may be able to gain some insight into attitudes, ideas, and ideals of these women, as later chapters of this study attempt to show.

The initial account of the modest beginning of the community, then, serves effectively as a foil for the great achievements in later days that the authors are intent on telling. The sense of accomplishment, that permeates the early history of the community's foundation and *exempla* featuring outstanding women who were responsible for the eventual resounding success of the saintly monastery, ties the two parts of the texts together. One without the other would diminish the Sister-Books' literary merit.

b. Structural Devices

Attention to the basic rules of rhetoric by the authors account for the internal structure of the books. Some texts are surrounded by a prologue and epilogue (such as *W* 68 and 85). The Gotteszell author begins by saying, "Those who want to give praises and thanks to the Lord for the overflowing graces ... should take to heart the words written here about miracles so that they may participate here and in eternal bliss in the same consoling graces" (*G* 123). And as her epilogue, the same author makes use of a poem composed in rhyming couplets (consisting of a total of forty-eight lines) which reads in part:

> Nobody shall read this little book
> unless they notice with diligence
> that God does not leave unrewarded
> those who live according to his love (*G* 147b.1–7).

In the Oetenbach text, the lengthy history section starts with a prologue and ends with an *Explicit*, each containing the biblical image [Eph. 2:20] of Jesus Christ as the cornerstone of this monastery (*O* 218, 237).

At times an inconsistency in structuring reveals to us that divers authors and editors were at work, as was the case in the Weiler text mentioned above. Likewise, series of short episodes in the Töss Sister-Book as well as entries with independent endings, with the closing formula Amen (*T* 84, 86) and an *Explicit* or *Dis ist uss* (*O* 248; *T* 33) suggest several hands.

Structural planning becomes evident also in the use of foreshadowing, such as: "I will let you know" (*E* 4); and "as you will perceive well hereafter" (*G* 137). Similar attention to an over-all plan is suggested by authors when they refer back to something they related before: *als da vor geschriben stet* (*K* 119; *U* 363, 407).

The authors of the Sister-Books also claim a careful selection of the material on hand (*U* 381). They speak of shortening their tales (*U* 374); excuse themselves for a necessary omission, such as, "we must omit [some things] because of the length of this tale in order not to let displeasure arise, *das da von icht urdrüsz wahse*" (*G* 145; *T* 61; *K* 105; *D* 41). Anna von Munzingen uses the cliché, "one neither can nor wants to write all this" (*A* 156). Katharina von Unterlinden directly refers to rhetorical terms, when she explains her procedure as "*prolixitatem, matrem fastidii, euitantes*" (*U* 385). The authors thus mind the eminent rhetorical rule that the audience must be entertained (that is, Horace's concept of *delectare*).

The rules for tight structuring are set aside, though, when the authors digress by inserting material that is often not directly related to the subject matter. It is thus that some standard monastic tales, *Klosternovellen*, are given a place in the Sister-Books to provide moral teaching as well as entertainment. And it is this rhetorical device that enabled the Gotteszell author to integrate the *jubilus*-hymn into her text (*G* 127–130).[25]

---

25. Concerning *Klosternovellen*, see Krebs (1904, 94ff.).

6. One Body of Literature

The individual characteristics of the nine Sister-Books also highlight their inherent similarity. Each text was compiled between 1310 and 1350; each text originated within the limited geographical boundaries of the southern area of the Dominican province of Teutonia; each text, furthermore, deals with one specific women's community. The unique historical context for the compilation of these works is also identical: this was a time for each of these communities to take stock, to recapture their origins and past achievements before they would be forgotten, and to celebrate the current community of saintly sisters.

The Sister-Books were usually composed in more than one editorial process by one or more monastic women. These authors, editors, and compilers made use of traditional tales about their monastery's early history as well as its more recent past. They integrated pre-written *exempla* as well as orally transmitted tales into their works. It is generally acknowledged that the Sister-Books are compilations of a number of different texts written by different women authors at different times preceding the final editing of each work.

Given the complicated genesis of these texts, it is nevertheless not accidental that the Sister-Books represent "a homogeneous literary form."[26] With the exception of the Gotteszell and Weiler books (because of their poor manuscript tradition), each text starts with a chronicle. In it the authors relate the foundation history of their monastery, making sure that the number of miracles attached to the story qualifies the beginning of each community as an undertaking divinely authorized. Each text also contains a series of accounts of individual sisters of the community. These entries, typically varying in length, are, nevertheless, similar to each other. With its underlying theme of praise and thanksgiving uniting the two parts of the book, each text constitutes a tribute to a saintly community of women.[27]

And while the nine texts differ slightly as to their literary significance and as to their cultural and socio-historical relevance, such differences pale in comparison with the many similarities. It seems

26. Regarding several authors of the Sister-Books, see also Peters (1988c, 102); Gehring (1957, 14).

27. Haas (1987a, 297) thinks that some of these texts may contain some intentional propaganda for the particular monastery. See also Ruh (1978, 593); Zoepf (1914, 28).

appropriate, therefore, that the Sister-Books be recognized as one body of literature.[28]

THE LITERARY GENRE

Depending on a work's classification, the critical measuring rod can yield drastically different results. Throughout the reception history of the Sister-Books, the contentious issue of the genre of this *corpus* has interfered with its interpretation. In an attempt to solve this problem, I will briefly scan some potentially appropriate genres.

1. Mysticism

Coincidentally, many manuscripts of the Sister-Books were discovered at the same time as those of medieval German mystics. This led some nineteenth-century scholars (starting with Carl Johann Greith, 1861) to include the Sister-Books automatically among the works of Dominican mystics – albeit, compared with the male "masters," as a second-rate sample of late medieval mysticism.

There is little doubt that the Sister-Books stand within the mystical tradition. Passages of religious fervor describing an ascetic life, accounts of raptures and the occasional reference to someone's mystical experience are not infrequent, as a few examples will illustrate. In the Gotteszell text we read of Margaretha von Rosenstein:

> And finally she came to the grace that she could neither see nor talk, so that she had to be carried from the dormitory. And when the sisters saw this behavior, they were greatly astonished what God had done with her blessed soul in this long while, for her body was so insensible that she lay like a corpse. And the sisters who were with her saw that she had lost consciousness. Then they wanted to examine and better perceive God's miracle, and they pricked her with needles. She reacted as little as if she had been some piece of wood. And when she came to again, she was asked both privately and publicly, but she did not want to tell anybody about it (*G* 139.30–42).

In a rapture, Ernst Benz explains, persons often experience a complete temporary loss of their senses, thus reaching a state of catalepsy. Following a hagiographic topos, the scene quoted typically depicts the effect of this special state as well as the total lack of understanding on

---

28. See also Acklin Zimmermann (1993, 34).

the part of the bystanders. Their pricking with needles was a common test (cf. *W* 68) when on-lookers suspected a person of having been en-raptured.[29]

A rapture may also entail an out-of-body experience following which the soul is typically reluctant to return to earth.[30] The Töss author explains that Ita Sulzerin's soul after a rapture hesitated, not wanting "to return again into her body, hovering for a long time over the body"; for to her noble soul the body appeared "contemptible and ignoble" (*T* 81; cf. *O* 241). In the Adelhausen text, Else von Vacken-stein's body is shown "shuddering" and "shooting up" at the point where her soul was ready to come back after a rapture (*A* 157).

Raptures may lead to a mystical union (also called *die genad jubilus*[31]), an experience that remains incomprehensible even for the sister herself (*W* 75; cf. *U* 353, 389; *O* 267). Elisabeth von Kirchberg defines the *jubilus* as follows:

> One should know that whoever wants to come to the grace *jubilus* ... must be completely free in heart and mind from all attachment to passing things and must have complete, uncontaminated purity ... . But note what the grace *jubilus* is: It is a grace that is so immeasurable and great that nobody can hide it and yet nobody can fully describe it in its sweetness. It is so abundant that heart, soul, and mind, and all veins of the human being are inundated with ineffable sweetness so perfectly that no one is disciplined enough to contain oneself in this grace. Perfect love shines through in this grace with divine light. This is the *jubilus* (*K* 105.11–24).

The author here makes use of terminology typical of the mystics by naming detachment and purification as prerequisites for this grace which flows into the human being as an unwarranted gift of love; its awesome effect is such that no tongue can tell nor can the recipient remain silent.[32]

---

29. Benz (1969, 226ff.). Kieckhefer (1984, 153) refers to such episodes in the life of Catherine of Siena.

30. See Dinzelbacher's comparative study (1985c) of such scenes with near-death experiences.

31. Ringler (1980a, 105); Langer (1987, 150). Grundmann, in his essay "Jubel" (1978), discusses the origin, meaning, and semantic change of the term *jubilus*. As used here, the term offers an example of the later development of *jubilus* in the meaning of mystical rapture.

32. For an excellent discussion (aimed at the English-speaking reader) of the MHG mystical terminology, see Schmidt (1985, esp. 22–26).

Mystical terminology also includes the mystical kiss, as exemplified in a bizarre Adelhausen episode about a sister lost in contemplation under an overturned tub (*A* 155). In somewhat more abstract terms, the Töss author explains mystical union as becoming "one will and one love" with God (*T* 73).

Passages like these understandably led interpreters to classify the Sister-Books as a work of mysticism. And yet, these paragraphs are of a descriptive nature and told by an observer. An experiential aspect is usually lacking. If we spoke of mysticism as a genre, the authors of the Sister-Books would have to be characterized as biographical (rather than autobiographical) mystical authors.

Aware of the inadequacy of this classification for the Sister-Books, recent interpreters have employed the term "mystology" or "mysta-gogical" literature. In other words, they see in the Sister-Books mystical teaching rather than a direct expression of mystical experiences. For in spite of many mystical key terms used throughout these texts, Ringler claims, mystical experience in the Sister-Books appears "only as a derivative." Elisabeth von Kirchberg – perhaps a mystic herself – may be an exception, since throughout her work she shows herself capable of defining different "graces" and dividing into categories intrinsic parts of someone else's mystical experience without sounding flat.[33]

The genre of mysticism, then, if seen in the restrictive terms of mystology and mystagogy, comes close to classifying some passages in the Sister-Books. It does not, however, do justice to the entire work, because this category does not equally cover the chronicles nor most of the *exempla*.

2. *Historiography*

English-speaking writers, when they mention the Sister-Books at all, refer to them as "Convent Chronicles," thus placing the emphasis on the historical component. Historiography (although it had not yet become a discipline of its own but was grouped with rhetoric in the seven liberal arts) was a field of special interest during the late Middle Ages. In Germany, historical works in the vernacular were composed as early as the mid-twelfth century, and their popularity, stimulated by the mendicant friars, greatly increased during the thirteenth century. In a medieval context, historiography comprises both secular and salvation

---

33. On mystical passages in the Sister-Books, see *Frauenmystik im Mittelalter* (1985, 388); Ringler (1990, 89, 104); Acklin Zimmermann (1993, 167).

history, for the events of history were interpreted in view of what was understood as the only true reality, that of the world-to-come. Typically, therefore, it is difficult "to draw a sharp dividing line" between history and hagiography. In other words, history-writing, especially during the later Middle Ages, becomes generally more and more "like story-telling." Miracles and other unusual happenings, reported as having been witnessed by some well-known person, are often integrated into secular history. The extremely popular "Golden Legend" (the *Legenda aurea*, circa 1264), for instance, counted as a medieval work of history.[34]

The Sister-Books do contain some glimpses of events that happened outside of the cloister walls, such as references to an interdict (O 270), to local battles (T 23, 77f.; W 80), and to a certain ruler (such as Emperor Friedrich II in A 154; E 2). But in general these authors work on a small scope, having no intention of speaking about any of the major events of their time, concentrate almost exclusively on their own monasteries.

The Sister-Books' chronicles, of course, represent medieval historiography. They belong, in fact, to a special category, the so-called "monastic foundation histories," *Klostergründungsgeschichten* or *Historiae fundationum monasteriorum*. Such chronicles, originally a genre of medieval Latin literature, but some also transmitted in MHG, were highly popular especially during the late Middle Ages, having started about 1150. Foundation histories typically abound in legendary traits and are of minor historical value. As Karl Münzel explains, the monastics often created their own history in answer to the enthusiasm with which the late medieval reading audience devoured such works as an entertainment.[35]

---

34. On medieval historiography, see Brincken (1988, 304–306); *Deutsche Chroniken* (1936, 9); Lotter (1979, 308). On the eschatological concept in medieval historiography, see Grundmann (1934, 421); Ott (1984, 186). Schmid (1963, 98) speaks of *Geschichtenschreibung* versus *Geschicht-schreibung*, that is, story-writing versus history-writing. See also Horst Wenzel (*Höfische Geschichte: Literarische Tradition und Gegenwartsdeutung in den volkssprachigen Chroniken des hohen und späten Mittelalters*, Beiträge zur Älteren Deutschen Literatur 5 (Bern and Frankfurt, Main and Las Vegas: Lang, 1980) p. 54: "absolute' Faktentreue [kann] kein Ziel der mittelalterlichen Historiographie sein."

35. On foundation stories, see Honemann (1983); Däniker-Gysin (1958, 17); Patze (1977); Münzel (1933, 37ff.).

These chronicles were usually written to celebrate an individual monastery or as a favor to a founder's family, and more so than ordinary medieval historiography, foundation histories usually had a special spiritual, edifying effect. The "necessary ingredients" of this genre are also present in the Sister-Books. Monastic foundation stories contain a foundation legend (such as a vision or miracle); speak about actual steps taken for the building of a monastery (such as purchasing or being given a lot); and relate a miracle as a proof of the saintliness of the community in question.[36]

Münzel, who only talks about monks' monasteries, does not list as a characteristic the onerous trips to the papal court that the women had to take to become accredited members of an order (A 154; E 7; O 224f.). Such journeys constitute an essential part only of the nuns' foundation history since monks or friars typically start by belonging to an established order.

Nevertheless, the Sister-Books' chronicles are clearly in line with this particular genre of historiography; they are *not*, as Wilhelm Oehl wanted us to think, "typically female, without a trace of objective history writing."[37] Rather, the chronicles belong to the tradition of the medieval monastic foundation histories. Medieval historiography, then, is related to what the Sister-Books represent, but this genre does not exhaust these works' complexity.

3. Hagiography
In hagiography, which is "one of the principal genres of medieval literature," God-given saintliness lies at the centre of interest. In Hippolyte Delehaye's classical definition, hagiography is "part biography, part panegyric, part moral lesson." Hagiography or legend-writing (the terms are used interchangeably) were most popular under the form of the *vita*.[38]

---

36. On various aspects of monastic foundation stories, see also Honemann (1983, 1239f.); Münzel (1933, 48f., 56f.). The MHG *Das Stiftungs-Buch des Klosters St. Bernhard*, Fontes rerum Austriacarum 6, ed. H. J. Zeibig (Wien 1853), for instance, shows a number of striking similarities with the Sister-Books chronicles: finding the site through special divine revelation, a nobleman who declares himself interested in founding a monastery, and the poor and hard life of the first nuns; it even includes the story (similar to the Diessenhofen chronicle) that a raven provides a big cheese for the nuns' nourishment at a crucial moment.

37. Oehl (1924, 13).

38. On the characteristics of hagiography, see Delehaye (1962, 54); Weinstein and Bell (1982, 47); Scheibelreiter (1988, 285); Lotter (1979, 308).

From the early beginnings of monastic life, readings from hagio-graphic material, usually centering on the saint of the day, became an obligatory part of the daily routine in every monastery. Eventually, legends of saints, next to sermons, represented the most important spiritual nourishment for the nuns and monks, equal to that of the gospels and the Acts. Especially during the late Middle Ages, legends became the numerically most frequent literary expression of that time.[39]

Hagiography exerted no doubt a strong influence on the Sister-Books. And although *vita is* a misnomer for the average entry in the Sister-Books, which simply lacks a *vita*'s complexity, some entries could be referred to as *vita*-like. Similarities between the typical *vita* and some longer entries in the Sister-Books include, according to Ringler, the intention of praising God and edifying the audience, a catalogue of vir-tues, a series of episodes, and the *exemplum* character. But since most entries fall short of such a fully developed *vita*, König (1880) already coined the special term *Gnadenleben*, that is, "lives of grace," as a designation specifically for the Sister-Books. The term is helpful in showing that the Sister-Books do belong to hagiography but that, at the same time, their entries cannot simply be equated with the traditional *vita*.[40]

However, there exists within the genre of hagiography a prototype for the Sister-Books, that is, Gerard de Frachete's *Vitae fratrum*, "The Lives of the Brethren." Related to similar collections that proliferated during the thirteenth century, and standing in the literary tradition of such favorites as the sixth-century *Vitas patrum*, and St.Gregory the Great's *Dialogi* (593/594), Frachete's work came about by order of the General Chapter of the Dominicans in Paris in 1256. The task of com-piling and editing this collection was accomplished by 1260. Gerard de Frachete (†1281), the Provincial of Provence at that time, was named as the editor of the "Lives of the Brethren," which was intended as a

39. On medieval legends, see Steer (1987, 307). Among the specifically Dominican literature preceding the Sister-Books were St. Dominic's *vita* by Dietrich von Apolda, Vincent of Beauvais' *Speculum historiale* (circa 1250), and Thomas de Chantimpré's various *vitae*, and especially Jacobus a Voragine's *Legenda aurea*. Moreover, the Cistercian Caesarius von Heisterbach's work, *Dialogus miraculorum* (about 1220), and the Augustinian Jacques de Vitry's *Sermones vulgares* (before 1240) were among the regular readings in monasteries.

40. Ringler (1980a, 10); König (1880, 149). König's term was revived by Ringler (1980a, 6) in the slight variation of *Gnadenvita*.

chronicle of the origin and development of the Order of Preachers. All the friars were officially encouraged to send in relevant material. The work was revised between 1265 and 1271. The "Lives of the Brethren" consists of an introductory chronicle with a number of monastic foundation histories for individual convents, and of a long series of entries concerning virtuous friars, preceded by two lengthy *vitae* of St. Dominic and Jordan of Saxony. Critics agree that Gerard's narrative reveals "an almost fantastic love of the marvelous." Legendary clichés and monastic tales are an integral part of his work and go back most likely to the same legendary sources from which the Sister-Books are drawn. Petra Seifert's comparison (1985) of Frachete's work with the Töss text shows close similarities, in some cases even identical formulations.[41]

It has been generally accepted that the Sister-Books were patterned after Gerard de Frachete's *Vitae fratrum*, although a marked difference exists, not just because its content deals with women, but also in such areas as perspective, attitude, and tone.

4. The Sister-Books: A Genre of Their Own

This brief survey of the various genres, that the Sister-Books have been thought to be indebted to, yields the general conclusion that the authors, in different degrees of intensity, made use of diverse influences. But in spite of many unmistakable similarities of parts of the Sister-Books to each of the genres surveyed, this body of literature fits (in its entirety) best into the genre of hagiography and closely resembles its model, the *Vitae fratrum*.[42]

The Sister-Books, however, are not simply a female version of Frachete's work, as becomes obvious when their differentiating features are considered. These distinctive characteristics of the Sister-Books may be summarized as follows:

> The idea for the Sister-Books, as far as we know, originated with the women's communities themselves while the *Vitae fratrum* was centrally ordained.
>
> Each Sister-Book deals with only one individual monastery, since the cloistered nuns had neither the official cooperation of their order nor, due to enclosure, the liberty to move about collect-

41. On Frachete and his work, see Jarrett (1924, v–vii). Wehofer (1897, 24ff.) shows how the *Vitae fratrum*, which appeared within ten years of Aquinas' *Summa*, was, even then, severely criticized by many readers from within the Order of Preachers; the *Vitae* is "reeking of holy naiveté," as Schillebeeckx (1983, 242) puts it.

42. Ringler (1990, 103).

ing generally relevant material for the entire Second Order, even if they had intended to do so.

The Sister-Books have features that go beyond the typical legendaries, such as passages of deep spiritual content and examples of hymnic poetry.

And above all, the didactic element of the Sister-Books reveals a markedly non-authoritarian approach in as much as these female authors invite the reader and listener to participate in their thinking and feeling.[43] Instead of producing a carbon copy of the *Vitae fratrum* with a simple gender-change, the nuns deliberately set out to author a parallel but different work about saintly women.

The striking contrast between the Sister-Books' positive images of saintly women and the traditionally misogynist hagiographic literature is not be underestimated. The highly ambiguous legendary image of women that was at the disposal of the authors of the Sister-Books was either the idealized saintly virgin of the *vitae* who was impossible to emulate, or else the common harlot that showed up in many guises providing great entertainment for a male audience.

The MHG version of the *Vitas patrum*, available by 1300 and, according to Engelbert Krebs, known to the Dominican nuns, is a typical instance. It contains only two blameless women characters: a desert mother and the wife of a pagan. All other females are despicable: women persistently seduce monks; a saintly virgin after forty-five years as an anchoress is not able to overcome her vainglory; and even the devil appears in the image of a woman. In Vincent of Beauvais' *Speculum*, to name another example, woman is represented as "the confusion of man, an insatiable beast, a continuous anxiety, ... and a hindrance to devotion." And Gerard de Frachete's *Vitae fratrum* belongs to this tradition. While showing some saintly Dominican nuns, his work also includes episodes of loose women tempting friars. Donald Weinstein and Rudolph M. Bell point out that *vitae* of male saints "invariably [portray] women (other than mothers and most sisters) ... as limbs of Satan; [women] had no other function than ... to induce [the men] to sin."[44]

---

43. See also Ringler (1990, 104).

44. On the nuns' familiarity with the *Vitas patrum*, see Krebs (1953, 257). For the image of women, see *Vitas patrum* (1903, 306, 373, 380, 384, 388–390, 392). For women in Frachete's work, see *Vitae fratrum* (1924, 142f.); and on women generally in *vitae*, see Weinstein and Bell (1982, 98). Tuchman (1978, 211) quotes from

Such misogynist tales were the steady diet offered to monastics, both male and female, in their daily reading. This depressingly negative image of women in the popular legends is the backdrop that highlights the unique and novel achievement of the authors of the Sister-Books. They created images of saintly women with whom contemporary women could identify.

Thus, while the formal appearance of the Sister-Books, such as language, style, and structure, resembles the *Vitae fratrum*, there is a wide gulf between the Sister-Books and all of its predecessors. Legendary clichés are used, as demanded by the contemporary reading and listening audiences, but the clichés are not adopted indiscriminately. The villains, for instance, are no longer female but male, such as the vengeful father and the seducer, although notably a good number of positive male figures also play a role in these texts. But the Sister-Books are most typically characterized by the specific contents of exemplary saintly women and the authors' consciously feminine perspective.

Women in the Sister-Books talk directly about themselves, their own community, their values and attitudes, and also occasionally about the society they come from; mostly they concentrate on the God-given graces granted significantly to women as women. And while other medieval works "by women or based on female witnesses ... are usually filtered through male editing," as Kari Elisabeth Børresen finds, the Sister-Books are unusual also in this respect. Thirteenth- and fourteenth-centuries women *are* the subject, they *are* the authors, compilers, editors, and copyists, and they *are* the audience. The end result is a complex literary narrative in praise of successful and saintly women's communities. Granted that many diverse influences, as surveyed above, are integrated into this work, the finished product is, nevertheless, more than any one such influence and more than a combination of several. It is for these reasons that the Sister-Books cannot be consigned to any one of the existing genres.[45]

The Sister-Books, then, may be understood as a body of literature whose language is deliberately simple, whose structure follows the *Vitae*

---

the *Speculum*. Many sermons the nuns heard also dwelt on "the crimes of Eve, Jezebel, Bathsheba and other notorious women of the Old Testament"; the low opinion of women was "a clerical commonplace throughout the medieval centuries: ... the usual adjective coupled with *mulier* is *fatua*" (that is, foolish, silly), Bennett (1937, 121f.) explains.

45. Børresen (1990, 923). As far as we know, male editors of the Sister-Books, such as Johannes Meyer, came into play only from the fifteenth century on.

fratrum, and whose narrative, by using legendary patterns, conveys spiritual teaching, and, above all, whose every page celebrates the saintliness of sisters and of women's communities. These features combined with the exclusive feminine perspective make the Sister-Books unique. As early as 1952, Georg Kunze suggested, using the term "autonomy," *Eigengesetzlichkeit*, that the authors of the Sister-Books followed their own rules. His judgment is still valid. We can only do justice to the literary *corpus* that these nine texts represent by treating the Sister-Books as a genre of their own.[46]

46. Kunze (1952, 27). For attempts to define the Sister-Books, see especially Ringler (1980a, 13); also Acklin Zimmermann (1991, 75); Haas (1983, 50). Johnson (1989), in her study on "the medieval nun's self-image" which does not mention the Sister-Books comes to conclusions similar to those I have been able to reach. See also Penelope D. Johnson's monograph, *Equal in Monastic Profession: Religious Women in Medieval France*, Women in Culture and Society (Chicago and London: Chicago University Press, 1991).

The story of how the Sister-Books fared from the mid-fourteenth century to the present is paradigmatic of the reception of women's literature in general, and women's religious texts in particular. The typically biassed reaction to the Sister-Books throughout the history of literary criticism, therefore, serves as a case study.[1]

THE PERIOD BEFORE THE PROTESTANT REFORMATION

1. The Interaction of Women's Communities

Thirteenth-century Dominican women's communities (among them the women of the monasteries we are here concerned with) knew each other and were in communication with each other (O 231). Archival documents provide proof of business transactions as early as 1263, for instance, between the monasteries of Weiler and Kirchberg. Records of women who transferred from one monastery to another also exist (E 24, 26; O 236).[2]

From the fourteenth century on, some "traffic in books" (*Bücherverkehr*) was established between Strasbourg and Switzerland. Kurt Ruh thinks it possible that the Sister-Books exerted a certain influence on the Benedictine women of Engelberg (Switzerland), and Alois Maria Haas speaks of literary contacts between Töss and Engelberg aided by the Lucerne municipal scribe Johannes Friker. This "flourishing trade" in manuscripts was the result of a "well-developed infrastructure" of the women's communities in Teutonia[3].

Similarities among the texts and even some almost identical passages in different Sister-Books, while partly accounted for by the common treasure-trove of generally available legendary material they share, also testify to the circulation of manuscripts of early versions or parts of the Sister-Books among the monasteries. Moreover, the concept of plagiarism was unknown to medieval authors who copied freely from each

---

1. See Lewis, *Bibliographie* (1989).
2. Dinzelbacher (1981, 264f.); Peters (1988b, 101); Uhland (1961, 14).
3. Robert Durrer, "Das Frauenkloster Engelberg als Pflegestätte der Mystik, seine Beziehungen zu den Straßburger Gottesfreunden und zu den frommen Laienkreisen der Innerschweiz," *Der Geschichtsfreund* (1921) 127–218. See also Ruh (1981, 54); Haas (1984a, 116); Acklin Zimmermann (1993, 35).

other. Especially sermons and generally edifying material, was judged as *herrenloses Gemeingut*, "unowned public domain." Ruth Meyer is convinced, for instance, that the Diessenhofen women were in possession of at least some of the Töss material during the time they composed the Diessenhofen text. And Ringler asserts that the Kirchberg community knew the Engeltal Sister-Book and that the Engeltal monastery had some material from the Kirchberg and Gotteszell texts. Engeltal also owned codices that had come from the Weiler monastery.[4]

In brief, networking, as we would call it today, between women's monasteries in Teutonia and beyond must, therefore, simply be taken for granted. Connections also existed through letters, through the contact with itinerant preachers (such as Heinrich von Nördlingen) and with the friars confessors, through annual visitations, and also through monastery chaplains who kept in touch with each other. Muschg describes monastic life, especially within the Order of Preachers, as a large web of inter-communication.[5]

2. Copying and Circulating Manuscripts

Writing and copying in the Dominican women's scriptoria was, from the beginning, an essential part of the nuns' cloistered life. Some theological works written in the nine monasteries in question are preserved from the early fourteenth century on. But only one manuscript of a Sister-Book, a copy of the Engeltal text (today in the Nürnberg Germanisches Nationalmuseum), dating from the middle of the fourteenth century, is extant. As literature became an important means for spreading the idea of spiritual renewal of the monastic reform from the

---

4. Ringler (1980a, 371f.) believes that the exchange of codices accounts for textual influences and similarities. See Spamer (1910, 14) for the notion of *herrenloses Gemeingut*. In his study of texts of Eckhart and Tauler, Spamer convincingly shows that a gluing-together of texts (*Agglutinierung*, Grubmüller 1969, 202) was common during the fourteenth and fifteenth centuries. Spamer (120) also distinguishes between *Vererbung* or conscious borrowing, on the one hand, and *Zersetzung* or a more naive copying, on the other. As a result, the texts underwent a constant change.

Meyer (1995, 40 n.69) cites passages from the Anne von Ramswag- and Elsbet von Stoffeln-entries (*D* 41 and 33 respectively) that are comparable to the wording in the Töss Sophie von Klingnau entry (*T* 55f.). The parallel Ringler (1980a, 107f.) cites does not prove but might suggest a direct influence; both *E* 23f. and *G* 132 have a passage where King David harps while a sister's soul leaves her body. And see Tanz and Werner (1993, 256) regarding Weiler manuscripts.

5. Muschg (1935, 137).

late 1300s on, the copying of manuscripts greatly intensified. Typically, monasteries that had undergone reform attracted better educated women interested in learning and education. Such monasteries began to put great emphasis on a well-stocked library. As Werner Williams-Krapp notes, the size of a fifteenth-century monastery library was less a sign of wealth than of renewed emphasis on informed spirituality.[6]

The Sister-Books, like other works, were instrumental in strengthening reformist ideals. Most of the extant manuscripts of the Sister-Books, therefore, date from the fifteenth century. With few exceptions, such as the 1433 Adelhausen codex [F] 98 and the 1451 Vienna *codex scotensis*, they were written by women in the monasteries of the mendicant orders that had returned to strict monastic rules. In fact, in their reformist zeal the scribes were apparently so overworked that they made mistakes that still confuse modern scholars: texts are conflated, (as are the Kirchberg and Gotteszell books); pages from one codex are unwittingly inserted into the text of another (a passage from Mechthild von Hackeborn is found in the Weiler manuscripts; an Engeltal entry is copied into the Kirchberg book); and such errors are thoughtlessly repeated. But while these errors have occasioned editorial confusion and misinterpretations, they are also testimony to the increasingly lively exchange of manuscripts during the fifteenth century.[7]

Single manuscripts of the Sister-Books are quite rare. The 1433 Freiburg manuscript of the Adelhausen text (F[98]) as well as manuscripts of the Unterlinden book exist in separate codices. However, the combination of a number of texts with similar contents into a single, large codex was much more common. A collective codex or *Sammelkodex* is usually built on a broad theme, such as religious, moral, and ascetic instruction, and vaguely resembles an anthology. The Sister-Books are thus often bound together with extracts from Suso's works, translations of the Helfta mystics, hymnic poems, prayers, sermons, and the like.

The oldest collective codex extant (Y 74) which contains a Sister-Book manuscript (the Diessenhofen text) was copied by two scribes in the Diessenhofen scriptorium some time after 1424. It became part of the monastery's library until it was transferred to the Frauenfeld library

---

6. Williams-Krapp (1986b, 42ff.). See Wallach-Faller (1986, 339f.) regarding early Dominican manuscripts; Ringler (1980a, 43) shows that especially reform monasteries attracted highly educated nuns.

7. See also Williams-Krapp (1993, esp. 302f.).

menschen enpfahen die gab. Da begert sie sin von
ganczem irem herczen Das gewert sie der gut got
alls williklich das sie dar nach ymm an iren tod
alle tag vnsers herren lichnam gaistlich enpfieng
in ir sel vnd dar inn tet ir vnser her manigvalltig
genad Da mit er sie sichert das sie in werlich het en
pfangen gaistlich vnd doch het sie als gros be
gird vnsers herren lichnam ze enpfahen dus zu
dem altar Das sie vnser her trost vnd sprach zu
ir Do du zu dem altar gaist so enpfahest du mit
das du da sichst sunder das du globest Also tustu
och sust als dik ich mich dir gib got vnd menschi
gaistlich vnd sprach Bis tref mit dem mvnd dihi
begird hor est werp men mit dem selben wort
enpfand sie gottes als werlich in ir sele in alles
der süssikait vnd genad als sie in zu dem altar
enpfieng Darnach sprach vnser herr zu ir Ich
wil dich sterken mit minem lichnam vnd wil dich
trösten hadigen mit minem wiirdige blut vnd
wil dich trösten mit minem zarte sel vnd wil din
sel gros machen mit miner ewigen gathait In aime
ander mess sprach er zu ir als zu Sant Augustino
Cibus sum grandium crescab me. Bet sprach och zu ir ih
der messe Ich han din sel lebendig gemacht mit
minhem lebendige lib vnd gerainiget mit mime
rösenwerbe blut vnd getröst vnd glorificiert
mit miner wiirdigen sel vnd han din sel erlüch
tet vnd enzundet So macht och des ragus so
sie vnsern herre enpfieng licel ittm essen Er
ward och dik aigenlichen grossen wacht was
vnser herr der samnut guten vnd gnade tet
des ragus so sie vnsern herren vnpfingen vnd
von vil frowen sunderlichen Es ward och.

in 1869 after the dissolution of Diessenhofen. The earliest surviving copy of parts of the Töss book in a collective codex (now in Donaueschingen, [D] 452) equally came from this active Diessenhofen scriptorium. This manuscript gathers together not only *vitae* of relatively recent women saints, from Elisabeth von Thüringen (1207–1231) and Margaretha of Hungary (1242–1270) to Elisabeth of Hungary (1293–1336), but also the Töss book entries on Sophia von Klingnau, Mechthilt von Stans, and Jüzi Schulthasin – all Dominicans, with the exception of Elisabeth von Thüringen.[8]

The Katharinenkloster, a Dominican women's monastery in Nürnberg, played an especially important role in the preservation and circulation of the manuscripts of the Sister-Books during the fifteenth century. The community was a cultural centre during the late Middle Ages and a focal point for reformed Teutonia. Wilms tells the story of how the Katharinenkloster at first resisted attempts at reform: when the Dominican reformer Konrad von Preußen tried to force his way into the Katharinenkloster, he was almost killed by a large crucifix wielded by two irate nuns. But by 1428, the community willingly returned to a strict observance of the rule. The renewal of spiritual and intellectual interests in the wake of this reform encouraged the nuns to copy and lend out codices.[9]

Uniquely, about one third of the well-stocked library of the Katharinenkloster has survived intact (it is now located in the Nürnberg municipal library). These manuscripts constitute one of the largest known German collections of the time and together document the extent to which the internal monastic reform influenced the preservation and promulgation of books. About half of all the works in the Katharinenkloster library were written by the sisters themselves, the other half were either donated by individuals or were originally part of the sisters' own dowries. The collection also testifies to the books read in reform-minded women's monasteries.[10]

8. See also Meyer (1995, 4f.) and Grubmüller (1969, 182–187) concerning the Frauenfeld and Donaueschingen manuscripts respectively.

9. See Schneider (1975, 212); (1983, 70); Barthelmé (1931, 32); Wilms (1920, 146f.)

10. The Katharinenkloster collection is the only medieval Dominican women's library available to modern historians. For a description of its holdings, see especially Schneider (1975, xiv) and Schneider (1983, 70, 73). The library contained, among other works, a copy of Hugo Ripelin von Strassburg's *Compendium theologicae veritatis* (around 1270), consisting of extracts from frequently read theologians. Schneider (1983, 79) claims that this volume was "generally not counted among the books read by women," *im allgemeinen keine Frauenlektüre.*

Johannes Meyer, among others, strongly influenced the literary work accomplished in the Katharinenkloster. In his *Book of Offices* (*Das amptbuch*, 1454) and its supplement (*Das buechlin der ersetzunge*, 1455), based on Humbert of Romans' *Liber de instructione officialium O.P.*, Meyer provided detailed rules for building up, cataloguing and maintaining a monastic library. He also established an efficient lending system, regulated by a book mistress (*buochmeisterin*), to encourage the circulation of codices among religious communities. The Nürnberg Katharinenkloster's library catalogue is witness to Meyer's effective instructions. Indeed, study of several manuscripts has shown that the Katharinenkloster nuns administered a medieval inter-library loan system that operated throughout the Province of Teutonia.[11]

The codices containing the Sister-Books are strictly functional. The manuscripts are typically plain, although the occasional red underlining and some enlarged coloured initials are also to be found. Marginal notes, glosses, and pointing fingers draw attention to especially important passages as well as some doodles and caricature, perhaps done by bored children, suggest that the books were in use. But these codices bear little resemblance to more familiar medieval illuminated manuscripts. Scribes and miniaturists did not lavish on the Sister-Books the attention they accorded the precious parchment codices or *Prachtkodizes* regularly produced in the women's scriptoria. One reason undoubtedly was, as Helga Unger explains, that vernacular texts, whether religious or poetical in content, were typically less illuminated since not intended for sacred purposes. A further reason for the Sister-Books' simplicity may also have been that a general chapter of the Order of Preachers had stipulated that books ought to be modest and written for practical purposes only. But in the end, poverty and humility were sufficient reason for these Dominican women to write their own texts in simple, unadorned, mostly paper manuscripts.[12]

11. See Meyer in: König (1880, 202–204), with Fechter (1983, 478). A vigorous traffic in manuscripts during the period is also evident in the friars' monasteries (Kunze 1952, 39). As Kirchhoff (1853, 5ff.) explains, this important development in medieval intellectual life coincided with the beginnings of the universities in the mid-fourteenth century.

12. Unger (1986, 25). In his *Expositio regulae* Humbert of Romans sarcastically condemns manuscript illuminations: "Beauty [in books] is puerile, since juveniles are delighted by flowery letters, a variety of representations, and similar things" (*Opera* [Rome, 1888], 1:448, cited by Brett [1980, 305]).

A codex from the Katharinenkloster, manuscript [N] Cent.V 10a, however, is an exception. Collected and in some cases augmented by what Grubmüller calls Johannes Meyer's "reformist penmanship," it contains the Töss and the Diessenhofen Sister-Books as well as the only extant copy of the Oetenbach text. The three works were copied in the Nürnberg Katharinenkloster by Klara Keiperin and two other scribes, presumably around 1454. Although the other manuscripts in the codex are average in appearance (only fol. 85ra has a miniature of a monastery church), the Töss text (fol. 1–84v) shows twenty-three miniatures in deep blue, red, green, and gold, contained within the initials of entries on individual sisters.[13] The miniatures depict nuns, *putzige Nönnchen,* as one Nürnberg archivist recently called them, in various attitudes: in prayer, being nursed by Mary, chastising themselves, in company of a blond-haired child Jesus, and – my favorite – standing in a flowery meadow with outstretched arms as if in great joy (or perhaps suggesting a cross-like prayer posture). Individual figures of these miniatures have the "doll-like heads with red-painted cheeks" characteristic of folk art. The depiction of monastic women as readers, writers, and scribes makes these miniatures rare among medieval German illuminations. They have been identified as originating in the school of Barbara Gwichtmacherin, a nun at the Nürnberg Katharinenkloster around 1450.[14]

In addition to the Nürnberg Katharinenkloster, the Dominican women's communities of St. Gallen, Zofingen (Constance), and Altenhohenau, as well as the Augustinian women of Pillenreuth and Inzigkofen, among others (see Appendix), were responsible for copying and disseminating the texts of the Sister-Books. In general, the lending and

13. On Meyer and the Töss text, see also Grubmüller (1969, 179). Vetter (1906, xvif.) argues that the opening of the entries in this Töss manuscript varies slightly from the stereotype "*Wir hatten och ein swester*" in other preserved Töss manuscripts; this variation might reflect the illuminator's desire to choose a different initial with which to work. Schneider (1965, xxix) provides a brief biographical sketch of the scribe Klara Keiperin.

14. On folk art, see Karl Fischer, *Die Buchmalerei in den Dominikanerklöstern in Nürnberg*, Diss. Erlangen (Nürnberg, 1928), p. 73, as quoted by Schraut (1991, 100). See further Schneider and Zirnbauer (1965, 67–69); Schraut (1991, 113); a study of this illuminated Töss manuscript by Jane Carroll and Elisabeth Remak-Honnef is forthcoming. Art historians may also wish to explore the striking resemblance between the fourteenth-century wall-hanging woven by the nuns of Wienhausen near Celle (and now located in the *Domschatz* of the Halberstadt cathedral, Germany) and the illuminated figures in the Töss manuscript.

trafficking of codices during the fifteenth century was so extensive among communities of Dominican women that, as Christian v. Heusinger suggests, it might be impossible to ever trace them completely. The very survival of this body of literature (together with many other works) depended on the women's diligent copying and the vigorous exchanging of manuscripts. Credit must, of course, also be given to the friars engaged in the fifteenth-century monastic reform who encouraged the women's literary work and through their pastoral visits to various monasteries facilitated its dissemination.[15]

In surveying the surviving Sister-Books codices and their routes, however, it is important not to lose sight of the total picture. In relative terms, the sphere of influence of these women's texts, even during the period of the monastic reform, was limited. The Sister-Books have never had, what Ringler calls, "mass appeal"; Suso's *Büchlein der ewigen Weisheit*, which is contemporary with the Sister-Books, by contrast, has survived in no less than 337 manuscripts, 260 of which alone date from the fifteenth century. And the *Legenda aurea*, in both the Latin original and the translated versions, reached the highest-ever number of copies of any work before 1500.[16]

FROM THE LUTHERAN REFORMATION TO THE ENLIGHTENMENT

From the turbulent period immediately following the Reformation in the sixteenth century, no additional manuscripts of the Sister-Books have survived. Scribal activity stopped during this time of hardship and penury; the dissolution of many monasteries brought with it the loss of important libraries. The network of women's communities that had flourished for over two hundred years seems to have broken down during the sixteenth century. The drastic reduction in numbers witnessed by the Order of Preachers in the wake of the Protestant Reformation continued unabated.

---

15. Heusinger (1959, 138).

16. Ringler (1990, 89). On Suso, see Williams-Krapp (1986, 46), and on the *Golden Legend*, Brincken (1988, 307). Other examples: the copious manuscript tradition of the *Speculum virginum* (written ca. 1100), which is preserved in 56 manuscripts (Ancelet-Hustache 1960, 152), and of Elisabeth von Schönau's (†1164) work, parts of which exist in more than 150 manuscripts, some dating back to the twelfth century (Kurt Köster, "Elisabeth von Schönau," Verflex. 2:492). But also works of secular poetry, such as the *Minnesang*, often have a surprisingly meagre transmission (Ringler 1990, 90).

The Dominican writer Conrad Zittard provides one notable exception to this ebbing tide. In 1596 he compiled a work for "the women and sisters of the Order of Preachers in the German Province" so that they would "be strengthened in the Catholic faith against all heretics." His short anthology of Dominican writings (in the spirit of the Counter-Reformation, but with an emphasis on edifying miracle stories) contains some excerpts from the Sister-Books.

Even so, the next three hundred years show little interest among Dominican women and men and general readers alike in the Sister-Books, or in the literary tradition of which they are part. Sporadic traces of manuscript copies suggest that a few isolated monastics from various orders showed some interest in the works. As the complete listing of the Sister-Books manuscripts in the Appendix shows, partial reproductions were sometimes made for personal use or for the use of a particular community. But the paucity of interest could not support printed editions; indeed, occasional hand-written copies of parts of the Sister-Books were made, even some two to three hundred years after the invention of printing.

Of singular importance to the preservation and promotion of the Sister-Books was the work of the monks of the Carthusian Order, who never having undergone internal reform had an uninterrupted tradition of interest in religious literature. Their decisive influence on the ascetic and mystical literature of the Middle Ages is well known: Ruh calls the Carthusians "the great mediators of vernacular mysticism."[17] Thus, the monks of the Carthusian monastery in Freiburg made a copy of the Adelhausen text ([F] 99) in the seventeenth century, and the Carthusians of Ittingen, Austria, were responsible for copying, translating, and publishing several texts from the *corpus* of the Sister-Books during the seventeenth and eighteenth centuries. The provenance of the Einsiedeln codex ([E] 694) containing both the Töss and Adelhausen texts is also the Carthusian monastery of Ittingen. The scribes of Ittingen equally wrote codex Y 105 with the Diessenhofen Sister-Book in the mid-seventeenth century, preserved in the Thurgauische Kantonsbibliothek, Frauenfeld, the famous Carthusian author Henricus Murer (1588–1638) being among the four men who worked on this manuscript.

---

17. Ruh (1982, 27). For example, the Carthusian Johannes Landspergius' publication of the complete works of Gertrud von Helfta was instrumental in the transmission of her *Exercitia spiritualia*, of which no other manuscripts survive.

THE NINETEENTH CENTURY

Many medieval manuscripts that had survived the Reformation in Germany fell victim to the so-called period of secularization in the wake of the peace treaty of Lunéville (1801) between France and Germany. This treaty gave France possession of the left bank of the river Rhine. As a consequence, the German state compensated the rulers who had owned land west of the Rhine for their loss of power and possessions by nationalizing the property of the Church and its religious orders on the right bank and by transferring these ecclesiastical holdings to the secular princes. Needless to say, this expropriation caused great hardship, especially for the cloistered women's monasteries.

The church property thus secularized included a large collection of medieval codices and art. At the time, such priceless items were viewed as the outmoded relics of an unenlightened era, and many unique treasures were carelessly dispersed or destroyed. The tabernacle, chalices, and other art works in silver and gold from the Gotteszell monastery, for instance, were shipped to Stuttgart to be melted down. When the Kirchberg monastic library was to be transferred in 1806, the chief librarian Schott declared that its catalogue "contained nothing but the junk of old Catholic theology which is not appropriate for a royal library." Johann Christoph von Aretin, the Bavarian official who oversaw the dismantling of monastic libraries at that time, told what he called the "amusing," but true story of some coachmen who, while transporting the manuscript collection of a secularized monastery to a state library, used parchment folios on the ground to prevent the coach wheels from sinking in the muddy road. In an atmosphere so indifferent toward things medieval, especially anything religious, entire monastic libraries were lost; from many women's monasteries known to have had very active scriptoria during the Middle Ages not a single manuscript has survived.[18]

Yet during the secularization of the early nineteenth century and precisely due to the curators' fine-combing through monastic libraries, a few alert scholars rediscovered some valuable medieval literature, among others also works of mysticism and manuscripts of the Sister-Books. Not sure of the genre of the Sister-Books but recognizing the language of mysticism, scholars then classified these works as mystical writings. Read as works of mysticism, however, the Sister-Books soon

18. Erzberger (1902, 268) who also quotes Schott's dismissive comment (294). Fromm (1989, 356) retells von Aretin's anecdote.

became the object of unbridled scorn. The early critical reaction of Deacon Fr. Cless is typical: in his cultural history of Württemberg (1807) he emphatically declares that the authors of the Sister-Books show "an inclination to the wildest excesses ... a pseudo-mysticism ... a poisoned imagination." His judgment was to set the tone for much nineteenth-century criticism of medieval women's writings. It betrays what Haas aptly calls *kleinkarierte* prudishness, a collective petty-mindedness that has lasted well into the twentieth century.[19]

Greith, later Bishop of St. Gallen, was the first scholar to print excerpts from the Sister-Books. In his *German Mysticism in the Order of Preachers (1250–1350)* which appeared in 1861, he showed himself fully aware that the publication of these texts coincided with "a time when the Middle Ages had a poor reputation." Quoting from and more often paraphrasing the manuscripts at his disposal, he declares the Sister-Books a "historical document of the spiritual fervor in the [medieval] Order of Preachers." Greith's work lacks critical discrimination. He nevertheless must be appreciated for having published some texts from the Sister-Books. In contrast, the supposedly comprehensive list of Dominican authors up to 1330 published by the renowned nineteenth-century Dominican historian, Heinrich Seuse Denifle, some twenty years later, omits mention of women writers altogether.[20]

The Protestant historian and theologian Wilhelm Preger who started publishing the first extensive study of medieval mysticism in 1874 must be credited with furthering interest in the Sister-Books. "Even if the history of mysticism were nothing but the history of an illness," Preger allows in his introduction, it would still merit attention. Women visionaries do not fare well in Preger's view: he thinks that it is mostly women who have visions (*Es erklärt sich aus der Natur des Weibes*) and that their visions often coincide with menstrual periods. Nevertheless, Preger's work is important because it contains a number of lengthy entries from the Sister-Books some decades before the first texts appeared in print. While both Greith and Preger are outdated, they were the first to provide many readers access to admittedly partial extracts from the Sister-Books. Still, classification of the Sister-Books

19. See Fr. Cless, *Versuch einer kirchlich-politischen Landes- und Culturgeschichte von Würtenberg bis zur Reformation* (1807, 2,1:457), cited by Bihlmeyer (1916, 66); and Haas (1988, 365).

20. Greith (1861, 291 and iv). He had already discussed and paraphrased sections of the Töss text in his study *Henry Suso and His School* (1860, especially 409–416). And see Denifle (1886b, 192f.).

among the works of mysticism is in part responsible for the dismissal of an entire literary *corpus* as second-rate mystical writing.[21]

The late nineteenth-century German philologists, on whose editorial work on the Sister-Books we still largely rely, also understood these works as part of the history of mysticism. Philipp Strauch's review in 1881 of König's edition of the Adelhausen book, for instance, claims, somewhat prematurely: "This text completes our knowledge of the mystical life in women's monasteries." König's edition is not without merit, but his commentary is often misogynist, calling the authors of the Sister-Books childishly naive and speaking of their sick and extravagant phantasies. And Roth, who edited the Kirchberg (and Gotteszell) texts in 1893, concludes somewhat grudgingly that the Sister-Books are "of a high value for the history of mysticism, in spite of some eccentric views," *überspannte Anschauungen*. Albert Hauck's ecclesiastical history of Germany first published in 1887 provides an early example of an objective approach; but he too remains unsympathetic. The nineteenth-century critical attitude toward medieval women authors, especially toward writers of religious literature, is at best patronizing, at worst disdainful. It is a legacy carried over into the twentieth century.[22]

THE TWENTIETH CENTURY

Although this brief survey concentrates on reactions to the Sister-Books, such reactions cannot always be isolated from the critics' general remarks about religious literature written by medieval women authors.

One current in critical opinion has continued uninterrupted into the 1980s; that is, a distinction between the male or speculative from the female or practical approach to mysticism, as discussed by the Jesuit Emil Michael (1903). While there is nothing in principle wrong with such a division, it does produce dubious, even objectionable conclusions. Walter Blank, for example, explains that practical mysticism was inevitably reserved for women, because women had only "a limited conceptual ability for speculative thinking," *begrenzte Aufnahmefähigkeit*

---

21. See Preger (1874–93, 1:iii, 139) and Preger (1874–93, 2:253–269). Denifle, in a review of Preger's still unfinished work (*Historisch-politische Blätter für das katholische Deutschland* 75 (1875) declares it the work of an heretic; see also Ruh (1978, 570) and Ruh (1982, 4).

22. See König (1880, 147) with Strauch, *AfdA* 7 (1881) 96; Roth (1893, 193); Hauck (2nd ed. 1911, 383–397); and cf. Ringler (1980a, 8).

..., *was das spekulative Erklärungsschema betrifft*. Moreover, the inter-action between the two kinds of mysticism is often explained away, by claiming that the men were obliged to provide the necessary theological corrective to the women. But Ursula Peters convincingly argues that, while men appear to be predestined to write theological *summae* and women to compose visions and become subjects of *vitae*, there were also examples of the contrary. Thirteenth- and fourteenth-century women, such as Beatrijs van Nazareth and Marguerite Porete also wrote theological treatises, and men like Suso and Friedrich Sunder feature in contemporary *vitae* illustrating their virtues and spirituality.[23]

Oskar Pfister offers a different approach to women's mystical writ-ing. His study of the Dominican mystic Margarethe Ebner, a contem-porary of the authors of the Sister-Books, was published in 1911. Pfis-ter, a priest and psychiatrist, believed that hysteria and religious idio-syncrasies were inextricably intertwined, and he argued that Margarethe Ebner's illnesses were the product of a repressed sexuality. Martin Grab-mann was quick to react against the tendency to explain these women's writings as "pathological hallucinations of an overwrought imagina-tion." Nevertheless, some traces of Pfister's negative psychoanalytical approach can easily be found through virtually all the twentieth-century criticism of the Sister-Books. Rufus Matthew Jones' short essay "Certain Women Mystics" contains some useful insights into the Sister-Books, in-cluding his suggestion that illness often is a fertile ground for true in-genuity; but he is also only too ready to add that "there is a large factor of hysteria and abnormality in evidence," and that there is "a trail of superstition and of self-torture over it all." Also Blank remains captive to terms such as "perverse" and "pathological." Finally, Mela Esche-rich's psychological study in *Deutsche Psychologie* (1916), adds a new note. Although she, too, maintains that many visions were symptoms of hysteria, she suggests that visions were probably used to express views that might otherwise have been branded heretical. Escherich also combines her psychoanalytical approach with an interest in the socio-cultural aspects of these works. Medieval women, she states, may have been attracted to the world of the monastery because it offered cultural opportunities, companionship with other highly cultivated women, as

---

23. See Blank (1978, 36). On male theology as a corrective to female mysticism, see, for example, Emil Spiess (1935) and Otto Langer (1982). Contrast the more critical approach of Peters (1988a, 46f.).

well as spiritual friendships with men through visits and correspondence.[24]

A socio-historical perspective also characterizes studies that might
be labelled neo-romantic. Some of these simply take the accounts in the
Sister-Books literally. This uncritical group of scholars includes men
and women: not only Wilms (1920), Oehl (1931), Muschg (1935), and
some studies by Grabmann during the 1910s and 1920s, but also Margarete Weinhandl (1921) and Anne Marie Heiler (1929). Commentaries
with phrases such as the "charming idyll" of the medieval nuns' life, the
"uplifting effect of these noble souls," and "the air filled with miracles"
in the monasteries as well as "our joy in these nuns' naive way of
expressing themselves" are patronizing and useless. Moreover, while
applauding each pleasant scene they nevertheless make snide remarks
about the intellectual limitations of the authors, the often exaggerated
emotion of the writings, and their "literary phrase-mongering,"
Schreibseligkeit. Oehl's condescension is typical: "Although completely
uncritical, womanly, and naively fantastic, these writings are highly
valuable and important for social history, for psychology, and for
literature; and some are of charming beauty."[25]

Among early twentieth-century scholars Herbert Grundmann represents an exception. His approach to his subject matter is consistently
fair. Grundmann's pioneering research into a variety of historical and
literary sources in the 1930s was instrumental in establishing the influence of the highly educated women – among them the early fourteenth-
century authors – in the rise of vernacular religious literature. He is
also among the few scholars of the time to credit the work of women
in monastic scriptoria for the survival of important medieval texts.[26]

---

24. See Pfister (1911). In an article in the 1980s discussing the important role
of the Sister-Books in art history, Johannes Werner, "Frauenfrömmigkeit: Zur
Entstehung der mittelalterlichen Andachtsbilder," *Das Münster* 35 (1982) 21–26, still
relies directly on Pfister for his generally denigrating remarks (see especially 23).
See Grabmann (1910/11, 43) for his critique of Pfister. Jones' (1939, 174f.) harsh
judgment might have stemmed from his apparent unawareness of recent German
scholarly works (such as Grundmann's 1935 study). But his views have perhaps
gained unfortunate influence through a reprint of his book in 1971. See also Blank
(1962, 172 and 1978a, 29); Escherich (1916, 153–155, 163).

25. Muschg (1935, 156) uses the term *Schreibseligkeit*. See also Gehring (1957,
22); and Oehl (1931, 197f.).

26. Grundmann, especially (1935), as well as the shorter studies published
during the thirties.

As one would expect, secondary literature on German mysticism, especially on the so-called Rhineland mystics, Eckhart, Tauler, and Suso, vastly outnumbers studies on the Sister-Books. Most critics refer to the Sister-Books only incidentally while discussing male authors. But often even casual mention of these women's texts betrays a real misogyny. Muschg, whose study is generally useful, nevertheless judges the authors of the Sister-Books as incapable of distinguishing genuine individual experience from convention and commonplace; he scorns the psychological trivialities of a time that debased religion into a plaything (*den seelischen Kleinkram einer ins Spielerische abgleitenden Zeit*). Rudolf Franz Merkel is quick to dismiss the cheap sentimentality in these texts which resort to frequent appearances of the child Jesus, just the kind of thing, he says, one would expect in books by women (*spezifisch frauenhaft*). Friedrich-Wilhelm Wentzlaff-Eggebert, who proclaims his study (originally published in 1943) "unprejudiced by religion," shows great respect for writers like Mechthild von Magdeburg; none the less he finds in the Sister-Books only trivial emotion, self-deception and other pathological symptoms, and spiritualist rather than spiritual attributes. He grants these women incidental success in poetic expression of religious experiences, saying that "with women, unlike with the masters of mysticism, the thought process does not interfere in their formulating an immediate expression."[27] Also James Matthew Clark, whose 1949 study aims at objective analysis, leaves his readers with conflicting views. While acknowledging existence of "an active intellectual life" in the Dominican women's communities, he nevertheless adds the corollary, "The friars had to express theological and philosophical ideas in a garb that would make them intelligible to women." In his ecclesiastical history of Swabia, Hermann Tüchle refers to the Sister-Books as "literary memoirs," the typical products of a "genuinely female need for loquaciousness." Josef Quint, who contributed an article on the Sister-Books to the *Reallexikon für deutsche Literatur*, compares them to Eckhart's works, judging them the "childish and naive" literary output of "pious and simple-minded nuns, ... strong in feeling" but otherwise thoughtlessly repeating what they had been told by the friars. The charge of verbosity had also been made by the French critic Jean Chuzeville: "Ces livres, dont beaucoup ne sont que des imitations

---

27. See Muschg (1935, 156 and 218f.). Merkel, *Die Mystik im Kulturleben der Völker* (Hamburg: Hoffmann & Campe, 1940), p. 65. Wentzlaff-Eggebert (1969, 4, 23, 66f.).

plus ou moins verbales et verbeuses des grands livres doctrinaux ... ." Another account of the (male) German "masters" of mysticism in 1968 by Louis Cognet, however, judges the Töss and Engeltal texts favorably and sees the Sister-Books as witnesses to "un très haut niveau de culture spirituelle." In view of these judgments, positive and negative, it is difficult to understand why renowned Dominican writers such as Denifle (1886b), Gabriel M. Löhr (1930), Pierre Mandonnet (1943) and Gundolf Maria Gieraths (1956), even in comprehensive studies, simply ignore the contributions these women made to the literature of the Order of Preachers.[28]

Two dissertations written in the middle of the century, by Kunze (Hamburg, 1952) and by Gehring (Michigan, 1957) undertook a more objective assessment of the Sister-Books as works of literature. Neither thesis was published, and both were ignored for over two decades. Both Kunze and Gehring relied on the comparative study (1904) by Krebs, with its meticulous collection of parallel passages from the medieval legendary tradition and the Sister-Books. Despite their refreshing approach to these texts as literature, also Kunze and Gehring are still only too conventional in their disparagement of the authors of the Sister-Books. Even Blank's essays, published in 1962 and 1978, which contain valuable insights, betray negative attitudes. The miracle stories in the Sister-Books are seen as the strange products of an "excited fantasy," their theological discussions trivial and untouched by the intellectual reasoning that was the hallmark of the preaching of the Dominican friars. Their special womanly disposition made the nuns search for a secure basis for their faith in inner experience, transposing speculation into asceticism. Finally, Max Wehrli's short discussion of the Sister-Books in his history of medieval literature deplores the "loss of *niveau* and originality" in what he calls "biographical reminiscences" (following Tüchle).[29]

Looking over this depressing critical record, one is compelled to ask with Peter Dinzelbacher: why this disqualifying of women?[30] But at times unintentional and certainly more covert than previously, a misogynist strain in modern scholarship undoubtedly continues. Still,

---

28. See Clark (1970, 4f.); Tüchle, *Kirchengeschichte Schwabens* (Stuttgart: Schwabenverlag, 1950), 2: 136; Quint (1958, 550f.); Chuzeville (1935, 169); Cognet, *Introduction aux mystiques rhéno-flamands* (Paris: Desclée, 1968), pp. 199f.

29. Blank (1962, 99f., 261f.); (1978a, 28 and 35); Wehrli (1980, 657ff.).

30. Dinzelbacher (1979c, 119).

these days, prospects for a fair treatment of the Sister-Books look better, especially in the wake of recent feminist scholarship in different disciplines. While the complete *corpus* has not yet been subject of a monograph, several critics have dealt with various aspects of these and similar texts. Two deserve special mention: Caroline Walker Bynum (since 1982) and Peters (since 1988) share similar yet independent and balanced approaches. More recently, dissertations on specific themes have appeared, including those by Rosemary Drage Hale (1992), Béatrice W. Acklin Zimmermann (1993), and Meyer's (1995) critical edition of the Diessenhofen text.

Much of the current research regarding the Sister-Books has been made possible by the enormous progress achieved since around 1970 by scholars who began to interpret these works from an expressly literary point of view. Their systematic study of the manuscripts yielded promising results, as has been demonstrated by Grubmüller (1969) for the Töss text, Müller (1977/78) and Ringler (1980) for the Kirchberg, Gotteszell and Engeltal books, and Geith (1980 ff.) for the Unterlinden Sister-Book.

Especially Ringler's work has been decisive. His concentrated study of several texts of the Sister-Books (and similar contemporary writings) opened new perspectives. He called attention to structure and language, and showed the authors' conscious dependency on the literary traditions of their time. A recognition of the rhetorical structure governing the Sister-Books makes all the difference between condemning or appreciating these deceptively simple works. Also the research of many other scholars of the *Forschungsstelle für mittelalterliche Prosa* at Würzburg University, led by the historian of medieval literature and theology, Kurt Ruh, has generally had a considerable impact. Several of their publications are devoted to medieval women's literature. Also among the ranks of the *Germanisten* stands Haas (Zürich), a scholar with an unparalleled knowledge of German mysticism and of the Sister-Books, which he sees as part of this wider field. He, too, combines literary scholarship with a deep interest in and knowledge of theology, philosophy, and medieval history; his approach to these texts is always fair, often imaginative. A staunch defender of medieval women writers, he suggests that labeling the nuns in the Sister-Books as pathological says more about the critics than the women they so criticize.

A number of comparative studies have also appeared, since the Sister-Books have attracted the interest of scholars in theology and history of religion. An example is the historian Dinzelbacher with numerous fair-minded publications on medieval women (1979ff.).

Scholarly debate continues on the proper methodology for the interpretation of medieval religious prose such as the Sister-Books. It is hoped that such controversies will produce the basis for a balanced approach to the study of these and similar texts.[31]

31. The many contributions of Haas, Ringler and Dinzelbacher relevant for the interpretation of the Sister-Books are listed in the Bibliography. Haas' approach, he explains, is guided by a two-pronged examination of the texts' "literarischer Zuschnitt" and "geschichtlicher Ort" (1987a, 234); see also Haas (1987a, 297). See Ringler (1985ff.); Dinzelbacher (1988a); (1993, 304ff.) for scholarly controversies.

The ubiquitous miracles, miracle stories, visions, and charisms of the Sister-Books have often provoked ridicule. A survey of these legendary commonplaces may provide some insight into how and with what intention the authors make use of them.

KARISMATA

Charisms in the Sister-Books are called "special graces" or *sunder gnad*, freely-given gifts from God. They are part of the language of hagiography with which the contemporary reading or listening audience would have been familiar. And although accounts of *karismata* (*U* 390) should not be taken at face value, each is imbued with significance, hidden but in many cases recoverable.

1. Auditory Sensations
a. Hearing a Voice

The miraculous reception of a verbal communication, the most frequently mentioned charism in the Sister-Books, can be traced back to the auditory revelations in the Hebrew Bible. A criterion in all saints' lives, audition or locution is also prominent in the Sister-Books. Notably, as the Oetenbach author points out, it is only those saintly individuals who, having achieved inner silence (being "at leisure," *muoze*), can be granted an auditory sensation (*O* 253).[1]

Nevertheless, auditions in the Sister-Books are frequent and repetitious. They are usually marked by the formulaic phrases "she heard a voice" or "it was said to her" (*K* 120; *A* 161, 164, 166; *O* 252, 266f.). The source of the voice is often vague: sometimes "in the air" (*O* 247, 251) or "sounding in her ear" (*U* 379, 427), or "from heaven" (*U* 405), or Christine Ebner even speaks of "a divine voice," *ein gotliche stimme* (*E* 5). The Unterlinden text is rather more explicit: Benedicta von Egensheim "heard the Lord Jesus Christ speak to her in her innermost soul ... . His sweetest words ... also resounded in her bodily ears" (*U* 352; also *U* 461). "God also spoke to her" (*K* 121), the Kirchberg author states unequivocally. The source of the voice that awakens Ita von Hutwil in Oetenbach is not disclosed; but the authoritative message,

---

1. See also Benz (1969, 413); Weinstein and Bell (1982, 150).

repeated three times, clearly shows it to be of heavenly origin (O 253). A voice can be as clamorous as an "army trumpet" (D 50). "Sudden," "terrible," and "like a loud thunder" a voice leaves an Unterlinden nun "very frightened and downcast," until committing herself to the divine will, the voice returns softly to tell her that her prayers have been heard (U 433; also D 39).[2]

Voices in the Sister-Books often go beyond those in the mystical writings of Suso and others, where a phrase like "'Jesus said to me' ... only applies to pious thoughts arising in the mind during prayer."[3] Their nature and purpose are more varied. A voice is said not only to answer prayers (D 27c; E 42f.) and teach its auditor how to pray (D 41, 44), inform (K 115; E 5), and even issue instructions (D 27e, 30, 33; E 28, 44; K 122), but also predict the death of a sister (D 43; E 15; O 247) and assure another she would be carried into "the ninth choir" of angels in heaven (K 113; O 252). Voices are said to help with personal decisions, such as when a nun faced with a difficult predicament is "answered in her soul" (K 119; E 29). A voice admonishes (D 46), consoles (A 172; D 29), and takes away temptation (D 42). A voice can also be a conscience stirring (T 73).

Voices sometimes reach beyond the auditor to the community: Adelheid die Eugsten in Kirchberg was "so filled with grace" that other sisters heard "something singing inside her which, they believed, was her spirit" (K 107). And the Engeltal author makes use of this charism in her effort to heighten the reputation of her entire community: to Else von Sessenheim "our Lord" supposedly said, "you are never closer to me than [when you are] in this community" (E 29).

b. Music
The auditory experiences is also musical. The women of the Sister-Books are said to hear "the sweet sounds of harps," *manigen suessen harfen klang* (T 82; E 37) and organ music (K 122). An Adelhausen sister speaks of a vision in which the child Jesus sang for her (A 176). Others hear angels singing (K 111; W 79) which is an audition that often accompanies or follows visions (E 42; U 360f., 400, 451) or raptures (E

---

2. In his discussion of "hallucination" in the "history of prophecy," Jung (1980, 461) explains that "psychic contents not infrequently come to consciousness in hallucinatory form"; we are then apt to say: "it occurred to me" or even "it was as though an inner voice said."

3. Vernet (1930, 220).

28, 40). Singing angels are a commonplace in medieval religious prose and have a long tradition; angels and music are, not surprisingly, next to inseparable in the Sister-Books.[4]

Angels are often heard singing along with the monastic choir during the Divine Office and at mass. Once, on the Second Sunday in Advent, standing in choir "at Matins, singing the antiphon *Benedicite montes et colles*," Margaretha von Rosenstein "heard the angels in the air singing the same antiphon with the community" (*G* 139; cf. *E* 38). Diemut Ebnerin in Engeltal even hears angels singing polyphony: On All Angels' Feast, she heard them in the responsory *Te sanctum Dominum*; and when they came to the verse *Cherubim*, "they sang with three voices. And that, she said quite sweetly, exceeded the human senses," *waz uber menschlich sinne* (*E* 32f.). A reference to "a beautiful *Kyrie eleison* sung [by angels] with three voices" in the same text suggests that the Engeltal women sang polyphonic music themselves (*E* 27f.). This need not be a poetic exaggeration: polyphony was, in fact, used in a number of women's monasteries as early as the twelfth century.[5]

The human choir accompanied by heavenly angels is, as Cipriano Vagaggini reminds us, part of the liturgy itself. Each Preface during mass, for instance, closes with the words "With all the angels in heaven let us sing our joyful hymn of praise," or a similar exhortation. The Sister-Books sometimes refer directly to the *Sanctus* that follows the Preface:

> [Heilrade von Horburg] heard ... with her bodily ears, as it were, two or three times, but at different times, a crowd of holy angels intoning an ineffably sweet melody on high and presenting in a most joyful rhythm with resonant voices the *Sanctus sanctus sanctus Dominus Deus Sabaoth* (*U* 458.38–459.4; cf. *T* 67).

Similarly, the Weiler author speaks of one sister who heard "angels above the choir singing the *Sanctus* with the community"; and they made "the most beautiful sounds with their voices and ringing with

---

4. For angels and singing, see Hammerstein (1962); Benz (1969, 433); Gérold (1931, 168f.).

5. On polyphony, see Coldwell (1986, 43). Hammerstein (1962, 59) argues that the "three voices" may refer not to polyphony but to the three-part division of the *Kyrie*. He does not, however, consider the first example (*E* 32f.) cited above. Moreover, manuscript studies by Yardley (1986, 26f.) have brought to light a "three-voice troped Agnus" and a "two-voice Kyrie" in a fourteenth-century manuscript (MS. 4) from Maigrauge, the Swiss Abbey of Cistercian nuns.

their wings" (*W* 82). The special musical effect is peculiar to this passage; angels with wings [cf. Is. 6:2] do not occur elsewhere in the Sister-Books. But the effect for listener and reader would have been incomparable: the human and heavenly harmony, as Christine Ebner says, was capable of producing nothing less than a "*jubilus* of the heart" (*E* 28). Perhaps this musical intertwining may reflect, as Reinhold Hammerstein suggests, "the mystical desire to unite the heavenly and earthly liturgy."[6]

In the end, even the music of the angels (and that of the cherubim and seraphim, see *W* 77) gives way to other-worldly music. Katharina von Unterlinden's remarkable description follows:

> One day, deep in prayer, [Elisabeth von Senheim] was suddenly divinely given to hear with her bodily ears voices singing, making heavenly harmony resound most sweetly and clearly through the air. The sweetness and delightful beauty of these voices was so great and ineffable that no musical instrument nor any song of this world could be compared with it. Most delighted by this magnificent heavenly melody, she was filled with sweetness and wonderful devotion (*U* 451.11–19).

This "heavenly harmony" represents, as Christine Ebner puts it, heaven itself, because it means "singing before the Holy Trinity" (*E* 15). "Celestial music," the tenth-century German canoness and playwright Hrotsvit von Gandersheim explains, is made by the seven planets and the heavenly bodies "in the same manner as instrumental music." It is the consoling and healing sound of this *armonia celestis* that is granted to some special sisters. Among them, Heilrade von Horburg is so overcome with "joy and exultation" that "her soul, as it were, began to dance in her body" (*U* 383, 400, 458). Also Adelheit von Hiltegarthausen of the Gotteszell monastery, taught a splendid *jubilus* during a vision, hears *des firmamenten klanck*:

> And there she was led to the rotation of the firmament, and from there came such sweet sound and music that it exceeded all senses. Later, when she came to, she told her intimate friends everything: If all the string music that this world could play and all the sweetness that anybody ever heard sounded together it would still not resemble that loveliest of sounds she had heard there ... (*G* 131.6–13).

---

6. Vagaggini (1976, 350–354). In his study "Jubilus" (1978), Grundmann speaks both of the *jubilus cordis* and the *jubilus oris*. See also Hammerstein (1962, 57).

The music of the spheres, understood as the supreme *auditio spiritualis* and granted only to select saintly individuals, can only be encompassed in hyperboles.[7]

2. Other Unusual Phenomena

Tokens of saintliness are often received during liturgical feast days or periods of illness (*W* 79; *K* 109, 114). Some texts speak of miraculous tastes and olfactory sensations; the legendary "odor of sanctity" and sweet scents are found in many versions (*U* 371, 380; *A* 173; *T* 20f., 92; *D* 14, 26; *W* 84, 85). Pleasant fragrances associated with sanctity in medieval legends may have been a reference to a saintly person's serene state of mind, Heinrich Günter claims.[8]

The Sister-Books make untiring use of the commonplace by which the piety of childhood inevitably engenders future sanctity. An entry in the Unterlinden book is the most detailed: "Filled with God's grace from the cradle," Agnes von Herkenheim never mingled with girls her age, "who filled their days with playing" and frivolous things; "from childhood on she only had one aim and desire, to crucify herself to the world" (*U* 385). Such precocious children typically spend their time praying (even through the night) rather than joining in children's games (*U* 422; *K* 107, 110, 118). Aron Gurevich believes that these images are connected with the classical topos of the *puer-senex*, here become the young woman wise beyond her age.[9]

When speaking of other "special graces," such as levitation, most authors feel it is necessary to add some explanation. Usually the experience is credited to a combination of a spirit of devotion and grace (*U*

---

7. Hrotsvit von Gandersheim, *Pafnutius*, ed. and trans. by Katharina M. Wilson (New York: Garland, 1989) pp. 98f. In *De Musica*, Augustine speaks of *carmen universitatis* ("the song of the universe"), a notion later appropriated by Bonaventure (†1274) in his *mundum quasi carmen pulcherrimum*. (See the discussion of "die Welt als Lied" by Curtius 1938, 20). Gérold (1931, 120–122) explains that the *jubilus* – as distinct from "the grace *jubilus*" – is originally understood as a highly melodic chant derived from the melisma of the liturgical *alleluia*; later it came to be used as an exalted poetic chant of praise and thanksgiving. Hammerstein's hypothesis (1962, 54) that such heavenly music can only be perceived by visionaries in the image of music already known to them should perhaps be amended: it would be more accurate to say that such auditory experiences are presumably rooted in music, with which the visionaries are familiar, but enhanced by musical imagination.

8. Günter (1906, 34).

9. Gurevich (1990, 18); Curtius (1963, 98–101).

341, 369). In Oetenbach, Elsbeth von Beggenhofen's great desire for God caused her to be levitated "far above the earth" until she implored God in embarrassment to let her down (*O* 269). "It was said," remarks the author of the Töss Sister-Book, that Elisabet Zollnerin's "spirit was sometimes so drawn upward into God that her body levitated in the air" (*T* 32, 36: *wol ainer elen hoch*).

A similar event is corroborated by a witness. When Beli von Winterthur was at prayer after Matins, another sister saw her "surrounded by a blissful light": "the divine Spirit had so absorbed all her strength that her saintly body levitated in this light and in the air" (*T* 41). Gravity here has ceased to operate; Beli is so filled with the Spirit that nothing can bind her to the earth. The example finds typical echoes in hagiographic literature. Its archetype, according to modern commentators, is fittingly Dominican: "One of the most famous levitators was Thomas Aquinas: his companions bore witness as the chunky Dominican floated 'two cubits' above the church floor while he prayed." In the Sister-Books, levitation is integrated as evidence of a sister's intense spirituality.[10]

The "gift of tears" represents a further "manifestation of grace." Witches and demons, according to traditional folklore, were noted for their inability to weep; saintly persons consequently weep profusely. Katharina von Unterlinden praises "the devout sound of crying" that could be heard when her community was in prayer (*U* 437). Some sisters, she explains, "truly having been liquified through the fire of divine love, cannot hold back their tears" (*U* 340). And Mezzi Sidwibrin in Töss, among others, cried "tears of love," *mintrechen* (*T* 29). Mezzi von Klingenberg, too, "had the great grace that, whenever mass started, tears ran abundantly down her cheeks" (*T* 45; 62; *O* 246; *D* 31, 41), and Margret von Zürich excelled in "vigils and steady praying, and because of her constant heart-felt tears her face was as if swollen" (*T* 36, also *T* 41, 55, 83).[11]

10. For levitation in the Sister-Books, see also *A* 160, 176, 187; *K* 106; *D* 40, 41. For an additional interpretation of levitation in the Unterlinden passage (*U* 341), see Glente (1988b, 261f.). On Aquinas as levitator, see Weinstein and Bell (1982, 150); see also Kieckhefer (1984, 155) for further examples from fourteenth century hagiography. Leroy (1928, 250), in an early study of levitation, argues that "According to very old traditions of various origins, the human body is apt, in certain circumstances, to elude the law of gravity." See also Underhill (1955, 185f., 376f.) and Thurston (1952, 30f.); WbM (1989, 321f.) cites different types of levitation and surveys the psychological explanations currently supplied.

11. Gehring (1957, 16); WbM (1989, 498f.) describes the criteria necessary for the interpretation of tears as a gift of grace. Dinzelbacher (1982b, 68) quotes as his source for demons' folklore: H. v. Hentig, "Über das Indiz der Tränenlosigkeit im

The charism receives a dramatic account in the experience of an Adelhausen nun who

> could not weep by nature. And when she saw the exceeding weeping of the sisters she had a great desire to weep. And once when she was in her devotion she became so serious about this that a tear appeared in her eye. And with this, she was enraptured. And it was as if two angels came from the heavenly kingdom and brought a golden bowl and received the tear in it and carried it up and brought it before our Lord (A 186. 27–187. 4; see also A 173, 184).

The gift of stigmatization has its origin in the intense contemporary preoccupation with the humanity of Christ and his suffering. St. Francis was in 1224 the first known person in history to have borne the marks suggestive of Christ's wounds. In the Sister-Books, the charism clearly expresses the nuns' empathy with and imitation of the passion of Christ. "Holy women imitate Christ in their bodies," and although St. Francis was the first stigmatic "almost all late medieval stigmatics [were] women," Bynum observes.[12]

The Gotteszell author, who is usually reticent about charisms, provides a vivid example that I quote in part:

> And especially [Adelheid] had the great desire to become aware and experience how great the pain was that our Lord felt when the crown of thorns was lowered onto his divine head and cut into his brain. And this heart-felt love and desire was strongly present in her mind for many a year. And then an angel came to her bed and beat her so bitterly that, in a quite patient and disciplined voice, she cried out because of the great and miserably unbearable pain .... And thereafter on her head were found deep furrows and marks that had remained there from the bitter blows (G 126.34–127.3).

Hexenprozess," *Schweizerische Zeitschrift für Strafrecht* 48 (1934) 368ff. The "gift of tears" was significant in the lives of Thomas Aquinas, Suso, Catherine of Siena, Margery Kempe, and many others, see Vernet (1930, 124). Almost every entry in Ignatius of Loyola's spiritual diary refers to the infused gift of tears. On "spiritual" tears and on a "theology of tears" in patristic writings and in medieval German literature, see Heinz Gerd Weinand, *Weinen in der deutschen Sprache und Literatur des Mittelalters*, Abhandlungen zur Kunst-, Musik-, und Literaturwissenschaft 5 (Bonn: Bouvier, 1958). See also Moshe Idel, "Weeping as Mystical Practice," in his *Kabbalah: New Perspectives* (New Haven: Yale University Press, 1988), pp. 75–88.

12. Bynum (1986a, 423f.). See also Underhill (1955, 267).

The stigmatization is strictly untypical: the position of the marks are changed (they usually appear on the chest, the hands, and feet); still, the visible "signs" are nevertheless proof of her stigmatization.[13] In a similar passage in the Töss text, Mechthild von Stanz's body is marked in part by stigmata after her rapture:

> [Mechthild] saw the streams of water and blood running down from her heart. And when the bell rang for Matins ..., it went beyond all her strength. And she could no longer hold back, ... and she cried out so loudly as to make many sisters come to her. Not wanting to say anything, she still said: "I am so very sore!" And then the sisters led her to her bed, for she was love-sick [minwund] in a blessed and saintly manner (T 64.35–65.4).[14]

Some sisters receive the five wounds without being visibly stigmatized (A 168; cf. A 183; D 40); others are marked by temporary stigmatization (K 106) or experience the pain of Mary's sorrows and Christ's passion (K 110). The Weiler sisters discover Mechthilt von Hundersingen during her final illness with "a rose-coloured sore about as wide as a hand ... close to her heart" (W 72, 85). Its colour (see also W 68) typically identifies the wound's supernatural origin: contemporary religious prose often uses 'rose' to describe Christ's blood.

Luggi Löscherin in the Adelhausen monastery is said to have taken "our Lord's passion so to heart" that "suffering and pain so seized her that her heart became a fresh wound from which blood flowed." She "bore these stigmata for a long time." And whenever she was "troubled with some passing things a skin grew over them, and whenever she was not troubled by passing things they remained fresh." She did not "speak to any human being about this grace," except that she did once unknowingly (A 168). By contrast, a Weiler nun's stigmata are said to have been known among all the sisters of her community who interpreted her hemorrhages as the "sign" of a miracle:

> [Elisabeth Weiler] also had another sign [zeichen] on Fridays around None, when our Lord's passion came so close to her heart that blood flowed out of her mouth and filled the fair-sized basin held

---

13. Beyer (1989, 204) claims that the blows Adelheit received represent blows against a Church that chooses to follow worldly desire (financial and political) rather than the suffering Christ. The interpretation is intriguing but does not seem to be supported by the evidence.

14. Stoll (1994, 158–160) sees a parallel to Bonaventure in this Töss passage.

up to her. And she experienced this so precisely at the time of our Lord's death on the cross that you could be more certain it really was noon than you could with the horologe (*W* 68.28–69.5).

The illness is emblematic in hagiographic writing: flowing blood is "a sign of divine election," since blood is "the life force."

Medieval fascination with stigmata and stigmatization has never been satisfactorily explained. Modern interpreters have argued that stigmata were the product of a "crucifixion complex" or autosuggestion. To the Sister-Books' authors, such visible bodily "signs" prove unfailingly the sanctity of a human being.[15]

Some charisms in the Sister-Books have as their centre intellectual gifts. There are examples of glossolalia. Of two sisters speaking unintelligibly in tongues Elisabeth von Kirchberg writes: "it was neither Latin nor German, and nobody understood a word of what they said ... with a loud voice" (*K* 105; *E* 25), but all assumed that they were given an important message.

Prescience as granted the subprioress of Engeltal is not unusual; the women are often endowed with a profound clairvoyance: "For three years" before her death, "every day our Lord revealed ... secret and future things" to Elsbet Ortlibin, but she did not divulge them (*E* 38; cf. *K* 108f., 121). The women speak of an impending fire (that later sweeps through the monastery) and of other future events (*kunfftigú ding*) (*A* 188; *G* 146; *K* 112; *O* 245; *E* 29; *D* 40, 45). They also foretell the exact time of their own (*U* 366, 419, 433; *A* 168f.) or somebody else's death (*U* 430; *A* 173; *G* 124, 140) or the exact burial site (*U* 471).

Some women are said to have the gift of intuiting the spiritual condition of others (*A* 157). *Herzensschau*, knowing someone's heart, includes knowing a person's faults (*G* 124; *K* 121; *T* 34, 39; *O* 269; *E* 13; *W* 69). The life of St. Paul is the object of one extraordinary example in the Sister-Books (*G* 127), but usually the women of the community are the aim of this charism (*A* 181). Thus do some recognize the "worthiness" of a sister receiving communion (*W* 69; *O* 269). The Töss text praising a sister's purity, in an image presumably influenced by illuminated manuscript miniatures, describes her "body above the belt as pure as a crystal" (*T* 24; and cf. *T* 21, 83; *W* 70; *D* 9, 41). Similarly, the Gotteszell author writes:

15. On blood as a sign, see Weinstein and Bell (1982, 149). For the crucifixion complex, see Thurston (1952, 122–129); and cf. Pierre Debongnie, "Essai critique sur l'histoire des stigmatisations au moyen-âge," *Etudes carmélitaines* 20,2 (1936) 22–59; DictTheol. (1985, 488); WbM (1989, 470).

It was on a Pentecost Day that the lights in choir were all extinguished. And when the sacristan noticed it, she wanted to go and find a light to kindle the lamps. There another sister saw that the sacristan's heart was full of fire. And the sister who saw this understood that the Holy Spirit had sent the fire that he had sent to the apostles in fiery tongues to the sacristan ... (G 144.23–29).

The author, believing this sign to be an outward manifestation of knowledge and love well-deserved, declares that the sacristan "remained fully in this [grace] until her death," even though she herself never knew of the "miracle God had wrought with her" (G 144). The charism of *Herzensschau* is sometimes also bestowed on the entire community (A 188). "When the community went to Compline," all of the Engeltal women "saw that the heart [of Hedwig von Regensburg] shone through her garment like the sun, just as it does through glass" (E 22).

The "heavenly light" descending on a sister features in several other passages. "A light came over" Ita von Hohenfels in Oetenbach "and covered her from head to toe; and she experienced surely that it was God who filled her" (O 238). Elsbet von Cellikon in Töss is seen "standing before her bed at night, and her body was so transparent and such a blissful radiance came from her that there was no place in the dormitory where one could not have light enough to pick up a needle off the floor" (T 93; cf. T 36). The image of this saintly woman radiating light captures the essential human likeness to God that, in hagiographic writing, is reflected in the halo.[16]

Hagiography needs unusual signs to depict the unusual saintly women the authors wish to present; the exaggerated number of such charisms are simply part of the Sister-Books' hyperbolical style. But even though, the ubiquitous charisms are often overwhelming. A reader can easily sympathize with what is said about Sister Elisabet Zolnerin in the Töss Sister-Book: "Hearsay has it that she had so many graces that she had to fend them off to keep her sanity" (T 41).

On the other hand, there are some women without such special graces. Margret Finkin in Töss, asked at the end of her life what "God had wrought with her," gives the following answer: "What shall I tell you? It seems to me, it was quite enough that God gave me the grace that I never fretted about what I was supposed to do as part of the

16. For other instances of this phenomenon, see O 263f.; A 159, 160, 162, 174, 178; E 20, 30, 35; K 114, 115); cf. Kieckhefer (1984, 154) for further fourteenth-century examples. On the halo in hagiography, see especially Thurston (1952, 162–170).

order['s rule], but rather that I was always eager and happy to do it" (*T* 34). Charisms have their place, the author seems to say, but they are not essential for spiritual well-being.

MONASTIC MIRACLE TALES

Called *Klosterlegenden* or *Wanderlegenden*, that is, monastic or travelling legends, "these little narratives passed from one convent to another, were told and retold, probably with such changes of name and locale as seemed expedient, and were chosen for their pictorial quality ...."[17] Frequently moralizing in intent but not without charm, they belong, like the *karismata*, to traditional legendary material. Their adaptability to the lives and works of monastic women made these stories attractive to the authors of the Sister-Books.

Some miracles in these monastic tales are specifically called "supernatural, *übernatúrlich*" or paradoxically "miracles that the Lord of nature wrought supernaturally" (*T* 62, 69), even though the incidents are usually of the homely kind: Heiltraut von Bernhausen, for instance, seeking to light a lamp on the flames of the kitchen fire, inadvertently soaked the lamp with water, made absent-minded "because of an abundance of grace"; the lamp, the Weiler author explains, nevertheless burned "contrary to nature" (*W* 74). Her words directly reflect Aquinas' definition of a miracle: "When God works in natural things against the inclination of their nature, it is a miraculous work." But whether such miraculous work happened in Weiler is another question, since fire that lights itself is a commonplace in medieval legends.[18]

Monastic miracles typically serve a practical purpose. Once "a cluster of infinitely many flies" gathered close to the new Unterlinden vault, settling firmly above the altar, and "could not be removed or chased away." When Sister Hedwig von Wingenheim noticed this "inconvenience in such a pious place, it pained her very much"; for she "worried that during mass the flies could accidentally fall into the chalice." But when she felt moved to make the sign of the cross over the flies, they instantly left, never to return again (*U* 372). Identical stories often reappear somewhat modified in different texts. When Alheid Ortlibin of Engeltal loses her way on the dark staircase of the dormitory, "the Lord appear[s] to her in a great light and show[s] her the way to her cell himself" (*E* 24). The same tale of miraculous rescue is repeated in the Weiler text, only slightly embellished (*W* 72).

---

17. Gehring (1957, 94) who is largely relying on Krebs (1904).
18. On this legendary cliché, see Günter (1910, 14, 57); Aquinas, STh. q.113 a.10.

Protection from harm remains a common motif in several such tales. Even in inclement weather, some sisters manage to "stay dry": Heilin von Gruen finds a dry path on her way to mass from her cell to the Kirchberg church in the middle of a severe storm (*K* 118); a Töss sister does not get wet in pouring rain (*T* 38); and Elsbeth von Beggenhofen's clothes remain miraculously dry after she falls into water (*O* 259). Sister Wila at the Weiler monastery is especially favoured in an unaffected if also naively symbolic tale. Once after Compline, Wila "was in great devotion." When after a violent rain storm "a veritable brook started to flow through the cloisters, she did not notice it." But, about to leave the choir, she fell into the water, "which came over her head." The sisters who hurried to her help, "all became wet and dirty, but she remained clean and never got wet" (*W* 72f.). The tale from the Diessenhofen book extols Adelheit von Ossingen's exemplary behaviour. Assigned to kitchen duty, she could not stay at mass. As she went to the kitchen, the author is careful to explain, "it was in winter and heavy snow had fallen on the path she took." On her way, Adelheid "heard the little bells ring" as a sign that "our Lord was being elevated." Then she knelt down in the snow, and "on that same spot, there was such beautiful grass, as if it had been summer when grass is at its most beautiful" (*D* 5).

Food and drink figure in other monastic tales. A preoccupation of medieval women, according to Bynum's comprehensive studies, the theme receives little emphasis in the Sister-Books, though. In the Diessenhofen foundation story a raven provides a large fish when the cook had nothing left to offer (*D* "Gründungsgeschichte"). And in the Adelhausen text, the following story is included:

> When the community was in this poverty, one day when they were supposed to go to table, the sister cellarer said to them: "Dear sisters, you have nothing to eat. Therefore, go into the choir and sing something, and ask our Lord that he advise you so that you will have something to eat." And this they did, and they all went together into the choir and sang *Gloria in excelsis*. After they had sung this, they were asked to go to the table [to see] whether God would not show them his mercy and grace. And when they had sat down at table and said a blessing, enough beautiful bread came to them so that they had it in abundance. And the youths who brought it were unknown to them and had never been seen before. Thereby they realized that they were angels, sent by God whom they had called to so eagerly in their distress (*A* 162.38–163.12).

On another occasion, when food was again desperately needed, a village woman brought the sisters two hundred eggs, showing once more that the community would be amply provided for (*A* 163).[19]

Miracles often echo New Testament stories. When the Kirchberg community "had no more than seventeen loaves of bread, our Lord nourished them for five days" with these, and there were more than sixty sisters (*K* 117). Walther, chaplain at the same monastery, is said to have changed water into wine while visiting a poor hermit (*K* 116f.; cf. *U* 474). And the Engeltal Sister-Book contains variations of the miracle of the loaves and fishes (*E* 9, 43).[20]

Other stories incorporate folkloric motifs, such as the never-empty pitcher:

> One sister [at Diessenhofen] was called Sister Adelheit Werlin. She was in charge of the wine. And at that time, the community had only one barrel of wine. And a sister lay severely ill and would have liked some wine. Then [the cellarer] did not want to deny it to her even though she had so little. And when she poured the wine out, she forgot to put the spigot back in. For our Lord wanted to do a miracle. And she went away and took the wine to the sister. And then she remembered what had happened, and she said: "Let me go right away, I forgot the spigot," and she feared that all the wine had run out. And when she got there, not one drop had run out of the barrel (*D* 6; cf. *T* 35).

This fairy tale-like episode is something of a charming aside; but the monastic tale sometimes becomes an integral element of the narrative. The lack of wine in the Gotteszell monastery on the eve of Pentecost threatens to jeopardize the celebration of the eucharist and the sisters' opportunity for communion the next day. After praying at the grave of a saintly sister who had died recently, the community unexpectedly receives the donation of *zehen mass weines*, "ten quarts of wine," from a woman burgher of the nearby city (*G* 137). A long-awaited communion day, so essential for the community's well-being, could thus be celebrated.

---

19. See Bynum (1987a and 1986b, 275). Nourishment arriving through the agency of a raven or of another bird bringing a fish is a typical legendary motif: see Günter (1910, 14 and 186).

20. See also Günter (1910, 22, 24, 97, etc.) and Thurston (1952, 385–395) for biblical analogues.

Other stories show other needs wondrously fulfilled. The money that was lacking for the building of a choir in the Adelhausen monastery church suddenly appeared from nowhere (*A* 163; cf. *U* 478). Eligenta von Sulzmatt who dearly wanted three coins to buy herself prayer beads (a so-called *paternoster*) but did not want to ask the superior at Unterlinden for money, turned around to find the coins on the floor (U. 456).[21]

The authors' pronounced intent of using the Sister-Books both for instruction and entertainment is nowhere else made more obvious than in their telling monastic tales. The basic message is always to trust in God as a protector and provider. And no matter how commonplace these miracle stories might have been to the audience, their attraction lies in being applied to the kind of women and community settings with which the readers and listeners were familiar.

Visions

1. Narrative Visions

The supernatural is inscribed in the very forms of medieval thought, its words and its images. "Popular taste," in the Middle Ages, Delehaye remarks, was "instinctively drawn toward all that is marvelous and appealing to the senses."[22] But the supernatural is also part of a rhetorical order. A complex set of conventions and expectations govern vision, miracle, and legend in the Sister-Books. Their significance is often revealed in the breach: the absence of vision can seem to violate narrative decorum itself.

A passage in the Töss Sister-Book provides a particularly telling example. In the figure of Anna von Klingnau the sisters of the monastery find "a true follower of the holy father Dominic." But "hearing about her perfect life" and "wanting to know about some special revelation of the things God showed through her," they were disappointed: "Then we heard great complaining from the sisters" who had known her during her life "that she had not wanted to tell them anything at her death ... . Yet we found a little how our Lord sometimes revealed himself to her" (*T* 38f.). Sister Anna's silence confounds expectations. But narrative sustains itself by making good

---

21. The "money from heaven" motif is common to many medieval legends and to fairy tales; see Günter (1910, 15). The Töss Sister-Book contains slightly different stories about golden shoes given as a heavenly reward (*T* 45) and a story of wish fulfillment (*T* 58).

22. Delehaye (1962, 60).

precisely such deficiency and perplexity. Hence, admitting that no miracles can be attributed to her, the author (unperturbed but following ample hagiographic precedent) manages to unearth "a little" to tell anyway: Anna's visions, auditory revelations, even a visit to purgatory accompanied by her angel, are all resourcefully deployed to complete the tale in the Töss Sister-Book. Christine Ebner similarly endows the saintly Diemut von Nürnberg with visionary credentials. "Never enraptured during all her life, nor ... grant[ed] any special graces," Diemut none the less is transformed into a *revenante* (one who supposedly returns to earth after death) who dutifully reports that "God had conferred three graces" upon her while she was alive (*E* 22f.; cf. *U* 335, 343f.).[23]

a. The Term Vision

Medieval authors rarely differentiate between a vision, a colourful dream, or an imaginary account inspired by scripture or meditation. Nor are visions, raptures, and apparitions clearly set apart in the Sister-Books. Whether a vision is "genuine" or invented can never be satisfactorily established. Its authenticity lies in the author's concerns and pre-occupations that the vision contents reveal to us.[24]

The authors of the Sister-Books also do not distinguish between corporeal and spiritual visions. Visionary experience proceeds simultaneously *mit vswendigem gesicht oder mit inwendigem* (*A* 178), that is, with both the bodily eyes (*die leiplichen augen*) and the spiritual eyes (*die innern augen, O* 250). Traditionally (especially to Augustine), the "outer" eyes are limited to sensual perception but the "inner" or spiritual eyes are what Julian of Norwich would call "the eye of my understanding." The inner eyes are capable of seeing into the divine mystery.

---

23. See Ludwig Hertling's brief discussion of this hagiographic topos in "Der mittelalterliche Heiligentyp nach den Tugendkatalogen," *Zeitschrift für Aszese und Mystik* 8 (1933) 260–268, esp. 261.

24. Rahner explains the Catholic Church's position on visions as follows: Christianity accepts in principle the possibility of visionary and auditory revelatory experiences, like those described in the Hebrew Bible. But the Church is very reluctant to accept any revelations. God's revelation in Christ remains definitive; to it nothing of any importance can be added. Visions do occur, but they need not come from God, except in as much as for the believer all good things emanate from God. And in no case can a "genuine" vision be objectively verified (Rahner 1948, 198). See also Dinzelbacher (1981, 217). Visionary experience may now be "induced" through neuroscience: see Michael A. Persinger, *Neuropsychological Bases of God Beliefs* (New York: Praeger, 1987).

The author of the Töss Sister-Book makes the opposition uncannily literal. Of the vision of a blind sister she says bluntly: "She must have seen it with her spiritual eyes, for with her bodily eyes she could not see" (*T* 86).[25]

b. Visionary Images and Visual Art
Visions find in art corroborating images and figures. The Weiler Sister-Book provides a particularly colourful visionary image:

> [Guta von Hohenheim] saw our Lord on Easter Day in his majesty, as he was risen from death. And he wore red clothes and had a red banner in his right hand, and a radiance went out from his face that illuminated all the world, as St. John writes of him in Revelation: *sicut sol in virtute sua lucet* [1:16] that his face shone like the sun in its strongest power (*W* 79.30–80.1).

Scriptural allusion is here supported by iconographic tradition: the figure of the resurrected Lord holding a banner is a standard symbol of Christ's victory over death in Christian art.

Painting and vision are directly conjoined in the Gotteszell Sister-Book: "There came the most beautiful little lamb that had ever been seen. And it was in every respect the picture with the banner and the cross, as one usually paints it" (*G* 138).

The sacrificial lamb here represents the New Testament image of the Lamb of God [Jn. 1:29] carrying the symbols of salvation. Christine Ebner also alludes to the banner, the sign of resurrection in art, when she writes of Anne Vorhtlin. Charmed by the play of natural sunlight one Easter Day Anne sees "our Lord in the clouds ... banner in hand," and Mary Magdalen kneeling before him, and "the sun playing upon him" (*E* 36). The following vision in the Unterlinden book is also inspired by painting. To Tuda von Egenheim, during prayer appeared the apostles Peter and Paul, "exceedingly glorious in face and garment, and yet as they existed when they were alive, as painted pictures of them clearly show us" (*U* 363). And gazing meditatively before a stained-glass window, Elisa of Engeltal is transported into ecstatic artistic vision:

25. On the "eyes of the soul," see Schleusener-Eichholz (1985). See also Fridolin Marxer's history of the spiritual senses, *Die inneren geistlichen Sinne. Ein Beitrag zur Deutung Ignatianischer Mystik* (Freiburg, Basel, Wien: Herder, 1963), pp. 48–79.

"Bowing toward the window on which our Lord's judgment is represented," she is "enraptured" and sees the Lord "sitting on a throne in
his majesty" with the twelve apostles and "all the world under him."
And "a brilliant radiance" comes from his face "as clear as if one
thousand suns shone from him, and the heavens stood open above him"
(*E* 39f.). The wording of this scene, from the redundant "brilliant
radiance" to the hyperbolical "one thousand suns," is an attempt to
express the beauty of light Elisa is said to have experienced.

Art historians have documented mutual influence that existed
between vision literature and visual art in the Middle Ages. Manuscript
illumination, painting, stained-glass, relief, and sculpture all exerted a
strong visual impression on the authors of the Sister-Books. Many of
the visions in these works were inspired by dominant themes in contemporary art, even though they may not refer directly to a specific
work of art. A vision of a head-and-shoulder portrait of Christ (*brust
pild*) that occurs repeatedly in these texts (*O* 264; *G* 145; *T* 78), for
instance, would make little sense if we did not understand its relation
to a similar half-figure in illuminated manuscript miniatures. And "the
right hand" that somehow appears disconnected in other visions (see *A*
167; *T* 33) is a common symbolic synecdoche for God in sacred art
deriving from the psalms.[26]

2. Miscellaneous Vision Contents

Readers who look in the Sister-Books for exotic images or for grandiose
around-the-world journeys will be quickly disappointed.[27] The visionary world of these works is the familiar world of their monastery, their
images the familiar images from Bible and legend. Only some exceptions occur: Juta Jüngin in the Weiler book is said to have journeyed
"to the grave of our Lord" [*W* 75). Enraptured to the Jordan River, an
Engeltal sister sees Jesus' baptism (*E* 7). And Alheit von Trochau from
the same monastery is "enraptured to Bethany on the day when he
commanded Lazarus to rise from death." There she finds herself at table
and sees "all the food that they ate." Then Andrew says: "'Let the
beautiful lover sit up here with the Lord'," – and this she does (*E* 13).

---

26. For studies concerned with medieval art and literature, see among others:
Panofsky (1927); Sauer (1928); Benz (1934); Wentzel (1959, 1960); E.H. Gombrich,
The Story of Art (Oxford: Phaidon Press, 1978); Vetter (1978); Belting (1990);
Hamburger (1990).
27. See Dinzelbacher (1989a).

Alheit is also witness to the final stages of Christ's passion "from the Wednesday in Holy Week to the eve of Easter" (*E* 11); and she claims that she stayed close to the suffering Christ, but does not describe the event further.

Visions of trees are common in medieval literature and art and can be found both in the Weiler and the Engeltal Sister-Books. In both cases, though, the trees are given an allegorical function. Christine Ebner's more elaborately described vision is of a linden tree, traditionally much beloved in German literature:

[Kunigunde von Eystet] went out of the choir after Matins at daybreak ... . There stood a large beautiful linden tree. It had all its leaves changed into morning stars; the ones below were larger and the most beautiful of all. This continued up to the middle [of the tree]. Then the stars changed. And the higher up they were the longer and narrower they became. [The leaves] toward the tree top became like the waning moon. They all hung there in their own strength, and whenever one came loose another one arrived in its place. When the natural sun rose, it shone its brightness on the stars. This created such a beautiful radiance that it exceeded all human senses.

Now she ... went under the tree. There she saw on the lowest branches two birds who were as large as Welsh doves and also had dove features; and they were as pure as a mirror and like a clear beryl stone in which one can see oneself.

This vision lasted until the second sign for Prime was given. Then the stars disappeared, and the tree regained its natural leaves. Then she went to Prime and could not forget her great vision.

When it then came to the silent part of the mass, a voice spoke to her: "Would you like to know what this vision means?" Then she said: "Yes, I would very much like to know." "It means that those at the first beginning of this monastery were the most saintly people, as rich in grace as ever could be found. Our Lord in his providence knows all things: ... Our Lord will always have somebody in here to whom he will grant special graces while the monastery is in existence. He himself will have those whom he gives special graces come here. And this is a proof to you that you will believe my words: the two birds that you saw signify that the two most saintly persons among you in this monastery will leave you shortly" (*E* 16.24–17.20; cf. *W* 76).

Needless to say, the death of two Engeltal sisters supposedly followed almost immediately. Although the visionary might be standing before a real tree, the tree as tree has no significance *per se* in this vision. Tree, birds, and stars only serve as a pretext for the real message of the vision spelt out in its second part. However, this vision contains an unusual detail. The imagery of light in the passage is, as Gehring observes,[28] based on a distinction "between *sunne* and *naturlich sunne*, that is, between the supernatural sun which is used to symbolize the Deity and its physical counterpart" (cf. *E* 36).

3. Visions of Light

The metaphors and visions of light, ubiquitous in medieval religious literature in general, have their origin in the Bible, as well as in philosophy and theology. Some of the light visions of the Sister-Books seem to be little more than direct transpositions of scriptural passages; others follow hagiographic convention; still others on occasion appear fresh.[29]

The power and significance of light occurs only against darkness. The women depicted in the Sister-Books, of course, spent much of their waking and praying hours in the dark of the night, a darkness so intense that a modern reader can scarcely imagine it. "It was a miracle," says the Gotteszell author, that one of the sisters "did not lose her mind for horror" (*G* 140; cf. *E* 24) when she prayed alone in a deserted spot at night. In such all pervasive darkness, light becomes extraordinarily significant. Its importance is perhaps best revealed in a startling comparison attributed to an Unterlinden sister: her children, Rinlinda von Biseck says, meant more to her than light (*U* 460). The beauty of natural light that overcomes darkness is expressed dramatically when Katharina von Unterlinden depicts a nun spontaneously exclaiming: *Ecce dies.* Joy in the brilliant colours of dawn that summer morning made her break the rule of silence (*U* 367). Also references to divine light in the Sister-Books, especially images of fire and of radiant light penetrating the darkness and illuminating "the whole world" (*W* 79), are pregnant with meaning.

Visions of light are the primordial experience of God and the transcendental world. For the author of the Weiler Sister-Book, God is "the most beautiful light of all"; and the meaning of a sister's vision is glossed precisely, when a voice explains: *daz liht ist die klar gothait,*

28. Gehring (1957, 55).

29. Blank (1962, 236 and 227) traces, for instance, *U* 360, 30ff. back to Ac. 2:1–4 and *U* 483, 22ff. to 1Tm. 6:16. And on the imagery of light, see Lüers (1926, 213ff.); Blank (1962, 187–197).

"this light is the clear godhead" (*W* 71f.). Katharina von Unterlinden speaks of the "divine light, ... the wonderful light of God" (*U* 351) and of "the light from heaven more brilliant than the sun" (*U* 379). The Diessenhofen author, recording a nun's vision, writes:

> Anne von Ramswag saw a round globe that was of pure fire. And in this globe of pure fire, she saw our Lord as he was in his childhood .... Then she saw him, as he was at the time when he was thirty years old. And with this vision, the globe of fire began to come closer to her so that she was set on fire by it, and that she became just like a fiery flame from this fire. Then our Lord said to her: "I was the little child, and I am the old God whom you love in all things." With that, she no longer saw the vision (*D* 41).

Images of the child Jesus are not themselves the end of contemplation, Anne is taught in a very special way, for in this vision of a fiery globe the visionary herself is set on fire and thus opened to the message of the awe-inspiring "old God."

The author of the Oetenbach Sister-Book describes the sight of the wounds of Christ radiating an intense beautiful light as a source of overwhelming joy and love for the visionary:

> And [Ita von Hutwil] saw shining from the wounds a light that was so beautiful and so large that she was unable to compare it to the sun. And when she looked into this light, it was in itself so large that she was unable to see the end of the flames of fire, neither above nor within nor at the side. And in these flames of the fire, she was given to understand what she could not formulate in words. And the light shining from his heart shone over her so that she stood within it, and she received so much divine sweetness, wisdom, and joy, and love, and she was so filled that she did not want to receive any more. And she was then given to understand that she felt like the souls in the heavenly kingdom that are so filled that they cannot receive any more ... (*O* 254.16–255. 4).

Such expression of exultation still has a didactic aspect: Ita is given to understand the fullness of beatific happiness.

Attempting to authenticate their accounts, the authors occasionally claim that the effect of a light vision was also witnessed by people other than the visionary (cf. *E* 4; *T* 23; *W* 83).[30]

---

30. For the importance of visions of light, see Blank (1962); Benz (1969, 326f.).

4. Visions of Jesus as 'Got und mensch'
The largest number of visions reported in the Sister-Books centre on
Christ as "God-Man." The preoccupation with the person of Jesus
among the women of the monasteries is revealed by the special attention given to the Incarnation. Each step of Jesus' life becomes a vision.
Jesus is often seen as a young man, usually at the age of thirty (*A* 171;
E 35), the ideal age of the human body to which medieval writers
thought one returns in heaven (STh. Suppl. q.81 a.1.). The Engeltal
prioress Anne Vorhtlin is said to have complained to the Lord, saying:

> "Ah, Lord, you promised me so much and now I suffer miserably."
> Then our Lord said: "I have never left you [even] for a while, I
> have always stayed with you." She lifted her eyes and looked at
> him: there he was in his beauty at thirty years of age, and he took
> three steps toward her and said: "You have to follow in my
> footsteps" (*E* 36.23–29).

The audience is left to assume that the prioress thereupon cheerfully
shouldered her burden, for the text abruptly turns to the next episode.

The Adelhausen entry on Else von der Neustatt contains an
account of a vision written in the first-person:

> "[The Lord] appears as a handsome lovable youth, and this room
> becomes quite filled with angels and saints. He sits in front of me
> and looks at me very benevolently. But the angels all stand before
> him. He never comes alone, the angels always come with him. And
> he speaks to me: 'I will come again and again and will soon take
> you with me and will never separate myself from you in eternity.'
> And he embraces me with an inner embrace." Then the sister asked
> [Else] what kind of a garment he wore and named several kinds of
> colours. Then she could not liken it to any colour except that she
> said that anything he wants appears on him. Then they asked her
> what she spoke with him when he was so benevolent to her. Then
> she said: "My soul bows toward him down to the earth, and I
> thank him that he acts so benevolently toward me" (*A* 178.29–179.
> 3).

The "inner embrace" Else refers to is synonymous with the "kiss" of
the mystical union; the vision entails an assurance of Sister Else's
salvation as well as foreboding of imminent death. Else's own spiritual
goals here effectively contrast with the other sister's more worldly
concerns. As Else remarks later: "[Jesus] can speak so that it penetrates
the soul and the ground of [my] heart" (*A* 180).

Visions can also reveal practicality. The vision of "our Lord [as] an old man" in the Töss Sister-Book has for its aim precepts on sensible eating. Ita Sulzerin, a lay sister, who suffered from an eating disorder (presumably "holy anorexia"[31]) so that "nothing attracted her but fasting," had forced herself to eat something the day before:

> And then, when night came, our Lord appeared to her in the dormitory in the image of an old man and asked her to go with him to the refectory. And he set [Ita] down at a table and stood before her and began *Gloria in excelsis* and sang all of it in such a rich voice that she imagined it possible that all the earth had heard it.
>
> And then he said to her: "Sister Ite, will you eat?" Then she said: "O Lord, I have nausea so that I do not like to eat."
>
> And then our Lord wanted to show her that he was pleased that she had overcome herself regarding food that evening, and he put some white bread before her, and when she tasted the bread, all the nausea that she had often had before disappeared. And for a time it did not come back (*T* 81.18–28).

Any expectation of a definite fairy-tale ending is curiously thwarted: the sister's nausea was cured only for a while. Such practical visions dealing with this-wordly concerns are in general rare in the Sister-Books.

The contents of vision at times extend their usual scriptural and theological patterns in unexpected ways. Using the device of "complementing," the writers create imaginative scenarios in which they attempt to fill in gaps they perceive in the life of Jesus. Thus in Töss, Adelheid von Frauenberg's "tears of love" are seen to effectively heal Christ's wounds (*T* 54). An Unterlinden lay sister, fetching water from the well outside of the monastery gate, encounters a leper and offers him a drink, only to discover he is "the Lord" (*U* 407). Elsbetlein of the Gotteszell monastery also speaks of a vision of "our Lord ... in the image of a leper" (*G* 143). These passages allude to Isaiah 53:4 and reflect contemporary preoccupation with leprosy. And Elisabeth von Kirchberg, generally quite restrained in her reports of charisms, has a nun see the unusual image of Jesus as a beggar that perhaps comes naturally to an author of a mendicant order. She shows, however, that a divine beggar's needs cannot be fully met by the cellarer:

> [Willbirg] also once was the cellarer. Then a man came and begged alms for God's sake. He was in height and build and colour just as it is said that our Lord was on earth. When she had given him wine

31. Bell (1985, 55f.).

and bread, she went into the kitchen and brought him some mush. When she arrived with it, she did not find him. Then she was sad in all her heart and asked every one she could where he had gone. And she went out into the outer yard and asked the gatekeeper if he had left through the gate. Then the gatekeeper and the others in the yard swore that on that day nobody had entered or left through the gate. Then she cried and wept ..., for she surely believed that it had been our Lord (*K* 113.37–49).

The narrative voice establishes its distance: Elisabeth von Kirchberg does not take any responsibility herself for the veracity of the event but quotes Willbirg who claims for it a visionary status.[32]

Many visions are inevitably influenced by the liturgy: after all, the celebrant of the daily mass is the representative of Christ himself. The lengthy extract from the Töss book that follows offers an example of a typical monastic vision; it also provides a glimpse of what the nuns' Good Friday service may have been like:[33]

One night after Matins when [Mechthilt von Stanz] returned to her bed, there came a quite honorable affable lord accompanied by a great host of lords, and one of the lords carried a large cross as pure as a crystal. And he spoke to her most benignly: "Sister Mezzi, do not be afraid. Nothing can happen to you. Follow me boldly without any fear!"

And that same lord with the magnificent cross went ahead into the choir and all the lords properly followed him, and they devoutly sang the song that is sung on Good Friday. And she followed them into the choir.

And then one lord went up to the altar and lifted the cross up very high. And the other lords sang very blissfully and genuflected for each verse and bowed, as is done on Good Friday. And when her heart was filled with great wonder, she looked up and saw our Lord descending from heaven onto the cross that the lord carried, right as if he stood in his passion with all his wounds. And she stood far away from our Lord. And our Lord looked at her with a loving face and said to her quite mildly:

"Sister, do you believe that I am truly God and Man?"

32. On complementary visions, see Tipka (1989, 240); Vernet (1930, 190f.) lists several *vitae* of thirteenth- and fourteenth-century saints who, such as St. Francis of Assisi and Elisabeth of Hungary, kiss lepers.

33. For the use of the liturgy in visions of monastics, see Benz (1969, 467–480).

Then she said: "Mercy, Lord, I believe it well."

Then our Lord said: "Then come here!"

But there were so many lords that she could not get close, and when our Lord asked her to come close, they all made room until she came before our Lord.

And then our Lord appeared very severe and said to her: "Sister Mezzi, do you not desire any consolation from me?" Then she said: "Mercy, Lord, not I."

Then our Lord said very sweetly: "Since you do not desire any consolation but mine and since you will let go of all other consolation, I will console you myself and will console you with my holy body and my holy blood and with my holy soul and with my holy godhead and will give you all the consolation that I gave my beloved disciples on Holy Thursday .... My much beloved and much blessed, you shall know that heaven is yours after you depart from this world. I am giving you my eternal blessing" (*T* 63.3–37).

Several aspects of this example are typical of visions in the Sister-Books, and may be generalized:

> The reference to Holy Week suggests that the vision took place at the end of Lent. The state of physical exhaustion that followed the severe ascetic practices of Lent often made the believer more open to extraordinary experiences. Several scholars have suggested that there is a clear connection between religious fasting and heightened visionary or auditory experience as well as a connection between visions and illness. Dinzelbacher argues that fasting and illness are factors that trigger visions (*Schlüsselreize*). The Töss author thus sets her account in a physical and psychological context in which visionary experience might make sense.[34]
>
> The vision is typically set after Matins, the liturgy of the nightly Divine Office. Benz claims that "ascetic vigils," held in the church choir during the early hours between this first Canonical Hour and Prime, often prepared the way for extraordinary experiences. Blank argues that in most cases deprivation of sleep and the surrounding darkness made the women psychologically overwrought and susceptible to autosuggestion and somnambulism. The authors of the Sister-Books would not agree; they clearly state on

---

34. For the connection between asceticism, illness, and visionary experience, see Zoepf (1914, 47); Benz (1969, 17, 38); Bernhart (1950, especially 176–180). See also Dinzelbacher (1985b, 80).

many occasions that charisms are gifts of grace alone, for "none have ever come to great saintliness by means of their own piety" (E 1).[35]

The vision then plays out the scene of a liturgical procession to the church altar with a shining cross leading the train.

The visionary image reenacts a late medieval topos showing "our Lord" in his most pitiful human condition, as the Man of Sorrows, that is "as if [sic] in his passion," with his five wounds visible and on the cross.

The visionary is said to have been singled out as an individual when the Lord calls her. A typical formulation elsewhere is, "she was given to see" (D 32).

The experience reaffirms and clarifies the theology of the eucharist. Through the eucharist the visionary is directly linked to the God-Man, and the divine presence in her heart thus becomes the source of graces and happiness.

Joyous, the visionary sees herself assured of her own salvation.

a. Images of the Child Jesus

The frequent references to visionary appearances of the child Jesus in the Sister-Books and other writings of the period have been ridiculed as typically female: many critics have interpreted such visions as pathological expressions of the nuns' repressed mother instinct. And yet, a preoccupation with the child Jesus – as a part of the renewed interest in Christ's humanity – is found not only in legends but in religious works by male writers as well, from Anselm of Canterbury and Bernard of Clairvaux to the fourteenth-century Dominican Suso. It is one of the most frequent motifs in medieval religious literature.[36]

Visions of "our Lord as he was a child" (T 88) can be found throughout the nine Sister-Books. Occurring typically during Advent (T 36) and around Christmas (G 124; W 74), the visions of the child Jesus are often set within the liturgy of the mass and are connected

---

35. Benz (1969, 48); Blank (1962, 266; 1978, 32). Wentzlaff-Eggebert (1969, 61, 67) maintains that these visions are considered gifts in recompense for a good life; but Haas (1987a, 238) correctly states that they represent *gratiae gratis datae*.

36. See Pfister's study (1911) on the image of the Christ child and the opposing arguments of Weinhandl (1921, 52) and Ruh (1990–93, 2:327). Among the many texts on the child Jesus preceding the Sister-Books, see Aelred of Rielvaux (†1167), *Jesus at the Age of Twelve*; Bonaventure (†1274), meditation on the "Five Feasts of the Child Jesus" and on the Circumcision; Ramond Lull (†1316), *The Book of the Nativity of the Little Child Jesus*.

with the elevation of the host during consecration (*D* 19, 31; *W* 72, 81).[37] The miracles, then, illustrate the nuns' faith in the personal presence of the divine in the eucharist. In the Töss text, for example, a sister is said to have seen in the communion wafer "our Lord ... in the shape of a small child" (*T* 81; cf. *U* 416); a passage in the Weiler book shows a host in which the image of the child is suddenly transformed into that of "a powerful king reigning in heaven" (*W* 75).[38]

If miracles conventionally represent a way of teaching and of reaffirming one's faith, then some may be said to have been "wasted." One of the visions of the child Jesus provides an example:

> Sister Irmengart von Dürenheim was a devout person. She saw during a mass our Lord as a small child in the hands of the priest. Then she offered her hands to him and said: "O Lord, now you know well that I have a firm faith. Why do you not show this to persons who need it so that their faith be strengthened?" (*W* 81. 10–14).

In a similar passage, the Diessenhofen author has a sister say: "My Lord, what do I need this vision for? You know well that my faith is not shaken" (*D* 8).

Many legends popular with medieval audiences contain the motif of the child questioned about his parentage. These stories may have found their way into the Sister-Books, as Ringler suggests, via oral tradition. There are several variations of the following story:

> Once [Gertrud von Herkenheim] hurried to the monastery gate because of the office she was charged with. Opening the gate, she immediately saw a most beautiful child, exceedingly handsome and comely, standing alone at the door. She looked at him closely, was most delighted in admiring his great beauty but assumed that such a small youngster could not say any words yet. Nevertheless playing with him she asked: "Dearest child, where are you from? And who are your father and mother, and what are their names?" He immediately responded with perfect words: "Pater noster

---

37. Child Jesus visions are discussed by Rode (1957, esp. 41ff.); Beyer (1989, 199–201); see also Gurevich (1990, 91).

38. See also Ringler (1980a, 187 and 1988, 153). Acklin-Zimmermann (1993, 73) understands this Weiler passage as a reference to the contemporary theological debate about the multi-location (or multi-presence) of the body of Christ (cf. Aquinas, STh. III, 76, 4f.).

himself is my father, and Ave Maria is my mother." Having said this, this most blessed youth was removed from her eyes and no longer visible (*U* 407.34–408.8; cf. *E* 32, 39, 43).

But the visionary is left with "incredible joy and exultation and burning with love" following her experience. Similarly in a vision of the "very blissful little child" that Else Schefflin in Töss supposedly had in the choir after Compline, the conversation proceeds as follows: "'Ah, my dear child, who are you?' There he benignly said to her: 'I and the Trinity are one, and this is as true as it is true that you shall never be separated from me'" (*T* 24). Theological teaching and a personal promise of salvation are here combined.[39]

Jesus is said to have appeared not only on the altar (*D* 47) and in choir (*D* 18); he was also supposedly seen in the kitchen playing with "cabbage dumplings" (*D* 24), at table (*D* 27), in the workroom (*D* 27f.) and in the sickroom (*D* 43; *U* 467; *G* 125; *T* 48; *K* 114). The child Jesus delighted the sisters and, at times, consoled and instructed them (*A* 171; *D* 1), and he always brought "great joy" through his presence (*D* 40; *T* 88). This proliferation of visions sometimes occasions careful, distant reporting:

> On St. Michael's day during mass, a sister called Mehthilt von Torlikon was in her prayers. And in her prayer she wept heartily. Then our Lord as a little child came to her. And just as is done with a crying child (whom one wants to silence and so one puts an apple in his hand), our Lord put an apple in her hand. Then she pressed her hand together firmly and imagined for sure to have clasped the apple in her hand, until she came out of the choir. There she had clasped her hand together so firmly that, for a long time thereafter, she had a mark on her hand (*D* 43).

The Diessenhofen author makes it quite clear that the vision only took place in the nun's imagination. However, she does not belittle Mehthilt's experience; rather, she provides critical insight into the way such stories were to be understood. Still, these visions, imagined or not as they may be, nevertheless remain crucial to the spiritual life of those they have graced. Elisabeth von Kirchberg uses a vision as an invitation to the *imitatio Christi*:

---

39. Ringler (1980a, 90f.); cf. also Lecouteux (1981, 278) for the didactic function of miracles.

[Irmlgart von Rosenvelt] once desired from all her heart to experience how much our Lord loved her. Having desired it so much, she saw our Lord as a small child running before her. And he played with her and said to her: "Do to me as I do to you." With these words our Lord gave her to understand how dear she was to him (*K* 114.26–32).

Six of the nine Sister-Books also include another popular moralizing motif especially prominent in Cistercian and Dominican literature.[40] In these visions the child Jesus or Mary or both are seen passing through the choir while the nuns are assembled in prayer. The Töss story reads: Once Ita von Sulz "also saw our Lord as a child going to the sisters in the choir, and when they bowed he embraced them, and whoever did not bow down deeply he passed up as if he could not reach her" (*T* 21; cf. *T* 82; *A* 177; *D* 20, 50). Such didactic stories are meant to induce fervour and adherence to the rubrics of the liturgical service. The moral aim is made more explicit when Katharina von Unterlinden shows Mary handing the child over to each of the nuns to hold, however sometimes passing over a sister "blemished with sin" (*U* 410). Other texts vary the pattern slightly: in the Engeltal book the event occurs during communion (*E* 27); in the Töss text it takes place during the communal reading of the Psalms (*T* 49); and in the Weiler Sister-Book the child is replaced with the Holy Spirit (*W* 84). In still other variations of this motif, the Lord and Mary appear in the monastery workroom (*U* 400f.).

Some visions of the Christ child are marked by special vividness. These accounts speak of a "lovable child" with golden locks walking through the choir (*T* 39; *W* 70); the child Jesus running around the altar, playing with apples (*U* 368); he appears in a red frock walking on the altar (*A* 172). Bihlmeyer, commenting on similar examples in the Weiler text, remarks that the emphasis on colour in these visions is characteristic of the female psyche. But as Jean Leclercq shows, such criticism is short-sighted: it disregards the "power of [the] imagination" by which medieval writers made "present the colours and dimensions of things, the clothing, bearing and actions" of the figures they depicted.[41] Moreover, critics of such scenes have overlooked the influence of medieval art as an important source of inspiration for these vis-

40. See Krebs (1904, 96).
41. Bihlmeyer (1916, 92); Leclercq (1961, 93).

Figure 6 Diessenhofen crèche, Liebenfelser Meister,
Lake Constance area, circa 1330

ions. For instance, a visionary scene in the Diessenhofen book picturing "St. Joseph, the donkey, and the oxen" (*D* 24; cf. *U* 403, 413, 431f.; *A* 170f.; *T* 88), seems related to a contemporary work of art that existed in this monastery at the time. In any event, the child Jesus was a favourite subject of Gothic painters and sculptors, so much so in fact that the Christ child is the child image *par excellence* in medieval art.

Finally, the frequency of reported child visions can be explained by a medieval custom (in some instances still practiced in religious communities today) according to which a cradle and a figure of Jesus were treated as religious objects during the Christmas season. Holding such objects facilitated meditation on the Incarnation in the same way that venerating the cross during Lent purified the self through spiritual exercises. And the unambiguously positive picture of the divine child provided a balance to the representations of the suffering man Jesus.[42]

b. The Passion

Late medieval Christology finds its literary and artistic expression in images of the passion. In this theological tradition, Christ is no longer the perfect human being, "the most handsome of all men" [Ps. 45:2], of the Romanesque era but the suffering Lord.[43] Images of the passion are not only ubiquitous in the art and literature of the Middle Ages but also closely interrelated; the written word stimulated artistic representation which, in turn, inspired literary creation.

The authors of the Sister-Books are themselves aware that a nun's adoration of Christ in his suffering is often kindled by representation in devotional art of the monastery. The Töss book refers to "a picture in which our Lord stood before [Pilate's] court" (*T* 27), and the Diessenhofen text mentions "a statue where our Lord lies in the tomb" (*D* 42). "Contemplative immersion" into such artistically represented

---

42. Extant are an early Diessenhofen relief representing a crèche, an oak-carving dating from around 1330, made by the so-called Liebenfelser Meister, to be seen today in the Frauenfeld Historisches Museum. The nativity scene in one of the initials of the Diessenhofen *Graduale (1312)*, fol. 18v, also seems closely related to this vision, see Knoepfli (1989, table 225). The *"infantia-*Christi" theme was first isolated by Wentzel (1960, 134–160). Elisabeth Landolt-Wegener, "Zum Motiv der Infantia Christi," *Zeitschrift für Schweizerische Archäologie und Kunstgeschichte* 21 (1961) 164–173 discusses this theme in late medieval manuscripts; see also Arnold (1980, 59). See Möckershoff (1983, 49) for references to the cradle as religious object.

43. Benz (1969, 517).

scenes increased the sisters' faith, deepened their worship, and engendered visions.[44]

Inspired by the *vir dolorum* of Isaiah 53:3, the image of the Man of Sorrows, the *Schmerzensmann,* is the most important *imago pietatis* or *Andachtsbild.* It concentrates emphatically on the physical pain and suffering, on the *liden* or *marter* (literally, "torture"), of Christ. The intense human agony embodied in these representations of the Gothic Jesus seeks to arouse compassion and to exhort the viewer to follow Christ's example.[45] "Praying before a picture of our Lord standing at the pillar," Hilti Brúmsin of Diessenhofen is moved to compassion so intense that "all her veins and limbs were inundated with such great pain and bitterness that she experientially experienced the passion our Lord had suffered when he stood at the pillar" (*D* 28). The tautological phrase *si empfintlich empfant* expresses the almost complete identification that joins Hilti to Christ. The passage from such experience to vision, the author implicitly suggests, is but a small step.

Descriptions of the suffering Christ provide some of the most powerful visionary images of the Sister-Books (for example, *A* 184; *U* 396; *G* 126f.; *E* 28; *T* 26, 49, 54, 76, 85, 88; *D* 4). Katharina von Unterlinden's depiction of visionary participation in Christ's agony is characteristic:

> For [Agnes] clearly saw in this said vision the Lord Jesus Christ, as it were, suffer again, seized by a crowd of Jews, cruelly bound, and most vilely treated. With terrible shouts and in tumultuous ways, they pulled him from one court of justice to another, mocking him, giving him a box on the ear and frequent blows; they spat into his face, crowned him with thorns, and scourged him with sharp instruments until blood flowed. Finally, after having been tortured [until he suffered] immeasurable pain and after he had become satiated with the disdain and mockery of the faithless, Christ was nailed most cruelly to the cross. The sister who saw all this also

44. Sauer (1928, 17f.) was among the first art historians to draw attention to the late medieval devotional art of the Upper Rhineland. The Engeltal author's somewhat ambiguous reference to *als sie den sarch an sach da unsers herren leicham innen waz* (*E* 13) could point to another artistic representation of Christ in a coffin. But the context suggests the meaning of "shrine" for *sarch,* that is, the tabernacle with the consecrated host, "the body of our Lord." And see also Winter (1951, 122). The term *kontemplative Versenkung* is borrowed from Panofsky (1927, 264).

45. See Belting (1990) for a comprehensive bibliography of this artistic theme.

heard clearly with her bodily ears how the Lord's most sacred hands and feet were pierced with nails driven in with frequent terrible hammer blows. After the vision finished, she remained life-less and motionless because of her soul's pain for a long time. For the sword of the bitterest passion of Christ, that she had seen in this vision with her spiritual eyes, had penetrated her entire soul with such pain of compassion that afterwards she could not live any longer ... (*U* 472.35–473.14; cf. *W* 72).[46]

The re-enactment of Christ's passion in front of this sister's "spiritual eyes" and "bodily ears" ends literally by killing her with compassion. Dying as a consequence of her visionary experience Agnes von Bilzheim becomes a second Mary, whose soul, too, was pierced with pain by a sword [Lk. 2:35].

In the Adelhausen Sister-Book Geri Küchlin is granted a vision of Jesus covered with fresh wounds, who exhorts her to "look what [he has] suffered" because of her (*A* 185). The audience is, in turn, invited to look at and to empathize with Jesus in his distress:

There our Lord appeared to [Margret Flastrerin], as when he had just been taken off the pillar, with fresh wounds and so wretched and miserable that his blood flowed everywhere over all his body. And he spoke to her: "O woe, you poor human being, how long do you want to remain in this empty forlorn life? Regard me and look at my many needs and at this anxiety that I have suffered because of you. And regard these fresh wounds and this rose-col-oured blood that I have shed for you ..." (*A* 170.10–17; cf. *E* 11).

Christ's thrice-repeated command to the visionary to look at him alludes to the biblical passage in which Pilate asks the crowd to look at this man (*ecce homo*) in the most degraded human condition [Jn. 19:5]. (*Ecce Homo* is another name for the image of the Man of Sorrows in art.) The image of Christ at the pillar goes back to "no other source biblical or patristic than the testimony of pilgrims to the Holy Places" who spoke of a "marble column to which Jesus was bound at the flagel-lation," according to Frederick P. Pickering.[47]

---

46. Similarly, another Unterlinden sister, while contemplating Christ's passion, "suddenly heard with her senses" the heavy hammer blows that nailed Jesus to the cross (*U* 415).

47. Pickering (1980, 9f.); see also Louis Réau, *Iconographie de l'art chrétien* (Paris: Presses universitaires, 1955–1959), 2:427–528.

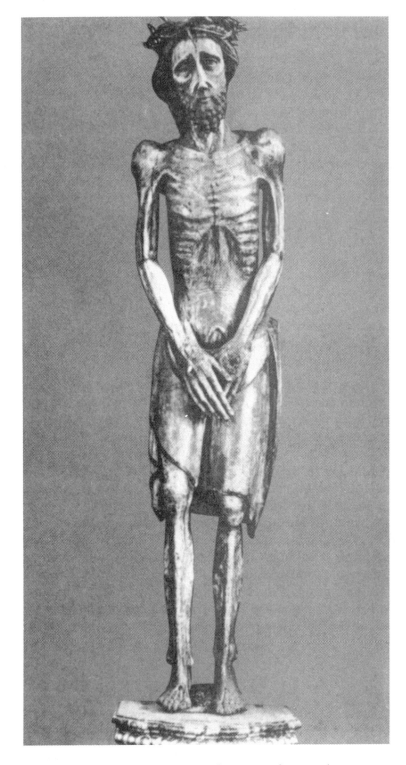

Figure 7 *Schmerzensmann,* Man of Sorrows, fourteenth century

Such unrelentingly grim scenes are occasionally softened, as when an Unterlinden sister's vision ends with a "gaze of the most dulcet God," an image that totally changes "all pain and suffering ... into joy and happiness" (U 396f.). And a Diessenhofen sister's painful vision of the suffering Jesus is followed by an image of his transfigured glory in heaven; Adelheit Rittrin's heart is then filled with "divine joy and sweetness" (D 22).

Other visions in the Sister-Books focus on the crucifix as the symbolic tree of salvation, a common theme in Gothic art. The Weiler Sister-Book provides a first-person account:

> One morning I went into the choir early. There I saw, standing before the altar, a green blossoming tree which was full of noble fruit. Then my heart and senses were drawn upwards, and I was given to understand that the tree was the cross and its fruit was the body and blood of our Lord (W 76.31–35).

This typological parallel that joins the biblical tree of life [Gn. 2:9ff.] and the salvific wood of the cross was used not only in the Good Friday liturgy but also in the monastic Divine Office from the ninth century on; and in late medieval art the tree-of-life is often represented as the *Gabelkreuz*, the tree-like cross.[48]

A number of hagiographic topoi relate to the passion of Jesus: the bleeding crucifix figures in the Diessenhofen Sister-Book (D 49); an art object that comes alive, typically after intense meditation, is described by Katharina von Unterlinden (U 447); in some visions nuns at prayer hear Christ's voice from the cross (A 161; T 24, 47; E 12; D 3, 34). Visions of nuns who claim they were embraced by the Christ figure hanging on the cross are instances of the so-called *amplexus* motif, presumably inspired by the Song of Songs ("his right embraces me," 2:6), and found both in art and in hagiography. Adelheid von Weiblingen of Weiler, for example,

> once sat by her bed. There she heard a voice: "You shall go into the choir." When she got there, she saw our Lord hovering high above the altar. Immediately she was pulled up to the cross and sweetly embraced by God in soul and body. And he said to her: "I will always be with you and you with me, and I will never be separated from you" (W 77.14–19).

---

48. On trees in visions and art, see Lüers (1926, 94); Benz (1969, 378–385); Franz Joseph Dölger, "Die Kreuzesmystik vom Baum des Lebens," *Jahrbuch für Antike und Christentum* 10 (1967) 16–21; Dinzelbacher (1990, 20); LThK 8:21.

Similarly, while Adelheit die Huterin, prioress at Diessenhofen, stood with two other sisters before our large crucifix, "it was to her as if" the Lord said to them: "Avete! This is the word he said to the three women when he appeared to them after his resurrection. And then our Lord moved his right arm from the cross and embraced them and pressed them against him" (D 44). Although relating the vision to an actual object of art in the monastery and to a biblical passage [Mt. 28:9], the author here distances herself from the scene she reports with her careful formulation "as if."[49]

Crucifixes with movable parts, where the arms of the figure were joined by hinges to the body, had been developed around 1300 to be used during the Good Friday liturgy in reenacting the entombment of the crucified Christ.[50] Legendary stories about Jesus reaching out with his hands from the cross, bowing his head, and pressing his head against a nun's cheek, also frequent in the Sister-Books (A 175, 185; E 12; D 30), may be cases of mutual inspiration between literature and art.

Visionary accounts of Christ's passion typically transpose this gospel story into the world of the present. The visionaries are said to be actual witnesses to the historical event. Such immediacy characterizes the sisters' reported experiences as "participatory visions." Inspired by art, visions of Christ's passion are moreover closely related to the nuns' daily readings (T 62) and their devotional practices, especially to the Canonical Hours which centered explicitly around the commemoration of Christ's passion.[51]

5. The Communion of Saints
a. Mary
The tendency of the Sister-Books to concentrate on the humanity of Jesus means that the veneration of the saints including Mary plays a

---

49. Günter (1910, 161); Vavra (1985, 227): "Bildwerke werden im gesteigerten Gefühlserleben zu auslösenden Momenten von visionären Schauungen". Ruh (1990–93, 2:93) lists a similar occurrence in Luitgard of Aywières (1:13).

50. Taubert (1969).

51. The term "participatory vision" is borrowed from Petroff (1979, 59). See Gertrud von Helfta, Spiritual Exercises, chapter vii, about the relationship between the individual Canonical Hours and the stages of the passion: Matins: Jesus is captured; Prime: Jesus before Pilate; Terce: Jesus is crowned with thorns; Sext: Jesus is condemned to death; None: Jesus dies on the cross; Vespers: Jesus is taken from the cross; Compline: Jesus is buried. See also Gertrud von Helfta's Legatus 3:46.

somewhat marginal role in the nuns' religious life, at least judging by the visionary accounts.[52] In the Oetenbach text, for instance, Mary is mentioned only once, in reference to an altar (consecrated in 1317) dedicated to her name. Nevertheless, the monastic tradition had, especially since the twelfth century, cultivated devotion to and imitation of Mary, a tradition continued by beguines in the thirteenth century. During the fourteenth century, devotion to Mary among the general public became more pronounced.[53] Accounts of Marian visions, however, were still relatively rare during the Middle Ages (they seem to have proliferated from the nineteenth century on). Typically, such visions appear, as Weinstein and Bell have found, in greater number in writings by men rather than women. In the Sister-Books Mary usually is pictured together with the Christ child.[54]

The visionary images of Mary in the Sister-Books also have parallels in the motifs of late medieval art. The Weiler author alludes to the popular image of *Maria gravida*, when she reports that a nun saw Mary "pregnant with the great God" (*W* 78).[55] The related art motif of the *visitatio* (which shows the two pregnant women, Mary and Elizabeth, each with a carved-out womb holding the figure of a child inside) does not have an explicit parallel in the Sister-Books. But it probably exerted an influence on this otherwise baffling image:

> On holy Christmas Day during mass, [Anne von Ramswag] sitting in her stall in choir ... felt as if her body came apart so that she could see into herself. And she saw two beautiful little children inside herself who embraced each other quite intimately and lovingly. And in this vision she was given to understand that the one little child was our Lord and the other her soul, and how she and God were united. And then her body closed up again (*D* 41).[56]

52. See also Lüers, *Marienverehrung mittelalterlicher Nonnen* (München: Reinhardt, 1923), p. 48f.

53. On Oetenbach, see Descoeudres (1989, 56). Devotion to Mary is also discussed by Kieckhefer 1984, 165ff.) and Wehrli-Johns (1990, 148). See Gössmann (1989b) for the complex and largely ambiguous role given Mary in medieval theology.

54. Benz (1969, 574) on the history of visions of Mary; Weinstein and Bell (1982, 132–137); Hale (1992, 156) on the nuns' devotion to Mary.

55. Krebs (1904, 95f.). See Lechner (1981) for a comprehensive survey and literature regarding this topic in art history.

56. Muschg (1935, 229); Knoepfli (1989, 237, table 224); Lechner (1981, 29). Notably, one such *visitatio*-figure (dated about 1300), today held in the New York Metropolitan Museum of Art, is attributed to Katharinenthal (Diessenhofen).

Visionary scenes of Mary in childbed (*U* 431f.) and literary images paralleling the *Maria lactans* motif in painting can also be found (*A* 171, 175).[57] The Töss Sister-Book provides an illustration:

> Then I saw our Lady. She was so very beautifully dressed and so lovely to look at and created so tenderly and so benignly that all tongues could not fully express it. And the coat she wore opened and let me see a sky-blue garment she had on. And she said: "See, I am wearing this garment because of you and your faithful work in the community." And then she said quite lovingly: "Since you so faithfully helped me raise my child, I will fulfill your desire and will nurse you with the milk with which I nursed my saintly beloved child." And she gave me her pure tender breast into my mouth. And then I saw her no more (*T* 54.18–27).

A further common motif in legend and Gothic art is "Our Lady of the Mantle," *Schutzmantelmadonna.* This image is based on early medieval German law according to which adults could legitimize or adopt children or grant protection to anyone in need by covering the person with their coat.[58] In the Adelhausen book, Mary is depicted protecting a friar and a novice under her coat (*A* 156; *D* 48); the Töss author describes Elisabet Bechlin's childhood dream vision of being protected by "the pure Virgin" and forever remaining "under our Lady's mantle" (*T* 87). Christine Ebner refers to this image twice: "It once came to pass" that when "they sang the sequence *Salve mater salvatoris*," Sister Elsbet Ortlibin "saw our Lady hovering over those who sang the mass, and she had embraced them all with her mantle" (*E* 38). Next to this conventional gesture of Mary, the author provides an unusual one showing Our Lady of the Mantle protecting against evil – and then suddenly raising her lilac mantle as a weapon to chase off the "fiend" (*E* 25).

Finally, the Sister-Books also contain images of the *Pietà,* "Our Lady of Sorrows." The German title of this image is *Vesperbild,* since it is during the Canonical Hour of Vespers that Christ's removal from

---

57. Bynum (1987a) cites many such instances in medieval literature in general.

58. On the *Schutzmantelmadonna* and the image's background, see *Lexikon der christlichen Ikonographie* (Freiburg: Herder, 1972; repr. 1990) cols. 128f; Angela Mohr, *Schutzmantelmadonna in Oberösterreich* (Steyr: Ennsthaler, 1987), p. 19; Krebs (1904, 30); Sauer (1928, 7); Hardo Hilg, "Mantel Unserer Lieben Frau," Verflex. 5:1221–1225; Christa Belting-Ihm, *Sub matris tutela,* Abhandlungen der Heidelberger Akademie der Wissenschaften 3 (Heidelberg: Winter, 1976).

Figure 8 *Schutzmantelmadonna,* Our Lady of the Mantle,
Lake Constance area, early fourteenth century

the cross was commemorated. The following scene is attributed to Mechthild von Stanz in Töss:

> Our Lord showed her ... how he was taken off the cross and laid into our Lady's lap. His body and face were so miserable that she said nobody could fully express [his suffering]. She also saw that our Lady's sorrow was so great and overpowering that [Mechthild's] human strength was no longer able to bear it so that she fainted with that great overpowering compassion she had with our Lady (T 66.9–15).

Mary's role in this episode is purely legend; but its unhistoric basis did not prevent this motif from becoming one of the major devotional themes of the late Middle Ages. It is not known whether the Töss community owned a *pietà* figure, but a Christ-torso originally part of a such a statue (about 1350) from the Adelhausen monastery is preserved in the Freiburg i.B. Augustinermuseum.[59]

Appearances of "God's mother" (G 124) or visions of her (U 400f.) have the function of consoling and healing the sisters (A 175; K 109, 110, 114; T 80, 83). In general, visionary images of Mary inspired by art remain prominent. In Diessenhofen and in Töss, sisters supposedly hear Mary's voice emanating from a picture (D 33; T 28). And Katharina von Unterlinden credits Mary, whose image was carried through the monastery at a time of crisis, with having saved the community and restored peace to the region (U 392). She also provides another dramatic example:

> Through the Lord's miraculous cooperation, a very joyful and in all respects worthy miracle happened to [Gertrud von Bruck]. She once stood in the choir before the statue of the glorious Virgin .... Suddenly she saw visibly with her bodily eyes the figure of the child Jesus sitting on his Virgin Mother's lap, lifting his hand and stretching it out to her. [And he] spoke in a clear and very sweet voice ... [assuring her of forgiveness of her sins and eternal salvation]. After this most gratuitous and joyful promise of the Lord, she was filled with joy and ineffable exultation and laid her right hand into this statue's hand, seizing it joyfully in faith. Then

---

59. See also Kieckhefer (1987, 75). For general comments on the *pietà*, see Sauer (1928, 14–16). Benz (1934, 40) argues that the medieval *pietà* should not be interpreted in modern terms, since it does not represent human suffering with which we are asked to commiserate, but shows the paradoxical way in which God reveals himself through suffering and death.

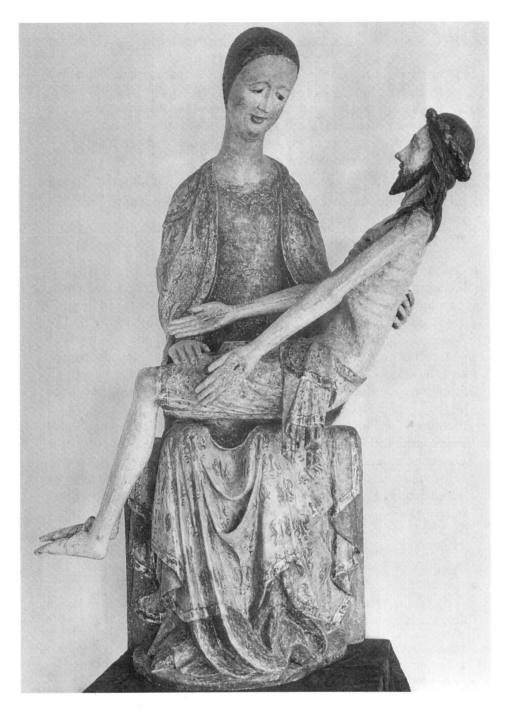

Figure 9 *Vesperbild*, Pièta, second quarter of the fourteenth century

suddenly, the hand of the youth remained in hers, somehow separated from his body by divine power. As a proof of the truth, this hand could later not be restored into the said statue, no matter by which means, although attempts were made very often. In that way, this saintly statue that was divinely deprived of a hand is still kept in the monastery today (*U* 414.6–31).

The audience is assured twice that it was divine intervention and not the sister's clumsiness that caused the hand of the statue to break – a statue that, in her eyes, had been alive.

b. Favourite Saints

One art object made a decisive impact on late medieval religious literature written by women. The so-called Christ-St. John statue shows "the disciple whom Jesus loved" resting his head "on our Lord's heart," as the author of the Diessenhofen Sister-Book describes it (*D* 41). The sculpture represents, as Hans Wentzel remarks, "a special achievement of German art," and draws its inspiration from the New Testament account of the Last Supper [Jn. 13:23–26], the Song of Songs 1:1, as well as medieval legends of John the Evangelist known in saintlore as the virgin saint. Images of Christ with St. John were also present in illuminated manuscripts. To judge by the fourteen versions of this much cherished sculpture that have been preserved (two from the Diessenhofen and one from the Adelhausen monastery among them), many more no doubt existed, especially in the women's monasteries which acquired it as a purchase or a donation. References to St. John, in one context or another, in the Sister-Books are manifold (*U* 449; *T* 38; *E* 32, 41; *G* 139; and especially *A* 173f.; and *D* 16, 21, 27e, 38, 39).[60]

---

60. Wentzel (1947, 22); Wentzel (1954, 658) also provides a list of all known Christ-St. John sculptures (cols. 664–666), as does Wentzel (1959, 155–176).; see also Wentzel's superb description of the Diessenhofen sculpture (1947, 14–16). Haussherr (1975, 89–95) lists many other sources from commentaries and sermons to the breviary text of the Feast of St. John (27 December), the writings of St. Augustine (for whom John the Evangelist is the model of contemplative life), and Albertus Magnus (who introduces the typological comparison with Jacob sleeping on the rock [Gn. 28:11]), to the *Legenda aurea*. Dinzelbacher (1979c, 120) suggests the pose depicted may owe something to the ancient custom of reclining at table. The sculpture's oldest extant version is kept today in the Cleveland Museum of Art, Ohio; see Greenhill (1971, 406–416). According to Vetter (1978, 40), the Diessenhofen monastery owned three sculptures of the Christ-St. John group, two

Figure 10 Christ-St. John sculpture, Diessenhofen, early fourteenth century

Figure 11 Christ-St. John sculpture, Adelhausen, mid-fourteenth century

Visions of saints are largely inspired by the *Legenda aurea*. Among others, St. Catherine of Alexandria was so much favoured by the nuns that an Adelhausen sister worries that she was too much preferred to other saints (*A* 156f.). The Diessenhofen book (written in the "Valley of St. Catherine") shows St. Catherine appearing as the patron saint of the sick Kathrin von Überlingen: The infirmarian "saw a beautiful affable lady come in who was clothed in pure gold, and she had a golden wheel upon her as a brooch. From that she understood that it was St. Catherine who went to sit before the sister, gave her milk from a bowl and served her as a maiden [serves] her lady" (*D* 15). The wheel suggestive of her martyrdom identifies St. Catherine in saintlore (*O* 243). In Engeltal an altar is consecrated in St. Catherine's honor (*E* 4). And Mechthilt von Stanz of Töss once "imagined" the refectory "filled with heavenly maidens" who are given bread from heaven by "our Lady and St. Catherine" (*T* 68). As an auxiliary saint, Catherine was the patron of philosophers and theologians. St. Gertrud von Helfta's vision of this saint, for instance, shows St. Catherine seated on a throne among fifty philosophers whom she had converted through her own divine wisdom, *ipsa spiritu divinae sapientiae*. C. Grant Loomis even suggests a historical basis because "the intellectual domination of beauty and brains appeared in most detailed form in the legend of Katherine."[61]

St. Agnes is called "the favourite virgin" by Christine Ebner (*E* 31). Also mentioned are Mary Magdalen (*K* 107; *E* 32; *D* 42), and St. Margaret who punishes a sister with a flash of lightening because she had not participated in a prayer to her (*T* 23f.). The Töss author repeatedly speaks of St. Ursula and her eleven thousand virgins:

> When the second bell for Matins sounded, she saw the choir door open and saw the eleven thousand maidens enter the choir, two by

---

of them still extant, and one small silver figure no longer traceable. One statue (today in the Musée Mayer van den Bergh in Antwerp, Belgium) was created by Meister Heinrich von Konstanz and donated, Knoepfli (1989, 231, table 212) explains, to the Diessenhofen nuns after 1300. See also Blank (1964/65, 70f.). Another such sculpture from the Adelhausen community is kept today in the Frankfurt/Main Liebieghaus museum).

61. On auxiliary saints, see Günter (1906, 111–125): The popular belief in the helper saints was especially wide-spread among the German people. Many of these saints are featured in the *Golden Legend*, although their explicit individual functions date only from the fourteenth and fifteenth centuries. Gertrud von Helfta, *Legatus* 4:57,1; Loomis (1948, 111).

two, and bow to the sisters in each choir. And they also came to stand before her, bowing benignly. And each carried a green palm leaf in her hand, and the leaves were radiant like shining stars. And an exceedingly sweet fragrance came from the palms, and the radiance was quite blissful, and the taste so sweet that it is ineffable. And thus they went back and forth in the choir until Matins was ended, rejoicing in great joy (T 30.27–31.7; cf. T 21).

Hearing, seeing, smelling, and tasting play a role in this joyful pageant. The Töss community was particularly devoted to this saint because of an acquisition of supposed relics of St. Ursula in the area of Winterthur.[62]

St. Dominic, too, is shown in visions alone or with Peter Martyr or St. Augustine (A 156, 158; E 43; O 243). In the Weiler Sister-Book, an appearance of St. Dominic starts as a dream vision but is then impressed on the visionary's waking senses:

> Then one night when [Guta] lay down in her bed after her prayer, she saw in her sleep that the most beautiful lord came down from heaven. He was clothed in a golden chasuble and was surrounded by the clearest light. He stood before her and said: "You shall be mine, I will not let you go to anyone else." Thereafter he wanted to depart from her. Then she fell [*sic*] after him before her bed, and there she saw him with her bodily eyes ascend to heaven. And with her bodily ears she heard a voice that said: "This is *sanctus Dominicus*". And the light and the good fragrance remained in her chamber for a long time. Thereafter, within three days, she was admitted and received into our monastery (W 80.8–17).

Ears, eyes, and the sense of smell are touched in Guta's vision. And St. Dominic's special rank as the Dominican nuns' "house saint" is underlined by the gold of his vestment and the light surrounding him; both are normally attributes of the divine. The vision apparently qualified Guta to become a Dominican nun.

Finally, the promotion of local saints in the Sister-Books is a feature not uncommon in medieval works. The Oetenbach author, for in-

---

62. Spiess (1935, 356). For another visionary's version of this legend, see "Liber revelationum Elisabeth de sacro exercitu virginum Coloniensum," in: Elisabeth von Schönau (1884, 123–138). The well-established medieval legend of the eleven thousand virgin martyrs accompanying St. Ursula may be, the eighteenth-century scholar Friedrich Carl Gottlob Hirsching suggested, based on a misreading of a manuscript containing the name XIMILLA. See *Historisch-geographisch-topographisches Stifts und Closter-Lexicon.* (1st ed. Leipzig 1792. Repr. Hildesheim: Olms 1972), 1:816.

stance, claims that their new monastery "was built exactly on the site" where the saints Felix and Regula had been martyred (*O* 271f.). Christine Ebner assures her audience through a vision account that the Engeltal church was partly constructed on St. Leuprecht's grave (*E* 27). Moreover, she reports a vision of St. Gervasius and his brother Prothasius whose relics were venerated not too far from Engeltal (*E* 33; cf. *A* 162). Some critics suppose that writers shrewdly calculated pecuniary benefits from telling such tales. Given these authors' over-all reverent attitude, such a ruse is unlikely, although there is little doubt that they were much interested in publicly propagating the saintliness of their individual monasteries of which they were truly convinced.[63]

These women see themselves as an integral part of the *communio sanctorum* (*W* 82). Examples show that they venerated their own deceased sisters as saints (*U* 452; *T* 38, 40, 69; *O* 235), and an Unterlinden sister uses a relic of the just deceased Elisabeth von Senheim to cure her own illness (*U* 451f.). Christine Ebner even describes friars of the Order of Preachers saying: "We should take along some earth from here to other monasteries because of the great saintliness we have found here" (*E* 7). And indeed, also the surrounding population held the monastery in high esteem, the Weiler author suggests: A blacksmith in the village "suffered greatly in his heart from always fearing that he would go to hell." But once he heard "a voice saying to him: 'If you want to be saved I will direct you to a safe place; come to Weiler, the monastery; on this homestead nobody shall be lost!'" (*W* 83; cf. *T* 35, 44).

Perhaps this author overstepped legitimate boundaries, Dinzelbacher remarks, when she ties an absolute assurance of salvation to one saintly community. But the author's claim may not have been exclusive, instead meant to encompass all monasteries.[64]

In the Gotteszell book, Sister Adelheit's rapture, which features four important saintly figures, engenders a remarkable *jubilus* poem, a highlight of this entire text. Its introduction reads:

> This saintly sister had so much love for the praise of God that for many years she desired to know how the saints in the heavenly land praised the eternal worthy God. Thus, on the high feast day after None when God's ascension was commemorated, her spirit

63. On relics of saints mentioned in the Engeltal book, see Schröder (1871, 66). On prosperity based on local saints, see Gurevich (1990, 41); Vauchez (1988, 541–544).

64. Dinzelbacher (1990, 26) notes with reference to *E* 7 that traditional Christian belief, of course, does not consider the earth sacred as such. Regarding the Weiler author's presumption, see Dinzelbacher (1981, 221).

was enraptured into paradise. There she saw the most blissful green she had ever seen and our Lord Jesus Christ in a brown garment. And he was tenderly inclining on his divine arm. And before him stood two patriarchs of the Old Law, Adam and Moses, and two highly praised lords of the New Law, St. John the Baptist and St. Augustine. And each one spoke his special praise. And they taught her how to praise her creator while she was here on earth ... (*G* 127.26–38).

The four saints of the vision and the poetic prayer initiate Adelheit into devotional poetry: Adam and John the Baptist stand at the beginning of the Old and of the New Testaments, and Moses and Augustine transmit the commandments and the Christian doctrine respectively. In claiming to be taught by these four men, Adelheit deliberately places herself and her sisters within a long and venerable tradition of sanctity.[65]

c. Angels

Visionary and auditory experiences are traditionally marked by the presence, the light, beauty, and song of angels. A "great crowd of angels in white garments" makes manifest visions of the Lord in the Engeltal Sister-Book (*E* 8, 35). The visionary angels conform to the traditional typology of perfectly pure heavenly creatures (*O* 244). They often belong to particular sisters, protecting them from harm or guiding them (*E* 12, 32; *T* 19, 21, 61, 64), although they are nowhere referred to as guardian angels. And as messengers of impending death, they follow an occupation that has etymological authority: The Oetenbach sister Elsbeth von Beggenhofen sees her angel who admits after a Jacob-like struggle [Gn. 32:26ff.] that she was close to death (*O* 261; cf. *E* 21). Angels also guide souls after death to their punishment (*T* 39, 43) or to

65. Saints that appear or are mentioned in visions not cited include the highly popular St. Martin (*E* 40), St. Blase (*T* 89), St. Lawrence (*E* 3); the apostles St. Andrew (*U* 429), John and Jacob (*T* 75), Peter (*T* 38), Luke (*U* 451; *G* 123); St. Augustine (*O* 243; *T* 14, 65) and St. Bernard (*T* 33). There are other references to the Order of Preachers, St. Dominic (*O* 243; *T* 12, 37), Thomas Aquinas (*T* 12), St. Peter of Verona (*U* 445f.; *T* 12) and the other martyrs of the order (*T* 13). And John the Baptist was supposedly instrumental in obtaining a dispensation for the Unterlinden sisters' tithe payment to the pope (*U* 479).

their reward (*T* 84; *W* 85) and stand by them when they are presented in heaven (*E* 23).[66]

d. The *Revenantes*

Many of the visions of the Sister-Books are attributed to *revenantes*, that is, former members of the community, now deceased, are said to have come back. These sisters generally give testimony to the unequalled beautiful rewards they received in heaven which is a feature of great importance. Formerly in monastic writings of the eleventh and twelfth centuries, going back to the *Dialogues* of Gregory the Great, souls returned from the dead to punish the living and to inspire fear of the Last Judgment. Art also is imbued with horrible images of death: torments of flesh, decaying corpses, skeletons surrounded by toads and snakes. And indeed, the visions of the Sister-Books at times show the same fascination with the horror of death. In an apparition of the deceased Elisabeth von Vackenstein of Adelhausen, her body is gnawed by worms after eighteen weeks of punishment (*A* 158). The Unterlinden author describes the cruel retribution upon a a young sister for expending her beautiful voice "more for glory in the world than for the glory of God" (*U* 361).[67]

Yet such instances are generally atypical for the Sister-Books. Usually the *revenantes* glow in heavenly radiance (*U* 398, 435, 440, 446f.). The much repeated phrase "after her death she came back" testifies to the salvation of the soul (*U* 398, 435, 440, 446f.; *E* 10, 20, 23, 25) and to her presence before God (*G* 131). Meritorious deeds are imprinted on the returning soul. So Sister Helwig of Gotteszell reappears "with a line of golden letters on her back, and on her heart in front, a cross with golden letters," her patient suffering rewarded "a thousand-fold in the radiance of his divine face" (*G* 132). The Gotteszell Sister-Book contains an elaborate description:

---

66. The guardian angel has its origins in the Hebrew Bible. The idea was developed in the Middle Ages by St. Bernard; in the works of Thomas Aquinas (STh 1.113.2, 5) it becomes part of a complex angelology. A special feast day for guardian angels in the ecclesiastical calendar is attested from the fifteenth century on. See Vernet (1930, 109); LThK 9:522–524.

67. On the imagery of death in medieval literature of visions, see Walter Rehm, *Der Todesgedanke in der deutschen Dichtung vom Mittelalter bis zur Romantik*, DVJS Buchreihe 14 (Halle: Niemeyer, 1928); Dinzelbacher (1981, esp. 260); Farmer (1985); Haas (1989b).

And the sweet consoler and mender of all wounded hearts had pity and sent before her eyes the soul of saintly Adelheit in a human image in order to make her rejoice. And [Adelheit] was decorated in extraordinary beauty that human senses cannot comprehend nor tongues can speak, except for this alone, that her heart was all covered with a wide golden brooch in which there were countless precious stones. And the stones shone and were radiant like the stars when they are in their lightest and purest power and blissful beauty ... . Then [this sister] saw on [Adelheid's] head three little crowns, one above the other ... . Then she saw on her back the most beautiful cross she had ever seen (G 133.30–134.1; cf. E 41f.).

Adelheit glosses the vision herself. The brooch, she explains to her friend, recompenses her deep suffering; the triple crown signifies her purity, compassion, and love; the golden cross acknowledges her meditation on the Lord's passion. In this painstaking exegesis, the gold and precious stones symbolize the earthly virtues of the nuns; they also represent heavenly *materia* for which the women are rewarded for the poverty they chose in this world.[68] The commentary then moves toward its didactic end: "'And therefore, dear sister,'" Adelheid concludes, "'farewell. For whatever you suffer on earth will be kept for you eternally as an immeasurable treasure and hoard.'" With this her companion is consoled, and "Adelheit's soul [flies] up again into the bosom of her desirous spouse where she enjoys the tender, eternal, true love" (G 134).

The *revenantes'* testimony goes beyond their obvious entertainment and teaching value; they bear witness to the acceptance of the deceased nuns in heaven as women. These visions, then, reveal the Sister-Books' authors' remarkable self-confidence. They convincingly declare women's capacity for sainthood. Even here and now, the *sanctorum communio*, Christ's mystical body, becomes for them a lived reality. By means of these vision accounts of *revenantes*, these authors provide proof that the Manichean heresy that excluded women from heavenly perfection unless they were somehow made male, was in the end as powerless as it had been insidious.[69]

68. See Christel Meier's valuable study of the allegorical use of precious stones in Christian literature, *Gemma spiritalis*, Münstersche Mittelalter-Schriften 34 (München: Fink, 1977).

69. The presence of women in heaven is discussed by Aquinas, *Summa contra Gentiles* 4.88; see LThK 4:651f. for the *sanctorum communio*. Hildegard von Bingen, Peter Lombard, and Aquinas fought to combat the heretical view of female imperfection: see Gössmann (1979, 297) and Gössmann (1987, 7).

6. The Devil

Opposite the communion of saints stands the devil figure as a necessary part of the didactic element of the Sister-Books. Although ignored in large stretches of the texts and not given the great importance found in contemporary legends, the devil in the Sister-Books, above all, never appears as the lascivious seducer he so typically represents in tales about saintly men (such as the *Vitas patrum*). A number of folkloric elements are integrated into the image of the devil portrayed here which make "the evil enemy" (*O* 267) into the single most active and colourful character in the Sister-Books.[70]

The devil's repertoire in disguises as well as his ruses are typical and manifold. "Terrifying in face" (*diabolus uultu terribilis*), the devil is shown carrying souls to the place of punishment (*U* 368). He is as obnoxious as flies; he causes large mice and "vipers and vermin" to show up; and he himself appears as a large horse, a wolf, and a threatening dog (*O* 240, 246f.; *T* 23, 46; *D* 50; *G* 126).

Tales of the devil's metamorphosis include the following scene from the Unterlinden text: While Tuda von Egenheim is at prayer, the devil appears "to her in the shape of a sow followed by piglets"; at the altar, "the sow turned as if in a puddle and the little piglets started sucking." When she realizes that "this was a deception by the impure spirit," Tuda makes the sign of the cross, and "the devil's concoction" flies away "like a winged animal, through the vaults of the choir, leaving behind a foul odor" (*U* 363, cf. *U* 416). The devil's notorious odor is deliberately contrasted with the sweet fragrance emanating from saintly sisters (*T* 53; *W* 84). The folkloric motif of the evil spirit suddenly growing to astonishing heights before the eyes of an "immeasurably frightened" sister occurs several times (*G* 126; *T* 31, 33).[71]

The devil also repeatedly poses as a sister and as a confessor (*U* 453f., 492; *T* 20, 52). And at one point in the Oetenbach Sister-Book, he seems to impersonate the Lord, when "two faces appear in a light"; to the visionary's exclamation, "'Mercy, Lord, do you have two faces?'" the Lord replies, "'Not me! The face you see is that of the evil enemy; and you shall be tempted by him'." But the light in this vision simultaneously attests to the divine presence and prefigures the outcome of the vision (*O* 214f.).[72]

70. For the paucity of devil appearances in these texts, see also Weinhandl (1921, 35); Ringler (1980a, 326). Günter (1910, 171) discusses the devil in legends.

71. Cf. Grimm's fairy tale *"Der Geist im Glas,"* and Goethe's *Faust*, part I.

72. The devil in the guise of a sister in the Töss book (*T* 52) is chased away when he is called "an evil rag," *du boeses fustuoch*, likely an allusion to Suso's dream of a dog playing with a rag in which Suso sees his own life foreshadowed (*Vita* I, 20).

As the typical trickster of folklore, the devil is heard "beating a drum or whistling" or pretending to bring "the roof" down (*T* 62). He is the poltergeist of legends and *vitae*, hurling praying nuns with such abandon that their fall can be heard in the entire building (*G* 136; *O* 264). In many cases, showing a crucifix, or mentioning the sacrament, or the help of an angel successfully chase the devil away (*T* 23, 80; *E* 12).[73]

Overall, the devil's main function in these texts is attempting to prevent the sisters from doing good and from praying, since he is *der boes nider aller guotten werken*, "the evil envier of all good works" (*T* 52). But on a more profound level, the authors also struggle with the problem of evil in the world. There are repeated references to Job. The Töss author explains that the devil's power comes from "our Lord" who permits him to trouble the sisters "in the same way as we read of blessed Job whom our Lord also, out of special love, decreed to be severely tormented by the evil spirits" (*T* 22; *E* 6).

The most severe diabolical torment found in the Sister-Books is an Oetenbach nun's doubt in her faith and a temptation of despair, *die anfechtung der verzweiflung*. For a period of ten years, Ita von Hohenfels is repeatedly tempted into thinking that nobody could ever be saved: "And all the time it was to her as if hell stood open in front of her and [as if] her chair were set next to Lucifer's chair." Then again, after a period of "peace and freedom in God," Ita was plagued by doubts in the divine goodness: "Then the evil enemy came to her in the image of a man and said to her: 'You say that God is good; but he is not. For he is evil and all evil comes from him. For he knew well, when he created the angel that he should become an evil enemy and that Eve and Adam and all humankind should fall by his counsel.'" Ita's temptation comes about through the basic unanswered question about the origin of evil. Ita is finally delivered after having been raptured into heaven where "she saw and realized and experienced" the goodness of God pictured through Christ on the cross (*O* 242f.; cf. *U* 454).

Whether the devil is presented as a malicious folkloric figure or as an embodiment of serious personal problems, the authors overall deliver the message that the women portrayed in these texts are successful in defeating evil. As the Gotteszell author says about Adelheit von

---

73. Weinhandl (1921, 64f.); Herbert Thurston, *Ghosts and Poltergeists*. Ed. J. H. Crehan (Chicago: Regnery, 1954) claims that "poltergeist phenomena ... cannot in fact be disputed" (p. 329). The Cologne beguine Christine von Stommeln (1242–1312), who was flung out of the house far into the garden, was also the victim of demonic forces. Cf. *Codex Iuliacensis* (1975, 88).

Hiltegarthausen, "the evil spirit became aware that, with her prayer, she was laying a trap and an ambush for his malice" (G 126). And the Weiler text illustrates this basic theme with the simple humorous image of a group of devils running away from an approaching Weiler nun, shouting: "Flee, everyone, flee! they are bringing a sister from Weiler!" (W 85). In the end, then, the lesson is unambiguous: The devil has no lasting authority over humankind because of Christ's salvific act.[74]

Concluding Remarks

Conventional, even commonplace, the visions of the Sister-Books nevertheless provide glimpses into the imaginative world of the women of these medieval monasteries, into their spiritual concerns, hopes, and fears, into their theological doubts and questions. Few of their stories or anecdotes betray an individual voice; but all of them speak with authority. Through visions and apparitions, these women claim divine inspiration which empowers them in their own ways of thinking and living.[75]

74. Vernet (1930, 226) explains that the decreasing threat of the devil was symptomatic for this time period.

75. See also Petroff (1986, 6); Ringler (1988, 154).

The Sister-Books mirror the authors' keen theological interest as well as the nuns' desire to deepen their spiritual commitment. Because of the hagiographic style of these texts, theology is transmitted not in theory but rather through *exempla* and legend, allegorical motifs and images. But the Sister-Books' legendary veneer also had the important function of diverting attention from the fact that, as women, these authors took part in theological speculation. Their simple style and seemingly naive faith in miracles afforded the authors some security against the raging Inquisition. For although cloistered women were protected from persecution, their words and acts were not immune to suspicion. A non-conformist Adelhausen nun was branded a heretic, *ein ketzerin* (*A* 154) by Dominican friars, and a Weiler woman's theological orthodoxy was officially scrutinized (*W* 70). A close reading of the Sister-Books reveals a profound preoccupation with theological and spiritual concerns that cover an astonishing range.

IMAGES OF GOD
1. The God of Creation
In her poetic hymn of praise or *jubilus*, the author of the Gotteszell Sister-Book offers a concise summary of the world view and faith of the nuns (*G* 127–130). A synopsis may prove a useful starting point for discussion:[1]

The creation of the world came about through the goodness of the eternal God who also created the angels for his praise, overthrowing "the proud ones" among them. Humankind was created through the "power, wisdom, and will" of the triune God. The divine Trinity consists of the Father, "the eternal out-flowing fountain," whose "unfathomable, blissful heart" gives birth to the Son, "his image"; the Son is both the Savior and Wisdom (Sophia), combining male and female aspects; the Holy Spirit – who, through Mary, created Christ's humanity – is the loving kiss, "the never-ending embrace" between the Father and the Son. Mary, God's virgin daughter, becomes, by virtue of her role in the Incarnation, God's spouse, the queen who is above

---

1. Lutz (1984, 111–114) suggests that hymns with a universal scope (like this *jubilus* poem) are based on the four cosmic psalms, Ps. 8, 28, 103, 107. See Lewis (1984–88, 5:164–174) for an English translation of this poem.

the angels and is the noblest of the saints. As in the Nicene Creed, Christ exists "before all ages": "I praise and honor the honor with which God the Father has honored your humanity that you have had with him before the world was created." The Son reveals the Father to us and ennobles humanity by becoming God-Man. His earthly suffering defines his virtue; the burial of his "pure divine body" illuminates the earth; he is at once divine and human, and through his resurrection and ascension he resides eternally with the Father.

The world that the Dominican women contemplated and sang about is a solid, well-ordered cosmological structure, created by God out of nothing (O 219). The creation of the world far surpasses the wonder of miracles. Asked whether she might have experienced any "special graces," a Kirchberg sister replies: "Yes, our Lord has done great graces to me in as much as he created heaven and earth" (K 109). Unique, the earth nevertheless remains insignificant in comparison with God:

> And there [Guta Jüngin] saw the formation of all things in God and how the creatures were related to the godhead. She also saw in one vision all the world, and she imagined that she saw far away a small boat in plenty of water: this is how all this world was compared to the great godhead with which [the world] was surrounded (W 75.4–8).

The vision conjoins the personal to the cosmic. But even though God's presence permeates this world, he is simultaneously separated from it by distance and divine otherness. The conclusion is unequivocal: "You shall put your heart and your love onto this creator and not onto the creation," the author exhorts her readers (W 74). The wonder of creation engenders the same insight: As she "stood in her prayer before the altar, and the stars shone clearly on her," Sister Elsbetlein of Gotteszell "greatly wondered whether the radiant shining was their nature or whether the stars thereby did a service and offered praise to God." In this "questioning within her own heart" she receives the answer: "all creation was created in order to praise God." The full understanding of the purpose of creation brings reproach and confirmation: if a creature without senses and understanding is created to serve God and may never expect any love or praise for it, how much praise and service do you, poor human being, owe your creator." For in as much as we are given body and soul, we "participate in everything that is good in heaven and on earth." Our "unwavering love" then must be our "clear faith and entire trust" (G 142; cf. T 77).

2. The God of Mercy and Motherly Love

Among the many attributes of God to which the Sister-Books allude including omniscience (*T* 74), ubiquity (*T* 21) and almightiness (*T* 12), omnipotence is conspicuously rare. One vision in the Diessenhofen Sister-Book of the all-powerful God does appear, depicted as Cecilie von Winterthur's first-person account:

> "I saw God in his power, and I saw the twenty-four elders [Rev. 4:4] sitting around him, and the four evangelists, and all the twelve apostles. And I saw so many angels and saints that they were innumerable. And I saw several sisters with our Lord whom our Lord treated quite tenderly and benignly. And the sisters shone just like the sun. And of the joy and beauty that I have seen, all tongues could not fully speak" (*D* 47).

Divine power is still seen as an aspect of a tender and benign God. But divine power also issues in divine justice. A God of justice and revenge presides over several scenes of the Engeltal Sister-Book. Punished for her lack of compassion, a lay sister sees the refectory filled with devils whom God "had given power over her," and the nun is almost driven to suicide (*E* 6). And Alheit von Trochau, believing her brother's childlessness constitutes a punishment for his sins, cries "See here, brother, don't you know that God's wrath, *die rach gotes*, lies on you?" (*E* 14).

Still, justice, too, is a sign of God's mercy: "If all the leaves that have ever grown and all the grass that keeps growing, if they all were masters of Paris, they could not fully speak of nor fully write about the mercy that lies in God and especially the mercy he has with human beings at their death" (*E* 33). When Elsbeth von Stoffeln goes into the orchard at Diessenhofen while the trees are blossoming, she gazes at the "beautiful pleasant blooming flowers" and thinks "how our Lord's goodness decorates all things"; thereupon "an inner voice tells her: 'God is the origin of all good. And he is *grundlos*, unfathomable mercy and endless goodness.'" God's profound mercy is not only an opportunity for theologizing, though. The "groundlessness" provides the basis for true spiritual growth. For God "has such a divinely kind and natural strength and eternal power that no human beings can ever, even for a short while, think of him without causing a vice to disappear and a virtue to grow in their souls" (*D* 33). The experience of nature leads to the contemplation of God's immense goodness; his mercy and benignity empower the human existence. Theology is not seen as an abstract pursuit for its own sake but rather as a basis for a better informed spirituality. Theology and spirituality in the Sister-Books are mutually dependent.

God in the Sister-Books, then, is the infinite, loving, divine presence. From him all graces come (*T* 17), graces available to all who seek
them (*T* 89). God is "the only good," *das ainige guot* (*T* 42), "the unfathomable good" (*T* 67), "the unfathomable godhead," *die grundlose
gothait* (*T* 39), the traditional "abyss of the profound godhead," *das
apgrunde der tieffen gotheite* (*A* 173).[2] God is the source of eternal love
for all human nature (*O* 251) and of the inexhaustible power to restore
(*O* 274); God's presence is found in the "secret and soft wind" (*U* 386;
cf. 1Kg. 19:12).

Following a tradition that stretches from the Hebrew Bible to the
Christian era to include the medieval mystics, God the Father is also
God the Mother in the Sister-Books. A prayer in the Töss book reveals
"fusion of masculine and feminine roles" in the God image: "'Ah,
beloved Lord, you are my Father and my Mother and my sister and my
brother ...'" (*T* 86). When Mechthilt von Stanz in Töss expresses her
wish to remain in constant prayer, she imagines herself "exactly like the
child that does not want to leave the tenderness of her mother's lap"
(*T* 61). This image of a motherly God is echoed in the Oetenbach
Sister-Book. God's presence in Ita von Hohenfels was so profound that
"she could not express it in words except with the example of a mother
caressing her only child with heartfelt love and pressing [the child] to
her heart." For thus did "God caress her soul in great holiness with
divine tenderness" (*O* 245).[3]

This image of a motherly God who nourishes her children is also
found in the Kirchberg book: Sister Eite experiences "such exceptionally high grace that she was given to drink from our Lord's loving
wounds – as this experience seemed to her," the author adds cautiously
(*K* 107). And a Töss lay sister heard in a dream vision "a voice saying
sweetly to her: 'Drink the water flowing from my heart'" (*T* 84). In
another variation on the *Deus lactans* image, Katharina von Unterlinden
speaks of Gertrud von Geiersperg, who has severely punished her body,
experiencing the sensation of being "poured upon and anointed from

---

2. Underhill (1955, 97) speaks of "the Unplumbed Abyss" as the God image
of later mysticism.

3. Since the Second Vatican Council, much has been written on feminine
attributes and feminine images of God in the Christian tradition. As early as 1949,
an essay by Cabassut drew scholarly attention to what was then a "little known
medieval devotion" (the article appeared in English translation in 1986). For the
discussion of another passage that conflates masculine and feminine attributes, see
Petroff (1986, 17).

the breasts of divine consolation" (*U* 418; cf. *O* 274). When Hilti Brúmsin of Diessenhofen in her prayer thinks of our Lord's passion, she desires "to know from our Lord what she should suck out of his wounds" (*D* 28; cf. *D* 11).[4] Nourishment flowing out of or being sucked from Christ's wounds, especially from his breast, symbolizes the free flowing of grace, Ringler suggests. Bynum warns, however, that readers must be on their guard not to "overemphasize ... the affective aspect" of this image of the nursing mother and child. Its purpose is more profoundly spiritual. The images of the *Deus lactans* are attractive to the women of the Sister-Books precisely because they enable them to see themselves relating directly to God without any priestly mediation. As explained in the thirteenth-century *vita* of Gertrud von Helfta, by drinking from Christ's wound, one's heart "is continuously able to receive, without any intermediary, the inflowing of [his] divine nature."[5]

The feminine aspect of Christ also underlies references to *die ewig wishait*, "eternal Wisdom" (*T* 33). As Felix Vernet explains, the equation of Christ with Sophia (Wisdom) was typical of Dominican spirituality whose best known exponent was Heinrich Suso. Suso's influence on the authors of the Sister-Books, especially of the Töss nuns, is apparent in this context. The connection between Jesus as Mother and the christology of Sophia is taken for granted in these texts.[6]

When the Kirchberg author declares that Elsbeth von Oettingen once "also saw our Lady in her most high worthiness within the Holy Trinity" (*K* 110), the modern reader is reminded of Carl Gustav Jung's discussion of the divine by which the "exclusively masculine character of the Trinity" is transformed by the unconscious into a "quaternity," the "fourth constituent" of which is the Virgin. The obvious reference in the Kirchberg text is to the belief in Mary's bodily assumption into heaven; but the phrase, "our Lady," was seen *within* the Trinity may

---

4. Specific literary examples of the *Deus lactans* image in Clement of Alexandria, Anselm of Canterbury, Bernard of Clairvaux, Guerric of Igny, William of St. Thierry, and also Catherine of Siena and the Helfta mystics, are mentioned in Bynum (1984a, 129–135) and Richstätter (1919, 170–173).

5. Ringler (1988, 158); Bynum (1984a, 134); Gertrud von Helfta, *Legatus* (1:16, 1).

6. Vernet (1930, 42). The parallel Sophia-Christ had no lasting impact, however, as Helen Schüngel-Straumann shows in her discussion of the feminine aspect in the divine: see "Alttestamentliche Weisheitstexte als marianische Liturgie," in Gössmann and Bauer (1989b, 12–35). See also Newman's studies of "Christ-Sophia" (1990 and 1992); Gardini (1987, 59); and Dinzelbacher (1988, 47).

suggest an understanding of the necessary inclusion of the feminine in the divine completeness.[7]

A God who encompasses both genders can be approached by women as easily as by men. Other saintly women had desperately desired to become male in order to partake in God's likeness.[8] But the women of the Sister-Books freely strove to emulate a Christ who fully integrates the feminine into himself. An *imitatio Christi* in the Unterlinden book is emblematic. When Adelheid von Rheinfelden saw herself take Jesus' own place in the gospel story of his baptism [Mt. 3:17], "a voice came from heaven into the ear of her who saw this" saying, "'She is my Beloved,' *Hec talis est dilecta mea*" (*U* 405). A biblical text is thus freely adapted to honor female spirituality. It is precisely the casual presence of the feminine in the imagery of God that impresses on the modern reader the matter-of-fact and self-assured femininity of the nuns in their relationship to God.

3. The Trinity

The mystery of the Trinity greatly preoccupied the authors of the Sister-Books, judging by their numerous references (*U* 353, 379, 382; *A* 156; *G* 129; *T* 39, 44, etc.). The theology of the Trinity was much debated at the time of the composition of these texts, and it was in 1334 that Pope John XXII initiated the Feast of the Holy Trinity.

---

7. Jung (1958, 62f.). Ann Belford Ulanov's gloss on the subject is useful: "Jung understands the Catholic dogma of the Assumption of Mary as theological recognition of the feminine in the Godhead ... . The Trinity becomes quaternity, as he sees it" (*The Feminine in Jungian Psychology and in Christian Theology* [Evanston: Northwestern University Press, 1971], pp. 318f.). See also Leonardo Boff, *Trinity and Society*, trans. Paul Burns (Maryknoll, New York: Orbis Books, 1988), pp. 103f. The vision of "the Trinity ... in the form of God Father, God Mother and God Son" attributed to St. Nikolaus von der Flüe provides a later parallel (Gardini 1987, 62). In her study of problems in theological anthropology, Gössmann claims that the Judeo-Christian God image has always had feminine connotations: "the concept of God and the Trinity as purely male ... has never existed"; during the history of Christianity, however, feminine aspects of God have been suppressed (1989a, 26).

8. Even the thirteenth-century Helfta writer, Mechthild von Hackeborn (*Liber* 1:19) asks God to change her natural sex so that she can become a true son of God (Bynum 1984a, 138f.). And St Perpetua, when she was about to die as a martyr, stated: *facta sum masculus*. "Fourth and fifth century hagiographic literature stresses that female saints are 'manly women,'" see Kari Vogt ("Becoming Male. One Aspect of an Early Christian Anthropology," *Concilium* 182 (1985) 72–83, esp. 78. On women's eschatology, see Gössmann (1988a) and Gössmann (1991, esp. 56f.).

Images of a trinitarian God, inspired perhaps by speculative preaching on the topic, predominate a sister's vision described by Katharina von Unterlinden, drawing attention to Augustinian thought. The excessive use of *conduplicatio* in this passage aims at underlining its special importance:

> Through the rays of an inner light, [Hedwig von Laufenberg] saw the profoundest mysteries of the undivided Trinity, knowledge, recognition, and insight of which undoubtedly, constitute eternal life. In this sweetness and in this peace surpassing all senses, she was led by grace and found worthy to pre-taste and have a foretaste of this ineffable goodness ... . With her intellect thus illumined and clearly enlightened, she understood and comprehended the Trinity of the luminous Godhead. Not even all the words and writings of the excellent teacher St. Augustine (in whose books this is most beautifully illustrated) contained that purest understanding with which she was uniquely illumined. The divine insight she received at that hour was by grace of a super-celestial anointing ... . As we have told, she indeed heard and saw in this divine vision the mystery of the highest majesty, of which to speak is not permitted nor right for a human being. As a result of the contemplation of this highest good she truly felt so filled and inundated with God's wisdom that she could have preached most lucidly and very clearly about the essence of the ineffable Trinity to the whole world. This she later firmly maintained (*U* 441.38–442.21).

Insight into divine mystery again proceeds out of a vision that at once includes and exceeds all the senses. And again spiritual insight overrides formal theology. Yet the author herself is more reticent: for Katharina von Unterlinden the sacred mystery (*archanum*) must remain ineffable; full understanding can only be achieved in eternity. Whether or not such passages imply a subtle criticism of the contemporary scholastic debates must remain an open question.

The images of the Trinity are generally traditional. For the author of the Diessenhofen Sister-Book the synoptic gospels on Jesus' baptism [Mt. 3:16f.; Mk. 1:9–11; Lk. 3:21f.] represent the principal source: Ite von Hollowe "saw our Lord in St. John's saintly hands, when he was baptized by him. And [she] heard the Father's voice: *Hic est filius meus dilectus*, and she saw the Holy Spirit in the likeness of a dove on his head" (*D* 24).

The Kirchberg text describes a vision of three young men seen by the leprous sister Heilin von Gruen. The scriptural echoes are again specific:

> [Heilin] saw three youths standing before her who were so ineffably beautiful that she recognized well that they were not human. And they were clothed identically and were in all things alike to each other. Then she thought of the Holy Trinity, as Abraham had seen it [Gn. 18:1–5], and [knew] that she was to adore the one God. And she kneeled down to pray. Then the mild God showed her his five wounds, and she fell prostrate, for then she was sure that this was the Holy Trinity (K 117.36–43; cf. E 33).

The reference to the story of Abraham at Mamre is commonly understood in Christian exegesis as an allusion to a trinitarian God. The image of the three identical youths is also found in late medieval art, originally influenced by Byzantine and Russian icons (manuscript miniatures of the theme date to the ninth century).[9]

Two other images of the Trinity, also common in medieval mysticism, are the fountain and light. They are part of a tradition that goes back to Egyptian sources. In the Töss text a rare *locus amoenus* is the site of Beli von Liebenberg's vision of the Trinity as three separate but reuniting streams:[10]

> She desired once so deeply to know something about the Holy Trinity. And then once, she imagined being led to such a most blissful beautiful field, where amiable special people were walking, and with pleasant flowers that were radiant all together like pure gold. And in this field was such a blissful pure fountain, and it was threefold, and it flowed back again to its origin, and its water was so ineffably sweet (T 31.11–17; cf. A 156, 178).

9. On the Abraham allusion, see Benz (1969, 495). For trinitarian images in art, see LThK 3:561; see also Hamburger (1990, table 197), listing the perhaps best known later example, André Rublev's icon of the "Trinity" (1411). The image also occurs – this time less statically – in the Engeltal text: "I saw the Holy Trinity in the form of three persons, and they changed into one person" (E 20; cf. E 7, 27). Katharina von Unterlinden, by contrast, interprets the originally trinitarian image of three young men in liturgical vestments and with "radiant red faces" as an image of the "angels of the Lord" (U 448).

10. On Egyptian sources, see Lüers (1926, 140f. and 213ff.). On the trinitarian fountain image, see also Ringler (1980a, 271). Nikolaus von der Flüe is also said to have had a vision of the trinitarian three-fold fountain (Amschwand 1987, 34).

The apparently simple vision granted Ite von Hutwil of Oetenbach attempts to make a complex theological mystery approachable to the audience: "And in that, there came a light toward her, and, above her, it was divided into three. And as it began to approach ..., it was only one light" (O 255).

Still, abstract ways of talking about the Trinity are not absent: the Töss author suggests that the Trinity is an example of how the soul can become one with God (T 39). The Gotteszell book, referring perhaps to recent theological debate, juxtaposes *drivaltikeit* with *einickeit*, "Trinity" with "unity" (G 129), in speculations about faith. To Elsbeth von Oettingen in the Kirchberg Sister-Book is also vouchsafed intellectual insight into the Trinity: "She came to such high and great understanding (because of her fervent love of God) that the Father, Son, and Holy Spirit are three persons, and yet one single God who is the creator of all things and who ever was and ever will be" (K 110). Such knowledge, the authors insist, is not granted to the merely curious; it is given only to those who love God deeply.

4. The Holy Spirit

The Holy Spirit is the force of love underlying all that comes into existence. The Spirit is the one who enlightens, empowers, and emboldens humankind to find its way to heaven, the one who teaches us "all things" [Jn. 14:26] (A 179). The Holy Spirit is the all-consuming fire that Gertrud von Colmar sees "coming from heaven with a thunderclap onto the saintly community of the sisters" of Unterlinden as they sing *Veni creator spiritus* at Pentecost. The fire fills "the entire choir" illuminating them so "with divine splendor" that they all appear "equally fiery." Thus do the sisters see "our Lord God himself the consuming fire, who consumed through his benevolent presence all the filth of vice" and inflamed the sisters "with love for him" (U 360f.; cf. K 120).[11]

The power of the Holy Spirit is often referred to in the Sister-Books (see E 42; D 37; W 84). It is the topic of a long passage in the Diessenhofen text (D 33) which I am quoting in full at the end of Chapter Eight since it constitutes an important example of the erudition of these women. The treatise is an *expolitio*, that is, a careful "polishing" of a single topic by repeating its essence in various ways. It touches upon a great number of articles of the Christian faith but always returns to the Holy Spirit that is its main theme. Structured like

---

11. See also Stoudt's interpretation (1991, 162f.) of this Unterlinden entry.

a sermon, it is a work of considerable speculative thinking – indeed, it represents the closest approximation to pure theology the Sister-Books have to offer. Its text reveals, as no other passage does, theological schooling of these women. The passage, presented as a revelation granted Elsbet von Stoffeln, takes the form of a hymnic meditation on the Holy Spirit.

5. The Son of God

Christ remains the centre of the spiritual world of the Sister-Books. The numerous images of Christ concentrate on his humanity. Christ is the mediator to the Father, *wie der sun alweg pittet für den menschen* (*O* 256); he is "true God and human being," *mensch* (*T* 27, 63), whose Incarnation has saved the world (*U* 441; *G* 129). "How the divine nature and the human nature are united" (*O* 256), a question that engaged so much of medieval theological speculation, also is raised by the authors of the Sister-Books. But again, their response takes not the form of a treatise but an unaffected image:

> Thereafter this human being asked God how big his love was for human beings. [And Ita von Hutwil] considered God's miracles, how wise, how great, how beautiful, how almighty he is in all things. And when he was so great in her because of all the miracles, she saw the image of a human being [*eines menschen pild*] that was crucified and was very small and said: As big as I am, I became small so that you might love me (*O* 253.26–254.6).

God's supreme gift to humanity lies not in any special grace but in the Incarnation. "What else do I have to give you? For I gave you today my dearest Son," a "soft but loud voice" declares to an Unterlinden sister (*U* 459). And as she offers a sacrifice "for God's sake" in her Oetenbach community, the "heavenly Father" says to Elsbeth von Beggenhofen: "I gave you my Son" (*O* 266).

The Incarnation is the consequence of human sin. The Oetenbach author underlines the logic of the *felix culpa* by explaining that Ita von Hohenfels "saw and realized and experienced our Lord's passion" and was given to understand "how the joy we have from his suffering is more blissful and greater than we would have had if Adam had not fallen" (*O* 243f.).

THE QUESTION OF THE SOUL

Questions about the nature of the soul intrigue many of the authors. They wonder about the relationship between body and soul and about the appearance of the soul. The dilemma of human identity and the unity and division of body and soul engage Katharina von Unterlinden in particular. Disparaging images of the body, "this decomposing matter" (U 358), abound. The terms used – "prison of the body" (U 350; kerker ires leibs (O 270), "flesh incarcerating" the soul (U 384) – are drawn from Platonism. Many of the questions about the soul, such as the fate of the body after death, were in fact topics of heated philosophical debate during the thirteenth century. Katharina, however, defers not to contemporary theologians but to the authority of St. Augustine:

> [Gertrud von Rheinfelden] wished very much to know the truth of the word spoken by blessed Augustine that all limbs of the human being after resurrection shine like the sun in God's kingdom [Mt. 13:43] and sing his praises equally. The benevolent Lord granted her wish. For when, on the feast of this saint, the antiphon *Adest dies celebris* was most solemnly sung in the choir, she was suddenly put in wonder and ecstasy and made worthy to truly understand and experience the truth of this said word, and how it will be fulfilled in the future. Then, immediately coming to, she could barely explain in spoken words the certainty of this mystery, as she had received it (U 432.11–22; cf. U 352).

Once again a decisive insight is ultimately ineffable.[12]

The dilemma of body and soul seems to be resolved only in the person of Mary. Jüzi Schulthasin of Töss is said to have "understood clearly about our Lady, how great a joy she had before all other creatures in God's humanity; but how our Lady's soul is united with the divine essence she did not at all understand." Nevertheless, she was able to comprehend "that our Lady went to heaven with body and soul" (T 76). This popular belief in Mary's bodily assumption into heaven, reflected also in a vision by the twelfth-century Benedictine Elisabeth von Schönau and recounted in the *Golden Legend,* is the topic of much discussion during the Middle Ages. Even so the theological crux again remains unresolved.[13]

---

12. For examples of contemporary theological debates that match those of the Sister-Books, see Bynum (1989, 188–196) and Bynum (1991b). Ancelet-Hustache (1930, 432 n.1) cites several possible sources from St. Augustine underlying the allusion in this Unterlinden passage.

13. See "Visio Elisabeth, quam vidit de resurrectione beate virginis matris domini," in: *Visionen* (1884, 53–55). See Gössmann (1989b, 82–84): this tradition underlies Pius XII's dogma of Mary's assumption, 1950. Söll's formulation in the Handbook of Mariology (1984, 125f.) shows that the text of the 1950 bull was

The many images for the human soul found in the Sister-Books are often traditional. The soul is seen radiating in clarity (*K* 120; *T* 24f.), "a pure crystal," *ein lawter cristalle* (*W* 70), "a shining magnet" (*U* 387), "a light like a round globe" radiant, and colourful, and even playful, *mit ainer spilenden froed* (*T* 44, 19), and, perhaps most commonly, a small child (*E* 40; *D* 41). This last image is explored by Anna von Munzingen:

> And when grace was so abundant in her, [Berchte von Oberriet] desired from our Lord that he let her see with her bodily eyes the miracle that was in her soul. Then ... it was to her as if grace came out of her mouth. And this grace was the most blissful child ever seen by human eyes. And for a long while, she had great joy with this child (*A* 171.32–172.3).

The personification of grace as a child leaving Berchte's mouth may have its origin in the notion of the soul-child being born through the mouth when someone dies, a common motif in medieval legend and painting. In the Adelhausen book, the soul is also seen as a beautiful rose leaving a sister's mouth at death (*A* 156). Patristic writers often speak of souls as children or "small people" (*kleine lútli*, *A* 166) endowed with the faculties and senses of the mature human being (cf.the frequent "the eyes of her soul" and "she heard in her soul").[14]

Assumed into "the highest joy," the soul that was beautiful during life on earth appears "exceedingly beautiful in heaven" (*T* 44, 45). The human soul is held in high esteem by God because she was sent directly from God:

> Then [Diemut Ebnerin] was again enraptured into heaven and saw our Lord in his clarity. And unceasingly, sparks came from him that were bigger and more beautiful in their radiance than the natural stars .... Then he gave her to understand that these radiances were souls he was sending from his godhead into human bodies (*E* 34.5–11).

A divine little spark, *ein klein geneisterlein* (*O* 255), the soul in the end reunites with the divinity. This absorption into the divine is experienced in communion itself. Juta in Gotteszell sees "our Lord and her own soul being intimate with each other in ineffable tenderness ...

---

based on quasi-historical sources of apocryphal accounts of the assumption. The theological difficulties with this relatively recent Marian dogma are explored by Gössmann (1990, 21f. and 30–35).

14. See also Schleusener-Eichholz (1985, 953–958).

united together in such playful joy as is impossible for human senses to conceive" (G 145). By its very nature, then, the soul becomes God's dwelling place on earth. Mechthild von Waldeck hears "our Lord" saying, "I will truly unite you with me" (K 118), and also in the Oetenbach book: *do si ... sich mit got vereinet het* (O 272, 252, 267). And an Engeltal sister declares: "It is as great a miracle that God lives in me so fully as it is a miracle that my heart is not bursting" (E 34).

The unity between the divine and the soul is often expressed in metaphors of the body. For the author of the Oetenbach Sister-Book, this unity is so complete that it resembles "a person [who has] locked together her two hands" (O 263). Elisabeth von Kirchberg, in a traditional image, suggests: "it was to her just as if she were pregnant with our Lord," *wie sie unsers herrn swanger were.* The image is carefully interpreted to show that the sister is "full of our Lord's grace" (K 113; cf. K 106; O 238). Christine Ebner provides a more homely image, saying of an Engeltal sister, she was "like a barrel full of sweetness" (E 31).[15]

Through the grace of God the "noble soul" may come to resemble "his only begotten Son" (T 68). "God is in me and I in him; he is mine and I am his; he belongs to me and I to him," declares Else von der Neustatt of Adelhausen in language infused with the imagery of religious writing and courtly poetry: "My soul is beautiful, proud and high-spirited, for God has opened his grace to me, and I am loved by him" (A 180). Ite von Nellenburg of the same monastery becomes aware of the deification of her soul, although, as she puts it, her body was still in the way: "Everything about me is God's, and between me and God is nothing but my body" (A 160). Such ideas could easily have aroused suspicion of heresy.[16] For although the context suggests the sanctification by grace, such favourable interpretation would not have prevailed had the authors of the Sister-Books not been protected by their cloistered communities. After all, the uncloistered beguine Marguerite Porete in Paris was burnt at the stake in 1310 for similar pronouncements in her book, *The Mirror of Simple Souls.*

---

15. For the image of pregnancy, see Lüers (1926, 151f.). The thirteenth century mystic Hadewijch expresses the same idea in "Allegory of Love's Growth" (1980, 346): "For that brought God down into Mary, / And he would yet acknowledge the same in one / Who could hold himself so humble in love: / He could not refuse his sublimity to him, / But such a one would receive him and carry him for as long / As a child grows within its mother."

16. Grundmann (1935, 416).

The divine aspect of the soul receives more elaborate poetical and theological treatment by Sophie von Klingnau in the Töss Sister-Book:

> And then the sister admonished [Sophie] in all confidence and asked her in all earnestness that she tell her how the soul was made. Then [Sophie] answered saying: "The soul is a very spiritual thing so that she actually cannot be compared to any bodily things. Yet because you desire it so much, I will give you a parable with which you can understand a little her form and her shape: She was a round, beautiful, and transparent light like the sun, and was of a golden red colour, and that same light was so exceedingly beautiful and blissful that I cannot compare it to anything. For if all the stars in the sky were as large and beautiful as the sun, and if they all shone as one, the splendor of all of them would not be comparable to the beauty of my soul ..." (*T* 57.25–35).

The excellence granted the human being by virtue of this splendor goes even beyond that of angels. A short poem composed "in her heart" by Hedwig von Regensburg, during a period of great distress as a beguine "in the world," centers on this idea:

> Christ speaks to the pure ones:
> "Spouse, you shall love me,
> For you are closer to me than an angel.
> This I want you to be aware of:
> I suffered death for your sake;
> Never did I do this for the sake of an angel" (*E* 22.11–16).

The soul must be tended to as a precious gift from God. Sophie von Klingnau berates herself, "contemplating the lack of faith" she had shown to God by "not taking good care of the noble and worthy treasure of [her] noble soul for which he had spent his holy blood on the cross and that he gave into [her] trust" (*T* 56). The noble soul, given freely by God and redeemed through Christ, bestows dignity but also responsibility on human beings.

THE HUMAN RESPONSE

The only adequate human response to a God of Love, according to the Sister-Books, is total trust: *Wol alle die die got wol getrawen* (*E* 31). Their probing questions reveal that it is more than theoretical knowledge these women seek; they are eager to live a conscious spiritual life. Intellectual insight should engender fervour and devotion. Knowledge of the truths of faith carries no value in itself, but only in as much as it directly elicits action in the human soul: knowing and living are wholly intertwined. Such harmony is perhaps best expressed by a balance of "understanding and devotion," *vernunft und andacht* (O 270), that is a motif of these texts. It explains why the sisters are so deeply interested in questions of theology. On reasoning insight they found their spiritual commitment; intelligence and piety need to be combined.

1. Letting Go

In order to live a life that reflects the dignity God has bestowed on the soul, a human being must "completely free herself from attachment to passing things," *genczlich frey sein ... von aller anhaftung zergencklicher ding* (K 105). For only the fully detached soul can be filled with grace. The call for inner detachment from things transitory is a leitmotif: "the heart that rests from all worldly and passing things is the one that is entered by the Holy Spirit" (K 119; cf. A 172, 174). Indeed, such detachment represents a profound "alienation" when God's spirit and [Ite's] spirit "become one spirit," and she was "so united with him that she lived in him alone," thus "removed and alienated [*geüssert und gefremdet*] from all exterior things that nothing impeded her" (O 252). Letting go (*lassen*), being detached (*kein anhaftunge haben*), being free, unfettered, unencumbered (*ledic sein*) by mutable things, being empty (*blos*) of desire, are all central to monastic life itself. "Letting go for God's sake," *lassen durch got* (O 266), represents a profound separation. "You shall separate your heart from all passing things and not let it be attached to anything, and not seek for anything but explicitly for God," an Oetenbach nun is exhorted by "a voice" (O 253). These notions spring from a rich theological tradition. "Letting go" out of love for God also underlies much of the influential writing of the contemporary Meister Eckhart.[17] In the Adelhausen Sister-Book, for example, the idea of detachment is seen metaphorically through the image of the pyx, the small golden container for the eucharistic wafer: "Then a voice said to [Metze Tuschelin]: 'If you are as detached and empty of all passing things as this pyx is [empty] of all things, except for me alone, then I will actually live in you as in this pyx'" (A 161).

This emptying is paradoxically also a filling up. Through detachment the soul is filled with love. The consequences can be intensely physical: an Adelhausen lay sister "burned so hard with love that her

---

17. For the terms *lassen*, *Gelassenheit*, *ledig sein* ("letting go"), see especially Eckhart's sermon *Qui audit me* (1977, 213-217).

body seared just like a bundle of straw" (*A* 165); the heart of a Kirchberg sister "was so drawn up into God" for three full days that "she served the community at table with her eyes closed"; when this same woman is, nevertheless, distracted from the divine service through a dog's barking, she cries "with all her heart" because she finds herself still so far from her goal (*K* 105f.).

The Oetenbach text explores the theme of detachment in an allegorical vision. It is attributed to a burgher of the nearby city, and thus disconnected from its context; yet this loosening also enlarges the scope of the vision:

> To a good person in the city of Zürich were revealed all the ways in which good people searched for God. And he was shown a high mountain full of people. Some of them were loaded with earthly goods so that they could scarcely crawl on all fours around the foot of the mountain. Others went up tired and slowly. Some went up easily, some flew up. And among all those who went up the mountain, nobody went up as easily as Sister Elsi von Beggenhofen. And on top of the mountain, there was nobody but her and two other persons who were bare [*blos*] of all earthly things in their desire, and they had come to a perfect life. And they drew from the fountain all the good they wanted, and the more they drew the more they found (*O* 269.13–24).

The biblical sources of this ascetic ideal [Mt. 6:33; Lk. 12:31] are made clear in a passage from the Töss book. Elli von Ellgue "well took the word to heart: *Querite primum regnum dei etc.* , Seek first the kingdom of God, and all else will be thrown to you, *úch zuo geworffen*" (*T* 83). Not to let go may bring swift reprisal, all the more ominous in the following Diessenhofen excerpt for being directed at an affection that is unnamed: While Gerdrut von Herblingen was in prayer, she heard a voice commanding her: "'Tell this person to let go [*lassen*] of [her] special love, and I will release her from her illness. And if she does not do so I will chastise her greatly.'" Gerdrut, hearing the pronouncement three times, told this person what she had heard. But the sister "did not want to let go. Then our Lord put his hand heavily on her with great chastisement so that she then was forced to let go of what she had not wanted to let go" (*D* 30). By remaining non-specific, that is, by identifying neither the person nor whatever it is she wanted to hold on to, this passage sounds all the more ominous.

2. Prayer

The communal liturgical prayer of the women is supplemented by personal prayer and devotional meditation.[18] The biblical admonition to incessant prayer [1 Th. 5:17], "night and day," is assiduously heeded (*D* 45; cf. *G* 126, 131, 132, 138; *O* 244; *K* 115, 119; *T* 20, 23, 60, 85, 86). The dark hours between Matins and Prime in particular are devoted to private prayer in which the nuns gained special strength and peace through meditation (*A* 173; *O* 242, 265). Humility and responsiveness direct the self in prayer (*A* 174, 184; *T* 24, 72; *D* 41, 44). The sisters pray everywhere, in a quiet corner of the church, in their dormitory, and in the workroom (*A* 160f.; *T* 26, 56; *D* 4, 27f); and so absorbed are they in their meditation that the bell ringing for one of the day's activities is felt as an intrusion (*D* 27a). In the Diessenhofen Sister-Book, Adelheit von St. Gallen's own prayer, as she bows before the Lord while passing a crucifix, is emblematic: "'Lord, I offer you a tired body, a loving soul, and a desirous heart,'" *Herr, ich opffren dir einen mueden lib, ein minnend sel vnd ein begerendes hertz* (*D* 20). God's expectations for prayerful souls are simple but no less exacting, the Diessenhofen author writes: "Praise me, then I will come; love me, then I will stay; have peace that I am; be merciful, then I, with my mercy, will never be separated from you" (*D* 27c). Praise, love, and inner peace, all these will bring a person closer to God, although God can also be found when seemingly far away: When an Adelhausen nun asks Sister Gepe "how she experienced God," she replies in words anticipating St. John of the Cross' "dark night of the soul": "When I lose God in all my senses and in all my mind so that I do not know where he is, then it seems to me that I really experience him" (*A* 160f.).

The women of the Sister-Books can also be found absorbed in petitionary prayer for both "passing and spiritual things" (*A* 154, 159), for the sick and for those in distress (*U* 418f.). They know that such prayers are answered, sometimes in unexpected ways (*D* 29, 33). They also show wise discernment in the objects of prayer. Jüzi Schulthasin of Töss, for example, asked to pray on the occasion of a joust, refuses, saying "with hard words that she had prayed enough for the serious [war just past] and did not want to be troubled with [the jousters'] arbitrary noise, *mit irem muottwillen schall*" (*T* 78). And just as she is about to relent, the joust is called off. When the Adelhausen sisters

---

18. Petroff's term (1986, 6) is helpful since the adjective distinguishes this practice from non-religious meditation exercises.

Figure 12 Gothic crucifix, circa 1330

heard that the founder of their monastery was about to die, they gathered and eagerly called to "the Lord" to come to his help. While they were "commiserating over his soul," he died, unknown to the community.

> Still lying on his bed, he became alive again and said: "I was dead, and the judgment of condemnation had been given to me. And then I was led to the gate of hell. There the women of Adelhausen came and saved me. For God listens to the prayers that they said on my behalf. Thus God has given me back my life so that I improve and do penance." And he sent for his confessor and told him his sin.

The author's comment is unequivocally triumphant: "Thus the Lord listened to the community, as always when they seriously asked for any worthwhile cause" (*A* 186.5–18). The efficacy of prayers may also be self-legitimating.

A large number of such petitions is comprised of prayers "for the souls in purgatory" (*E* 26; *U* 371, 399, 404, 470; *G* 124, 139, 146; *T* 43, 58, 83; *D* 41) that had become common in the late Middle Ages. Indeed, in the nuns' eagerness to rescue suffering souls, we may detect what Jo Ann McNamara calls "a certain competitive edge." The number of souls saved and the difficult cases resolved seem extraordinary. A Töss sister supposedly was assured to have helped "too many to be counted," *ain unzalichy menge* (*T* 31); the devil is upset that in Diessenhofen the sisters' intercessions saved so many souls (*D* 30); a former "citizen of Niniveh, ... the most miserable soul in purgatory" is rescued by another sister from this monastery (*D* 22).[19]

The saying of multiple prayers is also typical of the late medieval devotion. The repetition of certain prayers innumerable times is well documented. The Töss sister who "genuflected daily two hundred times, and in addition ... prostrated herself, *starke venien*, thirty times on her bare knees" is not unusual (*T* 61f.).

We read of 500 daily or even five times 250 *Pater nosters* (*T* 50); of four Psalters recited daily (*D* 45; *U* 421), and about three times fifty *Ave Marias* prayed on another occasion (*T* 84; cf. *T* 69, 70) and 300,000 *Pater nosters* that one sister prayed in her lifetime, finishing just before

---

19. On prayers for souls in purgatory, see Wilms (1923, 100); McNamara (1991, 217). Prayers for the "poor souls" was one of the main concerns of German Dominican monasteries at that time ("ein epochenspezifischer und regionaler Schwerpunkt"), WbM (1989, 148).

her death (*U* 410f.; cf. *U* 344, 370).[20] Sometimes these multiple prayers, *unmessige unmüde gebete* (*G* 123), were said in the round number of one thousand: Among the many other prayers she offered the Lord daily with a sincere heart, Anna von Wineck "also prayed one thousand, sometimes two thousand *Ave Marias* on a single day, most devoutly and without skipping even one day until her death" (*U* 426; cf. *U* 345, 458; *K* 106, 109; *T* 18, 28, 47). Multiple prayers are much favoured by the Virgin. To Beli von Lütisbach in the Töss monastery, who prayed one hundred fifty *Aves* daily, "our beloved Lady" shows "how pleasing her service was to her" by appearing in a snow-white dress," and declaring that "the white dress" she is wearing is woven "with the *Angelus* that [Beli] pray[s] so often with devotion" (*T* 84). For the choir nuns in particular, multiple prayers were a means to live up to the gospel demand for charity [Mt. 25:35ff.], Peter Ochsenbein suggests.[21] Cloistered life could not always accommodate practical acts of mercy, and the nuns had to resort to spiritual mercy that entailed saying hundreds of prayers every day, occasionally using the so-called *paternosters*, that is, a string of rings or beads that facilitated the counting of prayers (see *G* 136; *U* 456; *T* 33f., 80).

Devotional meditation on the contents of a prayer avoids the sheer repetition. It is a characteristic form of spiritual attention in the Sister-Books.[22] Margret Finkin of Töss "always got up before Matins" to read three *Paternosters*, "as our Lord Jesus Christ [had] prayed on the mount [of Olives]." Her meditation on the *Our Father* has a triadic structure:

the first one was about the misery his tender heart had when he had removed himself from all human company, wanting to be with-

---

20. This sequence of the *Ave Marias* was a devotional prayer which, in later centuries, developed into the rosary. Gorce (DTC 13,2:2903) explains that the word *rosarium* (next to the term "the Psalter of Mary") was used from the thirteenth century on (in Thomas of Chantimpré's *De apibus*) for the devotion that consisted of saying 50, 100, or 150 *Ave Marias*. Hinnebusch (NCE 12:667–670) in his history of the Rosary debunks the myth that it started with St. Dominic. See also Anne Winston, "Tracing the Origins of the Rosary: German Vernacular Texts," *Speculum* 68 (1993) 619–636.

21. Ochsenbein (1988a, 370f.).

22. The MHG *betrachtung* and the Latin *contemplacio* can both refer to contemplation and meditation, in as far as these two terms overlap (Langer 1987, 105); but the MHG terms *betrachtung* and *die genad contemplativa* are slightly different (see discussion below).

out help from any creature in all his needs; the second was about the great need his woeful heart had when he went from the protection of his heavenly Father into all the merciless evil power of his enemies; the third about his leaving the consolation of the Holy Spirit when his passion and suffering came to the highest point. She practiced this contemplation until Matins (*T* 33.28–34.6).

Kathrin von Stein at Diessenhofen supposedly prayed five hundred *Pater nosters* in addition to many other prayers every day; but "she especially meditated on our Lord's passion for each *Pater noster*" – and "that was quite a lot," the author adds laconically (*D* 50).

Elisabeth von Kirchberg is unequivocal in her praise for meditative practice over multiple recitation (*K* 110). Eite von Holzhausen, she says by way of example, "prayed only one *Pater noster* between Matins and Prime" (*K* 109), but meditated on it for several hours. And Christine Ebner says categorically of another nun, "she said no more than three *Ave Marias* because of her great devotion" (E. 26). Indeed, indiscriminate repetition of certain prayers were sometimes in conflict with the liturgy. Gertrud von Herkenheim who delighted in meditating on Christ's passion was warned (and so implicitly are the readers and listeners) that there were liturgical limits against dwelling too long on a single subject. For when this sister continued to mourn Christ's dying even on Easter morning, "the benevolent Lord" is shown to have appeared to her saying: "'Why are you sad and crying on the day of my resurrection and joy? For, truly, I rose from the dead today. But not only am I risen, but you, too, have risen today in order to live eternally with me in glory'" (*U* 408f.). Thereafter, the mystical idea of "rising with Christ" filled Gertrud with exuberant joy.

Meditative prayer, actively encouraged in the Sister-Books, can bring not only "peace of mind" and "inner joy" (*U* 390) but also a heightened perception in which all things, "the grass, the trees, and also the monastery buildings" appear as if "newly resurrected" (*U* 397f.). Only rarely are such associations between nature and devotional meditation made; but also Christine Ebner speaks of an Engeltal sister inspired by "an immensely beautiful" apple tree in bloom (*E* 21).

The subjects of devotional meditation also encompass "our Lord's childhood," *únsers herren kinthait* (*T* 39), Christ's five wounds, *die hailgen fünf minzaichen*, that is, "the signs of love" (*T* 46, 50) and his passion (*A* 154; *O* 256; *E* 33; *T* 45, 62, 93). The Gotteszell text describing how one of the sisters "honored with prayers ... the path that led our Lord to Jerusalem, ... and she threw many flowers ...

toward our Lord" and imagined each step of his way (*G* 144; cf. *D* 33) reveals *in nuce* the pattern of devotion that was to develop during the fourteenth century into "the Stations of the Cross." Miracles and joy, too, grow from meditative prayer: Absorbed "in an intense meditation on our Lord's passion, ... a quite blissful light hover[s] over a nun" in Töss, "just like a shining star" (*T* 36; cf. *T* 71).

Meditation is indeed a form of *imitatio*. Elsbet Bechlin of Töss shows her sisters the steps in "spiritual meditation" (*T* 89f.) that brings "much special consolation" (*T* 45); it inspires the nuns to offer up their own sufferings to Christ (*E* 37). Diemut von Lindau of Diessenhofen receives instruction in a dream vision during Advent: "She was given a rope ... braided out of red and green silk." When she asks what it meant, "she was answered: 'The red silk means the high godhead, the green means the humanity of our Lord'"; they are "braided together as one" symbolizing "the two natures, the divine and the human nature, [as they] were united." She was then admonished to "braid and unbraid this rope" while meditating on Christ's hypostatic union (*D* 31).

In meditating on biblical passages, the women in the Sister-Books also pray for a clearer understanding of the gospels. There seems to have been considerable interest in the exact hour of recorded events in Jesus' life. Unable to sleep "during the holy Christmas night," Gertraud von Berge hears "a voice saying overly loud: 'This is the hour in which God was born,'" whereupon she falls "prostrate before her bed thanking God" (*W* 82; cf. *U* 411; *D* 40). The women also try to imagine themselves in the world of the gospels, a preoccupation they share with many contemporary writers. They try to empathize with Jesus suffering on the cross (*A* 183; *D* 28); with Mary's distress at his passion (*K* 110; *T* 66). They imagine the apostles at the first Pentecost (*A* 166); and one of the women supposedly learns how St. Paul [Acts 9:9] felt during the three days when "God ... had struck him down" (*G* 127). A literally understood *imitatio*-ideal seems here carried to the extreme.

Contemplation in the mystical sense of the word is rare in the Sister-Books. Often referred to as "the contemplative grace," *die genad contemplativa* differs from the visualization of a scriptural word or event characteristic of meditative prayer by being a gift that is divinely infused into the soul. The human share in this mystical grace is restricted, as Elisabeth von Kirchberg explains, to opening the self in and to silence: mystical contemplation is granted only to those who are in "the desert and at rest" (*K* 109), to those who can say, "I am resting in God," *min ruowe ist in Gotte* (*A* 182). The language of the Constitution for Dominican nuns, revised according to the Second

Vatican Council, is similar: "the nuns ... should prepare the way of the Lord in the desert by the witness of their prayer and penance."[23] For Elisabeth von Kirchberg *die gnad contemplativa* also encompasses "the grace of divine in-flowing" (*der gotliche einfluss*) that follows this grace of contemplation. "The grace is such that the human senses are drawn up into God," she says, "admiring and gazing at the unfathomable wonders" of the divine "in the mirror of eternity." The mystical ascent is then completed by a mystical descent: "At times, God lowers himself, in turn," she continues, "into the soul and flows in with his grace" (*K* 105; cf. *K* 108).

Prayer and devotional meditation nevertheless have one goal: conforming human volition to divine will. When Ita von Hutwil states, "'Lord, I permit you to do with me as you will – except that I never be separated from you; make me blind, lame, leprous, as you will,'" the Oetenbach author illustrates the attitude of a truly spiritual being (*O* 254; cf. *K* 118). For guided by the spirit, Ita's life became prayer. Similarly Hedwig von Herrenberg of the Kirchberg community is "much motivated by the spirit [*geist*]. This is a true sign of the right spirituality [*geistlikeit*] and the right innocence. She [is] so very spiritual [*geistlich*]" that even when asleep "she truly sensed that her spirit guarded her, as one person diligently guards another" (*K* 111). This nun is fully in tune with her unconscious, as we would perhaps phrase it today.

3. Communion

The eucharist is the centre of devotion for the community of sisters. The most intimate human response to divine love is made possible through communion. Of special significance for the women of the Sister-Books was the sacrament of communion, the communal partaking of Christ's "body and blood" offered in the mass as bread and wine, rather than the eucharistic celebration as such. Communion causes such concentrated love in a person "that all present [are] bettered by it," Christine Ebner declares speaking also of the communal benefit of this sacrament (*E* 32; cf. *T* 80). The power of the eucharist thus extends beyond the individual leading to a salvation in which all humanity

---

23. For contemplative grace, see also the article in LThK 2:288f. The term desert *(einod)*, here denoting silence and solitude, is used again in a late fifteenth-century devotion meant for nuns; it consists of "going into the desert with Jesus" and comprises a series of prayers, readings, contemplations, and castigations (Rapp 1985, 356). See also *Book of Constitutions* (1987, 58).

participates. The thirteenth-century devotion to the eucharist, according to Bynum, was "the most prominent, characteristically female concern." Communion is quite simply "receiving God" (*A* 175) "as he actually is" (*T* 74); this "life-giving sacrament" (*U* 459) means the uniting of the soul with the divine. The women firmly believe the communion wafer to be (and not just to symbolically signify) Christ. Receiving communion means for them being "offered our Lord into the mouth" (*T* 60, 62).[24]

Christ's real presence in this sacrament occasionally produced doubt for some sisters. Tempted to leave the order at Engeltal, the lay sister Jewt von Unzelhoven walked out of the church rather than take communion one communion day. When she saw "a fiery wheel hovering above the roof of the choir," like Ezekiel's fiery chariot [Ezk. 1:10], Jewt returned to church. There a further vision is said to have taught her "that a small tube went from heaven into the chalice and carried the sanctity there" – a frequent image in contemporary prose used to explain relation of the divine to the human. This vision reassured Jewt of the holiness of the eucharist (*E* 26).[25]

But if doubt renews faith, faith engenders its own displeasing extremes: "Once a sick sister was given our Lord. But he was heaved out of her, together with a terrible vomit. And then [Margret] truly proved her heart's desire and drank [the vomit] as quickly as if it had been the best wine" (*T* 27). While the contemporary audience, much less squeamish, presumably greatly appreciated this heroic deed, modern readers will no doubt find the episode nauseating. However, it draws on stock motifs whose overall purpose is doctrinal and moral. For through her extraordinary act the Töss sister affirms the strength of her conviction in the divine presence and the power of the eucharist.[26]

24. For the importance of communion among late medieval women, see Bynum (1984b, 181); Vauchez, "Dévotion eucharistique et union mystique chez les saintes de la fin du moyen-âge" (1987, 259–264). Except for one passage in the Kirchberg text, only the communion wafer is mentioned in the Sister-Books (*K* 106). For the Church's general practice, see Winter (1951, 81). The Catholic belief in the "real presence" of Christ in the eucharist is well presented by Karl Rahner "Die Gegenwart Christi im Sakrament des Herrenmahles" in his *Schriften zur Theologie* (Einsiedeln: Benziger, 1962), 4: 357–385.

25. See also Acklin Zimmermann (1993, 67). Christine Ebner herself also has a vision of a fiery wheel, in that case said to symbolize the Holy Spirit (*E* 42).

26. The same story, for instance, is told by Caesarius of Heisterbach in *Dialogue* 8.33); see also Gurevich (1990, 207, 256).

Many of the spiritual and ascetic exercises of the Dominican women as well as the *karismata* of the Sister-Books center on communion. The short entry on Ite von Kloten in the Diessenhofen text is illustrative:

> One day, when the community was to receive our Lord, she was very sick so that she feared she could not get to the altar. And when the time came that she was to receive our Lord, St. John the Evangelist appeared to her, took her off her stall, and led her to our Lord. And when she had received our Lord, he led her back to her stall (*D* 16).

Communion days and spiritual or visionary experience are profoundly interrelated (cf. also *E* 26; *T* 62). Receiving the eucharist often brought with it the "grace *jubilus*" during Eite von Holzhausen's life in Kirchberg (*K* 107). And when Mechthilt von Hundersingen in the Weiler monastery "received our Lord's body, ... her entire heart was kindled, and all her blood began to boil and flow together, as if it desired to touch the divine body – as one also reads of the Jordan in which our Lord was baptized" (*W* 70f.; cf. *U* 352f.).

The receiving of the sacrament by lay people proved an intractable problem for medieval theologians. In the ninth century, the daily communion that had been recommended by Augustine and Jerome was no longer the usual practice because of the wide-spread fear that it encouraged unworthy partaking in the sacrament. When theologians during the High Middle Ages recommended the faithful to receive "frequent" communion, they meant two or three times a year. Thirteenth- and fourteenth-century synods eventually made at least the Easter communion obligatory. There was little agreement among ecclesiastical authorities, and their recommendations were not based on theological but moral grounds. Bernard of Clairvaux claimed that daily communion was a privilege of priests; all others were restricted to a few feast days. Aquinas suggested regular communion on Sundays, but Albert the Great "argued that frequent communion might encourage superficiality of spiritual response in women, who were by nature given to 'levity.'"[27]

The frequency of communion apparently varied from one monastic community to the next. The Sister-Books do not provide us with

27. See Browe (1929, 2f., 5, 11, 13f.); Winter (1951, 15, 44). See also STh 3.80.10, ad 5; Albertus Magnus, *Commentarii in IV Sententiarum* 13. art.27, in *Opera omnia*, ed. August Borgnet (Paris: Vivès, 1894) 29:378–380; *Liber de sacramento Eucharistiae*, 6.4.3 in *Opera*, 38:432 (1899), both cited by Bynum (1987b, 128f.).

specific information as to how many times the sisters were permitted to receive the eucharist. Humbert of Romans suggested that the sisters receive communion fifteen times a year, "as the Brethren having the care of the Sisters provide, and at a time when there are sufficient confessors so that the [Sisters] may be prepared." His recommendation, meant as a favour to the sisters, occurs, curiously enough, in his short chapter entitled "Communion, Washing of the Head, and the Tonsure," and is part of Humbert's instructions to the sisters to "wash their heads and cut their hair" seven times a year.[28] Such matter-of-fact treatment of communion days stands in sharp contrast to the highly charged emotional engagement about the sacrament revealed by the women of the Sister-Books.

According to the Sister-Books, special communion days *were* set aside (*U* 476; *E* 26, 30). They were much awaited, thoroughly prepared for (*G* 143f.), and appropriately celebrated by all the sisters (*D* 2). Although the restriction on the number of communion days applied equally to the order's friars and the laity at large, the paucity of communion days proved a particularly heavy burden in communities of women, who witnessed the priestly celebrant in daily mass taking communion, but were themselves forbidden access to this sacrament. The sisters "always had a great desire to receive our dear Lord often" (*O* 263) and felt overwhelmed with graces through communion (*T* 62), but requests for change were denied, Christine Ebner shows. Alheit von Trochau's appeal to Friar Conrad von Eystet "that he give her our Lord ... at a time when the community was not to receive [communion]" was rejected (*E* 13).[29]

Communion was not only restricted in frequency, but also to sisters under the minimum age; not everybody in the community was, therefore, able to receive the eucharist. Changes in these equally arbitrary rulings had to be nothing short of the miraculous. When the community of Diessenhofen "was about to receive our Lord one day," Williburg von Trossingen, one of the sisters who had entered the monastery at a

---

28. Humbert (1259, ch. 12).

29. Two twelfth-century theologians, Hildegard von Bingen (†1179) and Rupert von Deutz (†1135) in particular, emphasized the universal salvific power of the eucharist: see Bynum (1987a, 62). Regarding regulations for the friars, Tugwell (1987, 22) writes of an early fourteenth-century German priory that "ruled that the brethren must eat together in the refectory on the days for receiving communion – that is, about fifteen times a year". On the restriction of the eucharist among the Helfta women, see Gertrud von Helfta, *Legatus* (3:36, 1).

young age, "had a great desire to be permitted also to receive our Lord." But she was "so young that it would not be tolerated. And when the children were given to eat that morning, she would not take a bite." (Traditionally, and as a general rule prior to the Second Vatican Council, everyone wishing to receive communion had to fast from midnight on.)

> And when the priest blessed the hosts, he took as many as the [number of] the community members without the children. And after he had given our Lord to all the community, he had one host left over. Then he said: "There is still somebody or other here who is to receive our Lord." Then the sisters thought that our Lord had done a great miracle, and they brought the child there. Then the priest said: "Dear child, come here, our Lord himself has kept himself for you." And he gave her our Lord (D 7).

In the eyes of the author – and apparently of the community at large, including the priest, on this occasion –, petty church regulations could thus be divinely overruled. This reversal may not have been unique. It also "often happened" that the consecrated host was diverted from the altar so that sisters otherwise deprived of this sacrament could receive it, while the celebrant had to forego communion (K 117).[30]

Only the seriously ill were given communion (E 9) outside the regulated times, for the eucharist was thought to possess special healing powers over both "heart and body" (T 88). Anna von Klingnau at Töss finds speedy relief from a painful illness after she receives "our Lord " (T 60). But a dying sister's request to receive communion often produced a struggle between compassion and strict adherence to ecclesiastical rule. Again, it was only miraculous intervention that brought about change. The prioress of Adelhausen decided to let the dying Adelheid von Wendlingen take communion when she told her "how our Lord had appeared to her and [said] that she should receive him" (A 184). Others were less fortunate: patients in the sickroom were heard to cry out "with a loud voice: 'O woe, give him also to me!'" but to no avail (E 23).

The mystery of the eucharist is inextricable from the miraculous in the Sister-Books. The transformation of the eucharistic wafer into flesh and blood and its power as life- and soul-sustaining food, is a recurring vision in these texts. When Adelheit von St. Gallen was quite ill, she saw a lord come and sit down at her bed, " and [break] a piece of flesh

---

30. Browe (1938, 31–36) lists numerous examples of this legendary motif.

out of his hand" and give it to her into her mouth saying: "'This is my flesh and my blood'" (D 20). The repeated image of the work of art miraculously changing into "flesh and blood" before one's eyes also expresses the deep longing for the eucharist among these women. A vision of a cross that was brown and red like flesh is seen by an Oetenbach sister (O 238). An Unterlinden sister has a dream vision of a priest carrying a snow-white ivory chalice containing small rose-coloured pieces of flesh (U 490f.). A long-standing contemporary debate about Christ's real presence in the eucharist and the various competing materialistic interpretations underline these strange, "distasteful" images. The authors of the Sister-Books may have been trying to dispose doubts about the "real presence" by overemphasizing the material aspects of the eucharist.[31]

Their prayers for communion unanswered, many women were led to practice a new kind of prayer which, from the thirteenth century onwards, came to be called "tabernacle piety." For at that time, churches commonly started to keep a consecrated host, which always is "God himself," got selbs (K 118), in the church tabernacle, a custom to which the Töss author refers (T 27). It was before this tabernacle that the sisters, unable to receive communion, spent so much time in prayer. Exchanging their spiritual deprivation with physical closeness to the consecrated host, they nevertheless "received special strength from our Lord's body" (K 118).[32]

---

31. Cf. Bynum (1987a, 77): "it is the quality of the eucharist as [life-sustaining] food that is stressed." See also Meyer (1995, 198–200) for an overview of similar passages in legends and secondary literature, and Rubin (1991, 116) for the literary tradition of such images. Bynum (1989, 161, 169) suggests that such "distasteful" images violate "the boundaries between spiritual and physical," adding that although medieval male authors, such as Bernard of Clairvaux and Tauler, also speak of "eating God," their accounts lack "the immediacy of women's writing." See also Neunheuser (1963, 25f.).

Whether the repeated visionary scene in the Diessenhofen text (D 128, 166, 174) in which a piece of art is said to have turned into "flesh and blood," when a sister touched it, can be stretched to be a parallel to "the sacerdotal act of transubstantiation," as Hale (1992, 159) suggests, must remain open. While it is an intriguing interpretation, there are – at least in the Sister-Books – no other instances pointing to these women as celebrants at mass or even in a communion service. From among the Williamites, there are contemporary examples of women celebrating mass and intending to take over the hierarchy, see Müller (1991, 229).

32. On "tabernacle piety," see Browe (1933, 18); Neunheuser (1963, 37); LThK 9:1265.

The moment of the consecration during mass was also of special significance when, during the thirteenth century, the consecrated host came to be elevated and shown to the faithful. The elevation, announced by the sacristan's ringing of a bell (*W* 71), thus marked the high point of mass. The sisters who were required to keep their heads bowed (*W* 71, 84) were then invited to look up. The choir sisters in their stalls turned toward the altar (*A* 159), and lay sisters caught a glimpse of the elevated host through a special *oculus* (also called the "elevation squint"), the small window leading from the kitchen into the church (*A* 169). A Weiler sister whom the overcrowded choir had relegated to the rear of the altar during mass is alerted by "knocking against the wall giving her a sign that our Lord was being elevated" (*W* 81).

The highly charged moment of elevation was also marked by special graces and miracles. The Sister-Books share the commonplaces about host miracles current at the time. The elevated host is said to have once shone for Adelheit von Wendlingen in a "blissful light" in which she saw Christ's "divinity shine through his humanity" (*A* 184; cf. *W* 72). Many sisters claim to have seen the child Jesus when the priest elevated the host (*T* 81; *D* 31; *W* 81). And when Elsbeth von Stoffeln "looked at our Lord in the form of a wafer, he spoke to her, from the priest's hands" in words that echo the biblical description of the divine seen "face to face" in the hereafter [1 Co. 13:12]: "'Look at me and look at me eagerly, for you shall eternally see my face after all your heart's eagerness'" (*D* 33). From the twelfth century on, according to Joseph Andreas Jungmann, "the desire of gazing upon the Lord's Body ... brought about [the elevation, an] intrusion of a very notable innovation into the canon which for ages had been regarded as an inviolable sanctuary." The continuing debate concerning the relative spiritual value of seeing the host against partaking of it in communion was eventually resolved in the thirteenth century: most theologians agreed the eucharist was nourishment. The argument is dealt with in the Adelhausen Sister-Book. Anna von Munzingen describes a pious sister who annoyed the others by not looking at "our Lord" during the elevation of the host, insisting that she found him elsewhere (*A* 169). However, the superstitions that during the late Middle Ages came to be associated with the elevation of the host are nowhere to be found in the Sister-Books.[33]

33. Jungmann, *The Mass of the Roman Rite: Its Origins and Development* [1st ed. in German 1949], trans. F.A. Brunner (New York and Boston: Benziger, 1955), 2: 208. Dumoutet (1926, 19–21, 34, 37–74) provides a summary history of the eleva-

The period between communion days was often marked by intense frustration; the nuns' longing for the eucharist could not be stilled. In their "yearning for God," *gross begird vnd jämer* (D 40), the women compared themselves implicitly to the beggar in the legend of St. Martin. The following episode represents one of several reports of women who miraculously received communion: When Adelheid Ludwigin, who had "a great desire to receive our Lord,"

> was in this devotion, she saw a bishop standing before her, and he had a golden chalice in his hand, and said to her: "Would you like to receive our Lord?" Then she said: "Yes, with all my heart." Then the bishop gave her our Lord. Then she would have liked to know who this bishop was. Then he said: "I am Saint Martin." And then she saw him no more (D 8).

Spiritual communion thus miraculously fulfills the sisters' need, the authors claim repeatedly. During "the silent part of the mass" one day, Anna von Offingen experiences "such great desire for our Lord" that the sisters of Adelhausen see with their "bodily eyes ... the right arm of our Lord c[o]me from the heavenly kingdom," with "wafer in hand to offer" to her (A 167).[34] Elisabeth von Kirchberg's retelling of similar experiences attributed to Mechthilt von Waldeck is as expansive as it is detailed:

> And [the Lord] said: "Stand up and open the mouth of your desire. *Hoc est corpus meum.*" With these same words [that is, the exact words of the consecration rite during mass] she experienced God as truly in her soul in all sweetness and grace, as if she received him at the altar. Thereafter our Lord said to her: "I will strengthen you with my body and will sanctify you with my worthy blood and will console you with my tender soul, and I will magnify your soul with my eternal godhead." In another mass he said to her (as he had done to Saint Augustine): *Cresce et manducabis me.*"[35]

---

tion of the host during mass. On superstition concerning the host, see Dumoutet (1926, 31); Browe (1933, 49ff. and 1938, 100–117); Kieckhefer (1990, 79f.); Rubin (1991, 63).

34. As is the case with other Adelhausen passages, this particular episode in the Einsiedeln manuscript of the Adelhausen Sister-Book is more restrained ([E] 694, 168).

35. Acklin Zimmermann (1993, 101) explains that this is a direct reference to Augustine's commentary on John 25:12 (PL 35:1602) which deals with spiritual communion, a passage also frequently cited by Suso, Tauler, and Nikolaus von Strassburg.

God also spoke to her during the mass: "I have made your soul alive with my living body and crucified with my rose-coloured blood and consoled and glorified with my worthy soul. And I have drawn your soul into my godhead and have illuminated her and set her on fire" (*K* 121.1–14).

The words are carefully chosen to reveal the true understanding of the mystery of the eucharist with which the sisters of Kirchberg are graced. After all, only a few lines earlier the Lord had claimed: "'For many people receive my body and are yet not sure whether they really receive me; but those to whom I give myself are sure that they worthily receive me according to my mercy.'" But Mechthild von Waldeck, the Kirchberg sister chosen to receive this message, knows that this "exceptional grace" is more worthwhile than communion taken often merely as force of "good habit." The conclusion is inescapable: "When you go to the altar you do not receive what you see there but what you believe." And from then on, we learn, Mechthild is privileged to receive spiritual communion every day until her death (*K* 120). Again, several other women in the Sister-Books appear to have received similar dispensations (*U* 391, 398; *K* 106; *W* 79). Statements like these may have proved a serious, if only implicit, challenge to ecclesiastical rules.[36]

Finally, all these narrative elements – the solemn feast day, the liturgical setting, the remarkable light illuminating each event, and the joy and consolation the sister receives – come together in a vision of desire fulfilled in the Töss Sister-Book:

One day, on a high feast day, [Offmya von Munchwil] did not want to let the sister who nursed her stay with her. And during mass she developed such a great desire for the Lord. Lying [in bed], ... she saw a light, and in this light a fine tablecloth came down on her bed before her. Then she thought: "Ah Lord, what does this mean?" And looking up, she saw an even more beautiful light and in this light a beautiful paten came down on the tablecloth. Then with a devout heart, she thought: "Our Lord truly wants to show mercy to you," and her desire for God became even greater. And in this yearning, such a blissful light came down that she imagined

36. For spiritual communion, see also Gertrud von Helfta, *Legatus* (3:26, 1). Acklin Zimmermann (1993, 103ff.) speaks of these tales' possible challenge for the Church.

the entire room to be illuminated. And in this light our Lord's body lowered itself onto the paten. Then she became immeasurably joyful, but yet she worried, for she did not know how he would become hers. And then, for the fourth time, came the most beautiful light she had ever seen. And in it came a right hand and gave her our Lord, just as she would have received him at the altar. And then she was full of grace and consolation ... (*T* 32.22–33.4).

At a time when nobody except an ordained priest could touch the consecrated host, the "right hand" of God here does the work of the priest who was required to place the communion wafer into the recipient's mouth. God is thus shown to support the women by legitimizing and fulfilling their desire to overcome the sacramental restrictions imposed by ecclesiastical authority. The Sister-Books reveal these women's indomitable spirit amidst obstruction and deprivation.

4. Suffering

For the women of the Sister-Books, enduring pain (*we, ser*) and suffering (*liden*), both physical and psychological, is part of spirituality. Accepting to suffer engenders grace or, as the author of the Töss book declares, suffering "happens by grace" (*T* 66). Pain is a good and sweet word, full of graces, we read in the Engeltal Sister-Book:

> *We ist ein gut wort,*
> *we ist ein suzez wort,*
> *we is ein genadenrichez wort* (*E* 9.22f.).

To avoid suffering, on the other hand, is to misunderstand its nature and purpose. Hence, learning to suffer was considered important. When God sought "to work his great grace" in Jüzi Schulthasin in the Töss monastery, he "imposed upon her a severe illness." The thought of death was "quite intolerable" for her, and going "against her heart." Her refusal to accept this illness made her "hard-hearted." Only slowly and through prayer did she come to terms with her ailment (*T* 70). Jüzi's case provides an example for spiritually meaningful suffering: even though their very nature may rebel against pain, the women understood that free acceptance of such suffering has a salvific power. "Suffer and be patient,'" a voice commands Metze Tuschelin of Adelhausen, ailing and distressed that she cannot "observe [the rule of] the order," for "'I prefer your suffering to your doing'" (*A* 162).

These cloistered women speak mostly of physical suffering; but psychological suffering is not absent. All of them experienced the difficulties of living together in a community, the struggle of the individual will in its subjection to monastic obedience and divine will, many of them knew despair and doubt, and the "aridity" that comes with the knowledge of an absence of grace (*Min Herre, der ist geflohen*) (*A* 179; cf. *U* 424; *T* 71). But they knew that this pain, too, if "suffered gladly and patiently," would be rewarded by God.

"I suffer so much that I have experienced hell inside," an Adelhausen sister cries; but for that "God caused me delight so that I also experienced heavenly joy" (*A* 167; cf. *A* 169; *K* 109; *W* 71). Pain and suffering, these authors teach, are inextricably connected with divine consolation. Such close relationship between illness and special spiritual gifts, Joseph Bernhart explains, can often be found among intensely spiritual individuals. In many saints' lives overly abundant graces caused constant serious illness, as if human nature, like an overloaded fishing net, as Tauler puts is, can tear with the extra weight.[37]

The possibility that suffering may have been inflicted as a form of punishment is raised only to be left unanswered by the author of the Weiler Sister-Book (*W* 71). The Unterlinden text speaks often of the biblical idea [Rv. 3:19] that "the Lord disciplines whom he loves" (*U* 350, 379, 417, 440, 451, 468). The Gotteszell author's belief that God "greatly comforts" those who suffer and never neglects them (*G* 135, 145), however, predominates. In the end, those who suffer are divinely chosen, like Job, whose fate was allotted to him by God's "special love" (*T* 22). A Töss sister inflicted by "a despicable and obnoxious illness" is comforted by Elsbet von Cellikon: "'It is as if I saw and heard before God that he gave you this suffering so that you do not escape him but become exclusively his own.'" She "spoke these words with such certainty and eagerness," says the author, that the sick "sister was well consoled by them" (*T* 92). Suffering is a sign of divine love and election, it also prepares the chosen for the gift of "special grace" (*T* 52; *A* 177), for often a physical cure encompasses spiritual grace: "And at dinnertime, our Lord came to [Sister Wila of Weiler] and inundated her heart and soul with such graces that her body as well received strength and that the swelling went down and that she became completely healthy" (*W* 73).

Suffering also prepares human nature for death and the last judgment. The suffering of this earthly life is a purging of human failing

---

37. Bernhart (1950, 177, 184) refers to Tauler's sermon *"Ascendit Jhesus in naviculam"* and points to such famous saints as Hildegard von Bingen and Teresa of Avila who each spent a long life in constant serious illness.

and sin. If there were no suffering on earth, Anna von Munzingen explains, there would be an equal or greater amount of suffering after death: one Adelhausen sister, she notes, was so troubled about the suffering she would have to undergo after death that "she always desired that God purify her here so that she would not go to purgatory" (*A* 166). When asked why she has prayed that God might strike her friend with great suffering, Else von der Neustatt replies: "'I am doing so out of proper love, for you are dearer to me than other sisters. For whoever is spared here must do penance in purgatory or hell'" (*A* 181). The author here refers to an Augustinian notion that suffering in this life may prevent, in part, punishment after death.[38]

Precisely this purifying power of physical suffering underlies spiritual growth. To "suffer for God" is to ascend, step by step, in *imitatio Christi* (*K* 115; *A* 173). It is to understand the profound connection between the passion of the God-man and human suffering (*G* 138). So it is that the Lord gave Guote Tuschelin "such great distress and pain on account of his passion that [she] was confined to bed during all of Lent because of pain and because of the distress she felt on account of his passion (*A* 169). A vision of Christ makes an Adelhausen sister even want to increase her suffering although she was already wracked by almost unendurable pain (*A* 185). Adelheit von Frauenberg at Töss suffers her burden "devotedly and happily ... praising God specifically for each pain, and also because she was made to suffer in praise of his passion" (*T* 52). The author later has Jesus himself echo these words when he is given to acknowledge that Adelheit, indeed, has "suffered happily and patiently in praise of [his] passion" (*T* 54). The identification with Christ's passion through suffering reaches its climax when an ailing sister understands the great privilege she is afforded of dying exactly on Good Friday (*T* 94; cf. *E* 29; *K* 123). In this ultimate step the *imitatio Christi* is completed.[39]

5. Joy

Even in ascetic discipline and in spite of hardship and suffering, there is joy (*froede*). These women's spirituality is marked by "immeasurable

---

38. Le Goff (1984, 134).

39. Tipka (1989, 239); and see Bernhart (1950, 185). Weinstein and Bell (1982, 234f.) and Bynum (1989, 166) argue that the religious significance of illness and suffering is accepted more by women than by men. Langer (1985b, 29, 34) writes that the naive experiential spirituality often attached by the nuns to suffering was especially criticized by Eckhart in his *Trostbuch*.

joy" (*U* 379f., 390), the "great bliss and joy" (*K* 108), that comes in the possession of, and submission to, the divine. Their joy is so exuberant that some sisters cannot contain themselves (*K* 110, 114; *T* 54), and others are unable to go to sleep (*K* 119; *W* 82). "We often noticed" many graces in Sister Eite, says Elisabeth von Kirchberg; "for her face in such a grace was often so transparent and rich in graces that Friar Cmynt, who was our provincial, said ... that she was truly like a second Moses" (*K* 108). The passage gains in meaning both because the author herself implicitly claims to have witnessed Eite's glowing face and because of the friar's exalted comparison of this woman to Moses whose "face was radiant after speaking with the Lord" [Ex. 34:29f.]. Also Anna von Munzingen writes of "heavenly joy" (*A* 167) and of great and abundant joy (*A* 167, 170, 171, 187). In Diessenhofen Gerdrut von Herblingen heard a voice on *Gaudete*-Sunday saying "'*Gaudete in Domino!*'" When she asked: "'Lord, what should I rejoice about?'" the same voice told her: "You shall rejoice that I am your only love, and that I can give you everything that your heart may desire" (*D* 30; cf. *A* 172).

Grace and joy, then, are inseparable. Asked what she "experienced when God was in her soul," Else von der Neustatt replies: "'I experience all the joy and bliss that he brings along; he rejoices and widens my heart and opens and unlocks my soul with his divine grace.'" (The "widening of heart" in exalted spiritual joy is a deliberate reference to the *dilatatio cordis* in the Rule of St. Benedict, which underlies all monastic rules.[40]) Else's hyperbole, "everything becomes a praise of God," ends this passage of the Adelhausen text (*A* 180). The exultation of spiritual joy is perhaps most convincingly portrayed in Sophie von Klingnau's first person account of her vision in the Töss Sister-Book:

> And then I made the sign of the cross and wanted to lie down to rest and I read the verse: *In manus tuas.*[41] And having read it, I saw a light coming from heaven that was exceedingly beautiful and blissful, and it surrounded me and illuminated and shone through me altogether, and my heart was quite suddenly changed and filled with an ineffable and unusual joy so that I totally and completely forgot all adversities and pain that I had ever experienced ... .

40. RB 1980, Prol. 49.

41. "Into your hands, I commit my spirit," the beginning of the Church's evening prayer based on Christ's word on the cross [Lk. 23:46] taken from Ps. 31:5 and also used in the Gotteszell text (G. 144) quoted below.

And I imagined a radiance going out from me that illuminated all the world, and a blissful day rose over all the earth. And in this light that was my soul I saw God shining blissfully, as a beautiful light shines out of a beautifully shining lamp. And I saw that he lovingly and benignly linked himself with my soul so that he was truly united with her and [my soul] with him. And in this loving union, my soul was assured by God that all my sins were purely forgiven me and that I was as clean and as pure and quite without any blemish as [my soul] was when I came out of baptism. And through this my soul became so high-spirited (*hoches muottes*) and so full of rich joy that she imagined she possessed all bliss and joy, and that, if she had the power of wishing, [my soul] might not, nor could, nor would wish for more . ... (*T* 57.11–18 and 57.35–58.9).

The profound joy and wonder experienced by the visionary is at the same time indescribable: the doubling and even tripling of nouns, adjectives, and verbs suggests an apparent groping for the correct term, illustrating the basic ineffability of such an experience. The repeated "imagine" and the qualifying "as if" equally testify to the halting attempts at speaking the unspeakable. The term *hoher muot*, a highly charged term in medieval courtly poetry, stands for high-spirited and exalted joy.

LIFE IN TRANSITION

A preoccupation with the life-to-come is shared by all the authors of the Sister-Books. The ordered stringency of monastic life had but one ultimate goal, preparation for the afterlife. Elisabeth von Weiler's "mind and all her senses," for example, "were so completely drawn up into God that she said: 'I know better what one does and what it is like in heaven than in the Weiler community'" (*W* 68). The emotion is commonplace, but the words still convey the single-minded purpose animating these nuns, their constant striving "to serve the Lord Creator in an upright spirit and untiringly day and night," as Katharina von Unterlinden puts it (*U* 428). But if earthly life is, before all else, a preparation for the hereafter, it is not difficult also to believe that this life may be lived to "deserve" heaven.

1. A Religion of Reward

While the "eternal reward" (*T* 54) is ultimately a gift from God freely given, there is no doubt that some of the women in the Sister-Books thought in categories of a divine debit and credit. For Katharina von

Unterlinden "the Lord distinguishes with his largesse" those who serve him appropriately (U 357f.). This religion of reward is based on the gospel promise of a hundredfold return to those who relinquish all for the sake of the Lord [Mt. 19:29] – a passage to which Katharina von Unterlinden makes explicit reference (U 386f.).

The language of merit, reward, wages, recompense, retribution is especially pervasive in the Unterlinden Sister-Book. Terms used are *merces, premium, recompensari, remuneracio, retribucio* as well as the MHG *lon*. The biblical injunction is taken to apply not so much to the monastic life as a whole, but to the minutest daily actions and deprivations. An Adelhausen sister, it is said, feared that God would not recompense her for a good deed because she had done it only out of pity, and not with the ultimate goal in mind. But the author corrects her by having "St. Evangelist" say to her: "'You shall receive eternal reward for your pity, and you shall know that you will be seen in the abyss of the profound godhead'" (A 173). Mechtild von Colmar withheld her sighs during her painful illness in order to avoid sisterly pity that might have been "the detriment of the heavenly reward" (U 471). Anna von Wineck, also in Unterlinden, increases her net worth with her "admirable habit" of offering her accumulated merits to the Lord each Good Friday, saying,

> "take today from the hands of your handmaid this sacrifice of praise that she brings in devotion, and deign to look with kind eyes on it. For I offer you, most merciful and serene Lord, who do not need my goods, whatever I have done by your grace during this past year, that is worthy of you in observing the order, in daily prayers, and holy contemplation and finally all the good that I have accomplished well under your kindest guidance. And I request from my innermost that you bestow this good unto those living and dead, to whomever you want to – except to me – if this pleases your goodness" (U 425.28–38).

The passage has some nuances: it enumerates the diverse practices that were thought to increase one's celestial merit points; but it also shows an awareness that good is ultimately achieved only through divine guidance, and it betrays social concern. And even though Katharina von Unterlinden argues that "the Lord" does not need anyone's good deeds, she nevertheless concludes the episode with the expected formulation: "Thus this blessed sister ... made immense progress by gathering up treasures of an ineffable reward for the future" (U 426, 443).

Reward is less calculated in the Töss Sister-Book: God himself constitutes the eternal reward granted to those who "love God and serve him earnestly" (*T* 42, 53f.), the author explains, and "death is the time when our Lord wants to reward [the faithful] with himself" (*T* 44). Hence, the Töss author only rarely mentions merits (T. 43). On the contrary, she criticizes the habit of creating a business relationship with God, as it were, for the sake of a special reward: Elsbet von Cellikon, she says, "could not stand it when she heard that people would bargain with our Lord for some reward for their good works, and she said then: 'You ought to do it for the heartfelt love of God'" (*T* 92). For the Töss author, virtue is not a personal merit at all, but God working in the human being (*T* 52).

2. Sin and Salvation

The Sister-Books show that temptation and sin, even within a saintly community, are very much a part of the human condition. For many of the women, anxiety (*U* 396, 406, 461) and despair (*U* 454) and the "dense fog" of doubt (*U* 356f.; *D* 11) pose real temptations. An excerpt from the entry on Agnes von Effich in the Unterlinden Sister-Book reveals the deep anguish (*angustia, Angst*) that came to possess her:

> Although from childhood [living] in admirable purity and innocence and, according to her confessors, never contaminated with the blemish of a mortal sin, she was at the beginning of her conversion [that is, her entrance in the community] seriously beset by doubt, so that she almost fell into despair; and she feared that, according to God's secret council, she would be condemned after her death to eternal punishment. Under the weight of this temptation, she walked around all day in mourning, continuously sighing. ... For the anxiety of this most burdensome struggle increased daily and she found no rest (*U* 438.5–16).

Ita von Hutwil in Oetenbach is tempted by despair for six long years; "fully believing in her heart that she would go to hell with body and soul," *daß si mit leib und mit sel sölte in die helle faren*, she is freed from this shackling fear while receiving communion one day (*O* 248; cf. *O* 239; *U* 365, 406).

Sin is inevitably connected with salvation. The special grace whereby one sister in the Töss monastery was "assured of never being separated from God" (*T* 19, 27, 38, 88) or that another "would never go to the place of punishment" (*T* 31) or that a third was assured "that heaven is [hers]" (*T* 63; *E* 24) is a recurring motif throughout the Sister-

Books. Katharina von Unterlinden calls this assurance "a most magnificent gift" that one sister is reported to have received "secretly on each single day" (*U* 386), although many others were also granted this "consolation" (*U* 363, 404, 437). Promises of *Heilsgewißheit*, that is, assurance of "eternal bliss" (*A* 160) or of "immediate" passage to God, are numerous (*A* 159, 167, 173, 183, 184, 188; *K* 123; *O* 252; *E* 24; *D* 32). But the Töss author feels the need to admonish the sisters when she says of Jüzi Schulthasin that she "clearly recognized that faith is greater than the assurance [of salvation] and than the visions she had experienced; and then she directed all her life toward faith" (*T* 75). Despising all mercenary calculations, she teaches trust in God. This trust was expected to extend to the fear of death, and of dying without receiving the sacraments, in particular (*U* 379; *O* 242) – a widespread anxiety among the sisters' contemporaries. Once this fear is overcome, it is possible through grace to reach the spiritual peace, *inwendige ru und süssikeit* (*O* 265) that engenders true inner "freedom," *freiheit* (*O* 243).

3. The Reality of Death

Death, nevertheless, remains only too real. Death is part of everyday life for the cloistered women. Terrifying as it is, however, death is paradoxically also the gate to life. The "death struggle" that consumes Heilrade von Horburg is thus happy: "and she went confidently into death, not to be annihilated by it but to triumph over it in eternity" (*U* 459f.). Such a view of death also prevailed in medieval art until the end of the fourteenth century, when corpses were usually shown "with hands clasped and eyes open, ... young, radiant and transfigured, as though already in possession of eternal life."[42]

a. Deathbed Miracles

Special graces are often directly connected with death and dying. The Engeltal chaplain, for instance, is said to have witnessed "the sickroom full of white doves" shortly before one sister's death (*E* 8). A ray of light "about as wide as a hand" that a Weiler sister "drew in with her breath" reveals her soul "illuminated by divine grace" (*W* 85).

A contemporary audience clearly expected that a saintly sister's death would be accompanied by visions (*A* 155f.; *K* 115, 121, 122). In later medieval hagiography, the common vision of Christ at the

---

42. Vernet (1930, 131). Relief figures on Romanesque sarcophagi typically display such features.

deathbed was superseded by visions of Christ with Mary and the entire "royal household."[43] Thus it was that Mary and St. Catherine, together with "our Lord" and "the eleven thousand virgins [of St. Ursula] and the ten thousand knights [of St. Achatius]" were all present at Mechthilt's deathbed at Töss (*T* 68).[44] A lay sister in Töss is comforted by "our Lord and our Lady and the holy angels, the patriarchs and the prophets, the twelve apostles, the martyrs, the confessors, and the holy virgins" (*T* 81) – a quantity of people, some known through the mass canon, others familiar from legends, makes up for a meaningful vision content. Similarly, to an Unterlinden sister "appeared visibly" the Lord and Mary and "quite a large crowd of holy angels and other saints" consoling her in her death struggle and taking away "all trepidation and fear of a terrible death" with their "strengthening presence" and supplanting it with "ineffable joy" (*U* 382f.). Mary is sometimes encountered alone, more often "with her dear Son" (*T* 53; *E* 15, 20, 22, 31, 41); other saints as well, some alone, some in crowds, are part of the visionary death scene.

The "consolations" of the dead figure prominently in the Sister-Books. "But I do not want to forget" to write about the "saintly death" of Elsbeth von Oettingen, the author of the Kirchberg book announces, "for it was so pious and rich with graces." When Elsbeth "lay in her last breaths," her request that the sisters sing the sequence *Summe triumphum* brings them all extraordinary grace: for "then the spirit lifted her up, and all the while when we sang ... her hands and arms stretched out, and she gave to all the community open signs that she saw the Holy Trinity all this time" (*K* 110) – although what these "open signs" were is not clarified. Deathbed signs (*U* 385), speeches describing a spiritual experience (*K* 106), offering advice to the community (*K* 123) are typical. Crowded deathbed scenes follow the prototype of Mary's death in the *Golden Legend*. The dying Mary is there surrounded by the twelve apostles and is granted a vision of Jesus with hosts of angels, patriarchs, martyrs, confessors, and singing virgins.

Death itself is often succeeded by miracles: "a sweet scent" comes from the body of a saintly sister "as if from many roses" (*D* 26), or in what may be a symbolic account of "generative life," an oil-well springs up in a sister's grave (*E* 10).[45]

43. Dinzelbacher (1985c, 11).

44. According to legends, St. Akakios, one of the auxiliary saints, was martyred with his ten thousand soldiers; he was considered helpful at the hour of death (LThK 1:235).

45. Günter (1906, 155f.); Bynum (1991, 80).

For the burial, the deceased was wrapped in a shroud and lowered into a grave, often dug beneath the cloister's pavement, a tradition continued in some monasteries today. Hedweig von Herrenberg in Kirchberg "saw that, when a sister was about to be buried and the cloth was lifted up to put her into the grave, her body shone and gave a radiance just like the sun" (*K* 111). The image of the radiant corpse thought to represent decisive proof of the sainthood of the dead has its origins in legend and hagiography.

b. The Happy Death

A fearless and even happy dying is often to be found in the Sister-Books (*U* 345, 421, 466; *A* 161, 184; *T* 27, 41). At times, a certain serenity animates the accounts of death:

> In the hour of her death, when she was already breathing her last, her face with her eyes closed suddenly became serene. And all of us who were present saw to our great joy how, for about an hour, [Adelheid von Rheinfelden] smiled deeply. Thus this blessed soul was rescued in joy and exultation from the fetters of her body so as to eternally remain in the joy of immortal life (*U* 405.10–15).

Receiving special grace in the assurance of salvation, Richi von Stocken is consoled by Saint Dominic himself who appears to her saying that "it was his office to lead the sisters from this world"; whereupon Richi "laugh[s] so loudly" that she is heard "outside of the sickroom" and then she dies (*A* 158). Such laughter was a commonplace in the narrative of a saintly death. Indeed, a marginal note scribbled in a manuscript of the Adelhausen text questions why Sister Ite von Nellenburg is not also described laughing at death (*A* 159f.; [F] 98, 14v).

Music and angel-song were often heard at the time of death itself. Some heard "the sweetest string music in the clouds" or the playing of an organ at the death of a sister (*E* 38, 42; *K* 116, 121). Music at Diessenhofen even sounds stereophonic, as the angels are heard "singing in two places in the monastery" (*D* 17, 10; cf. *U* 424; *E* 42). The voices of angels also guide souls to heaven (*Seelengeleit*) (*W* 85; *T* 84; cf. *E* 37).[46] The dying sister herself may be heard laughing or "singing with a loud voice" as she anticipates her death, saying: "My soul rejoices that my eternal joy is approaching" (*T* 25, 41, 45; *E* 21, 15, 25, 43; *K* 110).

---

46. See Hammerstein (1962, 83f.).

Christine Ebner even recites a poem in rhyming couplets that a sister sang on her deathbed, which reads in part:

Jubilate, meditate,
Jubilate, contemplate,
Jubilate, speculate,
Jubilate, be at peace.

And the author explains, "she steadily sang these words at her death" and "scarcely stopped singing for as long as it would take someone to read the seven [penitential] psalms" (E 30.2–8).

Another Engeltal sister cries: "I will not die until King David comes to play my soul out [of my body] with the tunes of his harp"; Sister Berhte in Engeltal is ready to die after she "hear[s] the sweetest string music that ever a human being has heard" (E 23f.; G 132). The description of Sophie von Rheinfelden's death in Unterlinden is rich in scriptural allusion and liturgical echo. About to die, she bursts into song "as if drunken with heavenly wine," chanting the heavenly *jubilus* and continuing for many hours. Her resounding voice brings forth "the entire community of sisters" to see "with amazement this blessed sister dancing and singing the psalms [*tripudiantem et psallentem*] at the threshold of death."

Finally, when "the moment of dissolution was imminent," she "incessantly shouted a melodious *Amen.*" Asked by the sisters why she "repeated only this word so many times," Sophie, unable to speak, nevertheless replied: "'I can no longer speak; but as long as I live I will not stop singing the psalter. Therefore I keep repeating the *Amen* with varied sounds, for this way I can express what I have in my mind of heavenly things.'" Thereupon she "exhale[s] her blessed soul in order to be happily absorbed, eternally and without an end, into the abyss of eternal light" (U 434f.).

The paradoxical unspeaking speech that underlines the symbolic and didactic intent of this passage is a common enough theme.[47] Such saintly deaths are pictured as spiritually inspiring. The Oetenbach author refers to death as "sleeping blessedly in the Lord" (O 256); a Gotteszell sister who "departed from this world with such complete purity of heart, body, and mind that she will always be well remembered" (G 141). And Elsbetlein of Gotteszell, about to die, makes "the sign of the cross over the community, as if taking leave from them."

47. See also Gertrud von Helfta, *Legatus* (5:1,13).

Then lifting up her hands toward God, she cries: "'*Pater in manus tuas commendo spiritum meum*' [Lk. 23:46]." And thus does her "blessed soul" depart from her "pure body" and fly "to him whose spousal treasure she expected at the end" (*G* 144). The nun here blesses her sisters in community, as would a priest taking leave.

Such happy deaths are what a contemporary audience normally expected to read about; but they were no less well served by the depiction of unpleasant or even frightening scenes. For the authors never lose sight of their instructional role.

c. The Sting of Death

Some sisters are afraid of the devil's presence at their deathbed (*T* 31, 68; *E* 28); some ask God to let them "live longer" because they are not ready to face death (*K* 121); some are reconciled to have to "suffer death" as a sacrifice (*K* 123); others fearfully beg the community to assist them with prayers (*D* 25). Death is not always a pleasant occasion; a number of women in the Sister-Books experience "a severe death," *ein strengen tod* (*D* 40; *T* 39).

Ita von Hohenfels in Oetenbach is forewarned three times by "a voice in the air" of her impending death. Thereupon she felt "as if fifty arrows were shot into her body" which suggested to her "the pain and distress" of dying. Her "very severe death" soon after was so disturbing to her community that another Oetenbach sister asked in prayer for an explanation of such suffering. "Through [Ita's] distress," she is told, God wanted to "liberate other souls" so that they, too, could go "to the heavenly kingdom" (*O* 247). Miracles and visions are skillfully integrated into such scenes to obscure the harsh reality of an unpleasant death.

When a "most blessed sister" from Gotteszell who had led "such a saintly life ... that she did not know what a serious sin was" is about to die, her body is "so jolted that her bed [is] shaking" and "a terrifying look" steals "upon her face" that stays there until she dies. But immediately after her requiem mass, the deceased returns in "great beauty and joy." She explains she had suffered "such a severe death" because her soul was unwilling to separate from her body. The body, she says, lived "according to the will of the soul" until the sweet sounds of David's harp [1 S.16:23] finally allowed her to depart "tenderly and in joy and jubilation" (*G* 132). This legendary commonplace of the soul not wanting to separate from the body (cf. also *E* 20) sounds like a somewhat clumsy attempt on the part of the narrator to justify a difficult death that had the surrounding community scared.

Still, the terror of death is steadfastly faced. Already in her last breaths, Adelheid von Torolzheim in Unterlinden sees a "terrible thing" that so frightens her that "her face change[s] miserably, as if her eyes [had been] pulled out of their sockets and set to circling horribly." She attempts to jump over the headboard of her bed where she is lying but is restrained forcibly by the sisters. The scene ends peacefully and Adelheid's "serene face" shows her to have been "consoled most benignly by the Lord"; but death's terror remains a warning to all (*U* 417).[48]

4. The Hereafter

An insatiable curiosity about the afterworld is characteristic of the culture of the Middle Ages. Late medieval thinkers were much troubled by the question of the abode of the souls of the departed, and the Sister-Books often reflect this preoccupation. Their visionary accounts suggest three places in the other world to which the soul could be taken: a place of punishment, limbo, and heaven.

Visions of "the place of punishment" refer to *fegfúr* (literally, "a cleansing fire"), *wise* or *weiß* (used to refer to both purgatory and hell), but the authors rarely use the MHG word *hell* (*T* 39, 73). It is to purgatory that the sinful soul goes after death (*T* 43, 58); there the souls are "punished for each sin" (*O* 269). Enraptured and led to "a beautiful heath," Ita von Hohenfels sees "the place of punishment and the evil enemy." She sees "severe punishment and pain" inflicted on the different sinners, religious and lay, and the punishment meted out for sins both small and large. And there she sees "so many evil enemies ... humming around her like [horrible] flies" (*O* 240). From a beautiful spot in nature, she also safely beholds the different degrees of suffering inflicted on souls.

The entire episode stands in marked contrast with the vision of horror granted Adelheid von Rheinfelden in Unterlinden. "Enraptured in the Spirit in ecstasy and led by an angel to the places of horror and punishment filled with miserable cries and wailing of the miserable ones," she sees "an infinite crowd" of women and men, "monastics of different orders" harshly pressing against each other and suffering "because of this huge crowd."

---

48. According to an oral tradition, Nikolaus von der Flüe's face became permanently disfigured through a vision of the Trinity: Bruder Klaus was "*also grusam anzesehen, dass alle so in ansahend ein schrecken ab im namend*" (Durrer 653 and 86), quoted in: Amschwand (1987, 239f.). See also C. G. Jung, "Bruder Klaus," *Neue Schweizer Rundschau* 1 (1933) 223–229, esp. 225f.

All these were given, as their guilt demanded it, the hardest and most various torments. Their numbers increased and decreased at some moments depending on the crowd of souls standing back or arriving through death .... There she saw a woman set on fire like glowing iron who rose from the flames and looked at the one who saw this with a grim and most ominous regard as though intending to attack her. But [Adelheid] made the sign of the cross against her, so that she immediately fell into the fiery flames and could not harm her any more. She saw much else of which she later did not want to speak to anyone.

Having come to, she immediately began to hear the noise of something like a large army joyfully hastening by at a fast pace. Opening the window in front of her, she saw a large crowd of blessed souls, who had been rescued from the punishment of purgatory, brilliant in immeasurable light and flying through the air freely to the heavenly kingdom in inestimable joy. She also saw these most saintly souls go, two by two, through the air together, and others follow. Innumerable trains of angels accompanied these with honor and very great delight. Besides, one also heard there an unheard-of sweetness of heavenly harmony ... (*U* 399.30–400.27).

While 'hell' is not used in this passage, this two-part vision concentrates on both infernal horror and on eternal bliss. The power and sadness of punishment are revealed in images, of turbulence, a constant coming and going in the place of horror that bespeak the restlessness of the souls. In its second part, however, Adelheid hears the rattling of weapons, as if from a large clamorous army. They are souls released from purgatory. This image of souls with weapons, such as flails and scythes, recurs in German religious painting from the late Middle Ages to the Baroque period.[49] Such souls typically come to the rescue of their benefactors. This, then, is the thematic link that joins the two parts of the vision: her habitual prayers for the souls in purgatory guarantee Adelheid's safety. As such this didactic tale becomes emblematic of the preoccupation with purgatory, that Jacques Le Goff has documented. For here, too, we find the characteristic combination of joy in earthly values and an exuberant creative spirit with an acute fear of death and of hell. Purgatory offers new hope for the other world, made possible through the God-Man's redemption.

---

49. See Lutz Röhrich, "Religiöse Stoffe des Mittelalters im volkstümlichen Erzähl- und Liedgut der Gegenwart," in *Volksreligion* (1990, 455) with illustrations.

Purgatory also focusses attention on individual souls thus echoing a growing individualism.[50]

A soul may also be taken to an in-between world sometimes imagined as a beautiful natural setting (*A* 158; *O* 240). For Diemut Ebnerin it is the earthly paradise, the land-of-milk-and-honey or *Schlaraffenland* of German folklore: "Enraptured into the earthly paradise, *daz irdisch paradis*," she sees "Elijah and Enoch" who talk with her and "show her the wonders therein." There she also sees "several trees" with "fruit on one side and blossoms on the other," and fruit "fallen off a long time ago" that was as fresh as that which was about to fall (*E* 33). The passage reflects venerable medieval topoi. Heaven is reserved only for "the perfect"; the "earthly paradise" thus represents an attempt to accommodate "the just."[51]

The Töss Sister-Book also contains a brief reference to the "Limbo of the Fathers," called *vorhell*, that is, "a place above hell" to which "the worthy soul of our beloved Lord Jesus" descended in death (*T* 54). This place was thought to be one of the "temporary stopping places" where the Old Testament Fathers awaited salvation. A tale about Adelheit von Trochau in Engeltal imagines the "Limbo of Children, *limbus puerorum*" as "the place where the unbaptized children go." When she asks why these children flee from her and despise her, they answer: "'We do it because we came here through original sin, and we will never see God's eyes'" (*E* 10).[52]

In its passage to heaven after death, a soul is seen in a dream vision travelling on a ferry over "the ever-purest water" on her way to God (*T* 27).[53] Dream-like, too, are some of the rare images of heaven the texts contain. Christine Ebner credits an Engeltal nun with the following account:

50. See Le Goff (1984, 230ff.); McGuire (1989b, 61ff.); Haas (1989b, 206). See also Schmaus (IV,2, 1959, 511–520) who provides biblical passages and patristic doctrine on "purification after death."

51. On the "earthly paradise," see Le Goff (1984, 136f.); Dinzelbacher (1979a, 23); Ruh (1990–93, 2:286). Christine Ebner may have been echoing Mechthild von Magdeburg (1990, IV, c.27, 147f. and VII, c.57, 302ff.) who speaks of "Enoch and Elias ... in sweet paradise."

52. See also Le Goff (1984, 285, 258ff.). The *limbus patrum* as well as the *limbus puerorum* is also alluded to in Dante's *Inferno* (2:52 and 4:24, 52–61): "those souls who are suspended."

53. This image might represent a contrasting parallel to the "fiercely dangerous" river which, in Germanic mythology, a soul had to cross on her descent to *Hell*. See Howard Rollin Patch, *The Other World According to Descriptions in Medieval Literature* [1st ed. 1950]. Repr. (New York: Octagon Books, 1970), pp. 61f., 79.

"Dear children, I dreamed last night that a handsome youth came to me and said that a king had invited me to his court where I shall be from now on. Then I said in return: 'It is a long time that I came from the court. I no longer know how to behave there, and I also do not have nice clothes.' Then he said: 'Do not worry about this. The King to whose court you are invited can teach you well and will give you nice clothes'" (*E* 21.9–16; cf. *U* 371).

The courtly imagery is conventional: royal splendor was a significant part of medieval visionary images of heaven, embodying a world of beauty unknown to most but desired by all.[54]

For the women of the Sister-Books heaven is a place of "eternal joy and special reward" (*O* 247, 256; *T* 68) where the angels sing *Gloria in excelsis* (*E* 42), and where – as the Töss author claims, alluding to contemporary scholastic dispute about angels[55] – one hundred thousand souls find room on "the tip of a needle" (*T* 74). It is also the eternal life imagined in the biblical terms [Gn. 32:30], the place where the soul beholds the divine face and enjoys "the gaze of God," *die beschoew Gottes* (*U* 399; *G* 132; *T* 74, 95; *O* 218, 255). The Last Judgment, *der jungste tag*, is mentioned but not detailed (*T* 47). And in a trinitarian vision in the Unterlinden Sister-Book, life in the "homeland" is knowledge and understanding in a world of utmost peace (*U* 441f.).

Visions of heaven in the Sister-Books rarely encompass more than the soul's rapture in "great bliss and joy" when "seeing the heavens opened" [Jn. 1:51] and seeing "God truly as a human being and as God, as he is" (*K* 107f., 110; *U* 468; *O* 241; *D* 39; *W* 76). A description of Ita von Hohenfels by the Oetenbach author is a unique attempt to picture the soul in heaven:

She saw how the blood and flesh of Jesus Christ was united with the saints and with the souls. Thus through each soul, God's blood and flesh shone with special radiance as well as her saintly life, as it had been on earth (with suffering and special purity or whatever virtue she had especially practiced); all this was shining especially, radiant through our Lord's blood and flesh. And this union that she saw was so great and blissful, how the blood and flesh of Jesus Christ surged into the souls and how the souls again surged into his flesh and blood, just as if they were one (*O* 243.2–11).

54. Dinzelbacher (1979b, 33f.).
55. STh Ia q. 52 a. 3.

A lasting union of the soul with Christ's body and blood, as in the sacrament of communion, becomes a symbol of lasting heavenly bliss.

In the end, this "starry kingdom" (*U* 386) with its radiance (*O* 254) and "eternal joy" (*U* 364; *E* 15, 18, 19) is nevertheless unimaginable, exceeding human understanding: after her rapture, an Oetenbach sister is left severely ill "because of the miracle that she had seen in the heavenly kingdom" (*O* 241). Nevertheless, the same text contains a dialogue between Elsbeth von Oye and God about the fate of another Oetenbach sister who had just died. To her anxious question, God replies:

> "She was carried into the hidden treasure vault of my divine Trinity ... . The barrenness turned to marrow and playful joy in the gaze of my divine nature. Into the innermost ear of her soul I instilled the sound of the playing harp of my eternal word. As pleasant as it is for me to continually drink from the streams of blood of my crucified Son, as burning was my thirst for the playful presence of this soul" (*O* 273.11–274.3).

The Dominican friars' *cura monialium* has traditionally been discussed from the male perspective with the nuns seen as passive recipients of the friars' teaching and preaching. Nor can the dependency of Catholic lay people on the ordained male clergy for the administration of the sacraments be challenged. It would, then, be anachronistic to assume that the authors of the Sister-Books criticize the hierarchical structure of the Church they considered divinely sanctioned. Nevertheless, the Sister-Books lend a voice to women which differs from the traditional male view and adds new aspects to the complex history of the pastoral care of medieval women monastics by Dominican friars.[1]

THE PASTORATE OF WOMEN

1. Parish Priests and Live-in Chaplains

As beguines, the small groups of women living a communal life, were under the legally binding jurisdiction of a parish. Parish priests, the *leutepriester*, however, were notoriously little educated at that time and unable to provide adequate religious instruction. To compensate for this deficiency, the bishops sent friars of the newly founded Order of Preachers into the parishes to preach.[2]

The Engeltal Sister-Book gives testimony to the strong influence the Dominican friars' homilies could have on lay people, especially on women, such as the beguines who were highly interested in theology and spirituality. As Christine Ebner explains, the founders of her community were directly stimulated by mendicant preachers to live a common life: "There was a small community of beguines in the city"

---

1. Ute Stargardt, "The Beguines of Belgium, the Dominican Nuns of Germany, and Margery Kempe" in *The Popular Literature of Medieval England* (Tennessee Studies in Literature 28), ed. Thomas J. Heffernan (Knoxville 1985), pp. 277–313, esp. p. 291f, speaks of the "very receptive" nuns dominated by "the influence of Eckhart, Tauler and Suso." Only a few recent studies have discussed the relationship between the medieval friars and the nuns. See Peters (1988, esp. 110–188); McGuire (1989).

2. For the parish jurisdiction, see LThK 8:398–400. About the wide-spread and well-known incompetency of late medieval parish priests, see Oediger (1953, especially 46–57); Neumann (1960, 123f. and 143); Lutz (1984, 162). Jacques de Vitry's *exempla* (1914), for instance, contain instances of priests not knowing any Latin (no. 104) nor being able to read (no. 106).

of Nürnberg, "in the district of the priest of St. Lawrence," and they were "obedient to him as their rightful pastor." But one day, after a friar's homily about the great "reward our Lord would give for purity and voluntary obedience, they went to this woman Alheit, the *rotte* player," and eagerly asked her "to become their *magistra.*" Alheit "immediately granted them this saintly request. And going into her house, each one separately laid all she had before her feet" (*E* 1f.). As beguines, with their "reputation spreading in the country" and beyond, they themselves started to teach other "pious women who came to them" for counselling. This lasted for several years: "I do not know the number," the chronicler says (*E* 2).

Eventually beguine communities typically left the pastoral care of their parish priest, a move for which they needed official permission only a bishop could grant. One such group document is preserved in which Bishop Heinrich von der Tanne absolves the Diessenhofen sisters, upon their request, from the parish's jurisdiction. Freed from parochial restrictions, the women could search for a more adequate spiritual guidance than what the *leutepriester* offered. They were permitted to choose a chaplain of their own (a privilege that was later restricted by the 1321 General Chapter).[3]

The better-educated friars thus represented a "heavy competition" for the parish church because their growing influence on the faithful also resulted in a financial loss for the pastor, as historical documents for the Oetenbach community show: donations, that would otherwise have gone to the parish coffers, were made to the women after they had moved out of the parish. Also the Weiler women, in the early days of their communal life, had a long-lasting dispute with their parish priest Albert von Nellingen over property and burial rights. Financially many parish priests were harmed by the beguines and hence opposed their way of life.[4]

The communities' chaplains, on the other hand, were much appreciated by the women. They had either been invited or had volunteered to share their life. The early Engeltal community had as their chaplain a "rich priest [of Vilseck], called Ulschalk" who had been "a great sinner openly for many years." But when he saw the sisters' "saintly

---

3. For the Diessenhofen document, see Pfister (1964, 291). Regarding the juridical and canonical aspects, see Neumann (1960, 123); Müller (1971, 18); Scheeben (1961, 106 n.15).

4. Sutter (1893, 13); Halter (1956, 35); Borst (1978, 290); Uhrle (1968, 9).

life, he asked them to receive him" as "their chaplain" (E 3). And the Winterthur beguines were strongly supported in their constructing a church, living quarters, and an administrative building by Hug, "a respected priest, ... a pure, godly man." Hug later "became their [chosen] chaplain" after the women had settled near Diessenhofen (D "Gründungsgeschichte").[5]

Two chaplains are especially highly praised and even honored with entries of their own in the Sister-Books: Kirchberg's Chaplain Walther, who was as saintly as a desert father (K 116), and her Friderich, the "old chaplain" in Engeltal, "godly in all his doings, ... decorated with all virtues" (E 15, 40). Live-in chaplains remained in place, even after the sisters' incorporation into the Order of Preachers, as decreed in Humbert's constitution. In each monastery, an appointed chaplain (in most cases a secular priest) was to celebrate daily mass and be available for emergencies, such as administering the Sacrament of the Sick and officiating at burials (E 9, 19, 21, 27; W 85). If no friars were available, chaplains were also entitled to hear confessions and distribute communion. The chaplains, like the sisters, became subject to supervision by representatives of the order after the women's communities had officially become part of the Order of Preachers.[6]

2. The Order of Preachers: the Women's Own Choice
Around 1240 the fledgling beguine communities, the Sister-Books report, were ready to seek incorporation into an established order.

---

5. The Engeltal author refers to Ulschalk's not having lived as a celibate at one time in his life (see E 38). In spite of the eleventh-century Gregorian reform that had introduced celibacy for priests, even as late as the thirteenth century, secular clergy were often married, and arguments for and against the priests' celibacy were forcefully presented by theologians. See Jean Gaudemet, "Le célibat ecclésiastique. Le droit et la pratique du XIe au XIIIe s.," Zeitschrift der Savigny-Stiftung für Rechtsgeschichte. Kanonistische Abt. 68 (1962) 1–31, esp. 29f. Regarding the Winterthur women, see also Langer (1987, 37). The Sister-Books mention further chaplains by name, such as "herr Walther" in Oetenbach (O 224f.), Burkart von Wangen in Diessenhofen (D 27e, also "Gründungsgeschichte") and chaplain Heinrich in Engeltal (E 40). Others are listed in historical documents, such as the friars Sigeward and Diemo for the Weiler community (Uhrle 1968, 9) and the secular priest Walther for Oetenbach in 1239 and 1261; a second leutepriester Rudolf lived in Oetenbach between 1272–1301 (Halter 1956, 22).

6. Christine Ebner's entry on Friedrich Sunder consists of excerpts from the vita of Friedrich Sunder (ed. by Ringler 1980a, 391–444). For the role of a chaplain in women's monasteries, see Wittmer (1946, 21); Däniker-Gysin (1958, 19).

Specific reasons are not given, but presumably the women felt a need for official protection. It may have been unwise for the authors to mention their founders' fear of persecution for heresy since the Sister-Books were composed during the critical period that followed the execution of the beguine Marguerite Porete in 1310 and after the 1311/12 Council of Vienne had spoken out against the beguines.[7]

Not many choices were open to women wanting to join a monastic order. But the texts indicate that some options were still available. In fact, both in Oetenbach and Diessenhofen, women were eagerly sought as monastics by two competing mendicant orders, the Order of St. Francis and the Order of Preachers (*O* 223; *D* "Gründungsgeschichte"). And Christine Ebner explains that Cistercian monks actively wooed the Nürnberg beguines to become associated with their order: "There came seven abbots of the grey order and asked this saintly community, seriously pleading with them," and they said that "if they joined their order they would treat them with great benevolence" (*E* 3). (This episode relates to a time before 1228 when the Cistercians closed their doors to women.)[8]

The Order of Preachers became the women's final choice. "During that time it so happened," Christine Ebner explains, "that the preachers from Regensburg travelled in this area; then the women pledged "they wanted to be in their obedience" (*E* 7). The Oetenbach sisters became Dominicans because they appreciated being "taught well and in a saintly manner" by the preachers friars of Zürich (*O* 222). The Töss women, the Sister-Book shows, were impressed by the apostolic way of life of "our ever-saintly Father St. Dominic" and the example of his "saintly order" with outstanding men like "the glowing sun St. Thomas [Aquinas]" and the "many saints in this order" (*T* 12f.). The author clearly aims at placing her monastery in this illustrious tradition. And the Oetenbach chronicler speaks of Gertraut von Hilzingen, "a respectable woman" of Zürich who lived "close to the Preachers' convent."

7. See Daniela Müller (1991) for further details on the precarious contemporary scene.

8. Regarding women's choices, see also Freed (1972, 321ff.). In other texts, however, there seems to be a congenial relationship between the two mendicant orders: (see also Däniker-Gysin 1958, 19). The Töss sister Ita von Sulz, for instance, is said to have had a barefooter (that is, a Franciscan friar) as a confessor (*T* 20). And in Oetenbach, Elsbeth von Beggenhofen consulted with "wise men from other orders" (*O* 263) which may include the Franciscans. See also Meyer (1995, 292). Concerning the Cistercian Order, see LThK 10:1386.

There she saw "such great saintliness in the friars of the Order of Preachers and such diligent observance [of the rules] of their order that she gained a burning desire also to lead such a religious saintly life" (*O* 218f.).

Individual Dominicans also play an influential role. In Unterlinden, Friar Walther, *lesmeister der prediger zü straßburg*, first encouraged the women of the fledgling community and gave the habit to the foundress Benedicta von Mühlhausen (*U* 347f.; cf. also ms.[Guelf.]). In Kirchberg, the accidental arrival of Johannes von Wildeshausen, then the Dominican General, supposedly made the sisters "humbly desire the Holy Order from him" (Kirchberg mss. [S], and cf. [A] and [Wa]). This story sounds exaggerated, however, since the misogynist Johannes Teutonicus is unlikely to have encouraged women to join the Order of Preachers.[9]

Some individual women, too, were inspired by the Dominican spirituality. Beli von Liebenberg first met a Dominican friar at her mother's house:

> At that time, the Order of Preachers was still unknown here. And then came a friar, called Friar Aquillus; and he was one of the first friars to come to a German land. And when they saw him, they wondered to what kind of people he belonged. And when they heard what his order was, and [having listened to] his sermon, they received him with great honor into their home. And as this blessed sister listened to his words, she followed his advice to the extent that she came to this monastery (*T* 30.7–13).

Beli joined the Töss sisters when they were about to start their first community at the Töss bridge. Also the rich Swabian widow, Ita von Hohenfels, sent out messengers "to inquire where the poorest and best people lived"; this was "where she wanted to go." Thus Ita became a member of the Oetenbach community (*O* 231). In the eyes of the surrounding population, then, a Dominican monastery seemed to best realize the religious ideals of the time.[10]

The new Order of Preachers in contrast to other monastic orders, Langer suggests, offered the women an organized life conducive to their developing an individual spirituality. Having opted for St. Dominic's

---

9. Wilms (1967, 19) identifies Unterlinden's Friar Walther as the Strasbourg Prior Walther (†1258). Regarding Teutonicus, see also Krauss (1894); Müller (1977/78, 46).

10. Ironically, historical documents show that the Oetenbach monastery, here praised for its poverty, turned into a distinctly wealthy community toward the end of the thirteenth century, see Langer (1987, 93f.).

order, the sisters were then intent on obtaining official affiliation with the Order of Preachers.[11]

WOMEN AND THE HISTORICAL *CURA MONIALIUM* DEBATE

As far as their monastic life was concerned, the women depicted in the Sister-Books unexpectedly had to live through precarious times. They found themselves in the middle of a long-ranging debate, during the thirteenth century, between the popes and the Order of Preachers concerning the spiritual care of monastic women. The Sister-Books, in fact, document several aspects of this controversy from the women's point of view.

1. Women Denied Spiritual Care

Dominican women's communities soon by far outnumbered the men's monasteries. The rapid growth of women's monasteries brought about a crisis for the Dominican friars for whom the task of the *cura monialium* was becoming a growing burden. The General Chapter of the Order of Preachers, meeting in Paris in 1228, thereupon ordered that no additional women's monasteries were to be incorporated into the order, a decree strongly supported by Jordan of Saxony: "Under pain of excommunication we prohibit any of our friars from laboring for or procuring that the care or supervision of nuns or any other women be committed to the friars, and if anyone will presume to act contrary, he will be subject to serious blame." Misogyny played, no doubt, a part in the Dominicans' refusal to continue their work among the nuns.[12]

The Oetenbach Sister-Book contains a most telling passage on how this crisis affected their own sisters: "From the beginning," that is, before their official incorporation, "the devout spiritual sisters" had all their spiritual needs met by "the friars of the Order of Preachers in Zürich [that is, this community did not have a chaplain]; and that had been their greatest consolation." However,

11. Langer (1987, 67); see also Borst (1978, 284).
12. The text of the decree is quoted by Brett (1984, 59). Decker (1935, 51) notes Jordan of Saxony's ambiguous opinion of women: Jordan showed himself a real patron of some women (especially the St. Agnes monastery in Bologna) while not promoting other foundations. But his decision was simultaneously based on the too heavy workload for the friars. The *cura monialium* left to his order by St. Dominic not only concerned Dominican women but also included some beguinages and many women's monasteries of other orders.

now it so happened that in all countries of christendom very many women's monasteries were started that wanted to live according to the way of life of the Order of Preachers and under their rule and teaching. So that the order would not be burdened too much with the women's monasteries, the reverend saintly Jordanus, the first Master after St. Dominic, had forbidden his friars in the large general chapter to care for these monasteries. And for this reason, the preachers of Zürich as well no longer wanted to hear these poor good sisters' confessions nor preach, and they removed themselves from all their tasks.

Thus the sisters "were much burdened," the chronicler continues, "for nobody wanted to care for them. And in this need they remained for a long time." Only when the Dominican friars "were then told that the barefooters wanted to care for" the sisters, they started again to look after the sisters "and returned to them on the eve of the feast of the Holy Cross in the fall." This period without a priest, that is, without the sacraments, had lasted "from Easter to fall" (O 222.10–224.6). In the end, the Oetenbach author suggests, it was the competition with the Franciscan Order that made the Dominican friars return.[13]

2. Sisters Actively Seeking Incorporation

After Pope Gregory IX had agreed, in 1239, with the Order of Preachers' decree against the *cura monialium*, Pope Innocent IV overruled Jordan of Saxony's decision in 1245. He issued papal bulls again entitling the nuns to all the privileges of the order by simultaneously subordinating them to the Dominican Order's general and provincials. This move, not to be read as a rare pro-feminine stance by the Holy See, rather mirrored the pope's fear that the *mulieres religiosae*, if left unsupervised, might deviate from the orthodox teaching of the Church. But whatever the pope's motifs were, the 1245 papal bull started "a veritable pilgrimage of German monastic women" to the papal curia to obtain official incorporation; within five years, in the province of

---

13. The period here referred to lasted precisely from March 30 to September 13, 1236, after the Chapter of the Order of Preachers at Bologna in 1235 had enforced Jordan of Saxony's 1228 Decree, Halter (1956, 18) explains. Wehrli-Johns (1980, 94) suggests that the nuns' material well-being was probably also affected because the friars used to encourage townspeople to make donations to the Oetenbach community. Langer (1987, 32) finds that such rivalry with the Franciscans often determined the Dominicans' policy.

Teutonia alone, thirty-two women's communities became officially part of the Order of Preachers.[14]

The women themselves had taken the initiative to seek incorporation into the Order of Preachers hoping the pope would overrule Jordan of Saxony's decision against the *cura monialium*. The Sister-Books give witness to these women's extraordinary task of personally travelling to the Holy See in the hope of convincing the pope of their need for affiliation. The difficult journey to the papal court to obtain the desired bull of official incorporation is described of the newly elected prioress of the Engeltal community: she went on foot, accompanied only by a sister and a lay brother, and with the help of a Dominican friar she was granted the incorporation without any problem (*E 7*). The Adelhausen chronicler writes about the Sister Countess von Sulz who took it upon herself to acquire the community's approbation (ms.[E]). A similar tale is told of the Unterlinden sisters (ms.[Guelf]). But only the Oetenbach Sister-Book offers a somewhat more explicit travelogue of such a journey to Rome:

> In those days, they did not yet have any confirmation from our Holy Father, the pope, as each monastery is supposed to have. This caused them much distress. For they were so poor that they had no goods that could be sent to Rome as an aid to having their monastery confirmed and incorporated into the order by the pope. Consequently they elected a saintly sister, Hemma Walaseller, who took along a companion and their secular chaplain, called Lord Walther, who was an old respectable man. The [community] entrusted these three persons with obtaining their confirmation from the pope. And right away, they committed themselves into God's mercy on the way. They had nothing to ride on so that, putting all their trust in God, they walked to Rome ....

The text does not give any further detail about the hardships of this journey. The author concentrates instead on how the community at home accompanied the delegation with their fervent prayers and pious vows; and then the chronicler concludes:

---

14. For the papal reversal of the policy, see Goodich (1981, 20); Köhler (1982, 280). The question of heresy is only of marginal importance for the Sister-Books, hence not pursued in detail. For a thorough study of the contemporary scene, see Leff (1967); Lerner (1972). Grundmann (1935, 249, 251) describes the incorporation of women into the order.

Thus they came to Rome. And at that time, great lords were there, who had great goods to give to whoever was useful to them in their affairs. The poor women of Oetenbach had nobody but these two sisters. And God, who never abandons those who trust him, helped them so that they were quickly given attention according to all their wishes. And the Holy Pope Gregory IX granted them the confirmation when we counted the year 1239 from Christ's birth, in May on the feast of St. John *ante portam latinam.* Then they left, before many a great lord who had been there long before them (O 224.10–226.2).

Since the Oetenbach delegation was successful in being confirmed, the author only alludes to the corruption at the papal court. No more needs to be said. The incorporation into the Order of Preachers was given to Oetenbach on July 12, 1245 by Innocent IV.[15]

3. The Continuing Effect of the Debate

The discussion about the *cura monialium* within the Order of Preachers, however, did not subside. The Dominican General, Johannes Teutonicus [von Wildeshausen] (1241–1252), renewed efforts to free the friars from the pastoral care of women. Even some six hundred years later, the Dominican historian Denifle heartily approves of Teutonicus, writing: "If only the friars had stuck to their conviction!" Denifle blames the later decline in learning among the preachers, their neglect of their real vocation during the fourteenth century, on their involvement in the *cura monialium,* while conceding that there may also have been small benefits for the friars. Recent scholars view the *cura monialium* decidedly as a give-and-take between friars and nuns.[16]

15. The bull for Engeltal, dated October 10, 1248, is preserved (Schröder 1871, 61). The historical document pertaining to Adelhausen is dated June 12, 1245. Concerning improprieties at the papal court, see also Raymond of Capua's *vita* of Catherine of Siena written about a century later: "... the holy virgin bewailed the fact that at the Roman Court, which should have been a paradise of heavenly virtues, there was a stench of all the vices of hell" (1960, 138).

16. See Brett (1984, 621) on Wildeshausen. Denifle (1886a, 643) is contradicted by Hinnebusch (1966, 399): "such a contention would be hard to prove, since so many other factors are involved in the decline of Scholasticism." Scholarship and pastoral care could be successfully combined; these critics cite Dietrich von Freiberg (†1310), Meister Eckhart, Nikolaus von Straßburg and Johann von Sterngassen (each a fourteenth-century Dominican). See also Frank, "Die Spannung zwischen Ordensleben und wissenschaftlicher Arbeit im frühen Dominikanerorden," *Archiv für Kulturgeschichte* 49 (1967) 164–207; Scheeben (1961); Ringler (1980a); Grubmüller (1986); Haas (1987b, 155).

The earlier papal decision was again reversed in 1252 in favour of the friars. Pope Innocent IV gave in to the demands of the Order of Preachers and agreed to release the friars from the obligation of the nuns' pastoral care. The women, consequently, while not losing their recently acquired incorporation into the Order of Preachers, could no longer count on the friars' spiritual care. Many women's monasteries were thus left without the sacraments for an extended period.

Intensive lobbying at the papal court by the Dominican sisters (and their relatives and patrons) and the death of Johannes von Wildeshausen which, according to Edward T. Brett, produced "a void in the anti-feminist forces which was left unfilled," accounted for the fact that the *cura monialium* was eventually resumed. The Dominican Chapters in Milan (1255) and in Florence (1257) once again officially reversed the papal decision of 1252, decreeing that the Order of Preachers would not abandon the spiritual care of the sisters in monasteries already incorporated into the order.[17]

The task of creating a much needed general constitution for all women's communities, that would simultaneously regulate the *cura monialium,* was at that point given to Humbert of Romans. Humbert's constitution of 1259 clearly spelt out the First Order's duties, apparently to the satisfaction of both the friars and the nuns: The Order of Preachers took responsibility for annual visitations to both women's and men's monasteries, and the Dominican friars were to function as the nuns' preachers and confessors. Thus Humbert of Romans' constitution finally decided in favour of the spiritual care for women monastics. The *cura monialium* was then confirmed by Pope Clement IV in 1267. In the history of the Dominican Order, 1267 is the date when the stormy relationship between the Dominican men and women was legally settled.[18]

Thereafter, following the advice of the Teutonia Provincial Hermann von Minden in 1286/87, the pastoral care of the Dominican women was given only to especially learned friars (*fratres docti* or *hoh lessmeister*). Although this directive does not imply that only scholars were charged with the nuns' *cura monialium,* it does suggest that the

17. Brett (1984, 65).

18. Däniker-Gysin (1958, 45) explains that Humbert was also responsible for a reform of the Dominican liturgy and strongly favored a *numerus clausus* for women's monasteries. Humbert is thus considered "the true founder of the Second Order" because of this accomplishment (Fontette 1967, 127). See also Decker (1935, 101ff.); Bennett (1937, 65f.); Pfister (1964, 286); Tugwell (1987, 16, 18).

sisters were generally so educated that the order could not send just any preacher to them. It was undoubtedly a move that the theologically demanding sisters greatly benefitted from (O 263; G 124).[19]

A period of more or less congenial cooperation between the friars and nuns began that stretched from the late thirteenth to the middle of the fourteenth centuries at which point the Black Death in Europe interrupted all aspects of a normal life.

THE *CURA MONIALIUM* IN PRACTICE

1. The Order of Preachers as Superiors

The incorporation of a community into the Order of Preachers gave the friars a certain amount of power over the sisters. How this control by *únser maisterschaft*, "our superiors" (T 18) is exercised, is mentioned sporadically in the Sister-Books. The Oetenbach author speaks of a transfer ordered by Friar Hermann von Minden (Provincial in Teutonia 1286–1291 and 1293–1294) of four sisters to another monastery to help with the start of a new community (O 236). The authors also mention regular visitations of superiors of the order to the individual monasteries, naming some well-known Dominicans in the process. The consecration of an altar in Diessenhofen was the immediate reason for a visit by the illustrious Albert the Great:[20]

> God provided for us a great fortune in that the high teacher and worthy Bishop Albreht came to us. He was a light of christendom and a friar of the Order of Preachers. He blessed us, and he blessed the main altar in the choir in honor of our Lady, the noble queen of the heavenly kingdom, and the good saint John the Evangelist (D "Gründungsgeschichte").

Meister Eckhart supposedly visited both Diessenhofen and Oetenbach (D 41; O 263). The Oetenbach text refers to the sisters' pastoral care by "the prior of the preachers" of Zürich, believed to have been Hugo Ripelin of Strasbourg (O 220). In Engeltal, Bishop Niklaus von Regensburg spent Christmas with the community (E 27); and a reference to "Mosburger's mass" suggests that the fourteenth-century Domi-

---

19. See also Scheeben (1964, 103f.) on the *fratres docti*.

20. Muschg (1935, 133) dates the transfer in Oetenbach to 1294; and see Halter (1956, 51ff). The Diessenhofen book reference to Bishop Albreht is generally assumed to allude to a visit by Albert the Great which, however, is not clearly documented (Meyer 1995, 282f.).

nican *lesemeister,* Berthold von Moosburg, celebrated the eucharist at the Engeltal monastery (*E* 28). The Kirchberg author speaks of "Friar Cmynt who was our provincial" (*K* 108), identified as Edmund [Emynt] (†1278), Provincial of Teutonia.[21]

But in general, the Sister-Books are more surprising for omitting the names of so many contemporary friars considered important representatives of the Order of Preachers today and who are, in fact, documented as having been in touch with several of the monasteries concerned. Neither Suso, Elsbet Stagel's spiritual friend, nor Tauler, the popular preacher who travelled throughout the Lake Constance and Strasbourg area, is given a place in these texts.[22]

2. The Spiritual Guidance by the Friars

Consoling the sick (*E* 38) and the suffering (*O* 220), occasionally administering the Sacrament of the Sick and even burying a sister (*U* 376f.), the friars generally showed themselves as good pastors. They also celebrated mass on high feast days: Diemut von Lindau in Diessenhofen sees Friar Conrad's hands radiant as gold during mass on Christmas Day (*D* 31; *O* 246). Their main official function, however, was to preach, and there is little doubt among the authors of the Sister-Books that the friars' preaching played an enormous role in these women's spiritual life (*G* 126; *T* 28f., 35f.). Before communion days, the friars were

21. While he is rarely mentioned in the Book of Sisters, Meister Eckhart was, in fact, actively engaged in the *cura monialium* as a vicar in Strasbourg between 1314 and 1322/23 (Langer 1987, 41–46). Ruh (1982, 326), continuing Grundmann's line of thought (1935), credits Eckhart with having consciously aimed at preserving the valuable ideas of the *mulieres religiosae* (such as the notion of individual perfection, love of God, and spiritual poverty) by reformulating them in a theological language. Ruh's view is considerably more appropriate than the derogatory premise of Langer that Eckhart functioned as a "corrective" for the nuns' emotionally charged spirituality (1987; cf. also Blank 1978, 28). Hugo Ripelin became famous for his *Compendium theologicae veritatis* (1265–1270), see Zeller-Werdmüller and Bächtold (1889, 220, n.1); LThK 5:519f. Müller (1977/78, 48) identified the provincial Edmund as the Provincial of Teutonia (1249–51 and 1266–69).

22. For a similar observation, see Krebs (1904, 94ff.); Walz (1967, 19ff.). Among those omitted, are especially Friar Reiner (†1281, buried in Unterlinden), Konrad Gurli von Esslingen, Ulrich von Strassburg (1272–1277 Provincial of Teutonia) and his disciple Johannes von Freiburg (†1314) who were connected with the women's pastorate in Teutonia during the time covered in the Sister-Books. Pfleger (1937, 40) writes that visits of Albert the Great and Eckhart to Unterlinden are documented for 1269 and 1322 respectively. Regarding Tauler, see Grabmann (1926, 478). Regarding Suso, see Kirchberger (1930, 251); Spiess (1935, 371); Borst (1978, 298); Haas (1987a, 278).

also available as confessors (*pichtiger*) of whom some are especially singled out by the authors, such as Friar Eberhart, *lesmeister* at Freiburg, whom a Kirchberg sister in distress especially called to the confessional, *peichtvenster* (*K* 106; cf. *T* 38, 39). And Offmya von Munchwil in Töss, "when going to confession," never failed to remember "that the confessor sat in God's place" (*T* 32).

Settling the nuns' nagging questions of faith was arguably one of the most important tasks for the friars, the Sister-Books suggest. Thus, Elsbeth von Beggenhofen in Oetenbach was greatly troubled about how to understand the essence of God (*daß got nit ein söliches wesen hette, als man von im seit*) following an encounter with "the evil spirit" (*O* 267). A Weiler sister is pictured discussing Scripture with a friar, *ein leßmeister von prediger orden* (*W* 70).

The friars especially assisted the sisters with proper discernment. The Diessenhofen Sister Anne von Ramswag asked Meister Eckhart to help her interpret her spiritual experiences (*D* 41). Because of the highly inflammable social atmosphere at that time, some of the women, even inside the monastic community, continued to be afraid of being accused of heresy.[23] The Diessenhofen author herself, for example, was so worried about Anne von Ramswag's visions that she writes: "After her death I went [to consult with] the *lesmeister* Hugo von Stoffenberg" who was able to assure her that he "could not find any error in what [Anne] had told him" (*D* 41). Other sisters too are shown asking the preachers' assistance in interpreting visions (*E* 24f.; *T* 75). Even the prioress Anna von Selden in Adelhausen was fearful that her mystical experiences might endanger her, and "hence she asked her confessor whether she was right or wrong" (*A* 154; cf. *O* 263). And Jüzi Schulthasin in Töss, intent on living a true *imitatio Christi*, discusses with Friar Hugo the Provincial a subtle dilemma: Jüzi's "love was so great" that she wanted

> to suffer voluntarily with God all the passion that he suffered for us. And as a consequence of her courageous attitude, she was often in such pain that she thought she would not leave a particular place alive. And this, at times, made her afraid; [she wondered] whether, if she then died, she herself would be responsible.

Friar Hugo permitted her to continue, adding that "if she thus died he would answer for her before God." And he then said: "'Die, just die!' And because of this, she was consoled and had no more fear at all" (*T*

70.32–71.8). Her confessor's offer to shoulder her responsibility (patronizing though it was from today's perspective) was gratefully accepted by Jüzi, as was his later advice during one of her arid phases to accept from God "both sweet and sour," a suggestion that Jüzi followed "as much as she could" (*T* 75, 79).

An especially urgent case in Engeltal required the arbitration of a Dominican superior, who in this case was the "prior at Regensburg": Alheit von Trochau was told in a vision that she had never been properly baptized: "The preachers came and said they had read about" such cases, and they decided that she must have "received a baptism by grace" but should now "be given the Christian sacrament (*E* 11), a decision the nuns promptly acted on.[24]

As the Sister-Books show, the friars were often touched by the saintliness of the women, impressed by the nuns' "compelling image of living faith," Elizabeth Alvilda Petroff states in a similar context. Friar Albrecht von Bello speaks of an Oetenbach sister "as pure as an angel" (*O* 244); and of Elsbeth von Beggenhofen's confession, Prior Friar Johannes says, "it was the highest perfection he had ever heard of a human being" (*O* 267). Confessors also testify after a sister's death that her soul must have gone straight to heaven (*U* 462; *T* 94). In a study of late medieval women's *vitae*, John Coakley concludes, some of these women impressed the friars "as veritable loci of the divine."[25]

3. The Nuns' Reaction to the Friars

Due to their high esteem for the Dominican Order, most women fully accept the friars' spiritual guidance. The preachers friars so impress one sister that she prays for years that her own brother might also enter the Order of Preachers (*U* 444ff.); and an Oetenbach sister has a vision of the perfect lives led by two of the friars (*O* 249). The busy cooks in Diessenhofen, offering the visiting preachers a delicious meal when their own community was starving (D. "Gründungsgeschichte"), not only serve as a good example of monastic hospitality, but also suggests the deference of some of the nuns toward the friars. In the Töss Sister-Book, it is said of the old Sister Mezzi Sidwibrin:

> She was also very eager to hear God's word. And when there was a homily [given by a friar] ... she sometimes nudged the sisters sitting next to her, saying: 'Listen, listen! Don't you hear? What a

---

24. Beyer's otherwise pointed insight (1989, 208) into Alheit's vision ignores its outcome.

25. Petroff (1994, 139); Coakley (1991, 245).

miracle!' And she often sat like this, expressing admiration with words and gestures. And sometimes she lovingly flattered the men who preached so well (*T* 28.25–30).

Notably the author, conscious of the awkward scene she describes, repeats five times in this context that Mezzi was of a great simplicity (*guotter ainfaltikait*).[26]

An occasional passage also suggests a closer relationship between a friar and a nun: "A preacher called Friar Conrad von Eystet was, for a long time, in charge of the spiritual care" of the Engeltal monastery. He "had a great love" for Alheit von Trochau "because of her saintliness." She simultaneously had the gift of grace "that, wherever he said mass, be it far or near, she saw our Lord's body in his hands." Moreover, Alheit also perceived "whatever he did against God," and she kept it in mind to tell him "when he again came to her" (*E* 13). As a friend, Alheit considered it her duty to make the friar aware of her telepathic knowledge of his failings, the pastoral care thus being reciprocal. The Diessenhofen author, too, speaks of the good relationship between Anne von Ramswag and Friar Hugo von Stauffenberg, "who was a relative of hers and to whom she was quite close" (*D* 41).

There are cases, however, where the reader senses a much more reserved and, at times, a critical attitude toward the friars. In the story about the seriously ill Adelheit von Hiltegarthausen, the author of the Gotteszell Sister-Book relates that "It also sometimes happened that reverend fathers, such as high *lesemeister*, came to the monastery to console her. And when they then sat by her bed and began to bring forth sweet talk of divine devotion, she overwhelmed them with such profound words that they worried about answering her. And yet she was not educated with worldly, *irdischen*, books" (*G* 124). While

---

26. The verb *zartten* used in this Töss passage implies both 'flatter' and 'caress.' If Sister Mezzi, indeed, caressed some preachers (which could have been possible, given her naiveté or even feeble-mindedness, *als sy nit sinn hetty*, *T* 28), these episodes would have to have taken place before the enforcement of the nuns' strict enclosure in 1298, because thereafter such close contact between the sisters and anyone from the outside, including the friars, was no longer possible. The Töss author also ascribes to this particular sister the much quoted lines, attributed to Augustine and a commonplace in medieval literature: "Lord, if you were Mezzi Sidwibrin and I were God, I would nevertheless let you be God and would want to be Mezzi Sidwibrin" (*T* 29), cf. Vernet (1930, 185).

acknowledging the preachers' learnedness, the author simultaneously points to the friars' experiential shortcoming.[27]

Likewise, Elsbet von Beggenhofen in Oetenbach is said to have approached "her confessors and other preachers and knowledgeable priests of different orders" with a question, but "they never gave her any answer," until Meister Eckhart solved her problem: "He said that there was no need for worldly wisdom," and that her spiritual experiences "were purely God's work." And he recommended to her to "entrust herself to God in free detachment, *freie gelassenheit*. And she experienced that it was so" (*O* 263). The master's wise council, then, was far superior to that of other friars who, the author implies, were not all equally wise and helpful. Nor were they all equally acceptable to all the women.

The Sister-Books are no exception in the long line of medieval works by men and women writers who air their discontent with the clergy. As Grundmann explains, an anti-clerical attitude was often found during the late Middle Ages because the "high expectations of the purity and dignity of the priesthood" led to sharp criticism of individual unworthy priests. And although criticism of clergymen usually concerned secular priests, some passages in the Sister-Books implicitly also reproach the friars preachers. The women especially object that some friars interfere with their spiritual experiences. A Töss sister is quoted saying that if Friar Wolfram the Provincial "had not ordered [her] to fend off the graces, God would have done miracles with [her] that would forever be told" (*T* 67). Having first obeyed the friar, she then blames him for a loss of special graces. Similarly, a sister in the Engeltal monastery does not want to interrupt a vision for the sake of accommodating a brother, who was later himself affected by her charism (*E* 14).[28]

More importantly, some passages in the Sister-Books depict sisters not complying with orders given by friars. The Adelhausen sister, Else von der Neustatt, who was as knowledgeable as "a well-educated clergyman," is represented in a teaching dialogue with a younger sister where

---

27. While consultations with clergy and confessions normally take place through a grille or confessional window provided for such events, priests are permitted into the infirmary on condition that all rules be observed (Humbert's constitution, 1259, 18 and 36).

28. Grundmann (1935, 516f.). Among contemporary authors critical of the clergy, Vernet (1930, 194) singles out Bernard of Clairvaux, Denis the Carthusian, and Ruysbroeck. To them must be added women, such as Hildegard von Bingen, Mechthild von Magdeburg, Christine Ebner, Agnes Blannbekin, and others.

the question was raised whether it was better to listen to a preacher or to remain in contemplation; and the answer given was by no means unambiguous: one "might hear something imperfect" from a preacher "that were better not heard," Else explains (*A* 182). The Adelhausen Sister-Book also speaks of Elisabeth von Vackenstein's gift of knowing everyone's state of grace. When her confessor asks her to beg God to take this knowledge away from her lest she lose her mind over it, the sister does as advised but only after telling "this same confessor a sin he had never confessed" (*A* 157).

In another case, a sister's virtue is endangered. Anna von Munzingen explains that a friar, during confession, flattered Metze Tuschelin, and she started to feel attracted to him. However, a dream vision revealed to her how she was being robbed of her most precious jewel and gave her "to understand that it was her heart's love." This immediately made her withdraw from this friar (*A* 162). Comparably, the Engeltal author writes of one of the sisters (*fraw*): "There was a preacher who was very friendly to a woman. But the woman denied him her friendship with insulting words. He complained about this to our Lord while he had him in his hands" (*E* 13). The friar is shown in an even worse light when the author explains that the visionary Alheit von Trochau saw him using the sacred moment of consecration during mass to complain about this nun.[29]

The authors of the Sister-Books picture some women directly resisting the friars preachers. Typically the sisters' defiance is not expressed verbally but in their action: In Adelhausen, Adelheid von Brisach was scolded because once a week she neglected to attend the daily communal mass in the monastery. This happened, the author explains, because

> always on a Thursday night, she diligently contemplated the passion of our Lord and became so ill that she neither could get up nor attend mass on Friday morning. For that the preachers punished and reprimanded her in chapter, and she was accused of being a heretic [*ein ketzerin*]. Then she left the chapter in a happy mood, dancing and singing: *Laudate Dominum omnes gentes* [Ps.116]. And

---

29. A scene in the Kirchberg Sister-Book could easily be misinterpreted as depicting a sadistic friar who pretends to offer communion to a sick sister. But the point of this popular legendary story is, in fact, only that the sister is aware of his fraud (*K* 111). Cf. Jacques de Vitry's *exempla* (1914, no. 7); and Browe (1938, 36–40).

all the young children who were in the monastery ran after her and helped her sing (*A* 154.19–27).

This sister not only ignores the friars' severe accusation of heresy, she openly defies it, and simultaneously incites the children to take her side. Anna von Munzingen who introduces this passage with the phrase "she was also of a saintly life" has no further comment on the preacher's sharp reprimand, apparently respecting the sister's decision.[30]

The Töss Sister-Book gives a further example of defiance, this time even the entire community of sisters resisting the order of a provincial. Presumably reacting against the ever-increasing Ursula myth at that time, this provincial told the nuns to discontinue celebrating St. Ursula's feast. The community, however, claiming the authority of appropriate visions, continues celebrating the feast: "Thereafter we never neglected this office" (*T* 21, 30f.). Although, from our vantage point, the friar's advice was sound, the self-confidence of these sisters who collectively disobey their provincial's official order is not to be underestimated.[31]

WOMEN MINISTERING TO WOMEN

1. The Sisters' Own Pastoral Care

Such tales about the nuns' defiance in the Sister-Books raise the question whether the nuns really see themselves as dependent on the *cura monialium* as has been assumed. The pastoral function of a monastery's prioress has always been taken for granted (*A* 159, 188); she is considered a "quasi-pastor."[32] But, in addition, a number of especially erudite sisters are singled out in the Sister-Books for their good pastoral work, both inside the community and with people coming to the monastery. In Adelhausen, Sister Adelheid Geishörnlin counselled people in distress, and Elisabeth von Vackenstein "had so much grace that worldly people had great faith in her and sought her help and

---

30. Langer (1987, 146) argues that this passage shows a tendency away from the sacrament ("*asakramental*"), because Adelheid prefers her own religious experience to receiving communion at mass. He seems to ignore the fact that, for the sisters, the mass is also "a-sacramental" most of the time because of their limited access to communion.

31. Critics who mention this scene tend to mitigate it. Langer (1987, 99f.) wonders whether this order was a strict command or simply an exhortation; the latter, he argues, is more likely under the circumstances. Wilms (1923, 58) in retelling this episode omits its conclusion, thus ignoring the sisters' defiance.

32. Scheeben (1964, 105).

advice when in need"; moreover, Else von der Neustatt was able, through special grace, to solve other people's problems "as if she had been a well-learned priest" (*A* 165f., 157, 180; cf. *D* 29). The *exemplum* of Adelheit von Hiltegarthausen in the Gotteszell book describes a young friar who, after having sought but not found any help from his prior, came "to this woman with God's help" (*G* 126).

In Unterlinden, the author explains, the sisters cared for each other and for outsiders in their spiritual needs, since "the sisters had received from the Lord erudite and healing speech that could powerfully bestow the cure of health upon suffering minds." This was because "their own minds burned inside with the fire of divine love; hence their words consoled others and inflamed cold hearts" (*U* 343; cf. 352). Katharina von Unterlinden understands this ability of the nuns to offer pastoral care as a grace from God, as her entry on Agnes von Ochsenstein illustrates:

> She always admonished them severely and talked affectionately of God to the sisters and likewise to strangers at the window; [for] she had for many years the office at the grille. And she did so in such a saintly and conscientious manner that all monastic and worldly people who had come, left not little edified by her (*U* 354.18–355.12).

"There was evidently quite an 'apostolate of the window' at Unterlinden," Simon Tugwell also finds. In fact, because of Unterlinden's reputation, even illustrious people, such as Count Gottfried von Habsburg came to the nuns for spiritual help – apparently with good results, as a later vision reporting his salvation claims (*U* 447f.). Christine Ebner in Engeltal, documents show, was consulted even by the Emperor Karl IV. "Spiritual power radiated out from them to all the faithful and sometimes to the great and powerful," Leclercq sums up the medieval nuns' pastoral gift.[33]

The older sisters, in particular, were sought out for spiritual counselling (*T* 90, 92), whereas the most learned ones among them, like Anne von Ramswag in Diessenhofen (*D* 41), Sophie von Klingnau (*T* 55–60) and Jüzi Schulthasin (*T* 60–79) in Töss are apparently responsible for answering questions of a theological nature that arose in the community, such as those concerning the nature of the soul, the

---

33. On Unterlinden, see Tugwell (1982, 429). Ancelet-Hustache (1930, 447 n.1) verifies Count Gottfried's visit for the year 1271. Oehl (1924, 7) attests to Kaiser Karl IV in Engeltal. And see Leclercq (1981, 64).

Incarnation, purgatory, and heaven. Importantly, such mutual spiritual care among the nuns in the Sister-Books is shown as divinely sanctioned; for when Kathrin Brúmsin of Diessenhofen asks in prayer about how to pray, she is referred to Adelheid die Hutterin by "a voice saying: Go to this sister and ask her" (*D* 44).

Notwithstanding the fact that Humbert of Romans' *Treatise on Preaching* was quite unequivocal on the subject of women preaching, the Unterlinden author maintains that some sisters were so filled "with God's wisdom" that they could have preached (*U* 442). In the Töss Sister-Book, Anna von Klingnau is presented as a special example of how well a sister can both teach and speak of God:

> She rarely spoke a superfluous word, but God had given her the grace that she was overflowing with the sweetest words. And they were so good to listen to that hearts were rightly moved by them. For her words were flowing out of a full heart, as is written: The mouth speaks out of the heart's abundance [Mt. 12:34]. And because the sisters always found God through her, they quite often surrounded her, young and old ... . She also especially loved to talk about the lives and martyrdom of the saints. And when she was at a place where one did not talk of God, she found it unbearable. And she had a habit of bringing up God's word so skillfully that all other talk fell silent (*T* 37.20–31).

The Töss author also provides the example of Margret Finkin, whom she calls "a brilliant mirror of monastic life": she was able to "talk about God so pleasantly that it was most desirable to listen to her" (*T* 33f.). The Gotteszell author singles out Sister Elsbetlein who very much liked to preach – the term is actually used – and to talk about God, *Bredigen und von got reden was im die aller peste kürczweil* (*G* 142). Moreover, while not mentioned in the Sister-Books which predates this event, Christine Ebner preached to the flagellants when they came to Nürnberg in 1349.[34]

---

34. Humbert of Romans (1955, 47f.) writes: "The qualities requisite for a preacher in regard to his person are first of all, that he be of male sex," for St. Paul "does not want women to be permitted to speak" [1 Tm. 2:12]. Humbert gives four reasons for the exclusion of women from preaching: "First, a lack of intelligence, for in this woman is thought to be inferior to man; second, her natural state of dependency ...; third, the concupiscence which her very presence may arouse; fourth, the remembrance of her first error." On Christine Ebner's preaching, see Ringler (1988, 152); Tanz and Werner (1993, 256).

Counselling each other, and even confessing one's sins to a trustworthy sister was not unusual in these women's communities. The Diessenhofen Sister-Book contains the author's first-person account of Elsbeth Hainburgin: "I was told by a sister that she had opened her distressed heart to Sister Elsbeth and cried before her. When Sister Elsbeth saw this, she was moved by pity and cried with her and talked with her so wisely and well that this sister said: "I never heard a human mouth talk of God as well as she did'" (*D* 40). Similar to the story about Margaret Finkin of Töss, it is the nun's compassion and talking with (rather than down to) her sister in community that singles her out. The nun having received Elsbeth's instruction then knelt before her, asking her to pray for her, a gesture that resembles part of the ritual of confession. Also Katharina von Unterlinden explains that Hedwig von Steinbach "secretly revealed to a sister her biggest sin which she believed to be greater than all other faults," namely her envy of a sister in her community (*U* 393, 365f.).

In the early Christian centuries, Bernhard Poschmann shows, confessions were not necessarily made to a priest; rather, any saintly lay person had the power to forgive sins; and only during the Middle Ages confessions were eventually "clericalized." During the thirteenth century at least, there was still great uncertainty as to whether a priest was the only one authorized to administer this sacrament, Isnard Wilhelm Frank explains. Even Albert the Great writes: "confession to laymen is valid, if it is not motivated by contempt of religion, and in case of necessity laymen and *even women* have authority from God to grant absolution" (emphasis mine).[35]

Given the Church's severe laws prohibiting the ministry of women, it is surprising to find how much is actually said about the nuns' own pastoral functions in the Sister-Books. On the other hand, of course, no

---

35. Poschmann, *Paenitentia secunda. Die kirchliche Buße im ältesten Christentum bis Cyprian und Origenes*, Theophaneia 1. (Bonn: Hanstein, 1940, repr. 1964), pp. 463f.; and see also Poschmann, *Penance and the Anointing of the Sick*, trans. and rev. Francis Courtney. (Freiburg: Herder; Montreal: Palm, 1964), esp. p. 142. Frank (1984, 31). See also Henry Charles Lea, *A History of Auricular Confession and Indulgences in the Latin Church* (Philadelphia, 1896), in his chapter "Prolonged Struggle to Suppress Confession to Laymen" (1:217–226); he explains that the opinion in the Church of the High Middle Ages varied from one authority to the next. Likewise Schmaus (1957, 4,1:599f.) regarding *Laienbeichte*. And see Albertus Magnus (1651, 16:425); the original reads: ... *& hanc potestatem habet laicus in articulo necessitatis, & mulier similiter. Et per hoc patet solutio ad totum.*

matter how well trained and knowledgeable and saintly they were, the sisters were unable to provide for each other opportunities to receive the eucharist as often as they desired. To compensate for this deficiency, the authors speak of miraculous solutions.

2. Miracles Increasing the Sisters' Self-Reliance

Referring to one of the numerous traumatic periods during which the nuns were deprived of the sacraments, this time to an interdict imposed just before Elsbet von Beggenhofen died in 1340, the author of the Oetenbach Sister-Book tells a miraculous tale. She insists that, in spite of the absence of the friars, Elsbet was not forsaken at the time of her death but was given communion by means of a miraculous heavenly dispensation: "and as deplorable as the state of our spiritual consolation was at that time, God often gave himself to her" (*O* 270).[36]

Similarly, Katharina von Unterlinden maintains that, when her community was smitten with an interdict at the time of Ludwig der Bayer because the nuns sided with the king,[37] the sisters' desire for the eucharist was repeatedly and miraculously answered. Communion was divinely dispensed to them from the Lord's "most divine hands" or "by a heavenly messenger several times"(*U* 443, 449, 391). Of Adelheid von Rheinfelden she says specifically that she was "nourished sometimes, in a way perceptible by the senses, with the bread of life," claiming that the miracle was witnessed by others as well (*U* 398). And Hedwig von Laufenberg, the text continues, not only "receive[d] his precious body and blood" at the time of her death but also the sacrament of the Last Anointing" administered by "the Lord and King" himself (*U.* 449f.).

Similarly, the entry in the Diessenhofen Sister-Book of Sister Elsbeth relates that, in the absence of a priest, both the sacrament of reconciliation and communion were given to her by the Lord appearing as a bishop (*D* 40).

The final authority, then, the audience is to conclude, lies not with an ordained clergyman but with Christ himself. This is in fact the

---

36. This passage (*O* 270) corroborates a Zürich Chronicle according to which, in 1338/1339, the Order of Preachers, remaining true to the pope, had to leave the city of Zürich which took the side of Ludwig der Bayer. See Halter (1956, 48f.); Wehrli-Johns (1980, 97).

37. Venturino of Bergamo's letters of consolation to Katharina von Unterlinden and her community give witness to the hardship caused by this interdict. See Wilms (1920, 86f.); Geith (1984, 33).

strongly delivered lesson of a story in the Oetenbach Sister-Book: A sister portress accidentally let someone enter the cloister at the time, when the rule of strict enclosure had just been newly enforced for all female orders (by Pope Boniface VIII in 1298):

> And when she realized it, she was badly shocked, and with serious-ness and great sorrow she went to our Lord and confessed her guilt before him. Then our Lord showed his mercy and absolved her since she realized her guilt. And he said to her: "Do not be afraid, I have all the power, more than all the confessors and prelates" (O 265.8–12).

Since the Sister-Books teach by way of examples, miracles, and vision-ary images, this is a powerful message. It explains that, in the final analysis, petty rules and regulations have little sway.[38]

There is, then, no suggestion in these texts of a one-sided passive dependency of these women on the preachers friars' *cura monialium*. Nor is there any evidence that the *cura monialium* resulted in literary cooperation between the nuns and their Dominican pastors – a point that needs to be made clearly, for scholars have repeatedly suggested that any written work coming out of women's monasteries must have been inspired and aided by the clergymen in charge of the nuns. In the end, the authors succeed in convincing their audience that, through divine grace, these sisters, against all odds, were enabled to maintain an inner independence.[39]

Anna von Munzigen, in telling the following story in the Adelhau-sen Sister-Book, makes the point that even the friars may have been aware of the sisters' fearless self-confidence. Using the clever ruse of letting this crucial statement appear in a preacher's vision, the author makes her tale appear more objective and the message convincing. The final sentence reads, in fact, like the motto for the Dominican women's

---

38. Bynum (1987a, 139) reaches a similar conclusion from sources other than the Sister-Books: "... such an immediate and individual relationship between God and the soul could seem to bypass clerical authority."

39. For these sisters' independence, see also Haas (1987a, 292) and Grundmann (1935, 238). Peters (1988b, 187f.) also concludes that the Sister-Books were not co-authored; for the opposite view, see Kunze (1952, 42); Oehl (1924, 7). While it may have been the case that some women followed the advice of their confessors to write down their own experiences, this practice does not apply to the Sister-Books' authors. Two of the authors speak of being "forced by obedience" to compose their work (G 134; E 1), but neither one specifies an authority figure. It could be the prioress or indeed, her own conscience, that an author obeys.

self-reliance. Their confidence, however, is based neither on their own intellectuality nor even on their own spirituality but rather on the firm belief that "the Lord" supports them. The women depicted in the Sister-Books feel empowered through divine grace. The passage reads:

> And during that same night, ... there was a preacher two miles away. He saw [Richi von Stocken] walking in a meadow amidst flowers [that is, she had left her monastery's enclosure]. And he thought, if this is a sister from Adelhausen she will be punished for it. Then she turned around, quite angrily, and answering his thought, she said: "We are afraid of nobody, *Wir förchten nieman!*" (*A* 158.25–30).

The Sister-Books do not uphold the sharp division seen in earlier medieval works between "this world" and the traditional *vita religiosa*. The
lifestyle of the beguines had convincingly shown that the active and the
contemplative could exist side by side. To be sure, the commonplace of
exalting the monastic life can still be found. Katharina von Unterlinden, for instance, contrasts this world's darkness with the light of the
monastery (*U* 351). But in general, the stories in the Sister-Books about
the world and the monastery do not fit into a thoughtless black and
white pattern.

The world image in the Sister-Books is not a coherent one but is
composed of episodic scenes of the women's lives before they entered
the monastery. In viewing the different facets, stereotypes and "real-life"
experiences need to be distinguished – if it is, indeed, reality the authors
want to present.

THE WORLD

In the Sister-Books, the traditional reference to "this world" encompasses everything that had no place within the cloister walls. Glimpses
of ordinary street scenes as well as tales about violence are found. Of
the nine texts, the voluminous Unterlinden book best provides the
audience with extraordinary and detailed worldly episodes.

1. Religious Customs

Although an edifying or panegyric purpose typically underlies tales
about religious customs in the world, the *couleur locale* of such stories
may have equally attracted a contemporary audience. In speaking of
Adelheid von Torolzheim's early years and eager to depict her as a
child predestined for sainthood, Katharina von Unterlinden relates how
a priest is taking the viaticum to a sick person (which was a public
event for many centuries in small town Germany). In the priest's hand,
an "exceedingly beautiful youth, [his] hair curled and of brilliant golden
colour," suddenly appeared to Adelheid who, thereupon, violently pushed
the priest aside, intent on snatching the pyx out of his hand (*U* 415f.).

Another popular German tradition mentioned in the same book
refers to the blessing of common food brought into church by members
of the congregation on Easter Sunday (*U* 490f.). A less congenial
medieval custom is referred to in the Töss Sister-Book: after her

husband's death, Beli von Liebenberg, later a Töss sister, remained with his corpse in an ossuary until worms covered his body; "for he had been excommunicated [as a follower of the banned Emperor Friedrich II] and nobody dared to bury him" (*T* 30). This experience brought about Beli's conversion to monastic life, the author concludes.[1]

2. Dangers of this World
a. Fighting and Marauding

The outside world as presented in the Sister-Books was a dangerous place to be. Men, such as the sisters' fathers, brothers, or former husbands of sisters, often find themselves entangled in problems for whose solution the sisters ardently pray. Thus, Alheit von Trochau's father, for instance, had gambled away the family's fortune while on a trip to Regensburg (*E* 10). The siblings of many sisters were involved in feuds, battles, and other violent behaviour, while the nuns were concerned about these "worldly" brothers' souls (*A* 160, 169; *D* 29, 174). Two of Mechthild von Wingenheim's brothers had "set aside their fear of God and taken up robbery, homicide, and other nefarious works," Katharina von Unterlinden explains (*U* 368). Another nuns' brothers had been enemies for a long time, and she prayed "that they would not be killed through fratricide and thus die a miserable death" (*U* 392f.). A Weiler sister whose brother "was miserably slain dead" was especially saddened that God "had decreed that he should die without the Christian sacrament" (*W* 76). And Gertrud von Geiersperg's brothers, "endowed with rich goods and worldly honors, ... had been driven from their castles and lost all their possessions because they had offended the Roman king [Rudolph]" (*U* 418). Even in a clerical context, men could be subject to violence. The brother of an Adelhausen nun, "a Teutonic Knight, was innocently slain in an honest cause relating to his order"; his sister's vision later revealed him to be among the martyrs in heaven (*A* 171). Indeed, the generally bleak picture these tales give are only softened by the sisters' successful prayers on behalf of their relatives (*U* 444f.).

---

1. Adolf Franz, *Die kirchlichen Benediktionen im Mittelalter* (1st ed. Freiburg: Herder 1909; repr.: Graz: Akademische Druck-und Verlagsanstalt, 1960), 1:575–594. The custom of blessing ordinary food in church has been traced back to the seventh century and was reintroduced during the liturgical renewal of the 1920s. Pfister (1964, 287) identified Beli's husband as Heinrich von Liebenberg who died between 1238 and 1241; his remains were kept in the charnel house of Mönchaltorf. See Weinstein and Bell (1982, 110f.) regarding this legendary commonplace.

Wars were frequently fought in this world, some of them coming dangerously close to the women's monasteries – a reason why early communities, such as Unterlinden and Oetenbach, had moved back to the town to live within its protective city walls. The Diessenhofen author speaks of the menace of war (documented as a battle around 1312) when monastery property was severely damaged:[2] Margret von Fürstenberg "was greatly worried that the community would be destroyed because at that time there was a severe war in the country; therefore she was afraid that we would not be able to stay together" (D 51).

Danger also lurked from robbers and marauders sweeping the countryside. Agnes Wallaria of Unterlinden "was still in the world and married, and she owned sufficient amounts of goods and riches. And once, by God's permission, she was overcome by some powerful noblemen who damaged her possessions rather severely" (U 412). The same author, when including the following tale about the lay sister Heilrade's former life, specifically explains that there is more to such episodes than sheer entertainment value: "This is only told as a testimony of the saintliness and merit of these two people before the Lord." The story reads:

> She had been married in the years of her youth to an honest man, a resident of the village of Horburg. They were both righteous before the Lord, and all their neighbors testified to that; devoutly they did the works of mercy.
>
> Then strangers severely attacked this village one night and, being armed, they took away both people and booty. When they returned another night, they entered fully armed into the house of this man. They searched for him with burning torches and ran around everywhere, even near this man's bedroom, but by God's command they did not enter it. He and his wife were in there and called for help to the Highest with the greatest fear. After [the intruders] did not find the man by God's grace, they robbed everything they found, especially the horses, sheep, oxen, and many cows ... (U 457.2–17).

The story concludes in a happier vein meant to soften the horror: Having prayed through the night following this pillaging, the couple found at daybreak that all their cattle had been miraculously returned. Some real-life basis for parts of these tales may be assumed. Pillaging was such

---

2. Borst (1978, 289).

a routine event at this time in history that official chronicles no longer bothered to mention the episodes, Ancelet-Hustache explains.[3]

b. Vulnerability of the Individual

Women, during wars and raids, were particularly vulnerable since they were often enough considered free prey. Christine Ebner alludes to an apparently real experience of such gratuitous violence against women: During the time that Hedwig von Regensburg was a beguine, she experienced extreme distress, when "King Konrad had given his knaves power over religious women" (*E* 22). The author need not elaborate, since *Weiberhetze*, "the chasing and raping of women," has been a commonly known and routine war-time practice among soldiers.[4]

Travelling was also hazardous. The long narrative about Gertrud von Westfalen, especially "inserted" into the Unterlinden text, conveys some impression of how noble women travelled in mid-thirteenth century Germany: Wanting to join St. Dominic's Order in the Unterlinden monastery, this young woman journeyed in a carriage "from her distant home country [of Westphalia] to Colmar" in the company of her uncle.[5] For safety's sake, the party stayed close to a group of merchants, but they were still very distressed when caught one night without shelter on the dangerous road. The author then tells an entertaining miracle story, featuring among other surprises the "table prepare thyself"-episode of fairy tales, and explaining how Mary rescued the travellers (*U* 480–487). This narrative piece about the dangers of the road also functions as a fitting backdrop before which the courage of the women, who travelled on foot to the papal court, as outlined in the Sister-Books, appears even more extraordinary.

The Unterlinden author also inserts a story, here quoted in full because of its socio-historical interest, to suggest that some women "in the world" were not even safe in their own homes:

A devout virgin called Mechtild living in the suburb of Colmar had dedicated her virginity to God. A citizen of this city desired her as his lawful spouse. Therefore, one evening, surrounding himself with certain young fellows, he went armed to the house of this virgin. Having broken open the doors that late evening, he forcibly

3. Ancelet-Hustache (1930, 457, n.1).

4. Schröder (1871, 63) explains the ruler mentioned here is Konrad IV (1250–1254).

5. Ancelet-Hustache (U.1930, 482, n.1): the uncle is the Dominican Provincial Hermann von Havelberg, in office from 1251–54 and again 1260–65.

entered. He went into the girl's bedroom where she slept, and approaching her bed, he asked her and sought to convince her with promises and flattering words that she should consent to marry him. She answered she would never consent and added she would not ever marry him or anyone else. When he saw that he failed, he attacked her with threats and frightful terror and seriously threatened to kill her in order to make her marry him. He finally drew his sword out of its sheath and, putting it to the virgin's throat, he said: "If you do not consent right away, I will push this sword into your throat." But during all this, he could not force her to anything except that she assured him she would keep inviolate the vow of virginity she had taken. She would rather suffer even the cruelest death than give up the jewel of virginity. In her utter distress, the virgin then promised in order to escape death and so that this man would go away that, if ever she were to enter into marriage, she would prefer him over others. After he had heard this he got up, took his companions and disappeared. Thus this virgin preserved her vowed virginity, unshaken before the sword and the most frightful threats of the enemy.

This bad man then began untiringly to make the lies of his deceit work against the virgin and vowed that he had entered a marriage contract with her for which he called false witnesses. But the girl denied it most sharply. A judge summoned her to court. And finally the affair was brought before the [episcopal] court of Basel, and the virgin was forced to appear before the Lord Bishop in person. Her cause was here dealt with in great care. The investigation proved, with the Lord's help, that this man had no right over the virgin. Then she joyfully returned home.

The sisters of this monastery had pity on her because of her tribulations and anxiety and accepted her as a lay sister into their community (U 469.20–470.26).

This story of an attempted rape (where typically the victim becomes the accused) is told in a legendary version. The world here depicted is not the world of "pomp and luxury" but rather the milieu of a "common woman," whom the Unterlinden sisters later accepted "out of pity."[6]

---

6. I have borrowed the term "common woman" from Biller (1990, 127–157) to distinguish her from the typical monastic of noble descent. Katharina von Unterlinden specifies that Mechthild was accepted as a lay sister suggesting that she did not have the dowry required of postulants. Dowries were necessary to ensure financial security for the monasteries. The question of the dowry was not regulated

3. Women's Way of Life

a. Women's Dependency

Most stories in the Sister-Books deal with women of the upper class who, while kept dependent, were usually also protected by their kin – the exception simply proving the point. In her later years, the Unterlinden sister Sophie von Rheinfelden critically distances herself from the world of the nobility of which she had been a part: "While I was in the world, in childish naiveté, of course, I longed to be adorned in golden jewelry and to be called Lady by everyone, as noble girls are when they are handed over in marriage" (*U* 434). Her phrase, *quando nuptui tradebantur*, suggests the passive role of the noble woman. Many such references to women's dependency are contained in the Sister-Books. Parents or guardians decided whether to send a female offspring to a monastery, even "from her early childhood on" or to give her away in marriage, even if this were against her own will (*U* 378, 385, 410, 431; *T* 44). And few women were as determined and courageous as Elisabet Bechlin, later a sister of Töss, who defied her father: "When she was ten years old, she had the impression that her father wanted to give her to the world" that is, he decided to arrange a marriage for her. "Thereupon she quite boldly went to him saying, 'Father, you must know that, if you give me to the world, I will decry you on Judgment Day'" (*T* 87).

The power male family members, including siblings, had over a woman in the patriarchal society of the time is also shown with Guta von Hohenheim's example. Her brothers, the Weiler Sister-Book shows, were not sure what to do with her, but they were determined to prevent her from entering the monastery: "Sometimes they wanted to give her to the world, then again they wanted to put her into a hospital. But all this was nothing to her, for she instead would have liked to come into a cloistered monastery" (*W* 80). This passage also illustrates the limited choices available for women of nobility.[7]

---

until the Council of Trent (1545–1563). Until then, rules concerning dowry may have differed from one monastery to the next. See Thomas Mitchell Kealy, *Dowry of Women Religious: A Historical Synopsis and Commentary*, The Catholic University of America, Canon Law Studies, 134. (Washington D.C.: The Catholic University of America Press, 1941).

7. Bihlmeyer (1916, 80, n. 90) suggests that the Weiler passage could contain a reference to lay sisters in charge of the Katharinen Hospital in Esslingen since 1247.

b. Professional Women

With one notable exception, professional work for noble women, judging by the Sister-Books, seems restricted to nursing. Historically hospitals and hospice work had started to play a greater role since the twelfth century through the work of the Premonstratensian Order.[8] Beguines often earned their living through hospital work. And the Töss author explains that Adelheit von Frauenberg, while still "in the world," nursed a repulsive looking leper with great love, "for our Lord often appeared to her in the image of such people" (*T* 50; cf. *U* 425).

Only Christine Ebner writes about another profession, that of a woman musician; but she does so in a startling derogatory tone. Considering that aristocratic women instrumentalists in the contemporary courtly literature play a variety of stringed instruments, such as the harp, the rote, and the gigue, the reader finds this author's critical tone puzzling. For Alheit, later the founder of the Engeltal community, is explicitly depicted as a once shady character because of her involvement with music. Alheit, the text reads, was by profession a *rotterin* playing the stringed instrument called a rote.[9] Her background, as explained in the Engeltal Sister-Book, provides some clue to her predicament. As a companion of the Hungarian king's daughter (who became Saint Elisabeth von Thüringen, 1207–1231), the rote player Alheit had been sent from Hungary to Germany because, "with her string music, she was to comfort the child when she was crying." Having accomplished this task as a nurse, musician, and travel companion, Alheit decided to leave the courtly surroundings and settle in Nürnberg. Then the text reads: "she became a great penitent [*rewerin*][10] ... having been widely known for her sinful profession" (*E* 1).

Whereas otherwise in the Sister-Books, music is considered angelic and "divine," the cause for this performer's sin is playing worldly music

---

8. NCE 11:737; Wehrli-Johns (1986, 356f.).

9. Concerning the rote, see Gérold (1931, 184f.); Hans Hickmann, "Rotte" in *Musik in Geschichte und Gegenwart* 11 (1963) 992–995.; Hugo Steger, "Die Rotte. Studien über ein germanisches Musikinstrument." *DVJS* 35 (1961) 92–147); Keith Polk, *German Instrumental Music of the Late Middle Ages* (Cambridge: Cambridge University Press, 1992); both Steger and Polk overlook this passage in the Sister-Books in their studies of the *rotte* in medieval German literature. For women's role in Western music, see *Women Making Music* (1986, 4); Coldwell (1986, 42).

10. According to canon law, both "penitents" and beguines belonged to the *ordo de poenitentia*. See Wehrli-Johns (1990, 149f.) and Leclercq (1982a, 123) concerning the different names for beguines.

that the Church Fathers had judged a grievous sin. Indeed, the ecclesiastical authorities at that time looked at secular musicians as "servants of Satan." The accusation was based both on the minstrels' association with pagans, such as the musically skilled Saracens, and on the musicians' itinerant life which placed them outside of the ordered society the Church considered ideal. Especially women minstrels, who often painted their faces and wore colourful clothing in an attempt to resemble the Saracens, were ostracized like unrepentant prostitutes. The only exception to this outcast status, according to Edmond Faral, were minstrels, both men and women, who were hired at a noble court and thus had acquired a high and honorable position in society.[11]

Alheit's status, then, having left her steady engagement with the Hungarian royal court, dramatically changed for the worse. Degraded to the ranks of ordinary female minstrels, she was stigmatized as a sinful woman. Christine Ebner's story illustrates how easily a respectable woman could be defamed for causes beyond her control.

c. Women Rejecting Marriage

During the Middle Ages, Richard William Southern explains, "an unmarried woman was an anomaly in secular society." And although the Church had for centuries fought for a person's free consent to enter into a marriage contract, contriving a way to avoid marriage, if a woman was not so inclined, proved to be very difficult, the Sister-Books suggest.[12]

The most explicit tale about a young girl resisting marriage is again found in the Unterlinden text. Its main character, extraordinarily pious and exemplary, is Hedwig von Gundelsheim. The following novella-like insert into the Sister-Book is both of cultural and folkloric interest:

> In the village of Gundelsheim near the city of Rufach in Alsace was a family man, quite famous for his wealth, his family, and his descendants. He loved his daughter before all other children and engaged her, after she had reached marriageable age, according to worldly practice, with someone of his kind.

---

11. Faral, *Les Jongleurs en France au moyen-âge*, Bibliothèque de l'Ecole des Hautes Etudes 187 (Paris: Champion, 1910), p. 63. Concerning the status of medieval worldly musicians, see Rokseth (1935, 471, 474). Hartung (1982, 41, 61–71) cites patrological sources for the Church's view; cf. also *Das buoch der tugenden*, ed. Klaus Berg and Monika Kasper (Tübingen: Niemeyer, 1984), p. 448.

12. Southern (1970, 309); and cf. Goodich (1989, 130); Weigand (1981, 42f.). Regarding the Church policy, see Noonan (1973, 429, 431).

When the time of the wedding had arrived, the parents and relatives, both of the bridegroom and bride, came together, and the girl was led into the middle while the bridegroom stood nearby. Asked whether she agreed to marry him, she answered that she did not agree at all, adding that she was not ever to be tied in matrimony either to this or any other man. According to custom, a sword was brought where bridegroom and bride were supposed to put their thumbs to confirm the vow of marriage. However, she made a fist locking her thumb in so that nobody, even by force, could pull it out. But when some said that her entire hand would have to be placed on the sword, she showed such great resistance that [her hand] could not be pulled out or forced out of the fold [of her garment] with any man's strength.[13]

Then the parents became angry and started to hit [Hedwig] on both cheeks and to strike her mouth with fists and to pull her hair and tear her clothes. They declared that the bride had been enchanted so that she could not answer anything else. Thrown by her hair on a heap of thorns that pricked her, she was covered with blood.

While the parents were so cruelly raging against her, no word could be forced out of her except that she declared she would firmly adhere to the vow of virginity she had taken and would rather suffer the most cruel death than lose the jewel of virginity. When the bridegroom realized that the virgin persisted so firmly in her intention, he felt pity that she was punished so cruelly and resigned from the conditions of the marriage contract. Thus, those who had come together returned to their houses.

But the girl's uncle asked her father to let him have her so that perhaps with flattery, threats, or torture he could get her to agree. After having received her, he laid her across a horse, as one carries a sack to the mill. And thus he worked on her, almost a quarter of a mile, beating her back and sides so that, as a consequence of the incessant blows, blood in immeasurable amounts flowed out of the virgin's mouth and nose. Thus this dismal parricide led her into his house.

---

13. Ancelet-Hustache (1930, 374, n.1) states that these old customs were no longer practiced in Germany by the thirteenth century but may have survived longer in the Alsace. The role of the sword in marriage ceremonies and its magical power is also alluded to in O 230; see also Zeller-Werdmüller and Bächtold (1889, 231, n. 3); and *Handwörterbuch des deutschen Aberglaubens*, eds. Hanns Bächtold-Stäubli et als. (Berlin/Leipzig: de Gruyter, 1927–1942), 7:558. And see Lucas (1983, 71) on pagan wedding rituals before the Council of Trent.

More tortures from the hands of "this inhuman man, this ferocious man" continued for a long time until the young woman became seriously ill. The story then ends as follows:

> The illness increased. [The uncle] now feared he could become a parricide. He called his confessors, explained the case to them, offered retribution and asked for advice on what to do with himself and the girl in this danger. They came and assured him that those raging so inhumanly against the girl were parricides and worthy of public penance. They moreover gave the advice that if the girl escaped the danger of death and regained her previous health, she should be permitted to enter an order since they had heard how she could not be persuaded either through threats or flattery or torture to agree to marriage. This advice was heeded. When she had recovered her health she was taken to the monastery of the sisters of Unterlinden in the City of Colmar (*U* 374.11–376.16).[14]

This distressing tale follows a traditional pattern in accounts of women refusing to consent to an arranged marriage. The story material, seemingly dating from an earlier barbaric time, may even attest to late medieval torture practices. Weinstein and Bell affirm "the criminal dimension of female victimization" in cases where women were unwilling to conform, even at that time period.[15] Nor is the belief in magic that this story alludes to outdated yet, as other references to superstition in the Sister-Books suggest (*U* 361; *T* 79f.). And the Unterlinden book contains two further tales of this kind, although not as violent. Adelheid von Müntzenheim is helped in her plight by the bishop and enters the monastery (*U* 464f.). And Stephanie von Pfirt is smitten with a disfiguring illness for which she had asked in prayer and is promptly sent off to become a nun. She resided in Unterlinden for almost fifty years, suffering for the rest of her life (*U* 370). In the Oetenbach Sister-Book, the story about Ita von Hohenfels who outspokenly rejected marriage (after her first husband had died), also depicts her difficult struggle, when her friends attempted to force her to remain "in the world." In desperation, Ita took a knife, threatening to cut off her nose "in order to become repulsive to the world." Only at that point did her family and friends finally let her go (*O* 237f.).

---

14. Ancelet-Hustache (1930, 376f. n.1): Hedwig von Gundolsheim, historically documented, entered Unterlinden in 1239. She lived there, according to the text, for forty-two years, at one time holding the office of prioress (*U* 376).

15. Weinstein and Bell (1982, 97).

Besides showing the victimization of headstrong women, these tales also imply that unsightly features predetermined a woman for monastic life (cf. also *U* 423f., 436). Moreover, Ita's specific threat of self-mutilation belongs to a whole series of "various strategies [women] utilized in avoiding unwanted marriages."[16]

All the stories in the Sister-Books on rejecting marriage contain elements of heartless brutality. They are generally anchored in the tradition of early Christian legends of women who suffered horrendous martyrdom for the sake of their chastity. The most popular legend among them, the tale of St. Agnes, serves as the literary prototype for such accounts. Such legends were recopied and retold especially from the thirteenth century on. André Vauchez credits the influence of the mendicant preachers for making such *exempla* fashionable. The image of the heroic female in these stories presumably attracted the contemporary audience.[17]

d. Married Women

Once married, the woman was subject to her husband whom she had to obey or, as the Weiler Sister-Book suggests, she could incur his wrath: When Heiltraut von Bernhausen "was still in the world," she was married "to a man who impeded her a great deal in her graces and good works." On one occasion, she encountered, on her way to church, "a poor woman who asked her for alms in honor of our Lady." Since Heiltraut had nothing else with her, "she pulled a silken veil off her head and gave it to her." When her husband unexpectedly passed by and saw her, "she was very frightened, for she feared his anger." Patterned after the legend of St. Martin, the episode is given a feminine perspective, when the text further shows that Mary appeared to the husband explaining that Heiltraut had really given her scarf to "our

---

16. Schulenburg's study (1986, 46–51) on "the heroics of virginity" presents specific examples from hagiography – albeit from an earlier time period – of women's "sacrificial mutilation" for the sake of preserving their virginity. See also Dinzelbacher (1981, 260f.). Regarding children with physical deformities, see Goodich (1981, 24).

17. Vauchez (1988, 243f.). On violent legends, see Glasser (1981, 18f.); Dinzelbacher (1988b, 18f.). The cruel St. Agnes legend was attributed to St. Ambrose and added to the *Legenda aurea*, a collection that contains many other gory tales. Carlé (1980, 82) suggests that the attraction of these tales may have been the two disparate elements of the "sadistic scenes" (which at times came close to being pornographic) and the woman's successful fight (even if she had to pay with her death).

Lady" (*W* 73). According to medieval canon law, women in medieval marriages were legally subject to the whims of their husbands who were, in fact, permitted to use force. In Leclercq's delicate formulation, medieval husbands traditionally expressed toward their wives *"domination et estime."*[18]

While the Church herself had never recommended separation on any grounds, the Sister-Books feature a number of married women eager to dissolve their marriage bonds.[19] Using their narratives as *exempla*, these authors invariably imply that, in all such cases, the wish to be free was based on idealistic motives and not, for instance, on the fear of the enormous risk of numerous childbirths.

According to the Sister-Books, a woman had some options: She could devise to live in continence with her spouse in a so-called "chaste marriage" (*Josephsehe*), as told of Adelheid von Sigolzheim in Unterlinden. Having been married by her parents against her will, Adelheid contrived for twenty years "to preserve her virginity unblemished" by "staying away from her husband's bed at night" – which might explain why "her spouse hated her exceedingly," as the narrator laconically concludes (U. 473f.; cf. *W* 77).[20]

A woman's second option was to pray for her husband's death, an alternative shown in the following bizarre tale, told in her own words, about Eligenta von Sulzmatt of Unterlinden:

> "I constantly asked the Lord and Savior, when I lived in the world, to free me from the yoke of the marriage bonds in order that I could give myself to him more freely. And soon the Lord listened to the voice of my prayer. For a violent fever quickly snatched away my husband. He lived only a few days after the attack,

18. Leclercq (1981c, 104). Concerning canon law, see Goodich (1989, 130). See also Tuchman (1978, 217) regarding the brutality toward women, even among men of higher rank.

19. In his *Sermones contra Catharos*, Egbert von Schönau (†1184), for instance, defended the union between married couples which remains even after separation. See Leclercq (1981c, 106).

20. Leclercq (1981c, 107f.) explains that the chaste marriage is not only a hagiographic topos; speculative theology had argued for a long time that unconsummated love becomes more intensely spiritual. Brooke (1989, 131): the assumed chaste marriage between Mary and Joseph was widely believed in the Middle Ages to be *the* perfect marriage. See also Vauchez (1988, 442 and 1987, 203–209); Goodich (1989, 129f.). Kieckhefer (1984, 142f.) lists further examples from fourteenth-century hagiography.

piously received the Church's sacraments and departed from his body (*U* 455.37–456.6).

Similarly the Töss author explains that Adelheid von Frauenberg prayed to become a nun without, however, directly asking God for her husband's death. And the text continues: "Our Lord wanted ... to fulfill her desire and decreed that her husband should die" (*T* 50). There is no suggestion that the authors were flippant about husbands. These *exempla* simply teach that divine help was available for women to reach the goal of monastic life. Even in medieval canonization documents, Vauchez quotes, the death of a woman's spouse is referred to as "*une véritable libération*" which permitted the widow to enter a monastery.[21]

A wife could also choose to come to an agreement with her husband to separate, as is told of several women who later became members of monastic communities (*O* 231f.). The following example in the Unterlinden Sister-Book concerns "the most brilliant pillar of exceeding saintliness," as the author hyperbolically claims: "What was even more excellent and magnificent was the fact that, in order to enter the monastery of Unterlinden of St. Dominic's Order," Adelheid von Rheinfelden "left her young spouse, a warrior also very famous in worldly affairs, and her two small children." When her husband later decided to join the Order of Preachers as well, "he had left at home under the care of a wet nurse his two small children, a son and a daughter, who had outgrown their infancy." The story goes on to explain that the son died soon after his father's departure and that the daughter joined her mother in the monastery at a very young age (*U* 394f.).

This matter-of-fact account of the children's fate stands in contrast to a similar but more emotional story in the same Unterlinden text;[22] for, generally, the Sister-Books corroborate Weinstein's and Bell's conclusion that hagiographic accounts rarely suggest medieval parents were indifferent to their children:[23]

Then, divinely inspired, [Rinlinda von Biseck] left her husband, a noble warrior, distinguished and mighty in the world, excelling in

---

21. Vauchez (1988, 444). Concerning a husband's death, see also Atkinson (1983, 140).

22. The casual account of the son's death must be understood within a context of high infant mortality at that time and of death seen as a transition to real life. It could also be a literary device, Tuchman (1978, 49) observes: "in literature the chief role of children was to die."

23. Weinstein and Bell (1982, 242).

charm and beauty, and the eight children she had borne him, who were equally beautiful and in a young and tender age.

Although "she loved both her children and her spouse with highest loving affection more than her life, so that they were more to her than her health, pleasure and light," she did all this "for the sake of the Savior" because "the love of God in her heart could, in spite of all these emotions, not be diminished in its all-surpassing strength." Therefore, "she steadfastly bid goodbye to them and, covered with tears, commended them to almighty God. She herself died to the world completely and started to live happily for the Lord in this happy community."

Later her husband, "a magnificent man," also left "the pomp and luxury of the world" and entered "the venerable Order of the Teutonic Knights with his two young sons." Their six daughters were given to different Dominican monasteries. "The pious and saintly mother who had separated herself from the sweet company of her children and spouse kept only two daughters with her as a consolation" (*U* 460. 8–461. 5; cf. *U* 430; *A* 164). Rinlinda, then, strongly attached to an ideal husband and her children, abandons her family even though it tears her apart emotionally. "The anguish of leaving the world" after a conversion, Weinstein and Bell explain, is a commonplace in hagiography.[24]

There are further examples in the Sister-Books of women separating from their husbands and both spouses joining monastic communities (*A* 160; *E* 10, 15; *D* 33). In one instance only do we find the twist of a separated husband later regretting his decision. But even this story comes to its exemplary conclusion: Agnes' husband, Burchard von Wangen, "came to our homestead and became our chaplain, *únser caplän*, and lived quite virtuously until his death" (D. no. 35).[25]

The authors of the Sister-Books in some instances, then, implicitly depict marriage as the lesser good because it is "lost time voluptuously spent in the world" (*T* 56). However, these women also point out that marriage (recognized as one of the seven sacraments since the twelfth century) could equally provide a chance for a good, even a laudable life (*U* 428; *T* 28). Especially a passage in the Gotteszell Sister-Book speaks eloquently of the intrinsic value of married life:[26]

Sister Irmendraut [of Gotteszell] had been rich in the world, living so humbly and devoutly that everyone around her was improved

24. For conversion patterns, see Weinstein and Bell (1982, 101).

25. Borst (1978, 292) documents this chaplain in Diessenhofen for around 1260.

26. On marriage as a sacrament, see LThK 3:681; Emile Schmitt, *Le Mariage chrétien dans l'oeuvre de Saint Augustin* (Paris: Etudes Augustiniennes, 1983).

by her. And among other things, prayer seldom left her mouth; she also steadily pursued holy meditation. She freely gave alms; and she fled all the joy and frills of the world. She led this blessed life with her husband. And it often happened [to her] that God granted her great graces and she received divine consolation while her husband was sleeping with her in bed, *so ir wirdt bey ir an pette sliff* (G 134. 43–135.3; cf. *U* 481).

The author further explains that Irmendraut cared for lepers in her spare time, consoled the sick, frequently attended homilies given in her city – and all this with the blessings of her husband. Only as a widow did she join the Gotteszell monastery.

Marriage, this *exemplum* shows, can be wholesome and spiritual, for Irmendraut lived her saintly life not in spite of being married but in unison with her husband. And the text is quite explicit: even marital intercourse did not interfere with "divine consolation." Such affirmation of sex in marriage is rare in earlier medieval religious literature; it reflects, as James A. Brundage shows, "noteworthy changes in social attitudes toward both sexuality and emotional bonding" in the later Middle Ages, presumably as a reaction against heretical views that marriage was evil. The Sister-Books thus stand in the forefront of a new hagiographic trend begun in the thirteenth century.[27]

Stories about married women in the Sister-Books, then, fall into two categories. There are women who had to accept marriage but, once married, their only interest lies in avoiding their husbands. Most women eventually convince their spouses to adopt the ideal of a chaste

---

27. Brundage (1990, 71). Both Hugh of St. Victor (†1141) (PL 176, esp. cols. 479ff., 494) and Thomas Aquinas (STh Suppl. q.42 a.3) maintain that marriage was a sacrament and grace-giving. Weigand (1981, 51–54), however, is unable to locate any text among twelfth-century decretists that judges marital intercourse as completely free from sin; cf. also Katharine M. Rogers, "Medieval Attitudes Toward Love and Marriage," in her *The Troublesome Helpmate. A History of Misogyny in Literature* (Seattle: Washington University Press, 1966), esp. pp. 65–77; Leclercq (1981c, 102–115); Katharina M. Wilson and Elizabeth M. Makowski, *Wykked wyves and the Woes of Marriage. Misogamous Literature from Juvenal to Chaucer*, SUNY Series (Albany: New York State University Press, 1990), esp. pp. 61–121. On the medieval Church's attitude to marriage, see further McLaughlin (1974, 222–226); Dinzelbacher (1987, 236); Vauchez (1988, 442f.); Atkinson (1991, 153). Regarding the positive, even pastoral influence especially of married women on their spouses, of which the confessors were encouraged to take advantage, see Leclercq (1990, 87–97). For the views of the Cathars and Albigensians on marriage, see Glasser (1981, 20ff.).

marriage. Other women are depicted as exemplary wives and mothers equally succumbing to the appeal of a monastic vocation, who, although in great emotional pain, give up their worldly happiness. But while second in rank, marriage and parenthood are reflected in a positive light.

Notably, the Sister-Books also present a balanced view of the male partners. Husbands are mostly seen as reliable and affectionate and even as caring fathers. As Karen Glente shows, husbands in contemporary *vitae* written by clergymen are not treated that well. This fair view of men by the authors of the Sister-Books, therefore, might be particularly characteristic for medieval women writers.[28]

THE CLOISTER

Stepping beyond the stereotypical image of the soft worldly life versus the ascetic life inside the cloister, the Töss author contrasts the "you" of the monastic audience with "them" who live outside, explaining that the monastics really live a pampered life:

> God has decreed and put you into this life. There you have everything without any worry: You have good company – they do not; you always have good learning and teaching – they do not; nobody lays snares for you – they do not have this. They fight with each other, and one wants to get ahead of the other – you have your bodily needs taken care of without any worry. Everything is being prepared for you – they do not have this. You have God, if you want to – they do not: he is quite unknown to them, for one induces another one to sin (*T* 78.13–19).

But while life in the world is still likely to be sinful, the Adelhausen author also offers a sober reminder, as Wilms formulates it, that "the ideal of Christian perfection is not only attainable in the monastery": "You shall not think," Anna von Munzingen writes, "that you have been a spiritual human being only since you put on the religious habit"; rather, as far as she is concerned, "a spiritual human being" is someone who has "a desire for spiritual life," no matter where she is (*A* 164).[29]

Writing about women who question their chosen way of life, Christine Ebner includes the following dialogue:

---

28. Glente (1988b, esp. 260–264) explains that Thomas of Chantimpré, for instance, shows husbands mostly in a negative light, depicting them as rivals of Christ.

29. Wilms (1923, 25).

> After [Elsbeth von Sehsenham] had been in the monastery for some time, our Lord said to her: "Elsbeth, why have you come into this exile?" Then she said: "Lord, for the sake of your will." Then he said again: "Elsbeth, why have you come into this exile?" Then she replied: "Lord, so that I could be all the closer to you." Then he said: "You are never closer to me than in the monastery" (*E* 28.33–29.3).

This is the allure of life in the monastery. The MHG *ellende* ("exile"), used twice in this quotation, has the connotation of "being away from home, in a foreign land" but is here reversed to mean being close to God. The Lord's three-fold challenge in this scene follows the pattern of Jesus repeatedly confronting Peter [Jn. 21:15–17].

On their chosen monastic path, the women are encouraged to cut themselves off completely from the life they left behind to include their relatives. Else von der Neustatt of the Adelhausen monastery interprets this stiff exhortation [cf. Ps. 44:11] saying God would not tolerate any relatives since he demanded her entire heart for himself (*A* 181).[30] She accurately defines the medieval monastics' attitude; the gospel admonition that a disciple of Christ had to "hate his father, mother," and all relatives [Lk.14:26] was taken literally. Thus, when "the child" Elsbetlein in the Gotteszell monastery feels lonesome for her mother, who lived only "six miles away from the monastery" and whom she had not heard from "in three years," she hears "an answer being given to her" suggesting she overcome her worries in a spiritual way (*G* 141). The Weiler author illustrates the dilemma experienced by Heiltraut von Bernhausen whose sister had come to the monastery for a visit: Heiltraut was so glad that she said: "Lucky me, my heart-beloved one has come." But then she immediately added: "Oh, but then my heart-beloved Lord will leave me!" Thereupon "her distress and pain became so great that her heart was jolted and broke her rib so that all those around her heard it with their ears." This fracture is said to have stayed with her until her death (*W* 74). The reader is left to assume that the two siblings never got together. The author's lesson simply conveys the inner struggle caused by the demands of "the world" that a monastic needs to overcome.[31]

The following points raised about the monastic way of life are strictly limited to the Sister-Books. But since the authors had no inten-

---

30. Benz (1969, 53) speaks in a similar context of the *Heilsegoismus* of the saintly, today no longer understood as signs of saintliness but as selfish inconsiderateness.

31. The detail of the rib fractured through emotion is a motif in Grimm's fairy tale "The Frog Prince."

tion of depicting their day-by-day routine (knowledge of which they presupposed), aspects of their everyday life can only be glimpsed. The monastic rules and customs, a community's poverty and hardship, personal difficulties and problems behind the cloister walls are aspects of their monastic existence that serve generally only as a backdrop. Praiseworthy features of the ideal monastic life and special accomplishments of individual saintly women thereby gain a sharper profile. Intending to present the spiritual high points of their community life, the authors simultaneously permit us to read between the lines and thus gain a fuller picture.[32]

1. A Community's Composition

In addition to women separated from their husbands, women's monasteries traditionally counted a number of widows among their members. Many of them used to be, as is said of Beli von Liebenberg, *gar ain weltliche frow*, "quite a worldly woman," who simply sought refuge in a monastery (*T* 29; cf. *T* 17, 20; *U* 347, 350f.). Simultaneously, widows often brought a rich inheritance, thereby significantly contributing to the community's well-being (*U* 428, 467). Katharina von Unterlinden explains that, after her husband had died, Adelheid von Sigolzheim "hurried to Colmar calling on this monastery's prioress and offered her and all the sisters all movable and immovable possessions she had, giving it away for eternity, simply and unconditionally for the love of the Lord and Savior." But this noble woman also "humbly and pressingly begged to be received into the monastery as a servant in the kitchen" for the rest of her life, rather than be a choir sister. The author continues the *exemplum* stating that Adelheid even "ate together with the servants and always wore cheap and used clothing," because "she chose rather to be despicable here in order to be radiant in the highest glory with the Lord in heaven" (*U* 474f.).

Not all the widows, however, followed a vocation. Anna von Munzingen writes that in Adelhausen "there was an old widow called Sister Edelkint die Kuglerin"; this woman "had no taste for spiritual life, and she thought it very strange when the sisters were thus in their prayers

---

32. Claudia Opitz calls this method *"gegen den Strich lesen"* which she practices in her *Frauenalltag im Mittelalter. Biographien des 13. und 14. Jahrhunderts*, Frauenforschung 5 (Weinheim and Basel: Beltz, 1987). For a thorough account of late medieval women's monastic life (in England), see Eileen Power, *Medieval English Nunneries, ca. 1275–1535* (1st ed. Cambridge: University Press, 1922; repr. New York: Biblo & Tannen, 1964); see also Power's *Medieval People*, 1st ed. 1924 (Garden City, NY: Doubleday Anchor, 1954), pp. 73–97, and Parisse (1983).

and devotion." Her attitude changed when a light vision converted her (*A* 160). In many cases widows, due to their life experiences, become especially strong and active members of the monastic community.

It was also typical, within any monastic community, that some women were related to each other. Some siblings entered the community together as adults; others were brought as children when their mothers took the veil. The Engeltal author talks about the "faithful servant of God for about eighty years," Kunigund von Vilsek, who was the daughter of their saintly Chaplain Ulschalk, and who was even "honored by the pope himself" (*E* 3, 38). And Christine Ebner's own aunt, Sister Diemut Ebnerin von Nürnberg, treated "her brother's daughter" as her confidante (*E* 34).

Female children, furthermore, were an essential part of a medieval women's community. Some sisters entered the monastery at the age of three (*T* 48; *O* 234) and seven, eight, or nine (*A* 183; *K* 105, 109, 118), others around ten (*A* 172; *E* 24; cf. *D* 41; *W* 68; *U* 431). Many girls were oblated as infants in spite of an official, but rather vague ruling against admitting children. Seated separately at mealtime and occasionally joined at their table by old sisters, the children, too, had to eat in silence (*E* 8; *T* 34). When Adelheit von Frauenberg entered the Töss community, she handed her child to the novice mistress and tried not to worry about her. But "often she was very pained" when she heard that the novice mistress beat her daughter (*T* 51). Beating children was presumably not uncommon in a monastery. And while there is no reference to other beatings in the Sister-Books, Humbert of Romans even recommends severe whipping as a punishment for a nun's grave faults. These are again reminders that one must take into account the different mentality of an era far removed from ours.[33]

At a time when the average age of the population was very low, some of the nuns are said to have lived to a ripe old age, even by today's standards (*K* 111, 112). The authors speak of sisters dying at one hundred (*A* 176; *T* 85) and being around ninety (*T* 94). Else von der Neustatt reportedly spent seventy years in the Adelhausen community

---

33. Concerning whipping, see Humbert (1259, ch.20); and regarding the rule against admitting children, see Humbert of Romans (1259, ch.14); see also René Metz, *La Femme et l'enfant dans le droit canonique médiéval*, repr. (London: Variorum, 1985). Hale (1992, 166) found that in the Books of Sisters 58 out of 219 cases she studied were sisters who entered the community before the age of twelve.

(*A* 177). Of course, such longevity is presented as the noteworthy exception granted to saintly sisters.[34]

Membership in these Dominican monasteries was also granted to the so-called *fratres conversi* or lay brothers. *Conversi*, documented as early as the 1240s and 1250s, lived as part of the women's communities, pledged obedience to the prioress, and "served each of them as if their hired servant," as Christine Ebner says of one (*E* 2; *U* 403f.). The authors of the Sister-Books speak of these *conversi* in laudatory terms: he was "an upright and faithful brother to whom we are indebted in all good things, called Brother Bertholt der Mezier," states the Diessenhofen chronicler (*D* "Gründungsgeschichte"). In Engeltal a former Teutonic Knight served the nuns as a *dinstman* (*E* 4; cf. *E* 5, 6). The story about Brother Rüdiger in this same monastery, who was killed in an ugly feud with "an evil-doing man," ends with the assurance that he was so saintly that his grave "has since smelled like spices," *als ein aptek* (*E* 37).[35]

The picture generally conveyed in the Sister-Books is that of a large community of sisters of all ages and from different backgrounds. Ideally, the audience is to understand, individual characteristics faded before the uppermost goal of building a common monastic life. But while personal differences were evened out, secular class distinctions were typically upheld also within the cloister.

2. Social Ranking

Many entries in the Sister-Books start with the assertion that the sisters were of noble family background or related to the founder. The communities counted both free-born and noble women and daughters of burghers of the surrounding towns in their midst (*U* 336, 369, 394, 434, 460; *T* 17; *E* 16, 26, 37).[36] The Engeltal author specifies that one of

34. For low life expectancy, see Tuchman (1978, 52). Petroff (1979, 41), commenting on the "longer life span" of nuns, explains that "religious women were the only women who, regularly, lived beyond middle age" because they were not exposed to the contemporary health hazard of numerous child births.

35. For the institution of the *conversi* in Germany, see Krauss (1894, 302); Creytens (1949, 1–36). Concerning lay brothers in Dominican men's monasteries, see Decker (1935, 95). Müller (1971, 48) explains a community usually employed between four and ten *conversi* during the thirteenth and fourteenth centuries; the institution came to an end between 1480 and 1500.

36. For the identification of a number of the names in the Sister-Books, see the editors and/or historians and critics: Vetter (1906), for the Töss book; Bihlmeyer (1916, 87) and Uhrle (1968, 34) for the Weiler text; Ancelet-Hustache (1930) and Grundmann (1935, 193f.) for Unterlinden; Kunze (1952, 14) for Adelhausen; Halter (1956, 55f.) for

the women came directly "from the court of the Count von Hirsch-berg" and that another was familiar with courtly etiquette (*E* 21, 25). Editors and critics have routinely scoured archives as to the names and family backgrounds of the women mentioned in these texts. Indeed, his-torically speaking, Ernest W. McDonnell explains, "Medieval nunneries admitted only the titled and women of property – they were aristo-cratic institutions."[37]

Often archival searches also prove fruitless because the saint of noble descent had become a legendary stereotype which stated that no-bility by birth was typically overshadowed by a sister's acquired noble behaviour. It was thus clearly to the authors' advantage to portray these women as coming from the ranks of the nobility or otherwise powerful families. In speaking about Agnes von Herkenheim, Katharina von Unterlinden explains: "she was of noble origin, but still much nobler in faith and virtues," *nobilis progenie sed fide et uirtutibus nobilior* (*U* 384f.).[38] Subliminally, though, nobility of birth was still considered preferable (*U* 419, 422). The Töss author offers an elaborate example of this topos: Ite von Wezzikon, of "noble descent" and with "a very ten-der body," resented everything about the monastic life before entering cloistered life. She would "rather have suffered her head to be cut off than come into the monastery." When she later subdued her aversion "with God's help" and joined the community, the cliché reads: "the more tenderly she had lived in the world, the more severely she now lived in the monastery" (*T* 17). Similarly, Elisabeth von Rufach in Unterlinden learned "to despise all the pomp and voluptuousness of the world":

> The more she had led a delicate pleasurable life in the world, the more completely she despised and degraded herself in everything. On some days, she washed the dishes and kitchen pots with her

---

Oetenbach; Voit (1958, 10ff.) for Engeltal; Krauss (1894, 298f.) and Müller (1977/78, 48ff.) for Kirchberg and Gotteszell; Meyer (1991, 29ff.) for Diessenhofen.

37. McDonnell (1969, 89). Some women's monasteries in the history of the Preachers' Order consisted exclusively of women of high nobility, see Fontette (1967, 106); see also Ancelet-Hustache (1960, 154). Anneliese Müller (1971, 28ff., esp. 37) found for Diessenhofen that for the time between the thirteenth and sixteenth centuries the women had come predominantly from the nobility bringing along land holdings as their dowry.

38. Vauchez (1988, 204) explains that this "ambiguous" commonplace had developed from the eleventh century on after the hierarchy had become aware of "une véritable hagiocratie" in the church and then started to emphasize nobility of behavior.

own hands in the company of the servants and helped them diligently in all their work. She enjoyed herself in these kinds of tasks as if [she were living] in all riches (*U* 467.8–13).

This reversed rags-to-riches topos stands in strange contrast to the authors' repeated references to the personal live-in maids of some wealthy sisters (*U* 397; *G* 123, 146; *E* 17). But although such disregard for the ideal of voluntary poverty became a real issue during the decline of the monastic ideal in the late fourteenth and the fifteenth centuries, at the time the Sister-Books were composed, the privilege of keeping a personal servant was apparently not considered a problem.

The class system in society was normally accepted as God-given and therefore also reflected in the monastic communities. Passages already quoted, such as about the girl who narrowly escaped rape having been accepted as a lay sister (U. 469f.) and about the widow in Unterlinden disregarding the social ranking by insisting on being a servant (U. 474f.), suggest some such divisions. And the Töss author at times betrays, with a reverential attitude toward "the blessed and virtuous Countess Sister Adelheit von Nellenburg" (T. 93) that her class consciousness had not changed behind the cloister walls. Even the prioress was set apart in this rigid hierarchical order; for Anna von Selden in Adelhausen is praised for the special virtue of eating with the sisters (*A* 154). Historical documents show that the sharp class distinctions were eventually moderated, especially in the Order of Preachers, after a papal edict issued in 1285 forbade social ranking within monasteries.[39]

Communities were also divided into choir sisters and lay sisters, the latter usually illiterate and not obliged to regularly participate in the Divine Office. The number of lay sisters who routinely did the enormous amount of work in the monastery itself depended on the needs of a community (*T* 83). Outside work was normally taken care of by the lay brothers. It was seen as a sign of extreme poverty when choir sisters had to do the work of servants, as a telling passage on the early days of the Engeltal monastery suggests: "God then put them on trial as gold is probed in the fire. And they had to do heavy work and had

---

39. Historians explain that, with later acquisitions of land and other property, the monasteries even obtained bondsmen and bondswomen or serfs (*Eigenleute* or *Leibeigene*) documented as of 1274; see Däniker-Gysin (1958, 43f.); Heer (1947, 11); Krauss (1894, 308). Many medieval visionaries even transposed social ranks into a "feudal heaven," see Dinzelbacher (1979a, 35f.). For the changes after 1285, see Noffke (1990, 59); Vauchez (1988, 243f.).

to harvest their own wheat and wash and bake and do all servile work"
(*E* 3). While praising the nuns' humility, the author's message that such
lowly chores were beneath the choir sisters' calling is unmistakable, an
attitude typically shared by her contemporaries.[40]

In the Adelhausen Sister-Book, a different rank does not prevent the
choir nun Gisel von Unkilch and the lay sister Metze to trust in each
other. When Metze entered the herb garden, Gisel pulled her down
onto the grass, thinking that God had sent her because she desperately
needed to talk to someone in order "to cool off" [*erküelen*]. And they
talked from None until the bell rang for Vespers, even breaking the
rule of silence (*A* 165). However, when the Töss author, speaking to
the question of social ranks, insists that choir sisters and lay sisters were
not different in the eyes of God, we sense that perhaps there was a
special need for making this point:

> The good God also explicitly showed that he does not only want
> to reside with those whom he made join the order so that we
> should give ourselves only to inner spiritual things. He also showed
> himself loving to those sisters whom he made join the order so that
> they should faithfully serve the community (*T* 79.13–16).

Notably, the author teaches a fair attitude while explicitly placing
herself among the choir sisters.

3. Friendships
Confidential relationships between members of a monastic community
were fully accepted in medieval monastic life. As does Aelred of
Rievaulx's twelfth-century treatment on *Spiritual Friendship*, the Sister-
Books represent a rich source of information about monastic women's
friendships (*U* 393; *T* 39, 47, 55). The authors go as far as stating that
someone without a personal friend was to be pitied, for "she had
nobody special who could have consoled her or helped her" (*A* 174; *T*
48, 61, 90, 91, 94). They echo Aelred's words (based on Cicero) that
"without friends absolutely no life can be happy."[41]

---

40. Hildegard von Bingen (1098–1179), in a letter to the Magistra Tengswich,
justifies the class distinction within the monastic community: "Who collects his
entire herd of cattle, oxen, donkeys, sheep, and rams, into the same barn without
their running apart? Therefore, also here a distinction must be kept" (PL 197: 338).
For the number of lay sisters, see Hinnebusch (1966, 383).

41. Aelred (1977, 110). On friendship among nuns, see also Hale (1989); Acklin
Zimmermann (1993, 29f.).

Many women are singled out for having experienced a true bond of friendship (*U* 391, 393). Two Adelhausen sisters even called each other by their first names (*A* 155), an expression of extraordinary familiarity within German culture and within the monastic community in particular. (The Töss author, in contrast, presents it as a special virtue to call the sisters in community with the title "Sister" preceding their name, as Elsbet Schefflin did, even when addressing her own sibling, *T* 23). A personal friend, a *familiarissima*, usually became the first to be told of a religious experience (*U* 404, 450, 471; *A* 154f., 160). And Aelred's claim that "Prayer ..., coming from a friend, is the more efficacious in proportion, as it is more lovingly sent to God," is exemplified by two Engeltal women: they pray together and for each other, have visions about each other, and speak of special graces each one received; in short, they encourage each other in their spiritual pursuit (*E* 18). Exceptionally, as is said of Eligenta von Sulzmatt and her special friend in Unterlinden, on certain days friends even chastise each other (*U* 453). These authors understand well that friendships meet the psychological need for sharing one's experiences and insights with another human being (*A* 173, 181). Such intimacy also enhances the communal spirit, as friends are united in celebrating the monastic liturgy.[42]

Personal friends are referred to as "special" (*G* 131: *sunderliche freunde*, *E* 18: *freundin*), as "consolers" (*G* 133: *ir trösterin*), or as *gespilen*, "playmates" (*G* 137, *E* 18). And a close friend of Adelheit in Gotteszell was in great distress, ill-humoured and heartsick, after Adelheit had died, "because she no longer had anybody with whom she could sincerely lament" (*G* 133), which is presumably a reference to the "lamenting and crying in this vale of tears," as formulated in the *Salve regina*.

In general, the Sister-Books convey the impression that the women found pleasure in their communal living and enjoyed each other's company; they loved and respected, and even revered each other, and they were available for each other(*U* 342, 388). Of Mechthild die Ritterin, for instance, the Diessenhofen author writes: "She had exceptionally the virtue of common love which she practiced all the time. And whenever a sister needed her, she was always, night or day, ready [to help] in any way she could" (*D* 42).

The sisters are described as compassionate, as exemplified by Adelheit von Holderberg who was torn between keeping her usual silence or talking with a novice whose sadness she had noticed: "Then she was given to understand that it was our Lord's will that she should speak.

---

42. Aelred of Rievaulx (1977, 131). The *Speculum virginum* required that sisters address each other as "Sister", "Domina," or "Mater," see Bernards (1982, 139).

Then she took the novice and sat in the chapter room with her and asked her what was wrong." When the novice confided in her, Adelheid "spoke so mildly and benignly with her that she consoled her in her heart" (*D* 19, 29). Charity is more essential than remaining collected and silent, as the rule demands.

A separation from such a closely knit community, as was often required during an illness, was hard on any sister (*A* 167). But even then, the community supported the individual, stood by her in severe illness, actively helping and encouraging her, while equally sharing her fears and joy (*G* 132f.).

Friendship among these women also brings out a lighter side of the otherwise austere cloistered life. During recreation time, when the strict periods of silence are interrupted (in the common room around the stove in winter, in the orchard in summer), the sisters are eager to talk with each other (*U* 440; *T* 14). Some of them spoke of God so well that everyone was eager to listen (*T* 34); others, we learn, passed along gossip, *hinterred* (*T* 23). In this context, Katharina von Unterlinden wisely instructs her readers to make a conscious effort to live in "peace with all" (*U* 453), while simultaneously pointing out how essential it is in community living to guard one's tongue (*U* 411). It was also at recreation time that the novices got a chance to try a practical joke on the pious old Sister Margret Willin in Töss. This woman had "disciplined herself" all her life "by never looking out of a window." The young sisters, therefore, "sometimes tempted her by pretending they saw a miracle"; but even then "she never turned her eyes" toward the window (*T* 27). The tone with which the author uses *wunder*, "miracle," in this passage suggests a certain irreverence on the part of the monastery's youth.

Humourous passages in the Sister-Books were presumably not planned; and, of course, it is most unlikely that episodes we find funny today were meant to be witty. But there is a familiar tone noticeable here and there in the text. One Unterlinden sister is specifically singled out for her good sense of humour (*U* 376). In Töss, Elsbet von Cellikon calls herself "an old stick" (*T* 93). And of the noble Sister Ita von Wezzikon it is said "that she eagerly sang everything she knew although she did not sing well" (*T* 18). Especially the anecdote told of Anna von Klingnau may have been a favourite one among the contemporary audience: Anna loved to talk about God and got so carried away in discussion with another sister one winter's day that, when wanting to get up, she discovered that her garment had frozen to the garden bench (*T* 37).

But then again, the authors who write so positively about good friendships and companionship inevitably feel the need to warn their audience against giving too much attention to friends. Normally, friends must come second after the rules of the order (*E* 20). And in Adelhausen, Else von der Neustatt tells another sister: "I have seen that God looked at you angrily for you were too busy with your friends" (*A* 181; cf. *U* 427). To deprive oneself consciously of friendship for ascetic reasons is indeed admired (*T* 26, 41f., 69), as is the deliberate decision not ever to receive visitors at the gate (*T* 23, 91). But when such a step was taken, as in the case of the Diessenhofen sister Gerdrut von Herblingen, the author sympathizes with her because of the unhappy consequences of her decision; for Gerdrut remained "a poor, miserable ["exiled"] human being until her death," *ein armes ellend mentsche untz an ir tod* (*D* 30).

4. The Daily Routine

The important parts of the nuns' daily routine, their liturgical services and their manual work, are given much room in the Sister-Books. But for their surroundings, their clothing, and their meals, the reader relies on only sparse casual remarks.[43]

The monastery complex was by necessity relatively large to accommodate the great number of community members housed there at any time. The church choir, where each sister had her special place, was usually big enough, although occasionally severe overcrowding is mentioned (*U* 461; *T* 20). It had to hold the two choirs of sisters that alternated in singing the psalm verses (*U* 437). The monastery churches of Töss, Oetenbach, and Diessenhofen are known to have had a choir area so large that it exceeded the nave in length.[44]

The dormitory and cells, certainly in Unterlinden, were without light, for the sickroom is mentioned as the rare place with a "lighted lamp" (*U* 378, 447, 467). Nor were many rooms heated (*U* 440). Of one Töss sister it is told that she was so "badly cold," *sy übel fror*, that she warmed her feet in the hot ashes of the fireplace in the common room (*T* 51).

Details of the sisters' habits are barely mentioned in the Sister-Books. The Primitive Constitution suggested that the clothing "should

---

43. A "Book of Rules" (*Regelbuch*) of the Weiler monastery is extant for a later period; it contains minute details of the nuns' daily routine (Uhrle 1968, 59ff.).
44. Pfister (1964, 289).

be white, but not too fine or dainty a material"; each religious was to "have two tunics and two coarse undergarments" as well as "two mantles if the monastery allows it, one of which is lined with wool, a scapular, necessary shoes and stockings, and two veils."[45] As the Gotteszell Sister-Book reveals, there were nuns who apparently only had one garment all their life (G 140). And Katharina von Unterlinden speaks of the peculiar habit of Benedicta von Mühlhausen, seen as a special virtue: she "avoided putting on new veils and freshly washed white outer garments" during the day for work, presumably reserving them instead for "the time of the nightly Matins" (U 349). She also praises Adelheid von Rheinfelden's self-discipline because Adelheid "avoided reporting it to her servant if after Compline something was missing in her habit or headgear; she rather suffered, for God's sake, a severe deprivation than break by only one word the silence imposed at that hour" (U 397). Wearing the monastic habit properly has a highly symbolic significance for the nuns.

Only scant information about the nuns' nutrition can be found. The meals are taken with the community in the large refectory (T 18, 34). The Unterlinden author, praising the modest appetite of Agnes von Ochsenstein, mentions some food items: "Eating very dry barley bread, she rejected the white bread offered to her. Of apples, nuts, and other similar fruits, she never wanted to eat even a little" (U 355). She also mentions cabbage; and of the community's early days, Katharina von Unterlinden says, "one rarely saw eggs and even more rarely fish" (U 434). There were sisters who asked for special food or bought extra supplies (T 51, 91); for the daily menu was always simple, not only at the times of great deprivations (T 89). Sometimes the menu was enhanced by donations of food from outside the monastery (T 60; O 229f.). Children were occasionally bought extra sweets (T 90f.). And while wine had been, ever since St. Benedict's time, the usual monastic beverage, it apparently was served only rarely in some of these women's monasteries (T 40). Elsbet von Cellinkon is quoted saying that she "never bought any other wine but what the community drank" (T 91), a statement that suggests that other sisters at Töss might have added some wine of their own.[46]

An episode in Diessenhofen permits a glimpse into contemporary eating habits: One of the sisters had a vision during the communal meal

45. *The Primitive Constitution* (1969, 10).
46. About meals in medieval monasteries in general, see Zimmermann (1973, 38–61).

and was interrupted so that the vision ended when her neighbor "took the knife that lay before her." When the incident was brought "before the prioress, she then permitted each sister to carry a knife; for until then," the author adds, "we did not have individual but communal table knives" (D 27a). In Unterlinden, each sister is said to have carried a knife on her belt which she used at mealtime (U. 349).[47]

a. Liturgy

The sisters' communal worship dominated their daily life. "If the Liturgy were removed there would no longer be a Dominican Order," states Vernet.[48] No other activity of a monastic took up as much time and effort as the Divine Office. Days and nights were strictly regulated through the Canonical Hours, *die siben zeit in dem tag*, and all other work rotated around this divine service. Nor was a monastic's other work to be understood as apart from liturgy. For liturgy, properly lived as a public service to God, encompassed the entire life of the sisters. As had been the case in the centuries-old monastic tradition, the meticulously regulated daily routine helped these women in maintaining order and stability.

The observance of the Canonical Hours was considered more important than any "special graces" (K 110; U 398). Announced by a repeated ringing of bells, the Divine Office assembled the choir sisters in their stalls in the church starting with Matins at midnight (K 107, 109; U 436). In their Constitution, the nuns' gestures and posture during these services were strictly regulated. Rubrics guided them with such details as standing, genuflecting, and prostrating themselves. The Diessenhofen sister Diemut von Lindau is singled out for complying with such directions: For "around thirty years," this nun

> never sat down in choir, except at the times when she was supposed to sit according to the rules. And yet she was quite steadily present in choir, except at the times when through obedience she was to be at other places. When she was in choir, she either knelt or stood or again prostrated herself in honor of the presence of our Lord. And in these thirty years, during mass and the Divine Offices, she steadily had her hands raised up to God under her mantle. And she stood in great devotion at all times (D 31).

47. Ancelet-Hustache (1930, 349, n.1) speaks of this knife as "*une partie import-ante du vêtement féminin à l'époque de nos moniales.*"

48. Vernet (1930, 54).

The raising of hands [Ps.28:2], also found in contemporary paintings, was considered a sign of special devotion.[49] Again, a miracle related by the Weiler author makes the point that the sisters' deportment during liturgical services was designed to absorb both mind and body in the divine service:

> Once [Mechthilt von Hundersingen] was so ill on the Feast of Our Lady's Annunciation that she had to be carried to the choir where she sat on pillows. And when during the antiphon *Haec est dies*, the words were sung *Hodie Deus homo factus*, she felt such a strong force that she lifted herself up without any help and stood on her feet, and bowed down deep toward the ground, thus thanking our Lord with heart and body ... (*W* 71.17–22).

Among the different offices, the nightly Matins (*mette*, usually combined with Lauds) was the most demanding one (*T* 21, 61). Prime was the first day-time service in the early morning hours, and the other Canonical Hours followed roughly at three-hour intervals during the remainder of the day: Terce, Sext, None, Vespers. The last of the services, Compline, was solemnly celebrated just after nightfall and thus ended the day. The exact times for these liturgical celebrations varied according to the seasons.[50] Daily mass and sometimes even table blessings also assembled the community in choir (*T* 27, 60).

And just as the Divine Office lent a sense of the time of day to the monastics and the medieval society in general through the ringing of the bells for the Angelus and Vespers, the duration of time was also often measured by the length of a prayer. Something could "last as long as the *Responsorium*, with its usual slow pace ... festively sung by the saintly community" (*U* 432), or as long "as half a psalter" (*G* 138; cf. *K* 109; *E* 30), or else scarcely as long as an *Ave Maria* (*T* 49). Similarly, the entire year was divided, not only through the Church's solemn feasts such as Christmas (*G* 145), Candlemas (*G* 125), Easter (*G* 133), Ascension (*G* 127), and Pentecost (*G* 137, 144), but also according to the saints' feasts, such as St. Michael's Day, September 29, or St. Mark's, April 25, (*T* 13).[51]

49. For the precise direction in the Dominican nuns' Constitution, see Humbert (1259, 8ff.). An *Ordinarium* that contains all the rubrics for the nuns exists as an as yet unpublished manuscript in the München Staatsbibliothek (cgm 168); its provenance is presumably Oetenbach.

50. Wilms (1923, 26).

51. On the habit, starting in the thirteenth century, of giving dates in accordance with the Church calendar, see Kieckhefer (1987, 94). Even medieval recipes measure time with the *Ave Maria*, see Louise Gnädinger, "Taulers Leben und Umwelt," in her edition of *Johannes Tauler* (Freiburg i.B.: Walter, 1983), p. 177.

Besides feast days within the liturgical year, the repeated consecration and investiture services in women's monasteries are further high
points mentioned in the Sister-Books (*A* 164; *E* 8). The consecration service had become, by the tenth century, "a dramatic rendition of parts
of the liturgy of St. Agnes"; it had been influenced by "the same dramatic impulses that led to the development of the liturgical drama."[52]

Some other festive liturgical celebrations draw all the sisters into the
action. On Holy Thursday, they washed each other's feet (*W* 72), and
on Good Friday, when the cross was laid out on the steps of the altar,
the women went, presumably in a solemn procession, to individually
venerate the cross (*W* 81; *T* 62). Similarly in Advent, certain roles were
assigned to the nuns. The Töss author reports that Margret von Zürich
"was asked during Advent to prepare our Lord's bath, as we customarily do in order to spiritually make a house for him," thus providing
him with "everything that he was deprived of when he was on earth"
(*T* 36). Many of such small dramatic scenes are still practiced in a
number of monasteries even today. And it is in such a context that the
puzzling prayer of Adelhait von Frauenberg of Töss makes at least
some sense:

> She desired with heart-felt loving eagerness that all her body be
> tortured as a service to the sweet child. She desired that her skin be
> pulled off to make a diaper for our Lord, her veins to make threads
> for a garment, and she desired that her marrow be pulverized to
> make mush and desired that her blood be shed for a bath for him
> and her bones be burnt for a fire, and she desired that her flesh be
> used up for all the sinners (*T* 52.5–11).

Adelheid's appalling imaginative picture may have been influenced by
the quasi-liturgical play-acting and is, according to Haas, an example of
the drastic realism of the late medieval imagination which serves mainly
the purpose of representing things in as heroic a light as possible.[53]

---

52. Yardley (1986, 21). For the consecration service in the Roman Pontifical,
see Metz (1954).

53. See Haas (1984a, 112); cf. Hale (1992, 167). On the seminal significance of
liturgical ceremonies for the development of the drama, see Corbin (1960, 246);
Berthold (1932); Christine Klapisch-Zuber, "Holy Dolls: Play and Piety in Florence
in the Quattrocento," in her *Women, Family, and Ritual in Renaissance Italy*, trans.
Lydia Cochrane (Chicago and London: Chicago University Press, 1985), pp. 310–
329. On similar practices in modern women's communities, see Gropper (1983);
Möckershoff (1983).

Liturgical music played a major role in the nuns' worship, since the Dominicans typically sang the Divine Office and mass (*D* 19, 27e, 31, 47; *K* 110; *T* 21; *U* 340), and at least in the Gotteszell monastery also the table blessings (*G* 145). In the church choir, the choir nuns who could sing well stood in the front, the others were assembled in the rear (*U* 413). The choir was divided into two halves that alternated in singing the liturgical texts (*U* 409, 437; *T* 51). An Engeltal sister was reprimanded for having inadvertently sung both parts (*E* 14).[54]

How seriously the sisters took their singing in choir is illustrated with the example of Anna von Klingnau of Töss who was quite ill but, the author says, "she was always eager for choir. And when she could not stand, she sat in her stall and sang" (*T* 37). Formulations like *ad matutinem alacriter cantans*, "cheerfully singing at Matins" (*U* 360; *T* 26, 55) occur throughout. The sisters sang with voice and heart (*U* 461; *D* 50), as specifically recommended in Caesarius of Arles' sixth-century *Regula ad virgines*. The psalms as well as traditional hymns, such as the *Veni creator spiritus*, and the *Salve Regina* that concluded the day at Compline, are mentioned in the Sister-Books (*W* 71, 72, 84; *U* 345, 360; *T* 28; *K* 108).[55]

Singing the liturgy required training. Both in Unterlinden and Engeltal, Benedictine sisters, the "black nuns," instructed the Dominican women in "chanting the Divine Office" (*U* 365; *E* 26). In their early days, remarks the Unterlinden chronicler, they were eager to sing well, but in later years, their singing could often be characterized as "morose" (*U* 340, 397). The Engeltal women sang so well that, during the time before the rule of strict enclosure was enforced, they were invited out

54. This reprimand and the sister's reaction, often quoted as an example of the naive nuns' typical suggestibility, reads: "Then the prioress said to her: 'You act like a goose ... .' Then she fluttered with her arms and imagined she was a goose, until the prioress said: 'You are not a goose.' Then she quit her improper behaviour" (*E* 14). The context deals explicitly with the importance of this particular sister, Alheit von Trochau, in the Engeltal community so that the audience may well understand the opposite: Alheit acted in defiance to her superior forcing the prioress to take back her insult. Such an interpretation seems to be confirmed by the immediately following paragraph that speaks of Alheit's temptation to leave the monastery.

55. For general observations of the nuns' liturgical singing, see Wachtel (1938, 61f.); Yardley (1986, 22). See Caesarius, *Regula* (1988, xx). On the importance of the *Salve Regina*, see Hammerstein (1962, 51); Wachtel (1938, 12, n.21 and 22); William R. Bonniwell, *A History of the Dominican Liturgy* (New York: Wagner, 1944), esp. pp. 207–211.

to sing the Pentecost mass in a chapel in Reichnek; and the beautiful liturgy so inspired their noble founder, who had invited them, the author boasts, that he miraculously sang the mass along with them, "and he had never learned the letters" (E 6).

Liturgical singing, undisputed in these texts as an important form of prayer, is understood as divinely sanctioned (D 20). The Diessenhofen author explains that, while Berta von Herten "sang in choir in great devotion, another sister saw a golden pipe going up from her mouth to heaven," and at another time "a red rose" was seen before her mouth (D 12). And one Christmas Day, even the entire singing community was honored: "A sister saw a golden plate come down from heaven into the choir. And all the sisters who sang were listed on it. And when Matins was over, the plate went up to heaven again" (D 27d). Such miraculous signs were to underline the conviction that God must be pleased with the nuns' singing which also, as was shown, was thought to be in harmony with the angels in heaven. Since nuns' singing had not always been looked upon favourably, the authors' unreservedly positive attitude toward the women's singing in choir reflects the self-respect and independence of the authors of the Sister-Books.[56]

A dream vision during which a Diessenhofen nun saw a pontifical mass celebrated by John the Evangelist permits a glimpse of traditional liturgical practices: "The community sang quite well. And when offertory came, the entire community was told to go to the offertory [procession]. And when it was the novices' turn, the novice mistress took them with her. And then they came to the altar" (D 38). Similarly, a eucharistic celebration on communion day, vividly depicted in a vision by Katharina von Unterlinden, is of cultural interest:

[Hedwig von Laufenberg] was enraptured in the Spirit and saw with her spiritual eyes the Lord Jesus Christ before the altar in a priest's garments and celebrating a solemn mass. A glorious crowd of holy angels stood at his side ... who seemed to function as altar servers

---

56. McLaughlin (1974, 244) states that in the medieval double monasteries, somewhat earlier in time, "the sisters were not allowed to sing the offices lest their song, like that of the Sirens, arouse male passion." The women's own participation in music consists, as far as the Sister-Books go, exclusively in vocal music. External evidence cited by Halter (1956, 65), however (that is, a contemporary document referring to the Oetenbach community), suggests that people standing by the monastery church heard "string instruments and polyphonic singing in the choir" (do gigent und künternet man im kor); see Rats- und Richtbücher, B VI, 195/191, at the Staatsarchiv Zürich.

in inestimable joy. After the mass had thus been celebrated in sequence, the kind Lord Jesus turned his most benign face to the community of sisters so that all of them might approach to participate in the sacrament given by the Lord Savior's own hand. Then the Lord's Mother, the imperial Virgin, incomparably splendid in face and garment, came most reverently forward to the altar with her assigned bridesman, the holy archangel Gabriel. She humbly genuflected on the right side of the altar, while on the left side the holy archangel Gabriel similarly genuflected. The royal Virgin held forth a folded, snow white linen cloth holding it with her virginal hand, [and Gabriel] reverently accepted his part. Then, with their sacred hands, they both, as is the custom, held the cloth stretched out until this sister, who saw this, came forward first to receive the life-giving sacrament from the hand of the most dulcet Lord. Then all sisters approached in order and similarly received the most sacred eucharist most devoutly from the Lord Jesus Christ (U 442. 24–443.7).

With a different cast, this scene re-enacts a liturgical celebration, as it might have happened in women's monasteries at the time where the prioress, as does "the Lord's Mother" in the text, assumed an official function at the altar.

A touch of realism seems to underlie the Unterlinden author's remark that "the nightly and daily office in choir was usually observed by the sisters with a lot of fretting" (U 436), contrasting it with Adelheid von Rheinfelden's exemplary attitude; for this nun "never in her life experienced any tediousness, even if the singing was really morose. She also never was weighed down by sleepiness or numbness nor had she ever fallen asleep in choir or during a sermon" (U 397). The text implicitly reveals problems with sisters being exhausted or perhaps even bored by the liturgy. In a similar didactic vein, the Adelhausen author explains with a somewhat incongruous comparison that one sister was so devoted that she would not have missed a liturgy even for one hundred marks (A 183). Other exemplary sisters are said to have insisted on participating in the regular Divine Office even during an illness (T 57; A 167f.). In fact, the sick sisters were carried along to special liturgical celebrations, or else, angels spirited them to the choir, the Weiler author states (W 68; G 123, 135; K 110).

The mere fact that regular attendance in choir is stressed as a special virtue leads us to suppose some difficulty in this area (T 33, 61, 92). But in general, the sisters are praised in their dedication and perseverance.

Anna von Munzingen writes that the nuns "had a very great devotion to the service of God; and many were very happy to go to choir and went as eagerly as if they were to attend a great festivity" (*A* 188). A prime example for the nuns' enthusiasm for liturgy is a young sister, *ein kint*, in Gotteszell who was so eager to attend the Canonical Hour that rushing up to the church's choir she took "two steps at a time," (*G* 141) – a way of going upstairs no doubt considered improper behaviour for any monastic. Similarly, Beli von Sure of Töss on her way to choir, "really walked as if she were ready to fly" (*T* 42). Both incidents testify to a genuine love for the liturgy.

b. Communal Work
Manual labor besides intellectual work has always played an important role in monastic life. Hence the Dominican nuns' first constitution also stated: "So with the exception of the hours which the sisters ought to consecrate to prayer, to reading, to the preparation of the Divine Office and chant, or to study, they should devote themselves to some manual labor."[57] Such daily work was obviously necessary for a healthy balance in the choir sisters' lives but at the same time imperative for the community's subsistence and financial well-being, since the work contributed to the monastery becoming self-supporting.[58]

Judging by the frequency with which the nuns' commitment to "common work," *gemainen werken*, is mentioned in the Sister-Books, the authors see the importance of manual labor second only to the liturgy: "they sat in the workroom with such great devotion ..., as if they were standing in mass" (*T* 14, 29, 34). Many sisters were so dedicated to spinning or knitting that they only left the workroom when necessary; some even carried around distaffs to use in their spare moments, others spun while on duty at the grille, and some did so even when they were sick (*G* 138; *T* 18, 37; *O* 245; *U* 398). A passage in the Töss Sister-Book suggests that each sister had a certain amount of work to accomplish and was able to work ahead, as did Adelheid, for "most of the time, she was the first at common work. And she spun so diligently until her fingers were swollen. And, no matter by how much she exceeded spinning the week's quota, she still gave it all to the week's work" (*T* 51).[59]

---

57. *Book of Constitutions* (1987, 61); see also The Primitive Constitution (1969, 10, 20). For a comparison between these late medieval Dominicans and a typical contemporary monastic community, see the chapter "Work" in Cummings (1986, 43–70).
58. Monssen (1964, 128).
59. See also Caesarius' *Regula: pensum suum cotidianum* (1988, xiv).

Most monasteries also had large scriptoria that separated the writers and scribes from the sisters doing needlework. But in Unter-linden, also the writing of books "in a very elegant way," *valde eleganter*, took place in the workroom (*U* 411).

Work was normally accomplished in silence, as already prescribed by Caesarius of Arles.[60] Elisabeth von Kirchberg explains that no one "was supposed to or dared to speak" so that, even during their work, sisters did not need to take their minds off spiritual matters (*K* 106; *T* 37). On the other hand, some singing at work was apparently per-mitted, for in Töss Sophie von Klingnau "sat in the work room with the community, often singing the sweetest words of our Lord; and the sisters were very eager to listen" (*T* 59f.). And Mezzi Sidwibrin, the paragon of simplicity in the same community, sang, while spinning in the common work room, a song about *falsche minn*, ending with: "If caught in false love, rid yourself of it. May God make you scorn it" (*T* 29). Although still of a didactic nature, this song is the only one mentioned in the Sister-Books that is not directly related to liturgy or prayer.

Appropriate visions are again the means to highlight the great value of work. Heilwig von Rottenburg of Kirchberg, at the time ill in the sick room, is quoted telling the following vision to her community:

"I came before the community room and looked in there where the community sat at work with devotion, according to their habit. Then I saw that there were many angels, and they had great joy and bliss with the sisters. Thereafter I saw that a youth, who was loving and beautiful, attaching a rose on each sister's distaff. When he approached the door I requested that he also gave one to me. Then he said: 'I will give it to nobody except to those who are [at work] with the community.' Then he gave to each sister something out of a box. The fragrance was so ineffably sweet that nothing in this world can resemble it. I requested from my heart that he should also give something to me. Then he said again: 'I will give it to nobody except to those who are [at work] with the commun-ity.' I then fell down before the door from pain of heart so that you had to carry me away. But you imagined that it had happened to me from physical illness. Thereafter you saw how sick I was so that I rarely came to the community when they sat at work. And I requested that a pillow be put into the community room so that when I could no longer sit I could lie down and be with the community and thus receive graces."

60. Caesarius, *Regula* (1988, xviii).

Figure 13 Marienteppich, tapestry woven at Adelhausen around 1400

Ever after, Elisabeth von Kirchberg concludes, "every sick sister's straw mattress and pillow were carried into the work room, so that they could remain with the community" (K 112.9–31). Individuals united as a working community are so pleasing to God, this passage suggests, that they are rewarded by angels with special pleasures. Therefore, not even the sick community members should be excluded from this important part of the daily monastic life.

c. Offices[61]

A major concern of the authors of the Sister-Books is that gifted nuns offer their service to the community by holding an office. The demanding organizational tasks and the sheer logistics necessary in administering a large monastery had to be accomplished by skilled individuals.

First among the offices and the hardest of all is that of the prioress who could hold the office for a lengthy period of time, even up to twenty years (A 154, 172; E 12, 19, 31; W 70, 84; U 373; T 40). Like her, the subprioress is elected by the community (O 265; E 9, 38), and both could be re-elected several times (G 137, 140). Once in office, the prioress generally exercised almost autocratic power, and full obedience was given to her (U 424f., 474f.; D 27a). In fact, her decisions could only be reversed after she was succeeded by another prioress (E 12).[62]

An Engeltal sister is in awe of the prioress' office: "I would rather be sick to the end of my life than be a prioress" (E 39). But elsewhere in the text, a prioress is assured of divine help by these words: "I will be with you in all your worries and will protect you before all your enemies" (E 36). The duties of the prioress were seen to interfere with a sister's spiritual life. This dilemma is dramatized in the story about the Engeltal prioress Mechthild Krumpsitin, who was "elected away" to the Dominican monastery in Aurach:[63]

> When she went there, she could not silence the great devotion in her heart. One night, before her bed in her prayers, she was enraptured. Then a lay sister who was the guest mistress came three

---

61. For a complete list of offices typical for monasteries of the Order of Preachers, see Johannes Meyer's "Ämterbuch" (König, 1880, 196–206).

62. Fontette (1967, 104) speaks of an essentially democratic organization among the Dominicans. For lists of documented priorates in some monasteries, see Krauss (1894, 299f.) for Kirchberg; Däniker-Gysin (1958, 97–103) for Töss.

63. Aurach refers to the monastery of Frauenaurach, just west of Erlangen in the Nürnberg area, which the Engeltal sisters helped to establish (Schröder 1871, 63).

times to her saying she should come down to the guests. But because of the divine graces [Mechthild] could not perceive this world. Then the lay sister went and said about the prioress: "She is red under her eyes like a rose: she may have drunk wine" (E 19.10–17).

A prioress is expected to be available at all times, the passage suggests. The others' lack of understanding, here described in analogy with Ac. 2:13, points to various levels of spirituality within a community that a prioress had to reconcile.

High up on the ladder of importance was the office of the chantress, *cantrix, sancmeisterin* or *singerin*, since music played such an essential role for the Dominican nuns (U 340, 416, 437; T 46, 49; K 115; E 24; W 82). Her task included "organizing the choir, designating soloists, choosing the correct chants for the liturgical occasion, taking care of the liturgical books, making the table or weekly rotational chart, and assembling the music for such occasions as local saints' days," Anne Bagnall Yardly explains.[64] The Diessenhofen chantress is shown to have been so exhausted from her demanding work that one day she felt she could not get up for Prime. But when the first bell was sounded, "she heard a voice like an army trumpet that said: Get up! Get up! Then she got up right away and went into the choir and began [singing]: *Jam lucis orto sidere*" (D 50). Her conscience, like a loud trumpet, gave her no peace. In Unterlinden, Sister Mechtild, who was forced to move about on crutches because of an illness, was the best *cantrix* this monastery ever had. The following quotation describes her choir practice:

> The Lord had given her a strong and exceedingly sweet voice ... . For thirty years she held the office of chantress in choir, and she practiced it incessantly with the greatest alertness. Walking on both sides of the choir, she diligently admonished and solicited the sisters, not only through words but also through her example, so that they sang the psalms loudly and festively ... . At that time everything that was said and sung in choir was orderly and without mistakes (U 437.1–15).

The Töss author singles out Mezzi von Klingenberg as an excellent choir mistress: "God gave her the grace that, if on occasion she felt out of sorts, whenever she came into the choir and sang Matins she felt better" (T 45f.) – an apt description of Mezzi's personal fulfillment through a cherished profession.

---

64. Yardley (1986, 20).

The novice mistress trained the community's future nuns, instructing the novices in the liturgy and teaching them proper etiquette for the choir, among other things. When a monastery did not have a special children's *magistra, der kinde maisterin*, this office also entailed caring for the children who lived in the community (*E* 8). They were admonished to talk little, not to fight, and to avoid laughter in the chapter of faults (*U* 339). Based on the notion that Christ had never laughed, laughter was in general seriously frowned upon. On occasion this nun did not refrain from beating the young ones, *sin novizen maistri schluog fil úbel* (*T* 51; *U* 395). In the Diessenhofen book, Diemut von Lindau is held up as a model novice mistress, representing "before us the image of a strict life" (*D* 31).[65]

Because of the constant presence of sick people in a large community, the office of the infirmarian, *siechmaistrin*, was an especially onerous one (*A* 169; *K* 115; *G* 127, 138; *T* 47; *E* 27; *D* 15; *W* 68). As Christine Ebner explains of Anna von Weitersdorf in Engeltal, this office could mean "great trouble": "She was an infirmarian and suffered greatly from it, but it was not a dishonorable suffering. When she had finished [her turn] she thought she would never again take a big office" (*E* 26f.). And indeed, with the notable exception of only a few, many sisters apparently took on the office of the infirmarian only out of a sense of obedience (*T* 84). Moreover, the hardship of this office could be aggravated by the lack of understanding on the part of other sisters, the Gotteszell author explains:

> Once [Margaretha von Rosenstein] was ordered to be the infirmarian. There she had so much work that it was amazing. And once during wintertime, she made a bath for a sick sister after Compline, and the weather was quite cold and intolerable. And there, the garment she wore froze altogether. And then she went into the refectory which was heated, wanting to thaw her garment. Then the disciplinarian drove her to the dormitory and did not want her to remain until she was warm. And thus she went to the dormitory, with complete goodness like the little lamb that is God himself. And she stood at the window, which is turned toward the orchard, with her frozen garment and in miserable lamenting thoughts (*G* 138.38–139.1).

65. The San Sisto Constitution prescribes one psalm as a penance for those sisters who laugh "in a dissolute fashion uproariously," see *The Primitive Constitution* (1969, 12). For a well-documented chapter on laughter in a medieval monastic context, see Ritamary Bradley, *Julian's Way: A Practical Commentary on Julian of Norwich* (London: Harper Collins, 1992), pp. 49–54.

In addition to having to shoulder a heavy workload, Margaretha also was unfairly treated by the sister in charge of discipline. And while the *exemplum* emphasizes that she suffered patiently, her unspoken thoughts may not have been as forgiving.

The office of the disciplinarian, *circatrix*, was instituted for chastising, chiding, and admonishing lax community members. The Unterlinden author's definition suggests the austerity of this particular assignment:

> Rising in a virile manner in the zeal of God against all the sisters' negligence and trespassing of the rule and constitution, [the disciplinarian] never tires to stand before the house of the Lord as a wall. Neither fear nor love moved her to spare the sisters even in minor trespasses. She constantly admonished them in the chapter and often accused in one chapter all twenty sisters rather harshly (*U* 362.8–15).

As Tugwell explains, "It was the job of the *circator* or *circatrix* to tour round the monastic buildings, looking out for any infringements of the Rule or Constitutions. By the thirteenth century the disciplinarian was a well-established role in religious life."[66] In some monasteries, the subprioress had to punish misdemeanors (*O* 265). Such functions, one can well imagine, carried the additional burden of being disliked by the sisters in community (*E* 9).

Among other offices, one sister always was in charge of the "window," that is, the grille for communicating with people from outside the cloister. Referred to as the *fenstrerin* or the woman at the window, she had the double function of being present when the cloistered nuns received and talked with visitors (hence she is also referred to as *gesellin*, *T* 60f.) and, more importantly, of being available for people from the outside seeking pastoral guidance (*U* 355; *T* 18, 40, 60, 62). Therefore the Töss author explains, the guardian of the grille was considered especially virtuous if she immediately forgot the problems to which she had been exposed (*T* 61).

Contact with the outside world was also maintained through the office of the portress (*T* 23; *W* 81; *K* 113f.; *G* 146; *U* 449). The story of a portress in the Weiler monastery, who "was supposed to do service at the gate on Holy Friday," suggests how seriously the sisters were to take their official responsibilities: As Margaretha von Helbeunen went

66. Tugwell (1982, 430 n.111).

to the door by the cloisters, "a man came walking toward her," whereupon she wondered, "'O Lord, how did this man enter the monastery?' Then immediately, he showed her his five wounds and thanked her for her obedience, and she recognized well who he was" (*W* 82). The episode relates to the time after strict enclosure had been imposed on the nuns, in fact so strict, we are to understand, that even the visionary sight of a man is shocking. Enclosure limited the nuns to the monastery complex for the rest of their lives; its idealistic reason, Leclercq explains, was to provide the nuns with greater freedom for the divine service, *servire Deo liberius*.[67]

Among further important offices, the sister administrator, *hofmeisterin* or *schaffnerin*, is mentioned who works hand in hand with the prioress (*E* 25; *D* 5). Hers was an office especially characterized by busyness, *vnmuoss* (*D* 33). Then there were the sacristan, *küstrin* (*G* 144; *T* 45; *D* 20; *W* 71) and the guest mistress, *gastmeisterin* (*E* 19); the cellarer, *kelnerin* (*K* 113; *T* 21, 89; *D* 18; *W* 73); the bread mistress, *brotmeistrin* (*E* 43[68]); the cook (*T* 83); as well as the sisters who worked in the kitchen (*A* 169; *W* 74) and those who had to clean (*T* 82). Of the kitchen duty referred to as "the most despicable work," the Oetenbach author states that Ita von Hohenfels "washed the pots and bowls and carried water on her back from far away into the kitchen" (*O* 239). Having to haul water from outside into the monastery complex was apparently not unusual (*U* 407).

In addition, various tasks were shared by members of the community by taking weekly turns (hence the term *wuchnerin*, hebdomadarian). These rotating tasks could consist in some communities of presiding at the Divine Office, reading at table, preparing the church for the liturgies (*T* 28), some kitchen duties (*T* 81), and helping the nurse in the sick room (*T* 85).

Prior to the enforcement of strict enclosure, female monastic communities also had a so-called *terminiererin* (similar to the comparable office among the male mendicants), that is, a sister in charge of begging for food and alms for the monastery within a certain district (*termenie*). The person chosen for this office in the Oetenbach community was the

---

67. Leclercq (1982b, 129). On enclosure, see also Leclercq (1981b); Hinnebusch (1966, 135); Caesarius, *Regula* (1988, xxxiv); Philipp Hofmeister, "Von den Nonnenklöstern" (*Archiv für katholisches Kirchenrecht* 114 (1934), 3–96, esp. 68–96; see also Brennan (1985).

68. Kramer (1991, 202f.) draws attention to the symbolic meaning of this office in the Engeltal text.

simple-minded (*gar einfaltig*), but very successful Agnes von Zürich on whom the surrounding population enjoyed playing pranks (*O* 229f.).[69]

The offices were looked upon as duties that had to be observed with obedience, often for many years in a row or even life-long (*T* 40, 61, 84; *W* 74). There was ground for the entire community to rejoice, when a talented sister agreed to accept a difficult office, Christine Ebner writes (*E* 15). Some women, who were "wise and correct," were especially "much bothered with offices," *man bekümert sie vil mit ampten*; the community took advantage of their qualifications (*W* 73; *A* 159; *O* 260). Many nuns, such as Diemut Ebnerin who had spent over sixty-six years in the monastery, were likely to have held all "the biggest offices" by the end of their life (*E* 32). A lay sister in Engeltal held the administrator's office for a long time because "she was a skilled person for outside business" (*E* 25). The Weiler author offers the *exemplum* of Elizabeth Gebyn, presumably wanting to encourage others to serve: "Of graces I know nothing, but of great suffering I can speak well to you. When I was a young person I was afraid I would be bothered with an office, and I asked our Lord that he give me an illness that would protect me from busyness." She was immediately struck with an illness, this sister's report continues, "which you see on me and which I have had every day except on Sundays and high feasts" (*W* 79). The depressed tone of this passage suggests that escape into illness was not a wise move. Stressing the positive aspect of good service in the community, on the other hand, the Töss author relates a dream about the sacristan Margret von Klingenberg in heaven, "walking around in two golden shoes, saying: 'Look, these shoes I received for the steps I took to kindle the light in the chapel'" (*T* 45). Resorting to a fairy tale motif, she teaches that to have "suffered much trouble with offices" and still to have functioned obediently "with great diligence" is said to be worthy of great heavenly reward (*O* 272; *E* 25, 32).

But in the end, the authors of the Sister-Books seem to agree that offices held no attraction for a "devout person." Usually the nuns are shown as most reluctant to accept important offices, claiming that these would interfere with their chosen contemplative life (*A* 161; *O* 261; *W* 81f., 82). Preoccupation with worldly affairs, which is the very busyness they had intended to leave behind, would distract them from their spiri-

---

69. When the Töss author speaks of a simple-minded nun, she underlines that Mezzi Sidwibrin was "simple-minded by nature," thus differentiating between her nature and the monastic virtue of simplicity (*T* 28). On simplicity, see Grundmann (1978, 57); Leclercq, "Sancta Simplicitas," *Collectanea Cisterciensia* 22 (1960), 138–148.

tual concerns, they feared. Such apprehension about an office's heavy demands was no doubt real. Nevertheless, once again we are faced with a legendary topos. As Delehaye has shown, reluctance to take up a monastic office was recognized as a sign of humility; for holders of such high offices had to be "held up as a model of humbleness."[70]

The discussion about busyness versus being at leisure to attend to spiritual matters, *unmuoss* versus *muosse*, centering on the Martha-Mary dichotomy, is especially prominent in the Kirchberg and Töss Sister-Books. Elisabeth von Kirchberg presents the *exemplum* of Willbirg von Rotweil who "was also troubled all the time with offices, and yet she never omitted her spiritual exercises," thus having achieved the proper balance (*K* 115). The Töss author attempts a solution to the dilemma in her entry on Ita von Sulz, the monastery's cellarer. "Deeply sad-dened" by having to shoulder this burden, because "she feared that the busyness would interfere with her devotion," one day "she went into the choir and complained to our Lord"; and she was consoled when she heard the reply: "I am found at all places and in all things." Thereafter she accepted the office benevolently (*T* 21; cf. *T* 23).

d. Sickness as an Element of Community Life[71]

The presence on a daily basis of serious illness, *grosen siechtagen*, in a monastic community was the harsh reality often overlooked in the too idyllic picture of a medieval monastery. A historical study of the Engel-tal monastery concludes that the health of the members of women com-munities must have been very poor. The communities were notoriously overcrowded, many were poverty-stricken, their diet was inadequate. As a consequence, serious illness was a constant problem.[72]

The monastery's infirmarian, the audience is assured, happily took care of ill sisters like a mother of a daughter (*U* 343, 472), as the following *exemplum* from the Unterlinden Sister-Book suggests:

---

70. Delehaye (1962, 73).

71. See also Petroff's chapter (1986, 37–44) on women's illness based on *vitae* and medieval women's writing other than the Sister-Books.

72. For the historical basis, see Voit (1958, 22f.). Already Humbert of Romans' Constitution (1259, ch. 7) deals with the practical aspects of illness in women's monasteries, including the special diet and sleeping privileges granted sick sisters. And he warns the prioress not to be "negligent of the sick" so that they might "quickly regain their health."

We want to give the example of three sick sisters whom [the infirmarian Anna von Wineck] had taken under her special care and responsibility. One among them suffered miserably from epilepsy since childhood. Her face was terribly disfigured because of the force of her illness, and she was equally deprived of the use of her senses and mind. This servant of God served her always with devotion up to her death. She lovingly washed off with her own hands the sordid stuff and dirt that the illness caused. During the time when the sister was seized by this illness and yelled and foamed, she pressed her against her chest and petted her with motherly tenderness until she revived and the pain ceased ... .

She also served another sick sister, who similarly had lost the use of reason in her old age, as long as she lived with pious care ....

The third sister ... had dropsy. Her body was terribly swollen, and she lay paralyzed for many years. The saintly sister of whom we speak served her eagerly for God's sake. The Lord permitted that this paralyzed sister – although she, too, was undoubtedly saintly – became so impatient as a consequence of the hardship of a lasting illness that she neither obeyed nor pleased one of her servants. She also could not speak with her [nurse] peacefully but often scolded her loudly (*U* 423.34–424. 26; cf. *G* 135, 138).

That a single sister would be left in charge of such severely sick women is, one can only hope, authorial exaggeration meant to enhance the infirmarian's virtue. The author, by alluding to the Rule of St. Benedict (treating the sick as if "caring for Christ's wounds"), touches on the spiritual significance of the infirmarian's work.[73] And the didactic passage concludes with the assurance that this nun's selflessness in her work stood in direct relation to the divine consolations she received (*U* 425).

But as one would expect, if we assume an at least partially realistic representation, not all the sisters were reconciled to the constant presence of illness in their midst. And while some sisters are singled out as having visited the sickroom and felt special pity for the sick (*T* 61), many seem to have cared little or showed an outright distaste for sick members of the community (*T* 18, 47; *O* 260; *E* 5f., 24). Of the suffering Kunigund von Vilsek, Christine Ebner writes:

When [her friend] had died, [Kunigund] was commended to a maid who treated her quite harshly. One day she left her without food so that all her strength was gone. Then came two angels in the

73. RB, ch. 36.

shape of two beautiful youths. And one carried a towel around his neck and a large beautiful bowl with fish and nice bread. The other one carried a little pitcher with good wine, and he lifted [Kunigund] up and prepared a small table. And [then] they put her back down and disappeared (*E* 39.6–14).

This miracle story, replete with homely details, nevertheless provides a disturbing image of the abandonment of the sick.

Illnesses mentioned in the Sister-Books include epilepsy, senility (*G* 146; *T* 48, 93, 94), and dropsy (*A* 172; *W* 73), and they range from severe headaches (*G* 135, 140) and presumably allergic reactions to various foods (*G* 137) as well as digestive problems (*T* 32) and worms (*T* 22), to gout (*G* 135), tuberculosis (*T* 52), and paralysis (*U* 382; *A* 177, 183; *G* 145), which meant that some sisters had to be carried on chairs (*T* 36, 42), as well as advanced arthritis (*T* 53), intermittent fever for years (*K* 109), and spinal deformities (*G* 138; *T* 85, 93). Some other illnesses are not specifically diagnosed, such as Adelheit's ailment who was sick from childhood on and "bed-ridden ... for more than thirty years" (*G* 123).

The only medical cure or preventive measure that the Sister-Books list for any illness is that of "being bled," although we need not assume that nothing else was tried to alleviate suffering (*T* 18). Herbal remedies, for instance, were commonly used in monasteries, and in Töss, a "wise healer" was called to the monastery for consultation (*T* 66, 42).

The Sister-Books explain that sick sisters were transferred to the infirmary and offered special food, such as poultry and vegetables (*G* 127, 135; *T* 91f.; *E* 5). Depending on the severity of the illness, they were also dispensed from observing the rules of the order (*G* 140). But at the same time, some illnesses were not physical ailments at all. A Weiler sister was diagnosed by "a wise physician" as having fallen ill with love, which the community explained as being lovesick "for God, because she does not love anyone else" (*W* 69). The authors make use of this legendary motif of love sickness to underline an intimate connection between suffering and spirituality which is reflected in these texts.

The line between spiritually motivated ascetic behaviour and symptoms of medical disorders could sometimes become blurred. The compulsive finger-biting of a Weiler sister is, as is typical for medieval hagiography, represented as an ascetic feat (*W* 75).[74] On the other hand,

---

74. Both Marie d' Oignies and Christina de St. Troud, whose thirteenth-century *vitae* were composed by Jacques de Vitry and Thomas de Chantimpré respectively, are said to have suffered from the same ailment (Bihlmeyer 1916, 75 n.66).

the presumed ascetic behaviour of Ita von Hohenfels is unmasked by the Oetenbach author as an unhealthy deviation:

> [Ita] disciplined herself, and that was not enough. For she cut herself with knives down to her bones so that her flesh hung down from her body and her blood ran out fast so that one could tell where she had walked. And no matter how much she harmed herself, three days later she was always cured. *Her superiors forbade her this.* Then she did it with iron needles that she filed for herself. And no matter how much trouble she caused herself, *she imagined* that she was only serving God as other people served him (O 239.18–240.8).

The words I italicized show that the community in this case was alert, openly disapproved, and eventually put an end to such aberration.

As an illness, leprosy is a special case during the Middle Ages. "The good people," *die guten leut,* as lepers are called, were shunned by the community. The leprous Sister Heilin von Gruen of Kirchberg had to live "in a special little house" and attended mass from "outside of the choir." A vision of Heilin refers to the custom that lepers had to go around rattling a wooden clapper to warn people of their whereabouts; and it was, indeed, one of Heilin's greatest concerns not to infect anybody (K 117f.). Heilin's living apart from the community was accepted as a matter of course. As Saul Nathaniel Brody explains, the separation of the afflicted from society was officially sanctioned by the Church. Presumably Elisabeth von Kirchberg does not discriminate against Heilin and speaks of this leprous sister with great respect, even though medieval society generally assumed that "leprosy was a punishment for sin" and associated "with moral impurity." As a consequence, even the family of someone afflicted with leprosy at times suffered discrimination. In Engeltal, a prioress refused profession to Alheit von Trochau because her father was a leper, and the alleged sin of the parent was thought to reflect on the daughter. Only a new, apparently more enlightened prioress granted Alheit full acceptance into the community (E 12).[75]

The authors generally represent the sick sisters themselves as paragons of patience (O 240, 264), or even of happiness, during their suffering (T 85f.). Moreover, illness was conducive to prayer and stimulated the nuns' spiritual growth (G 123, 140; T 85f.; O 240, 264). And only in two instances are healing miracles mentioned in the Sister-Books (G 135f.; W 73).

---

75. On the treatment of lepers and the Church's attitude, see Brody (1974, 58f., 64f., 106); Tuchman (1978, 41f.).

e. Customs Surrounding the Dying

The medieval monastic community literally celebrated death as an integral part of life. In a monastery with around one hundred community members of all ages, death happened more or less on a regular basis. Some nuns' deaths were expected after many years of illness, others died unexpectedly at an early age, *ein junge froelichú swester* (D 17).

When a sister was close to death, someone knocked on a wooden board, especially reserved for such occasions, *tafel schlagen* or *taveln* (A 155; T 68; E 9; D 21). This sound, echoing through the monastery, brought all other activities, including the liturgical service, to a halt so that the community could assemble around the dying sister (U 411, 420; T 35). The audience is assured that, in the unlikely case, *won es ungewonlich ist*, that a sister died without the community assembled, this omission was compensated by angels coming to carry her off (T 84). During the Middle Ages, the presence of relatives and friends at someone's death was a matter of course.[76] The Weiler community, at one point, refused to sit down to eat because they feared that a seriously ill sister would die alone (W 73). A dying sister held off her final hour so that the nuns could conveniently gather around her death bed (G 139). The Töss author says of Ita von Tuengen that "when the time came that she was about to die, and the sisters were not aware of it, she very softly called them, saying 'Children, I am dying.' And only when the community arrived, did she depart" (T 35). In Diessenhofen, Adelheit die Zirgerin supposedly arranged her death in such a way that she would not interrupt the daily routine too much:

> And when she was about to die, she said to the prioress: "When is it most convenient for you that I die?" Then the prioress said: "The sisters are frightened, when they hear the knocking on the board at night." Then she said: "Do you imagine then that it is all right for me to die in the morning after mass?" Then the prioress said: "Yes, this is quite good." And when mass was sung in the morning, she was given our Lord. Receiving him with great devotion, she departed shortly after (D 29).

The prioress was to make sure the dying person was given the Sacrament of the Sick as well as communion.

---

76. Gurevich (1990, 186). Regarding death in the monastic community, see Leclercq, "La Joie de mourir selon Saint Bernard de Clairvaux," in: *Dies illa*, Vinaver Studies 1, ed. Jane M.H. Taylor (Proceedings of the Manchester Colloquium, 1983), pp. 195–207. Cummings (1986, 189) describes similar monastic practices today. See also Haas (1989b); Schipperges (1990, 60).

The sisters keeping vigil by the deathbed sang hymns, read a gospel passage or the psalms, and prayed the litany "according to custom"; and angels are said to have joined the community on such occasions (*U* 434; *E* 24; *K* 106, 112; *T* 25, 45, 93; *D* 10).[77] In a scene described by Christine Ebner, the community surrounding the dying sister suddenly prostrated themselves in a *venie* when she told them that "our Lord and his dear mother Mary had come" (*E* 16; cf. *T* 47). Descriptions of difficult deaths exist, as was shown, but are rare relative to the numerous miracles and to reports of women having died with a smile. Both the miracles and the smiles are legendary stereotypes surrounding the death of especially saintly persons.

A death in the community was followed almost immediately by the special Office of the Dead, and a requiem mass for the deceased was celebrated after the body had been transferred to the choir just before burial (*G* 132). Angels also sang during the requiem and at funerals (*E* 38; *D* 17). For the burial, the sisters carry candles on their way to the grave and pray and sometimes "greatly complain" at the loss of a beloved sister (*T* 49, 82; *U* 371).

5. Monastic Virtues

"To observe the order" faithfully encompasses everything that is expected of an exemplary nun, the authors agree. In the Sister-Books, the "strictest observance," *obseruantia strictissima* (*U* 343), entails both the rule of the order and the so-called evangelical counsels.

a. Observing the Order

Phrases such as a nun spending all her life "in burning devotion toward God and in observing the order with great diligence and seriousness" (*W* 72), or *den orden hielt sie fleissiklich und strencklich* (*G* 131, 140; *T* 14, 23, 40; *K* 107, 115), appear as a leitmotif in the Sister-Books. The "order and rule ... according to our Father Dominic," the basis for the monastic community, underlined all facets of life, making it meaningful. The Töss author writes:

> Everything [Belinum] was supposed to do as a part of monastic life she did quite eagerly and merrily so that she was a perfect proof of the fact that love is not a burden, since she strictly observed the

---

77. The Adelhausen author mentions the habit of taking special note at which psalm verse a sister passed away; this verse was then supposed to explain the dying person's fate (*A* 155f.).

order in all things, often with a sick body. For free love has the privilege of carrying heavy burdens light-heartedly (*T* 42.4–8; cf. *U* 367, 372).

Although observing the monastic order was not an easy way of life, it could be lived lightly through a sense of inner freedom, as stated in Katharina von Unterlinden's beautiful formulation that refers to a much quoted passage in the Rule of St. Benedict: she "did not simply walk but she ran, even flew on the path of God's command" (*U* 381; cf. *U* 423, 452).[78]

b. The Evangelical Counsels

The three virtues, *willige armuot und volkumne gehorsame und rechte lutterkait*, "voluntary poverty, and perfect obedience, and the proper purity," mentioned in the Töss Sister-Book, are a direct reference to the evangelical counsels (*T* 14). This particular triad, often thought to go back to the very beginning of monasticism, in fact dates from the late twelfth and early thirteenth century; until then, the counsels appeared in varying orders of importance, Adalbert de Vogüé explains. The Master and St. Benedict put obedience first; St. Augustine stressed disappropriation (as poverty should properly be understood). Both practically ignored chastity since it was traditionally considered "a threshold-virtue ... , an evident and unquestioned presupposition" for monastic life.[79]

In the Sister-Books, the praise of poverty is relatively limited in comparison with the enormous weight placed on obedience. Voluntary poverty means that the sisters selflessly gave away everything they had or received in favour of the community (*A* 187; *K* 107, 118; *T* 14, 20, 91; *O* 238). The Gotteszell text singles out Cristina who was extraordinary in her commitment to poverty, because her "one garment" was usually "so worn out that it barely hung on her and stayed up" (*G* 140). Of Juta, the same author says that she "gave away to her neighbor" even the things she needed (*G* 144). And Sister Hedwig in Oetenbach used to wash the nuns' habits and then lay them out in such a way that nobody knew whose they were, illustrating how little atten-

---

78. RB (Prol. 49): *curritur via mandatorum Dei.*

79. de Vogüé (1980, 3, 14, 4); see also Underhill (1955, 205f.). The term "counsels" rather than rule or law was chosen because New Testament teaching no longer stressed "thinking about God in terms of laws or obligations" (DictTheol 1985, 157f.).

tion was paid to clothing (*O* 229). The Töss author repeatedly makes the fine distinction between the voluntary monastic poverty they endured and the actual poverty of the poor:

> We also had a virtuous blessed sister, called Gertrud von Winterthur, who was so very compassionate with poor people that she was rightly called a mother of the poor and a special friend of our Lord's friends. And whatever she was given, she gave away totally to the poor so that we often imagined she was deprived of the necessary. She imagined herself unworthy to give merrily to the poor. She also imagined that it would be a great dishonor for her if anything were found of her [belongings] after her death (*T* 48. 31–49.4; cf. *T* 46).

Such a degree of social awareness, while in tune with the time, is otherwise not encountered in these texts.[80]

The counsel of obedience is represented in the Sister-Books as the most difficult one to observe, judging by the many problems reported and the frequent questions about obedience, and by the authors' lavish praise for obedient women. Obedience, considered in the western tradition the basis for monastic life, was literally understood as giving up one's own will. Anna von Munzingen reports that when Metze Tuschelin prayed to be spared the office of prioress, she was taught by a voice:

> "Go back to the chapter room and receive obedience. For you shall know that I prefer your obedience. It weighs more before my eyes than Abraham's obedience, for he sacrificed what was outside of him while you sacrifice what is inside you: that is, your own will" (*A* 161.18–22).

The author could hardly have found a more striking analogy to convince her audience of this difficult counsel: surrendering one's will, she says, is more difficult than Abraham's sacrifice of his only son [Gn. 22:2]. The Oetenbach author's definition reads: "This is the virtue that the human being wants nothing but what God wants," *daß der mensch nit wil, wan das got wil* (*O* 249; cf. *O* 253, 267).[81]

---

80. See Michel Mollat, *The Poor in the Middle Ages. An Essay in Social History*, 1st French ed. 1978, trans. Arthur Goldhammer (Yale: Yale University Press, 1986), esp, "A Fresh Look at the Poor," pp. 119–157. On poverty in the Sister-Books, see also Langer (1987, 82–95).

81. On obedience in the Sister-Books, see also Langer (1987, 95–100); Weinhandl (1921, 83).

In the monastic setting, "voluntary obedience" meant subjecting oneself to the authority and to the rule of order (*A* 179, 181; *T* 20, 40, 61; *O* 218). The nuns were taught, as an Oetenbach sister is quoted saying, that it was "easier to suffer death than to neglect obedience" (*O* 260). Obedience is even to rank above visions, as explained by Christine Ebner with the example of Hedwig von Regensburg who cuts short a visionary exchange through obedience to the rule: "Once our Lord appeared to her between the two signals given for Matins," whereupon she reminded him, "'Much beloved Lord, I am to read Matins now'" (*E* 21f.). Women exemplary in such unconditional obedience are said to have been rewarded with special graces (*K* 114; *G* 138f.; *O* 263; *E* 5, 43; *D* 9).

The enormous weight put on obedience is illustrated in a Diessen-hofen *exemplum* presenting Berta von Herten who wonders whether she should not have chosen a hermit's life like the recluse Guot. Her prayer for discernment is answered through a vision:

> Then she saw the walls of the refectory like glass. And outside of the glass was a little person who acted as if her heart was bursting because she so much wanted to come through the glass to our Lord. But she could not come through the glass. Then our Lord said: "Would you like to know, my dear daughter, who this person was?" Then she said: "Yes Lord, with all my heart." Then he said: "It is Guot from the forest. And the glass you see between us and her is her own will because she is not under obedience. And therefore she can never come as close [to me] as you because you are under obedience" (*D* 40).[82]

The difficult counsel of complete obedience, *vnder gehorsami sin*, to the monastic superior and ultimately to God is here extolled as also the most valuable counsel of all.

Obedience requires humility, hence these virtues are often paired in the Sister-Books. An Unterlinden nun had "the admirable grace of humility and obedience in her so that she not even once with a little word showed any difficulty obeying but submitted in all things to the will of the person giving the order" (*U* 434; cf. *U* 452; *O* 248). The great value of humility (*diemutikeit*) is frequently evoked (*K* 105, 107, 111, 114; *O* 253; *T* 57). Because of Gregory the Great's dictum that all vices were caused by pride, the high Middle Ages generally stressed humility as the root of all virtue.[83]

---

82. Leclercq (1982a, 122) explains that there had been women hermits from the beginning; but "in the thirteenth century and from then on, 'urban' recluses multiplied."

83. On Gregory, see Bernards (1982, 78).

In contrast to obedience, there is no indication in this particular *corpus* of literature that observing the counsel of chastity caused any problem. This is not to question the importance of this evangelical counsel; rather chastity is generally recognized as a prerequisite for the ascetic way of life. Leaving "the world" was tantamount for these women with renouncing male companionship in any form. And again, pride and licentiousness are seen as equally despicable (*A* 180f.). But as far as the Sister-Books are concerned, these sins of "the world" do not encroach upon the monastic life. As Katharina von Unterlinden states with a much quoted phrase by St. Gregory, there is "little wonder that, having tasted the spirit, all flesh is rendered tasteless" (*U* 421).[84]

But while chastity is a *sine qua non* for all monastic life, virginity, judging by the Sister-Books, was not in the same category. Although the value of virginity, both in a religious and secular context, is acknowledged, these female authors generally differ from the Fathers of the Church by not emphasizing virginity as superior to other virtues (*U* 354, 370, 415).

As evidenced in the Sister-Books, the Church's emphasis on the supreme virtue of virginity, in fact, caused a great amount of suffering, anxiety, and confusion in women's monasteries. Given the daily communal reading of hagiographic material that often contained the legendary commonplace of virginity as a condition for sainthood and, of course, given the sermons that the nuns were regularly exposed to, considerable fear was aroused among the numerous formerly married women who had become monastics.[85]

84. Gregory the Great, *Moralia in Job*, 36.
85. Vauchez (1988, 442) explains that virginity and sainthood were always inseparable in legends. On the ideal of virginity and its history, see Weinstein and Bell (1982, 99); see also Carlé (1980, 82f.); Salisbury (1991, 119); Lucas (1983, 19–29). Bernards (1982, 45) shows that in the Middle Ages the life-long fight to keep one's virginity was understood as a "bloodless martyrdom," also occasionally referred to as "white martyrdom" (NCE 11:313).

The old Germanic tradition that placed great emphasis on women's "sexual purity" was later easily assimilated into the Christian framework (Schulenburg 1986, 41). The most blatant example in medieval German literature of the invincible virgin is found in the character of Brunhilde in the *Nibelungenlied*. This early thirteenth-century MHG heroic epic (with roots in old Germanic mythology) presents the pre-Christian notion of virginal fortitude. In this tradition, virginity was tantamount to not being "subject to" anyone [Gn. 3:16]. It was understood as having the values of self-sufficiency, personal autonomy, and independence, an aspect that may also have contributed to medieval women being receptive to the Church's proclaimed ideal of virginity.

When she "heard in a homily that the blood of our Lord does not unite as lovingly and as devoutly with a sorrowful heart as it does with a virgin's soul," Mechthild von Hundersingen, who was formerly married, became so miserable that only the Lord's voice could console her: "'I will cleanse you with my rose-coloured blood [and will] crown you with my own virginity'" (W 71). The author here clearly wants to show that, in spite of what the friar preached, God does not discriminate against women who "had lived in the world." Similarly the Adelhausen author explains that sister Adelheit, a widow, was greatly troubled by the fact that she had lost her virginity, *magtuom*, a worry that made her "cry day and night." Only several years later is she consoled by a vision:

> Then an angel came and said to her: "Cheer up, God will answer your prayers as far as is possible." And he led her into the air. There were also other angels who had a wine press. And they laid her on it and pressed her so hard that she imagined not a drop of blood was left in her body. And they said to her: "We have pressed out of you all the blood that sinned in you; and we shall pour virginal blood into you, and you will become as similar to virgins as is possible. But you cannot become a virgin again." And when she came to again, she lay in a pool of blood (A 155.13–22).

The stark image of the wine press (*trotte*) is used to illustrate how Adelheit was freed from her anxiety about "the blood that sinned" in her, an allusion to the pervasive notion of moralists that sexual union, even in marriage, was sinful. The author suggests that heavenly intervention liberates these women from unnecessary worry. A vision also consoles the widow Else von Sessenheim, who "suffer[ed] day and night," fearing that she was less loved by Christ (E 29). Again the *exemplum* shows that she is freed of unnecessary anxiety by Christ himself.

Notably, fear and worry, in one case explicitly blamed on a preacher's homily, are overcome in the Sister-Books through divine intervention: Christ is shown siding with the women. Not the physical preservation of virginity, but rather the proper chaste attitude is crucial. Implicitly, then, these authors contradict the traditional concept of the diminished value of women who were no longer virgins. After all, chastity, not virginity, is the third evangelical counsel.[86]

---

86. On the presence of formerly married women in medieval monasteries, see Leclercq (1982b, 131f.). Bernards (1982, 51) quotes the *Speculum virginum*, circa 1100: *Vere magis placet Deo paenitens et humilis vidua quam virgo insolens et superba.*

c. Further Ascetic Striving

"Spiritual discipline" in the Sister-Books is typically referred to as fasting and abstinence and keeping vigil in prayer – practices recommended in the sisters' constitution that have the expressed aim of advancing the nuns in spirituality. Fasting, especially on communion days and for long periods of time, was very common (*A* 187f.; *K* 107, 111; *G* 132, 141; *T* 26, 51, 83; *E* 3). Katharina von Unterlinden also speaks of "the virtue of abstinence" (*U* 355, 359). And the Oetenbach author greatly admires a sister who, for forty years, had not eaten any fresh fruit or vegetables, *obs noch grünes dings* (*O* 268); other sisters were vegetarians for ascetic reasons (*G* 131). Customarily, Church law as well as the rules of their order required a number of days of fasting per year that the communities observed. But again, by praising an especially conscientious "angel-like" sister, *als ain irdescher engel*, for her strict observance of these rules, the Töss author draws attention to the fact that not all the sisters were equally keen on this ascetic exercise (*T* 34).[87]

Keeping vigil at night in private prayers and in "spiritual exercises" was an activity often enumerated along with other exemplary monastic virtues. As if respecting the women's privacy, the authors rarely specify the contents of these prayer vigils (*U* 378, 428, 436; *A* 188; *K* 105, 110, 111, 113, 115; *G* 123, 140; *T* 26, 39, 51, 83; *O* 268; *E* 18, 26). As an ascetic practice, the audience is given to understand, the vigil was especially weighty because the sisters voluntarily deprived themselves of "the sweetness of morning sleep" (*U* 381; *G* 141).

Silence, *swige*, was seen as "the sacred basis of the religious life" (*U* 367, 465; *K* 111, 113; *T* 23, 37, 43, 62). Katharina von Unterlinden illustrates the importance of silence with a homely image: "As the heat of the oven is preserved through its closed door, in the same way the grace of the Holy Spirit is retained in the heart through silence observed" (*U* 338). An Unterlinden sister is praised for having kept "the most severe silence, as if she had no mouth to speak and no ears to hear; this is how she mortified all her bodily senses" (*U* 427f.). The choice of words suggests the discipline necessary for observing silence. One Kirchberg nun reportedly asked God for muteness because she saw her tongue as a cause for sin; another was so accomplished in her habitual long periods of silence that "she made herself a stranger to all people all her life" (*K* 109, 113). But Elisabeth von Kirchberg is quick to challenge this behaviour, assuring her audience that being "mild and

---

87. The term "spiritual discipline" is taken from the *Speculum virginum* (Bernards 1982, 133). On fasting in the Constitution, see Humbert (1259, ch. 13).

friendly to all people" is also a virtue (*K* 114). Some Diessenhofen sisters often voluntarily increased the long prescribed hours of silence: silent during Advent and Lent, some never spoke on a communion day, "as still today many sisters have the habit of doing" (*D* 5, 40). The Gotteszell Sister-Book refers to the commonplace of remaining silent even when a fire broke out: "Once when the dormitory burnt, [Leugart] had the keys with which the sleeping quarters were locked. And when the community called for a long time [asking] where the keys were, she did not want to speak enough to point to the keys, until one of them found them near her bed" (*G* 138.1–5; cf. *G* 132, 137). Similar episodes, common in hagiographic texts, are also to be found (*U* 338; *T* 34).

In general, many women featured in the Sister-Books led a sensibly severe and busy life (*T* 20, 37, 61, 83; *G* 145). Their love of justice defined as "not being able to tolerate anything that was against God and the order" (*E* 9, 19) guided them safely. The much repeated stereotypical praise of these nuns' fasting, vigils, prayers, and chastising their bodies (*U* 362; *E* 17, 20, 43; *T* 14; *D* 29) may give the wrong impression as if these practices always came together. In fact, self-castigation is comparatively little emphasized in the Sister-Books. But of course, the mere mentioning of such corporeal exercises easily claim the modern reader's attention because of their perceived harshness.

d. *Disciplin*

The monastic life, if taken seriously, is austere. But the Sister-Books suggest – although again not all the reports of "discipline" should be taken at face value – that some women deliberately rendered their lives more difficult by their ascetic practices. The terms *disciplin* and *üebunge* are used in these texts for both spiritual and bodily exercises. The purpose of "corporeal discipline," the Unterlinden author explains, is "making the body serve the spirit" (*U* 362). And when Elisabeth von Kirchberg shows a monastic who "very often after Compline tied herself to a pillar and beat herself in praise of our Lord and in gratitude for his scourging" (*K* 106, 115), she touches on the spiritual meaning of self-chastisement. For castigation is understood by these monastics as a way of imitating Christ and of alleviating his burden.[88]

88. On *disciplin*, see also Gehring (1957, 155–158, 171–173); Langer (1987, 68–79). On practical *imitatio*, see Constable (1982, 10f.); Ruh (1990–93, 2:130). *Disciplina* traditionally only used for corporeal punishment had taken on a different meaning by that time, see Bernards (1982, 132).

Anna von Munzingen illustrates the *imitatio* idea with a vision Berchte von Oberried of Adelhausen had when she "was about to die and lay in her prayers, praising the passion of our Lord":

> It was to her as if she were led to a field where God was about to be tortured. And there was a big shout that she heard: "Will someone agree to be hanged and tortured for God?" Then she shouted: "Yes, I, gladly." And with this, death touched her. And this devotion remained with her until her soul left her. Then she was preoccupied with this word: "Lord, I am hanging on your back. You must not shake me down, I will never come away from you." And in this devotion she died (*A* 159.13–19).

The curious ending of this passage makes use of the folkloric *Huckauf*-motif, that is, the image of "the devil on the back" which perhaps is meant to picture Berchte's closeness to Christ. In a tone considerably more sombre, Katharina von Unterlinden writes of the rigorous and sometimes even cruel self-mortification the early sisters of her community imposed upon themselves, while stressing throughout that the nuns did so "for the sake of the Lord" and "in his name" (*U* 341f.). For her, the meaning of self-castigation is unambiguous: "They, too, shed their blood for the love of Christ; in doing so, they imitated his passion in their way" (*U* 342). Planned physical and spiritual discipline in her view aims at coming as close as possible to an *imitatio Christi*.

The wide range of acts of self-negation in the Sister-Books, encompasses watering down food (*T* 20), giving away special treats (*A* 166), never once drinking anything (*T* 51, 83), immersing oneself into ice cold water (*U* 476). In the Kirchberg text, Willbirg von Offeningen and also Chaplain Walther slept on boards and rocks or did not turn the straw mattress, thus making the paillasse next to unusable (*K* 113, 116; cf. *U* 388; *G* 141). Among the more severe measures, sisters wore iron chains or ropes around their bodies (*U* 356, 410; *K* 113) or a hair shirt, *ein herin hemde* (*U* 427; *E* 35; *K* 114); some whipped and even scourged themselves (*U* 340, 475; *O* 258, 262f.).

In Gotteszell, Adelheit von Hiltegarthausen, when she thought the others were fast asleep, "beat herself unduly," *unbescheidenlichen* (*G* 123f.) – the adverb ambiguously hinting at both disapproval and praise. And Elsbetlein in the same monastery, who was "only twelve years old, ... disciplined herself with a pole and with juniper rods" (*G* 141). Katharina von Unterlinden includes the legendary commonplace that one sister engraved a cross on her chest through devotion to Christ's passion (*U* 449). The Töss author refers to sisters practicing "discipline," such as Margret Willin who "had a pillow of willow-twigs and hard wicker-work under an old bed-covering; and as many stones as one uses for stone-flooring she had for her bed where she rested. She wore a hair shirt with frightful buttons and a strong iron chain around her body," and in addition, she "disciplined herself three times daily with a scourge" (*T* 26; cf. *T* 23, 40, 45). Geri Heinburgin's back was "as black as a veil" from such practice, the Diessenhofen author reports (*D* 26).

Such extreme self-mortification is representative of the "old school" of castigating the flesh, a practice that the authors associate with the exemplary life of the first sisters of their monasteries. Of these founding members they write: "Some beat themselves with iron chains, others with a scourge, some with juniper branches" (*T* 14; *E* 7, 17). The later nuns find this practice admirable, as the following report of the early days of the Unterlinden community indicates, but they themselves apparently no longer subject themselves to such discipline:

> In Advent and Lent, after Matins, all the sisters gathered in chapter or at other suitable places and scourged themselves, lacerating their bodies until the blood flowed, and they whipped themselves in a cruel and hostile manner. The sound of the beating was heard in the entire monastery, and it rose, sweeter than any other melody, to the ears of the Lord Sabaoth (*U* 340.25–32).

Self-castigation is described here with recourse to legendary patterns and is meant to enhance the saintly image of the early community.

Some are said to have disciplined themselves, even in later years:

> [Cristina in Gotteszell] was of such saintly life that she observed the order with all severity and serious diligence. And even beyond the rules of the order, she accomplished so many prayers and so much fasting and other good things that it was a miracle for her nature to tolerate it (*G* 140.10–14).

This nun's practice had apparently reached the limit of physical endurance, the text implies; and indeed, excesses occasionally had to be stopped by the superiors (*U* 339f.; *O* 240, 263). Significantly, excesses are also said to have been curtailed miraculously. The Oetenbach author is quite outspoken about Elsbeth von Beggenhofen who chastised herself together with a number of sisters "for God's sake" trying to find God's will through such exercises; however, God "gave her to realize that he did not want that of her"; she was stricken with some severe pain instead (*O* 263). And when Elsbet von Stoffeln in Diessenhofen offered to God in prayer that she might suffer cruel torture as a penance for her sins: "For that, I would gladly have all my limbs cut to pieces and all my veins pulled out," her thoughts are cut short by an answer given to her that her sins had already been forgiven without her going to such extremes (*D* 33; *T* 52).

The nuns' ascetic practices must be seen from an historical perspective. A "fascination with suffering" was characteristic of the religious sentiment of that epoch, leading to exaggerated forms of asceticism. Self-castigation was not only practiced by individuals but also publicly in groups. The actions of fanatic flagellants who roamed the countryside (in upper Germany, documented from 1260 on) is a case in point. This was a time, too, when corporeal punishment was a matter of course: children, students, and wives were regularly beaten, and everyday life was filled with bodily hardship; survival depended on overcoming one's physical weaknesses. And as far as the audience is concerned, Giles Constable suggests that such tales "may have served as a sort of vicarious release for feelings that could not be expressed directly." Moreover, the tales about rigorous bodily discipline in the Sister-Books again follow established legendary patterns. The writers present their audience with "heroines of Christian asceticism" in the tradition of the desert fathers, Haas suggests.[89]

Ascetic striving, in any form, was an integral part of the overall journey these women had embarked on as followers of Christ. The "practice of all virtue," *übung an allen tugenden*, could take many more moderate patterns. It could simply mean denying oneself comfort or even renouncing the aesthetic pleasure that the beauty of nature and art can provide (*O* 261; *W* 85). The Töss author offers the *exempla* of sisters who, while visiting the orchard, refrain, for ascetic reasons, from looking at the trees in blossom (*T* 27, 40). Metzi, an Adelhausen sister, wanted to see the "new paintings [that] had been made in the choir ... very badly"; but when her desire "went beyond all measure, she resisted so steadfastly that she decided never to look at them" (*A* 175). For ascetic reasons, she was determined to forego the deep joy she knew she would derive from art. But as the context explains, the sister was then divinely recompensed for her act of self-negation. Nature and art can be so pleasing to the senses, then, that their sight is made an object of self-denial. These women were by no means insensitive to the beauty of the natural and artistic world surrounding them.

89. Haas (1984a, 111). On the reception of such tales, see Constable (1982, 21). On a fascination with suffering, see Dinzelbacher (1981, 261). For a comparison of medieval castigation with the physical "tortures" of modern athletes, see Ringler (1988, 148). On group whipping, see Weinstein and Bell (1982,156); LThK 4:610f.

Elisabeth von Kirchberg defines the basic concept of asceticism by stating that one sister "was in such control of her heart as if she had it in her hands" (*K* 110). In the final analysis, neither self-inflicted suffering nor extraordinary "special graces" but only an inner *ker*, a turn-around, counts (*T* 26, 88). A radical conversion is called for, that is, "being truly changed from a worldly human being into a spiritual one," *von einem irdischen menschen in einen geistlichen* (*K* 107).

6. Difficulties of Communal Life

Financial problems were among the common difficulties in many monasteries. At the time of the priorate of Hedwig von Gundelsheim, for example, the Unterlinden monastery was unable to pay the hired harvesters or to employ additional farm hands to bring the wheat into the barn. Heavy taxation to which the nuns were subject was another severe grievance (*U* 478f.). Worries like these cause Katharina von Unterlinden to speak of "the heavy burden of the monastic life and the hard yoke of poverty" (*U* 349). For the community, such times of financial struggle resulted in daily deprivations. Some sisters readily accepted such hardship, as Adelheid von Rheinfelden who "never in her life complained about food or drink or about a poor bed, whether she was healthy or sick." And the author continues, "She never exchanged the food offered at table or demanded something else, even if she could not eat what was served" (*U* 397). By implication the audience is led to assume that a number of less virtuous sisters behaved quite differently.

Tensions are typical of any communal living, especially when a large number of people with divers backgrounds and differences in age and mentality live together in overcrowded conditions. Moreover, the unrelenting pressure of the continuous striving for an ascetic life no doubt made tempers flare up now and then. In brief, there was also a darker side of community life.

The Oetenbach chronicler mentions an open discord, *zweiung*, among the sisters concerning a move of the community to a new homestead (*O* 234). The Unterlinden author singles out the peace-loving Elisabeth von Senheim, who did not change her behaviour even in adversity: "She did not run away from suffering scorn and insults, always keeping a placid face and a calm mind. One never saw her angry, never fighting with another sister, never shortchanging anyone or doing injustice in word or deed" (*U* 450f.).

Reading this passage in reverse, as it were, provides an example of personality clashes among the sisters. Likes and dislikes among the nuns were inevitable (*T* 51, 67). In Unterlinden, Gertrud von Herkenheim "was sometimes excited by anger and bothered one of the sisters with bitter insults more than she had any business to. But then immediately she turned into herself, recognized her guilt, and accused herself very much" (*U* 477). Her repentance, while important to note, did not do much to remedy the disagreeable scene she had created in her community. A Töss sister, on the other hand, offered her serving of fruit in recompense to a woman she had insulted (*T* 60).

By showing sisters at fault, the authors admit that their communities did not quite live up to their ideal. Envy (*E* 5f., 18) and disobedience (*E* 24, 39), disregard for the order's rule (*T* 93), and superstition (*T* 79f.) are implicitly mentioned. The Oetenbach author even includes a scene of what one would today call sadistic behaviour on the part of a prioress, although at the time of writing, her attitude was presumably considered good pedagogy and an example of ascetic teaching: "Saintly Sister Hedwig" was bed-ridden, because she had hurt her foot and, since ailing sisters usually received a special diet, she too "desired some meat, for she had a good appetite, *wan si gar grob essig was.*"

> Then the prioress came and insisted three times that she eat meat. [Hedwig] said: "O woe, Lord, she insists so much but does not give me any." The sisters told this to the prioress. Thus the prioress came one day and brought her a beef shank and seriously ordered her to eat it; [but] it was dried out and so unpalatable that it nauseated her. Then a sister said: "Prioress, it is unhealthy and bad for her." Therefore she let it go. Through this, [Hedwig] became so glad that she never forgot this joy until her death (*O* 229.8–15).

Hedwig's unforgettable joy at the end was, it appears, caused by the nun who helped her in this predicament. To have discouraged the prioress from her questionable approach was a courageous move on that sister's part. Another almost Oliver Twist-like scene from the same text provides evidence of the harsh treatment of children:

> One day during a fast, the servant carried around the mush to the fasting sisters, and she gave some more to whoever wanted more. Then one of the children offered her bowl, but she did not give her any more. Thereupon the child laughed out so loud that the prioress and the other sisters became very angry. Then an old sister said: "Leave her in peace. She laughed from childishness, for she would rather cry and weep" (*O* 228.19–229.1).

Again, at least one understanding sister is shown to have taken the side of the mistreated person, this time against the community. Such sympathy seems to be lacking on other occasions: Ita von Hohenfels was disliked and hence painfully singled out by her sisters in community, although the author claims that, for ascetic reasons, she "was pleased that she was despised, *versmeht*, by many and that nobody paid any attention to her" (O 246).

Neither lavishly extravagant praise nor critical denigration can be accepted at face value, although there may be, in both cases, some kernel of truth. At the same time, the authors were well aware that one cannot draw a credible picture without mentioning some of the vexations of communal living with which their audience would have been familiar. The different degrees of perfection the Weiler author finds in her own community are perhaps emblematic. A vision shows "the community divided into three groups: the first one was perfect and united with God; the second one was saintly and practiced good works; the third one was frail and was promptly punished and bettered" (*W* 84). Negative aspects of community life needed to be included so that the unpleasant scenes could function as a foil against which the saintly behaviour of the especially virtuous sisters became more prominent.

7. *Dancing in Exultation*

It would be an unfair presentation of the Sister-Books to close this chapter on the life behind medieval cloister walls on a sombre note. Austere though it was, monastic life is not described as an unhappy one. In fact, a sensible ascesis may be understood as providing a basis for the deep liberating joy frequently mentioned. "Great joy" and inner happiness, as has been pointed out, are frequently represented as reactions to an overwhelming spiritual experience granted to someone whose story the authors tell. At times, such exultation found its expression even in dance.

Dancing, to be sure, has not been part of the western Christian tradition. In fact, Church authorities, especially during the thirteenth and fourteenth centuries, cast a suspicious eye on dancing. The Church felt she had to combat the "medieval passion for dancing" by speaking out against this "indecent habit." Even the liturgical dance was sharply criticized in patristic literature because of its proximity to ancient pagan cult dances. Nevertheless, minutely choreographed liturgical pageants, reminiscent of dances, remained common on special Church holidays, such as the procession on Candlemas (G 125).[90]

---

90. Rokseth (1935, 476); Hartung (1982, 64); Hammerstein (1962, 29, 48).

In medieval literature, a mere trace of the contemporary love of dancing survived in the topos of the heavenly or mystical dance. The Gotteszell author writes: "In heaven, there is a dance, alleluia; and God's spouses participate, alleluia" (*G* 135). Sung by the chantress, this joyous song apparently was the cause of Irmendraut's healing miracle:

> While the song was sung, this sick sister was kindled with such great joy that she stretched out her hands in a comely manner. And when the community saw that the sick sister was in such a state of tender divine grace, they ordered the chantress to continue singing loudly, until this sister became so deeply enraptured that she jumped off the pillow (where they had laid her) into the middle [of their circle] with quick straight legs. And then, in the presence of the community, she danced so lovingly in God's praise that all who saw and heard it felt longing and anguish for the joy that was so unknown to them (*G* 135.44–136.5).

Fearing that Irmendraut's ecstasy might end once the music stopped, the nuns surrounded her tightly to break her fall; but the illness did not return. Irmendraut's dance and the healing miracle became one.

Dancing ought to be more common, the Weiler author suggests with her story about Mechtilt Büglin, a "very old and sick" woman unable to walk by herself: "She got up off her chair, just as if she were dancing, went to the altar and said: 'The burning Seraphim and Cherubim stand before God and sing and dance and jubilate; we should rejoice with them and praise God'" (*W* 77).

The dance of ecstasy in the Sister-Books, while confined to the spiritual context of these works, is an expression of joy and happiness. In Adelhausen, Adelheid Geishörnlin was so filled with joy that she suddenly jumped up and turned like a spinning-top, *zwirbelet*, as is said twice: "The sweetness and the miracle she was granted was so great that she jumped up and whirled around the altar, and blood flowed out of her mouth and nose." Luggi, another sister, "standing below in the choir, saw how she whirled around the altar" (*A* 166f.). Asked about the reason for all this, Adelheid explained that her nature had to react to her excessive joy, *die vbrigen froyde*, or else she would have died. Also the Engeltal sister Alheit von Trochau is described "jumping and singing" for joy when she passed by "our Lord" in the monastery choir (*E* 13).[91]

---

91. The wording in the text is ambiguous: it shows the sister dancing either in front of an artistic representation of Christ or when passing by the tabernacle.

Finally, Elisabeth von Kirchberg intimates that dancing in these communities might not have been as infrequent as the few references to dancing in the Sister-Books lead us to suppose. Speaking of Mechthild von Waldeck's extraordinary spiritual experience, the author explains that it made her soul dance inside her body:

> So filled was her heart with deep devotion and lasting desire and divine love and the experience of God in her soul and much joy that she actually experienced that her soul moved inside her [body] as if she jumped up. And it seemed to her in true experience that her soul inside showed all the gestures that our sisters did on the outside when they were jubilant. And innumerably often she could not contain herself so that we became aware of it (*K* 119.20–25).

By way of a negligible simile, the author reveals that the cloistered women habitually expressed their feeling of happiness by abandoning themselves in dancing with joy.

While these spontaneous eruptions into song and dance might have been inspired by biblical passages [such as 2 S. 6:14 and Lk. 15:25], they are quite different from psalm singing and the measured liturgical movements in their proper settings. Pointing to the late medieval women's movement, Haas suggests that dancing at that time was a typical emotional outlet for women who often reacted to ecstatic raptures with dancing, laughing, and clapping of hands.[92]

Readers today might wish for more frequent scenes of spontaneity in the Sister-Books. Yet given the fact that the Church opposed dancing and that the authors may, therefore, have been reticent to talk about dancing at all, the few glimpses offered, must be appreciated, especially since this topic exceeds the scope and formal intent of these works. All the more, the depiction of the sisters' spontaneous dancing adds a significant feature to the image of the self-assured monastic women presented in the Sister-Books.

---

92. Haas (1987a, 240f.).

One of the dominant motifs in the Sister-Books is these women's love of learning. The Dominican nuns' intense interest in knowledge is not coincidental, since the Order of Preachers has, from its beginning, promoted studying and education as its very *raison d'être*. St. Dominic "was the first founder [of a monastic order] to weave study into the fabric of daily religious life, raising it to the status of a religious duty and placing it at the side of prayer as a service to God," William A. Hinnebusch explains.[1]

Informal learning had always been encouraged for monastic women in general. Caesarius of Arles' *Regula* (512) exhorted the nuns to learn to read and write and spend two hours studying daily after Matins. In Dominican women's monasteries, as had been stipulated in the Primitive Constitution and recommended by St. Dominic himself, studying became an habitual part of many sisters' daily activities. Although the Dominican women were at first not officially obliged to study, the first female members of the Dominican Order in Prouille in the early thirteenth century are said to have been both teachers and preachers, *educatrici et preadicatrici*.[2]

LITERACY IN THE WOMEN'S COMMUNITIES

Throughout the Sister-Books, literacy is taken for granted, at least for the choir nuns. Reading and writing was a necessary condition for admission to the Dominican Second Order, since "this ability was needed to master the psalmody and the lessons of the Divine Office."[3] An occasional illiterate nun is singled out in these texts as an exceptional case, where the authors hasten, as it were, to explain the specific circumstances for such an impairment. Adelheid von Weiblingen in the Weiler text, for instance, had "an eye illness, and she had never learned anything" (*W* 77). The Diessenhofen author reveals her lack of respect

---

1. Hinnebusch (1966, 123); see also Haas (1984b, 607); Mandonnet (1944, 85f.).

2. *Primitive Constitution* (1969, 20); Ceasarius, *Regula* (1988, iv). On Prouille, see Elm (1981, 12); on studying and manual labor, see Fontette (1967, 112); regarding the 1984 revision of the Dominican women's constitution where "'studying the truth eagerly' was inserted," see Noffke (1990, 59). In Humbert (1259, ch. 17) "reading" referred to praying rather than studying (ch. 17).

3. Hinnebusch (1966, 383).

for a sister unable to read, when she introduces a story rather bluntly with: "When [Kathrin Brúmsin] was a novice, she had an obtuse mind, *harten sinn*, for learning so that scarcely anything could get into her [head]" (*D* 38).[4] In their didactic vein and out of a sense of fairness, the authors of the Sister-Books state, however, that a lack of literacy does not imply a lack of virtues. Katharina von Unterlinden uses the legendary commonplace to explain that a monastic *illiterata* excelled before all others in saintliness (*U* 406f.). The Töss author shows a lay sister who learned the antiphon *Ave stella matutina* directly from "our Lady"; and she was able to memorize it and teach it to another sister (*T* 86; *U* 469).

Literacy at that time, of course, meant understanding Latin, the official church language and the language of culture throughout medieval Europe. In his treatise on education, *De Eruditione*, the thirteenth-century Dominican pedagogue and encyclopedist, Vincent of Beauvais, takes bilingualism, that is, knowing Latin and the vernacular, for granted at least among the educated including women. The knowledge of Latin, also in the monasteries discussed in the Sister-Books, was simply presupposed. The nuns' correspondence, such as with their provincial, for instance, was in Latin. Moreover, during a visit of Friar Peter of Verona, the so-called Peter Martyr, which Grundmann found documented for the Adelhausen community in 1244, the educated nuns conversed with him in Latin and listened to his Latin sermons. And while fluency of this standard may not have been routine, the liturgical Latin texts at least presented no difficulties to the nuns. The occasional exception is mentioned, as when Christine Ebner describes an audition noteworthy for its down-to-earth advice and refreshing wisdom: The "very old sister" Hedwig von Regensburg "wanted to skip choir" saying "she did not understand it. Then a voice said: 'Go to choir! You will understand it as little out here as you do inside'" (*E* 21).[5]

4. Gurevich (1990, 201f.) argues that "the contrast between educated people and the uneducated and ignorant was basic throughout the Middle Ages. The inability to express oneself in Latin, with few exceptions, was considered a deficiency and frequently mocked." However, it should also be mentioned that Engelsing (1973, 2) provides long lists of illiterate monks of the thirteenth and fourteenth centuries.

5. Literacy, at least up to the fourteenth century, does not necessarily mean both reading and writing; many could read but not write. See Thompson (1960, 85); Power (1975, 82); Boehm (1982, 155); Lucas (1983, 140). On Vincent of Beauvais, see Tobin (1974, 487). On the nuns' fluency in Latin, see Hinnebusch (1966, 384); Grundmann (1935, 463 n.51).

Judging by a few incidental passages and, of course, by the mere existence of these MHG texts themselves, the Sister-Books fall within the transitional period from the centuries-old exclusive use of Latin in written texts to a more frequent use of written German. Some passages witness to the fact that the authors, familiar with the Latin word, are groping for the proper German term, especially when it comes to biblical citations. Scripture translations were strictly forbidden at that time. But the authors often solve this problem by setting down both the Latin and the MHG phrase. In the following text passage, for instance, the Töss author has Anne von Klingnau report an exchange she had during a dream vision: "Then I said: 'Ah, dear Lord, who are you?' Then he said: 'I am called *Reparator*,' and this means in German: *ain widerbringer*, a Savior" (*T* 38). Messages the sisters receive in visions are often said to have been in Latin, or at least partially so. The Adelhausen author shows St. John the Evangelist making a sister read a Latin passage from Revelations [3:4f.]; and a *revenante* in the Gotteszell text supposedly had Latin phrases written on her garment (*A* 174; *G* 131; cf. *G* 139).[6]

The extraordinary use of the vernacular in matters related to religion always brings out the visionaries' startled reaction. An Unterlinden sister excitedly reports that she heard "the Lord speaking to her in German, *lingua theuthonica*," with a sweet voice (*U* 489). The Töss author, too, explains that a voice from above "sang such exceedingly sweet words in German, *tüsche wort*, that both the voice and words could not be compared to anything material" (*T* 72). The use of the familiar German heightens the spiritual experience.

While Latin as the Church language remained the general norm at that time, there had been tendencies within Germany since the twelfth century to soften somewhat the strict rule regarding the exclusive use of Latin in religious services, Hammerstein explains. Christine Ebner offers us an example of the spontaneous intrusion of German into the nuns' Latin liturgy during a night service:

> Their first chantress was called Heilrat. She was super-humanly beautiful and sang immeasurably well. She also studied very well and loved our Lord completely .... . When they came to the fourth Sunday of Advent, and when they sang Matins and came to the fifth responsory, *Virgo Israel*, and to the verse *In caritate perpetua*, she sang in German. And she sang so super-humanly well that they

6. Richter (1976, 51 and n.22) quotes thirteenth-century council documents that forbade translations of the scripture (Toulouse 1229, Tarragona 1234, Bézier 1246).

thought she was singing with an angelic voice. The verse meant the following: I have loved [*gemint*] you with eternal love [*minne*], through which I have drawn you to me in my mercy. Our Lord spoke this verse to humankind through the prophet's mouth.

This saintly community fainted out of great devotion and fell to the ground as if dead and lay there until they came to again. And then they completed singing their Matins with great devotion (*E* 6.30–7.7). The emotional impact of hearing the liturgy sung in their mother tongue, so dramatically illustrated in this text, constituted an unparalleled event in these women's life and enhanced their devotional fervour. The author's repeated use of hyperbole also gives the passage special weight. The description of the chantress as "super-humanly beautiful," for instance, is unique and must presumably be understood as a reference to Heilrat's spiritual beauty, for "corporeal beauty is, by its very nature, an evil," as Vincent of Beauvais, among others, had taught.[7]

German and Latin was also found side by side in the monastery libraries. A century later, Johannes Meyer would give minute instructions[8] to the book mistress in how to separate the Latin from the German codices. But even from the community's early days on, vernacular texts were at hand, as suggested by Christine Ebner: "When they sat at table, the *magistra* sat at the head. And when she had eaten a little, she read the table-reading in German. This was rare at that time" (*E* 2). This progressive attitude is specifically documented for Engeltal which was the community that later stood foremost in literary achievement, especially in the production of works written in the vernacular.

TEACHING, READING, AND STUDYING WITHIN THE CLOISTER

The *septem artes liberales*, that is, the *trivium* (grammar, rhetoric, dialectic) and the *quadrivium* (arithmetic, geometry, astronomy, music), that represent the formal school subjects during much of the Middle Ages, are not directly referred to in the Sister-Books. Speaking specifically about worldly knowledge does not lie within the intended scope of these texts.[9]

7. On the slow acceptance of German in the liturgy, see Hammerstein (1962, 54); LThK 2:267f. On Vincent of Beauvais, see Tobin (1974, 488). See also Kramer's comment (1991, 199) on this passage.

8. Meyer, in: König (1880, 202ff.).

9. Haas (1987b, 143) assumes that the well-educated sisters had had their formal training in the seven liberal arts. Tuchman (1978, 53) shows that educating noble women in medieval France "was encouraged by the Church" because it prepared young girls for possible monastic life.

The Sister-Books show that the nuns themselves functioned as teachers among each other; theological discussions within the community were apparently not rare (*T* 48). Sophie von Klingnau in Töss reportedly spent her life teaching theology (*T* 57–61; cf. *G* 133). Gehring suggests that the level of education in these Dominican monasteries was so high because the nuns welcomed rich women into their communities in order to benefit from their dowries; and upper class women "represented the higher levels of education and culture." These women then served as teachers, passing on their knowledge to the less educated community members.[10] Also Benedictine nuns were instrumental as teachers among the early Dominican sisters. They "worked hard for us, first bringing to us the knowledge of the Holy Scriptures," besides instructing the nuns in the liturgical chants, Katharina von Unterlinden explains (*U* 365). Experienced in the long tradition of Benedictine monasticism, these women were admired for their extensive learning and eagerly listened to by the members of the newly established Dominican communities (*E* 26).

Moreover, the nuns were intellectually stimulated by the homilies of the friars preachers (*O* 262). And as intelligent listeners, they in turn encouraged the friars to give speculative homilies, Gieraths suggests. A medieval homily was not the equivalent of an occasional sermon but was a means of expounding on the generally binding tenets of the faith. As James J. Murphy explains, the "*ars praedicandi* [after about 1220] clearly assumes an educated audience." Homilies, in fact, represented a focal point of medieval intellectual life and were conducive to continued learning.[11]

Schools for pupils from outside the community were not part of a medieval Dominican women's monastery. However, the young children in their midst were given proper schooling by the nuns. As Katharina von Unterlinden informs her readers, she had been raised in the Unterlinden community from early childhood and acquired, as her work

---

10. Gehring (1957, 5) following Denifle (1886a, 647).

11. On (mainly Dominican) homilies, see Gieraths (1956, 20); Völker (1963, 223); Murphy (1974, 310f.) See also Humbert of Romans, *Treatise on Preaching* (1955, 102). Halter (1956, 60) shows that the Zürich area benefitted by the relocation of the Colmar Dominican Philosophical Faculty (*Studium Arcium*) to Zürich in 1293–94. Ordered by the Provincial Hermann von Minden, this move had an immediate positive effect on the calibre of the friars' homilies and presumably directly influenced at least the women's monasteries of Oetenbach, Töss, and Diessenhofen located in this geographical region.

amply shows, an excellent education (*U* 480). Among the Töss sisters, Willi von Konstanz, who later wrote theological works, entered the Töss monastery at the age of three and obtained all her schooling there (*T* 48). And the Gotteszell author tells us about Elsbetlein, "a child who had been put into this monastery when she was in her twelfth year," who immediately manifested

> such a noble beginning that she never or rarely passed any time without either studying or praying. And when other children went to enjoy and entertain themselves, this child always studied and consolidated what she had learned. Thus she so much comprehended the Scriptures in her mind that she well understood what was being sung or read to her (*G* 141.15–21).

As an adult and a full member of the community, this Sister Elsbetlein became a teacher: "whenever she was not reading herself, she was teaching other children" (*G* 142). However, the Diessenhofen author suggests, the young girls were not always enthusiastic about school: When Anne von Ramswag "came to the monastery as a young child, she did not like to study at all. And when she was taught to read, she barely looked into her book." But then it so happened that, "one time, she opened the book and saw a little child lying in the book" (*D* 41; cf. *D* 40). A miracle is credited with having given this sister-to-be the zeal needed for learning, for the author continues: "Thereafter, with all her heart, she liked to study everything she was supposed to study."

Young members of the community were made to study the Psalter (*T* 34). The memorized psalter served the immediately practical purpose of enabling the sisters to participate in the divine services that were held in the monasteries during the dark of the night. Importantly, the Psalter also formed the basis for studying Latin. Thus, Humbert of Romans urged the novices to be diligent in learning the psalmody and the Divine Office. References to reading or praying the Psalter, *den salter lesen*, are numerous in the Sister-Books (*E* 3; *T* 40). A miracle story told by the Kirchberg author specifically encourages the reciting of psalms (*K* 115). And Katharina von Unterlinden, idealizing her early community, assures her audience that the sisters and novices knew and understood everything that was sung in the Divine Office (*U* 339).[12]

---

12. Humbert (1259, ch.15). Bell (1989,149) explains that around 1400 the Psalter was used "as an alphabet book." Illmer (1971, 177–179) argues that the memorization of the one hundred fifty psalms equipped the students with all the vocabulary and idioms necessary for understanding medieval Latin texts in general.

The importance of the texts used in the liturgy can hardly be overestimated as a source of knowledge in monastic education. According to Leclercq, the liturgy was "the medium through which the Bible and the patristic tradition [were] received". It is, therefore, little surprising that the office of the liturgical reader (*U* 393; *D* 40) played such a central role in the Dominican women's constitution.[13]

The authors of the Sister-Books take the constant everyday use of books for granted. Besides frequent references to the Bible and to *vitae* and legendaries, the authors mention Cassian, Jerome, Ambrose, Augustine, Gregory the Great, Bede, Bernard of Clairvaux, and Thomas Aquinas. Furthermore, the antiphonaries, evangeliaries, and pericopal readers (containing the sacred texts for the daily readings) were altogether indispensable for the liturgical services. Sisters in the sick room were read the gospel of the day by their nurses or friends (*T* 93). The Gotteszell author describes the bed-ridden Adelheit von Hiltegart-hausen with "a Psalter in front of her, and she had been reading in it" (*G* 125). The nuns listened to regular readings during *collatio* and in chapter which included texts of biblical origin, legends, and the "lives" of saints, the latter even used at the second Canonical Hour.[14] Some nuns are shown carrying around their own devotional readers for individual use in prayer. Of Elsbet von Klingenberg in the Engeltal monastery, it is said: "She prayed quite assiduously and especially she read much in the Psalter" (*E* 37); and Elsbet Mairin von Nürnberg was given "a long prayer that starts with *Ave Maria* which she read to the end" (*E* 41). The authors use miracle stories to encourage such individual reading of prayers. "As she prayed from her book, it turned golden in her hands," Anna von Munzingen says of an Adelhausen nun (*A* 173). And a lay sister is said to have found "stars and flowers in her book" that she used for meditation (*A* 165).

Communal reading had been strongly recommended in the Rule of St. Benedict and, more specifically, emphasized in the Constitution of San Sisto which states: "In the refectory there should always be reading during meals. The Sisters should listen attentively and in silence." The Weiler and Engeltal authors explain that some sisters were greatly

---

13. See Leclercq (1961, 87); Humbert (1259, ch.17).

14. For instructions on daily reading, see Humbert (1259, ch.6 and 30). Ancelet-Hustache (1928, 33); Pfister (1964, 284); Haas (1987a, 294) also stress these authors' book knowledge. For monastic readings habits then, see Steer (1987, 307) and for now, see Cummings (1986, 19).

stimulated in their devotion by the words of the table-reading; others were enraptured by what they heard read (*W* 71, 77; *E* 2). Some sisters who did not take their meal with the community in the refectory, such as the cook and the infirmarians, came in to sit close to the reader and listen (*T* 83, 48). The Töss author states that one sister's "heart was very moved when [stories] about our Lord's passion were read at table" (*T* 62). The fifteenth-century catalogue extant from the Nürnberg St. Katharinenkloster lists around three hundred and seventy different titles of books recommended for table readings.[15]

Table readings could sometimes be combined with learned lectures: In Engeltal, for instance, Cristin von Kornburg "had gained some knowledge and with God's grace she came to interpret large difficult books at table" (*E* 30). The verb *diuten*, "to make something understood to the people," used in this quotation could mean either interpretation or translation of the text.

Internal evidence suggests sizeable book holdings in the monasteries, some of it copied by the nuns themselves, others bought or donated. Metzi von Klingenberg, for instance, "donated many German books" to the Töss library (T. 45), presumably as part of her dowry.[16] These monastic book collections greatly encouraged individual studying which was something many women enjoyed. The Töss sister Margret Finkin relished "studying Latin or writing and giving herself to devout prayer; that was her steady busyness, *unmuos*, except when she had to do something else by obedience (*T* 34; cf. *T* 37). The Weiler author refers to her own reading which she made use of in her writing (*W* 70f.). And in

15. On monastic table reading, see RB (1980, ch. 38); *Early Documents* (1969, 8); Hauber (1914, 349); Ruh (1981); and, for a bibliography, see Baudouin de Gaiffier, "A propos des légendiers latins," *Analecta Bollandiana* 97 (1979), 57–68 esp. 60–68. See also Johannes Meyer in his "Ämterbuch" (König 1880, 205), suggesting that the reader was to prepare diligently for this weekly office so that she read "neither too softly nor too loud ... nor too fast", and she should announce what she was going to read and clearly indicate when she came to an end by saying "Explicit."

16. Bell (1989, 143) shows that a large number of fourteenth-century records identify women as book owners. The monetary value of books was exorbitant. Scholars often refer to the example of Ulrich, monk in Benediktbeuren who, around 1074, was given a vineyard by Graf von Bozen as payment for a mass text. And although paper codices during the later medieval period became somewhat cheaper, Robert I. Burns (Conference at the Centre for Medieval Studies in Toronto, 21 February 1992) suggested that the purchase of a book in the late Middle Ages was probably comparable to acquiring a medium-sized car today. On late medieval book prices, see also Boehm (1982, 154); Engelsing (1973, 13); Bell (1989, 140f.).

Töss, Anna von Klingnau is shown "reading the saints' lives," presumably in one of the popular legendaries (*T* 38; cf. *E* 23). Leugart vom Perg in Engeltal is singled out as having studied the trinitarian mystery with special care (*E* 7). A convincing portrait of a studious person is found in the Gotteszell book: Elsbetlein, because of "her desire" to study, "always kept busy reading the Scripture" which "she understood so very well that it ought rightly to satisfy any woman":

> And in the very cold wintertime, she studied during the night in front of her bed so much and so eagerly that she did not feel the bitter cold and paid no attention until the fingers of her hand got stiff where she held the book. And this lasted until her death. And whenever she got tired of reading, she gave herself to holy meditation and devout prayer (*G* 142.14–24).

The description of this sister's nightly studies has a rare realistic touch. Moreover, the text leaves no doubt that Elsbetlein's involvement with books apparently exceeded the standard set for a woman of the time. In much the same vein, the Adelhausen author states even more explicitly of Grünburg von Kastelberg that she "was an exceptional person in all things that concern a religious human being. She especially [had] exceptional knowledge in the Scriptures, more than any woman should ever gain" (*A* 167). Again, reference is made to limitations society has set for how far a woman should carry her intellectual quest. But, whatever these limitations may be, the women here presented are at liberty to ignore them. In this context, Ringler comments on the wholesome environment in these Dominican monasteries (as opposed to the oppressive atmosphere in some other communities); in the Order of Preachers, "women found a chance for self-realization like nowhere else in the society of their time."[17] By presenting monastic women who excelled in learning, the authors consciously make the point that the sisters were not only free from societal restrictions generally imposed on women but were, indeed, even encouraged to pursue their studies in the safety of their community.

The authors of the Sister-Books frequently use the Dominican friars, the so-called "learned people," as the measuring rod for the high level of learning that some sisters acquired. The Weiler author suggests that even the learned friars had to acknowledge the exceptional knowledge of some women in her community:

17. Ringler, as quoted in Bauer (1985, 375).

A lecturer (*leßmeister*) of the Order of Preachers succeeded in making [a devout sister] talk with him about God by telling her he wanted to verify her graces through the Scriptures. He [then] said: "This soul deals with the highest things that I ever heard from any human being" (*W* 70.8–11).

The Weiler author does not explain the contents of Elisabeth's superb understanding. Alheit von Trochau in Engeltal is said to have had the grace of being able to "interpret difficult books like a well-educated clergyman," *daz si die sweren buch als wol bedeuten kond als ein wol gelerter pfaff* (*E* 13). And the Töss book contains a lengthy passage that suggests a deep understanding of God that Jüzi Schulthasin had been given. This particular text, carefully composed around the key term *erkantnus*, that is, "knowledge, perception," and using the anaphora "she also perceived," *sy erkant och*, is surrounded by the twice repeated statement: "she knew this better than all the masters who studied it," *Und das kund sy alles bas denn alle die maister die ie da von gelernetend*, (*T* 72f.). Such a bold assertion testifies to the intellectual self-confidence of these monastic women.[18]

The Sister-Books' authors insist that all teaching and learning within their monasteries go beyond the mere acquisition of book knowledge. Due to their didactic intent, they stress the importance of learning to live the monastic way of life as a whole (of which books are only one, albeit an essential part). Thus Anna von Munzingen quotes one of the women saying: "When I accomplish the works of obedience, I go to my Lord Jesus Christ as if to my schoolmaster, and I listen and see what he teaches me" (*A* 159). Typically the desire for learning is spiritually motivated, that is, learning is valued because it can enhance devotion. Some of the most spiritually dedicated nuns mentioned in the Sister-Books are simultaneously represented as the most highly educated and cultivated women.

WOMEN AS AUTHORS AND SCRIBES

The Sister-Books themselves provide ample proof that the medieval Dominican women had a keen interest in writing. The trust that made these women set down their own stories attests to their basic faith in

---

18. See also Christine Ebner's reference to the "masters of Paris" (*E* 33; cf. *W* 75). Passages like this may reveal a competitive spirit between the spiritually enlightened nuns and the university-trained friars, remarks Andrew Colin Gow (University of Alberta, Edmonton, 1994); see also Kramer (1991, 199f.).

the value of the written word. Moreover, the authors' rhetorical skill and the ease with which they quote Bible passages and refer to patristic writings point to their generally cultured background. Whether this knowledge came from their own reading or from orally transmitted information – an unimaginably huge amount by today's standards – or both, is irrelevant in this context.

The scriptoria [*die schreibstuben*] of these monasteries produced a sizable number of books, many of them copies but also some newly written texts. The Töss author, for instance, says of Elsbet von Cellinkon that "she was able to write very well and loved to write good things" (*T* 91), a passage that could mean that this sister was an author or a scribe or perhaps both. And Willi von Constanz in Töss authored *ain schoen buoch* of theological content for the community: "But she especially showed that God lived so sweetly in her heart by being so eager and fond of talking of him and listening to talks [about him]. And whatever she heard she kept in her mind until she made a beautiful book for us" (*T* 48). The annual ten marks the Oetenbach sisters earned in the scriptorium by selling their work to other monastics, to secular clergymen, and perhaps also to interested people among the laity, played an important role in this at first notoriously poor monastery. This community only started to become financially viable after the rich widow Ita von Hohenfels entered the monastery and brought with her three young well-educated women, one of whom could write and illuminate manuscripts, another paint (that is, presumably a miniaturist), and the third do fine embroidery. The scribe among them, together with another copyist, turned the monastery's fortune around (*O* 231). The scriptorium in Oetenbach later became the largest and hence the most important workroom in this community (*O* 260).[19]

The office of the scribe was considered essential to the proper functioning of the monastery. Katharina von Unterlinden explains of Gertrud von Rheinfelden:

19. On the value of money the sisters earned, Hermann von Minden (ed. Löhr 1925, 162) suggests in one of his letters that three marks silver was considered enough for the annual upkeep of one sister. On scriptoria, see Hinnebusch (1966, 385): in the mid-1200s one of the provincials "prescribed that the copyists should write in the workroom where the other nuns did their assignments" – a recommendation apparently not observed in Oetenbach. Grundmann (1935, 462) refers to a decree of the General Chapter of the Order of Preachers in Trier (1249) that forbade the friars to have psalteries and other books copied by female scribes: *Fratres non faciant sibi scribi psalteria vel alia scripta per moniales vel alias mulieres.*

> She had received a good and competent scholarly education and administered the office of the scribe by writing for many years, with great eagerness and elegantly, the choir books necessary for the Divine Office as well as many other [texts]. Throughout her whole life, she never failed to work eagerly, for the benefit of all, in this and other tasks necessary for the monastery, but especially in her written work in which she excelled (*U* 431.5–12).

Making money from the production of codices took second place over supplying texts for the large communities themselves. Scribes provided the many copies of books necessary for the communal singing and praying during their liturgy. These liturgical texts must have been voluminous judging by the comment that the sickly Beli von Liebenberg took "two large books (to read Matins from) which she was unaccustomed to carry" (*T* 30). And Jüzi Schulthasin experienced so many miracles within seven years' time that, the Töss author explains, if one were to write them all down, they could not be contained even in a Matins book, *metibuoch* (*T* 70).

Much time and energy in these communities was spent on copying the texts and melodies for choir (*T* 51). Adelheid von Eftich in Unterlinden, for instance, "wrote many books in a most elegant way, especially for choir service" (*U* 411). And while as yet no traces of medieval Dominican women's own compositions or arrangements have been found (as we have of the twelfth-century abbesses Hildegard von Bingen and Herrad von Hohenburg), Hildegard Wachtel asserts that the Dominicans in particular are known to have introduced a number of new sequences (usually sung in D and G major) during the thirteenth century to supplement the existing hymns.[20]

The Unterlinden author praises the skilled scribes and tries hard to convince everyone of the value of literary work. She adds a typical miracle authenticating the virtue of diligent scribes by showing a scribe's hand appearing to one of the sisters "in a wonderful splendor, *mirabiliter refulgens*, like the clarity of the sun." And she concludes: "Not a little astonished by the novelty of this miracle, [Adelheid von Rheinfelden] realized from the heavenly splendor of this hand that the work of this [scribe] ... must be most pleasing and acceptable before

---

20. In her musicological study of four choir books from the thirteenth and fourteenth centuries in Adelhausen, Wachtel gives a detailed description of all the contents including the musical notation (1938, 18–48 and 80–82).

God" (*U* 431). Similarly, the Diessenhofen author credits a miracle, when Mechthilt von Wangen, a formerly illiterate woman, accomplished an unusual feat: "This blessed sister had never learned Latin nor known how to write; and yet, she wrote the four passion accounts in German with her own hand" (*D* 34). Since translating Scriptures into the vernacular was officially forbidden, this passage is a case in point that the authors' recourse to miracles is meant to protect them against questions raised by the ecclesiastical authorities.

The most beautiful piece that survives from the scriptorium of any of the nine monasteries in question is the elaborate codex, *Prachtkodex*, from Diessenhofen. It is the so-called *Graduale* finished in 1312, thus preceding the completion of the Diessenhofen Sister-Book by some decades. Its beautiful 314 parchment pages with forty-six large and many small miniatures and filigreed initials, contain the changing texts and melodies of the mass for the entire liturgical year. Its high artistic calibre, Albert Knoepfli maintains, places this codex among the three most important European codices in that particular style and of that period in time (the two others being the so-called *Manesse-Handschrift* and the *St. Galler Weltchronik*).[21]

Unfortunately, though, only a few other early manuscripts have been preserved from the nine monasteries concerned. Among the codices that go back to the fourteenth century, the following are known to have come from one of these communities: two breviaries and Ulrich von Straßburg's *Summa de summo bono* owned by the Adelhausen women; a *Ritualbuch* from Oetenbach, the *Ordinarium* mentioned above; and the oldest copy of Suso's *Büchlein der ewigen Weisheit* from the mid-fourteenth century Töss monastery, perhaps copied by Elsbet Stagel.[22] Many other books are extant from the fifteenth century. A number of devotional and theological works from the former Diessenhofen library as well as a few titles that originally belonged to Oetenbach have been preserved. The Stuttgart Landesbibliothek (currently in the process of cataloguing medieval material) has located seventeen manuscripts from the former Weiler monastery. And at least four

21. Knoepfli (1989, 173); for the description of this codex, see Knoepfli (1989, 187, n.2); and see the facsimile edition of this work, *Das Graduale von St.Katharinenthal [Diessenhofen]*, ed. Alfred Schmid, with its reviews by Mazal (1983) and Gerhard Schmidt, *Kunstchronik* 36 (1983) 436f.

22. Pfister (1964, 288f.) claims that the Töss monastery had a small, but steadily growing library as early as the thirteenth century which reached its high point during the fourteenth.

Figure 14 Graduale, from the Diessenhofen scriptorium, written in 1312

codices from Töss are kept in Zürich today.[23] None of the library catalogues of the nine monasteries have survived.

The Oetenbach chronicle is a witness to the high regard for codices among the nuns. At the time when the community was abjectly poor so that the sisters themselves helped to build a new monastery by pulling the stones, "harnessed in front of the cart" like oxen, the nuns "sent their books and other things they owned" once they were ready to move (O 226, 235). That is, even during the times of extreme hardship, the sisters had held on to the books as their most precious possessions. The chronicler does not reveal whether the community simply cherished their books as a source of knowledge or whether they were complying with official regulations, because the Order of Preachers, wanting to counteract the quite "lucrative" trading with books at that time, Hinnebusch explains, had issued a general ruling in 1236 that "interdicted all commerce in books."[24]

In general, manuscript-copying by women scribes in the various monasteries during medieval times, as documented in the Sister-Books, can be traced back to the sixth century; it is a historical fact that has not yet attracted our full attention. Perhaps female scribes have not been adequately recognized because, as the paleographer Albert Bruckner explains, male and female hands in medieval manuscripts cannot readily be distinguished. Hence, a male hand was usually taken for granted when we might, in fact, owe much of what has been transmitted of ancient and medieval thinking to female scribes. Grundmann credits women scribes to a large extent with having preserved the texts of the mystics as well as other medieval works.[25]

THE *DONUM SAPIENTIAE*

The possession of intellectual knowledge that cannot be accounted for by natural means is a "special grace." Leugart of Gotteszell, speaking of herself, declares that "our Lord gave her so many insights (*erkanntnüsse*]" that she "imagined he had forgotten all angels and saints and

---

23. For the enumeration of codices extant, see Däniker-Gysin (1958, 61f.); Gieraths (1956, 25); Haas (1987a, 281); Halter (1956, 63); Knoepfli (1989, 306, 179); Pfister (1964, 284, 289); Ruh (1981, 48f.); Schneider (1941, 133f.). Information regarding the Stuttgart Württembergische Landesbibliothek was kindly provided by Dr. Felix Heinzer (June 26, 1991).

24. Hinnebusch (1973, 206f.).

25. Grundmann (1936, 148); see also Völker (1963, 214 and 224f.). For early scribes among monastic women, see Hauber (1914, 351); Bruckner (1971, 441, 447f.); cf. also Wattenbach (1958, 445).

consoled her alone before all other creatures" (G 138). Some women, the authors explain, were granted a sudden, profound understanding and what Elisabeth von Kirchberg calls "divine illumination." Thus Eite von Holzhausen "came to such great understanding (*erkantnusse*) that she understood (*erkant*) God in himself, which is one of the greatest graces that ever can happen to a human being on earth" (K 107; cf. K 109, 118). And to Jüzi Schulthasin swept up in ecstasy is afforded not only theological insight but understanding into the nature of human existence itself:

> She was once enraptured into the heavenly kingdom, and from there she looked down to the earth. And she understood and saw that all the earth is so small. As small as the space that one hand can cover is compared to all the earth; [this is] as small as the earth is compared to the heavenly kingdom.
>
> She also clearly understood that each single star is as wide and as large as all of the earth together (T 76.20–25).

The Töss author here makes use of a common medieval topos that suggests the insignificance of the earth compared to the awe-inspiring universe.

Many other learning miracles, routinely found in legends, underline the prominent place attributed to learning in the Sister-Books.[26] The Diessenhofen author describes the dream vision of the novice Kathrin Brúmsin who had to admit to St. John that she did not know any Latin. The saint then took her by her hand, led her to a book with golden letters, and suddenly she was able to read twenty-four verses of a sequence. After waking up, she not only told her community about her dream, but she was still able to recite all these verses from memory. "Always after that she had a good mind for learning," the episode concludes (D 38). An illiterate sister in the early days of the Töss community, during one liturgical service, miraculously understood all the Latin words (T 46; cf. E 6). Of the elderly sister Tuda von Colmar, the Unterlinden author writes:

> She felt, richly flowing into her, an understanding of the Holy Scriptures of which she had been totally ignorant before [because] she had never been taught the letters from anybody; and for two

---

26. The *Vitae fratrum* contains similar episodes that belong to the topos of a small mind being miraculously changed, and a lack of interest in learning turning into great eagerness for studying (Wehofer 1897, 32).

continuous years, she remained in the possession of this miraculous gift. Then she was bereft of this grace because of a word she had spoken carelessly and arrogantly (*U* 429.16–22).

At one point in the Unterlinden text, the subtle differentiation is made between reading the Scriptures and understanding them. Katharina von Unterlinden explains that Elisabeth von Senheim was "divinely inspired," and "her intellect was illuminated" through a "truly new" miracle. For Elisabeth who had usually read the "daily hours" suddenly "began with deep and clear comprehension to understand the Sacred Scriptures in the book she held in her hands"; whereas before "she had not understood the sacred writing" (*U* 451). The acclaimed novelty of this story goes somewhat beyond the typical legendary cliché of the learning miracle.

The authors of the Sister-Books, as these stories suggest, understand true knowledge as a gift of the Holy Spirit, the legendary *donum sapientiae* [Is. 11:1].[27] Only divine grace can provide a knowledge that exceeds bookish learning. This motif, which has both a spiritual and a practical basis, accompanies the theme of learning in the Sister-Books. It corresponds, on the one hand, to the underlying deeply spiritual attitude of these monastic writers who take for granted that anything of great value, such as knowledge, cannot be credited to one's own accomplishments, but must be understood as having been freely given by God. On the other hand, realistically speaking, these late medieval authors were aware that, as women, they were only heeded when what they had to say was authenticated by visions.

This is why deep insights and special knowledge are routinely shown as having been provided or at least confirmed by miracles. Usually in these texts, some miraculous influence is said to have stimulated in these women a taste for learning, provided answers to certain theological questions, and even granted overpowering insights. Hilti Brúmsin in Diessenhofen, for instance, is credited with having understood through a vision "how all things had flowed out of God," and these were "such high and incomprehensible things," the author continues, using the topos of ineffability, that she herself was unable to set them down in writing (*D* 41; cf. *W* 74f.). In Kirchberg, Elsbeth von Oettingen is said to have received through grace "high illumination and divine understanding" (*K* 110), while the author of the Gotteszell Sister-Book asserts that Adelheit von Hiltegarthausen was taught by "the

---

27. Günter (1910, 13).

school master who is the beginning and source of all wisdom" so that her knowledge far exceeded that acquired from books (*G 124*). The authors thus support and authenticate their own literary and scholarly interests by pointing to divine illumination.

The notion of learning for the sake of learning is altogether foreign to these women. Rather, knowledge, just like silence and prayer, was one of the means for the nuns of getting closer to fulfilling their spiritual goal. The theme of learning in the Sister-Books illustrates the Dominican ideal, as expressed by the Oetenbach author, of maintaining a proper balance between reason and devotion (*O 270*).

A HYMNIC POEM TO THE HOLY SPIRIT

The following text is added, without any further commentary, as an appendix to this chapter on learning.[28] It illustrates the high level of literary skill and theological erudition in these Dominican women's monasteries. The hymn is taken from the Diessenhofen text and is said to have been received in an auditory revelation and composed as a poetic meditation. It is contained in the entry on Elsbet von Stoffeln and had, most likely, been written earlier as an independent text and then been included in the Diessenhofen Sister-Book:[29]

> Then a voice spoke in her heart: "Do you want to know what the Holy Spirit is? This I will tell you.
>
> The Holy Spirit is a creator (*würker*) who in his goodness created (*würkt*) all this: He created good will in the Father's heart so that the only-begotten Son of God was sent to earth. He created [Mary,] the sweet queen, according to his dearest will, and created the heavenly Jesus Christ in the maiden's womb, and created good will in the heavenly Jesus Christ so that he gave us his holy body on earth, and wanted to save us, with his death, from eternal death.
>
> He is a burning love that burned so heatedly for us in the heavenly kingdom that his love did not want him to stay there; but he wanted so lovingly to come to us on earth, that he did not want to be with us for forty years or a hundred years, but to always be with us on earth, and then to be eternally with us in heaven, unless we drive him out with our faults.

---

28. The poem was discussed above in Chapter Five: see p. 136f.

29. Meyer (1995, 243). While reminiscent of a sermon and, indeed, written in a very polished homiletic style, the passage may be influenced by but need not be the copy of a sermon, as Muschg (1935, 228) and Blank (1962, 13, 15) suggest.

He is a burning love that empowers [us]. This became evident in St. Peter: whatever he had heard of our Lord's sweet teaching and sermons and his wise instruction, and seen of his divine miracles, he was still so weak as to deny our Lord because of a poor wench. But when he received the Holy Spirit, he was so strong that he was able to withstand kings and emperors.

He is a burning love that makes [us] very wise. This became evident in the holy twelve apostles. They were so naive that they barely understood our Lord when he talked and spoke with them: 'We do not know what he is saying!' [Jn 16:18]. But when they received the Holy Spirit, they became so wise that in the blink of an eye they learned the seventy-two languages.

He is a burning love that makes [us] very bold. This became evident in many exalted saints who daringly dared to suffer all that the judges did to them.

He is a mild giver of graces who gives his grace so perfectly to many people that they leave father and mother and give up their own will, the better to comprehend his grace.

He is a mild giver of graces who gives his spiritual children such great love and such firm belief and such complete confidence that they are able merrily and with consolation to do works of which they scarcely heard tell before.

He is a mild giver of graces who does not deny his grace to anyone who desires it whole-heartedly. There were never any human beings so sinful that, when they were sorry for their sins and desired his grace, he did not fully give [grace] to them with complete blessedness.

He is a mild giver of graces who often gives his intimate friends his grace so fully in one hour that these people imagine that, if they had served our Lord for a thousand years and suffered all the tortures ever suffered by a saint, they would have been fully recompensed in this one hour.

He is a faithful counsellor. He counsels [us] to despise transitory goods that draw after them disagreeable goods and often eternal evil. And he counsels [us] to love virtue and a virtuous life that brings with it eternal bliss. And he counsels [us] to earnestly desire heavenly and lasting riches, and he counsels [us] to have a heart-felt yearning for the highest good.

He is an eternal light which has shone without a beginning and shall shine without an end, and a translucent light that illumined many dark hearts to divine understanding so that they could go the right way to the heavenly kingdom.

He is a heavenly light that shines in a heavenly way into the pure soul that locks her heart against passing love. He shines with much more heavenly light into the pure soul that opens herself wide toward him with love. And the wider she opens her heart and her desire and opens herself toward him, the more he shines with divine light, which is superhuman understanding, in that soul.

He is a sweet shining light that shines sweetly and radiates into the pure soul with such sweet illumination that the soul imagines that if she had this sweet illumination for a long time she would always have enough of the heavenly kingdom on earth. And this is the sweet illumination of which St. Augustine said: 'Lord, you lead me into a light and into a sweetness; if only I could have this for a long time. If that is not the heavenly kingdom, then I do not know what the heavenly kingdom is.'

He is a divine knowledge that makes [us] wise. This has become evident with many naive people who learned more divine knowledge in one hour than all the masters on earth could ever learn without his divine knowledge. He teaches [us] to think wisely of God and to speak sweetly and to act faithfully in his love.

He is a consolation to the unhappy. There has never been a human being so sad that, if only a drop of his consolation comes to that soul, the sadness does not disappear just like a thin leaf in a big fire.

He is a consolation to all those in sorrow. All of you who are sorry for your sins, I will console sweetly.[30] And if it were possible for a human being to have all the power and all the riches and all the lordship that all the kings and all the lords on earth ever gained, it would be just like a drop of water compared to the ocean and compared to all water in comparison with the consolation with which our Lord consoles the sorrowful.

He is a tender consolation [to] all those who love. All those who love him, he wants to console with himself, and wants to give himself to them to be felt so intimately that it has to remain untold by human tongues because it exceeds human senses by as much as the heavenly kingdom is above the earth.

30. This "I" refers to the voice speaking in the sister's heart and is presumably taken to be of divine origin.

He is an incomprehensible consolation to all miserable people. All those in misery, he wants to console with such incomprehensible consolation that no heart could ever think of it nor any soul contemplate it, except that it is a foretaste of the good to come and an incitement to greater misery.[31] Those who have and sense this incomprehensible joy cannot well speak of it and yet cannot well be silent about it. And it is hidden to those who have not experienced it. And even if they were told about it they would not know what it is.

He is a steady lasting consolation to those in [beatific] enjoyment of love. They shall have and enjoy him to the full, and yet they shall always hunger and thirst for him. And as much as God is almighty in contrast to a human being, by so much can he give more than all humans would be able to contemplate. And as much as God is wiser than human beings, by so much can he give more wisely than all humans are able to contemplate. And as much as God is milder and more merciful than human beings, by so much can he give more mildly and mercifully than all the saints and angels can desire" (*D* no. 33).

31. Consolation and reward for misery is so great that people desire to suffer still more, the text implies.

Epilogue

A close reading of the nine Sister-Books has yielded a kaleidoscope of female images. The authors present women of noble and humble descent, single, married and widowed women. Many of these women are shown to be non-conformists. We witness the fight of young women against parental authority, the insistence of widows not to be remarried, the struggle of married women for a "chaste marriage." Other women are portrayed feeling the need to separate themselves from their husbands and even from their small children – a context in which the authors never fail to praise the close and loving relationship between the spouses and children. In each case, the conflict with societal norms is motivated by the women's pursuit of spiritual ideals.

A number of the women described used to be beguines, at first living alone, later forming small communities; these small groups finally transformed themselves into full-fledged monasteries. Many women are depicted as initiators and leaders. The authors explain how these sisters eventually claim their right to belong to the order of their choice. In their relationship with the friars who officially minister to them, numbers of women are pictured as self-confident and independent thinkers. Many women function as spiritual guides.

Visionary images and legendary motifs are understood as an outward representations of an inner truth; through them the reader is made familiar with the ideals, the values, the theological concerns, and the monastic asceticism of the early Dominican women who are the heroines of these texts. Their ideas of the other world, their notions about God and the saints, the angels, and the devil are implicitly revealed. Their longing for the eucharistic sacrament is said to have been frequently satisfied by miracles. Miracles are seen as a proof that God is on their side.

The authors paint a picture of the austere routine of the nuns' daily life, convinced – and convincing the audience – that these women succeeded in achieving the goal they had set for themselves. Exploiting their various talents, the sisters are depicted as working hard at their assigned tasks – from cooking and cleaning, spinning and weaving, to writing, copying, and illuminating books, to studying and writing theology, preaching, and counselling. These Dominican monasteries generally maintained a high level of learning and education among their nuns. A few exceptionally gifted women are pictured whose knowledge and wisdom (usually understood as having been granted by grace) exceeded the norm set for women at their time and is said to have been, on occasion, greater than that of the university-trained friars.

While not ignoring internal difficulties in such communities, the authors explain that these women treasure each other's company and lend each other support. The texts offer attractive examples of women's friendships with close companions confiding in each other and encouraging each other in their chosen life style. Personal problems range from severe and chronic illnesses to doubts concerning certain aspects of their faith. Physical suffering was an integral part of medieval everyday life and equally so in the cloister. But these women understood illness as God-sent and hence usually bore it patiently, often finding themselves recompensed by a reaffirmation of their trust in God.

Some rare scenes reveal a genuine feeling for the beauty of nature, others permit us glimpses of spontaneous expressions of joy. Many more instances show the deep appreciation the women had for the works of art with which they were surrounded in their monasteries. Sacred music is represented as an integral part of daily life, playing an essential role not only in the divine service but often in visions as well.

As passages in the texts suggest, the nuns are highly respected in their local areas. Burghers and noble families brought them their daughters, made generous donations in exchange for prayers, and looked up to them as saintly women in their midst – an image the authors are keen on depicting.

The Sister-Books of fourteenth-century Germany thus add yet another example to our growing awareness that there has always been, parallel to the dominant male Tradition, a feminine tradition waiting to be explored. The history of how such books by female authors were received has given us an insight into the struggle for this tradition's survival. But survive they did (or at least some of them), revealing to us a multi-faceted and generally positive image of women. The women portrayed in these texts were intelligent, well-educated, dedicated to their monastic ideal, and are shown living a life of integrity and of a remarkable inner independence.

Appendix

THE MANUSCRIPTS OF THE SISTER-BOOKS

The following represents a comprehensive list of all the manuscripts of the Sister-Books known to be extant. The manuscript shelf marks and their current location are cited in full (the initial letter in brackets traditionally indicates the city or library where a manuscript is located). The brief descriptions are based on relevant secondary literature and on my comprehensive survey of the manuscripts.

The Adelhausen Text

1. [F] 98, fol. 1r–76r, written in 1433 by Johannes Hull of Strasbourg; it is kept in the Stadtarchiv of Freiburg i.B. (indicated by [F]).

2. [E] cod. 694 (919), 133–215, made by the Carthusian Matthias Thanner in 1606 and copied in 1731; it is kept in the Benedictine Stiftsbibliothek in Einsiedeln (see Lewis 1990).

3. [F] 99, 1–22, incomplete, made in a Freiburg Carthusian monastery in the seventeenth century.

4. [F] 107, 268r–287v and [F] 108, 199r–212v, two identical pieces with texts from Johannes Meyer's 1482 "Excerpts" of the Adelhausen Sister-Book.

5. Two eighteenth-century copies of [F] 107: a "house chronicle" (1729) by Sister Ursula of the new Adelhausen community (König 1880, 144f. and 150), and a copy (1761) by Gregorius Baumeister of the St.Peter's monastery (König 1878, 291).

The Diessenhofen Text
(See Meyer, 1995, 6–21 and 42–53.)

1. Cod. Y 74, fol.1–103, presumably the oldest manuscript, after 1424; its provenance is the Diessenhofen monastery itself; it is kept in the Thurgauische Kantonsbibliothek in Frauenfeld (indicated by Y).

2. [N] Cent. V 10a, fol. 84vb–118va, part of the collective codex compiled by Johannes Meyer (1454), copied by a scribe of the Katharinenkloster, Nürnberg; it is kept in the Stadtbibliothek of Nürnberg (see also Blank 1962, 69).

3. [G] cod. 603, fol. 446a–571b. The collective codex was copied in the Dominican women's monastery St. Katharina in St. Gallen, presumably in 1493; it is kept today in the Benedictine Stiftsbibliothek of St. Gallen (see Greith 1860, 74f.; Grubmüller 1969, 174).

4. [Ü] cod. 22, fol. 285a–320a, part of a collective codex, written during the early 1500s; its provenance is the Dominican monastery of St. Katharina, Zofingen (Constance); it is kept in the Leopold-Sophien-Bibliothek in Überlingen, Lake Constance (see Grubmüller 1969, 175f.).

5. [Bs] cod. A VI, 39rb–41rb, contains four excerpts from the Diessenhofen Sister-Book (*D* 21, 27e, 38, 39). Dated 1493, it came from the Sisters of St. Claire in Gnadenthal (Basel); it is kept in the Öffentliche Bibliothek der Universität Basel (see Grubmüller, Verflex. 2:94).

6. Cod. Y 105, a 1643 codex, Henricus Murer's *Helvetia sancta* which contains twelve entries of the Diessenhofen text, *Zwölff Heylige Kloster-Jung-frawen zu Diessenhofen*; it was written by four scribes, the Carthusian Murer of Ittingen (Thurgau) among them. It is kept in the Thurgauische Kantonsbibliothek in Frauenfeld. Cod. Y 105 also includes a chronicle which goes back to early sources in the Diessenhofen library.

7. [E] cod. 695, written before 1666, is a copy of Y 105 by a scribe of the Benedictine women's monastery in Münsterlingen (Thurgau). It is kept in the Benedictine Stiftsbibliothek in Einsiedeln.

8. Four additional fragments of the Diessenhofen book are: the mid-fifteenth century ([K] St. Peter pap.21, in the Landesbibliothek in Karlsruhe; the sixteenth-century ([C] V698 in the Zentralbibliothek, Zürich; Y 75, dated 1720, by the scribe Anna Bögin of the Diessenhofen monastery, kept in Frauenfeld; [We] cod. I 3, in the archive of the monastery "Maria Zuflucht" in Weesen.

The Engeltal Text

1. [N2] cod. 1338, 66 fol. is the oldest preserved manuscript of all the Sister-Books, dated mid-fourteenth century and written in the Engeltal monastery itself; it is kept in the Germanisches Nationalmuseum in Nürnberg.

2. [W] cod. scot. 308, fol. 84r–119v, a collective codex, dated 1451, kept in the Benedictine Schottenstift in Vienna (Wien). Among others, this *codex scotensis* contains also manuscripts of the Gotteszell and Kirchberg Sister-Books. Copied by Johann Propst von Biberach, it was designated for the library of the Augustinian women's reform-monastery of Inzigkofen, Württemberg (See Otmar Wieland, *Gertrud von Helfta: ein botte der götlichen miltekeit*, SMBO 22 [Ottobeuren, 1973], 24–29; Ringler 1980a, 16–63).

3. A third manuscript, listed in the late medieval library catalogue of the Nürnberg Katharinenkloster, has presumably not survived (Ringler 1980a, 82).

The Gotteszell Text

1. [Mz] cod. 43, fol. 28v–59r, dated 1451 and written by the scribes of the Nürnberg Katharinenkloster; it is kept in the library of the Bischöfliches Priesterseminar in Mainz (see Müller 1977/78; Ringler 1980a, 91–104).

2. [W] cod. scot. 308 (234), fol. 18v–44v, also dated 1451, is kept in the Vienna Schottenstift. See Engeltal 2. above.

The Kirchberg Text
(See Müller, 1977/78, esp. 43–45; Ringler, 1980a, 91–110.)

1. [Mz] cod. 43, fol. 4v–28r, dated 1451, kept in the Bischöfliches Priesterseminar in Mainz. See Gotteszell 1. above.

2. [W] cod. scot. 308 (234), fol. 1v–18r, dated 1451, part of the collective codex in the Vienna Schottenstift. See Engeltal 2. above.

3. [S] cod. hist. 4° 330, 199 pages, dated February 12, 1691, compiled and copied by Pius Kessler OP, then chaplain at Kirchberg. Presumably going back to an earlier text, [S] is apparently the only complete version of the Kirchberg Sister-Book. It is kept in the Landesbibliothek in Stuttgart (see Ringler 1980a, 92).

[S], pages 29–198 only, was excerpted (ignoring the chronicle) and paraphrased in modern German, see Anton Birlinger ed., "Die Nonnen von Kirchberg bei Haigerloch," *Alemannia* 11 (1883) 1–20.

4. [A] 4° cod. 94, part 2; pages 1–5 and 18–97, represents two fragments of the Kirchberg text based on [S]; it is kept in the Staats- und Stadtbibliothek of Augsburg.

5. [Wa] cod. MS 51, pages 1–127, 1860, based on [S], hand-written in New High German; formerly of Kloster Walberberg, now kept in the Bibliothek St. Albert, Bornheim-Walberberg.

The Oetenbach Text

[N] V 10a, fol. 118v–141v, part of a collective codex compiled by Johannes Meyer in 1454; it is kept in the Stadtbibliothek of Nürnberg. Its 19th-century editors, Zeller-Werdmüller and Bächtold (1889, 215), assume it represents an unfinished copy of the Oetenbach Sister-Book. See also Diessenhofen 2. above.

The Töss text

(See Grubmüller 1969.)

1. [N] Cent. V 10a, fol. 1–84v, part of Johannes Meyer's 1454 collective codex in the Nürnberg Stadtbibliothek. See Diessenhofen 2. above. This is the only illuminated manuscript in the entire fifteenth-century manuscript collection related to the Sister-Books. See Chapter 3 above, p. 64.

2. [G] cod. 603, fol. 163a–328b, a collective codex, presumably 1493, copied in St. Katharina, St. Gallen. It is kept in the St. Gallen Stiftsbibliothek. See Diessenhofen 3. above.

3. [Ü] cod. 22, fol. 127a–183a, an early sixteenth-century collective codex (altogether 320 folii) whose provenance is St. Katharina, Zofingen (Constance). It is kept in the Leopold Sophien Bibliothek in Überlingen. See Diessenhofen 4. above.

4. [Sa] 171, pt. 2, fol. 1r–93, seventeenth century, part of a collective codex copied by Sister Maria Katharina Dulliger of Hermetschwyl and illustrated by folk-art miniatures. It is kept in the Benedictine Stiftsarchiv of Sarnen (letter from the archivist, Adelhelm Rast OSB, Sarnen, May 10, 1990; see also Greith 1860, 74; Grubmüller 1969, 177f.).

5. [E] cod. 694, fol. 1–132, a seventeenth-century copy of [G] cod. 603; it is kept in the Benedictine Stiftsbibliothek in Einsiedeln (see Grubmüller 1969, 177).

Other partial manuscripts are:

6. [D] cod. 452 (L.187), fol. 102v–128r, the most important among the incomplete Töss manuscripts and the oldest, dated ca. 1440, presumably copied in Diessenhofen. It is kept in the Fürstlich Fürstenbergische Hofbibliothek in Donaueschingen (see Grubmüller 1969, 182–187).

7. [C] cod. 162 fol. 273v–274v, fifteenth century, a short fragment of the *vita* of Margaret Finkin (based on [G]); in the Zentralbibliothek of Zürich.

8. Contained in Y 105, it is an abbreviated and alphabetized version of the Töss Sister-Book, dated seventeenth century and made by Carthusians in Ittingen (Austria). It is kept in the Thurgauische Kantonsbibliothek in Frauenfeld. See Diessenhofen 7. above.

The Unterlinden text
(See Geith 1986.)

1. [Col] cod. 508 (926), 141 parchment folii, dated after 1485, entitled *Catharina de Gueberschwihr, Vitae primarum sororum de sub tilia in Columbaria*; it is kept in the Bibliothèque de la Ville de Colmar. First published by Matthias Thanner in 1624 (augmented by Elisabeth Kempf's *vita*), reprinted in 1725 by the Benedictine Bernardus Pez, librarian in the Melk monastery (*Bibliotheca ascetica*, volume 8).

2. [P] cod.lat. 5642, a shortened version presumably copied by a French-speaking scribe, it used to belong to the Ursuline Convent of St Loys de Poissy. It is kept in the Bibliothèque nationale de Paris.

3. [Guelf.] 164.1 Extravagantes, 2r–141r, late fifteenth century, written in an Alemannic dialect of MHG. It is kept in the Wolfenbüttel Herzog August Bibliothek of Wolfenbüttel.

The Weiler Text

1. [N] Cent. VI, 43b, 1r–16v, part of a collective codex, second half of the fifteenth century, written by Klara Löffelholzin, one of the many prolific scribes of the Katharinenkloster in Nürnberg (its original ownership entry reads: *Daß puch gehort in dz Closter zu Sant Kath pdiger Orden zu nurmberg*). It is kept in the Stadtbibliothek of Nürnberg.

2. [M] cgm 750 fol. 59r–76r, part of a collective codex, written 1454–1468 by Anna Ebin in the Augustinian monastery of Pillenreuth near Nürnberg; it is kept in the Bayerische Staatsbibliothek in München (see Ruh 1956, 172–176).

3. [Gr] Scrin. VIII, ser. V, n. 11, fol. 40r–66r, part of a collective codex, dated circa 1500, originating in Steinen in der Au (since 1570 a Dominican nuns' monastery). Owned by the Dominican Friars of Graz, it was donated to the Graz Universitätsbibliothek in 1990.

NOTE: [M] and [N] are closely related. Moreover, each of the three Weiler manuscripts is attached to a short MHG excerpt of Mechthild von Hackeborn's *Liber specialis gratiae* (1.18) suggesting that the three Weiler manuscripts go back to the same source, although not necessarily in a direct lineage.

FIFTEENTH–CENTURY MONASTERIES

Several other fifteenth-century women's reform monasteries (other than the ones where the Sister-Books originated) played a crucial role in the circulation of the manuscripts. Brief descriptions are provided below.

Altenhohenau

The monastery of Altenhohenau in Bavaria, founded in 1235, was reformed in 1465 by Dominican nuns from Nürnberg. The library catalogue of the Katharinenkloster, listing book donations to Altenhohenau, shows that the women of Altenhohenau participated in the late fifteenth-century book traffic. Altenhohenau was dissolved in 1803 but revitalized by German Dominicans from California in 1923 (Schneider 1975, 217; LThK 1:380).

Gnadenthal

Gnadenthal started as a beguinage in 1282, became a monastery of the Sisters of St. Claire in 1285, and is listed as one of the reform monasteries in 1447. It was dissolved in 1530. Through the work of its early sixteenth-century archivist, Dorothea Schermann, its scriptorium and archive became well known (Bruckner 1957, 173ff; Heusinger 1959, 136).

Inzigkofen

An Augustinian monastery whose library had a renowned collection of German codices (*gemain Teutsch Liberey*), mostly written by nuns and especially famous for its works of mysticism. Its most important early scribe was Anna Jäckin. Only some thirty codices have been preserved after the monastery was closed in the early nineteenth century (Ringler 1980a, 40, 49).

Katharinenkloster in Nürnberg

The Katharinenkloster was the focal point of nuns' literary activities during the fifteenth-century reform movement. Through its well organized book exchange system, the Katharinenkloster was in touch with a great number of monasteries. Among the impressive collective codices from the Katharinenkloster are also some containing manuscripts of the Sister-Books (Schneider 1965, as well as 1975 and 1983; Ringler 1980a, 45f.; see also Chapter 3 above, esp. pp. 62–64).

Pillenreuth

The Augustinian monastery of Pillenreuth near Nürnberg accumulated important library holdings, exchanging manuscripts with Engeltal perhaps as early as 1360–80. Pillenreuth underwent an internal reform in 1422. Mainly through its prioress Anna Ebin, the monastery reached a literary high point in the middle of the fifteenth century. It also maintained close literary connections with the Katharinenkloster in Nürnberg and Inzigkofen (Ringler 1980a, 49–59.)

St. Katharina (St. Gallen)

St. Katharina in St. Gallen started as a beguinage in 1228, taking the Rule of St. Augustine in 1266; it was later incorporated into the Order of Preachers. Having undergone an internal reform in 1476, it established close contact with the nuns of the Nürnberg Katharinenkloster who forwarded codices to St. Gallen for copying (Hauber 1914, 361).

St. Katharina (Zofingen, Constance)

St. Katharina in Zofingen was a Dominican monastery, reformed in 1497 by Dominican nuns from St.Gallen who also built up their new library. St. Katharina's book collection, a Zofingen chronicle of 1501 reports, also included a Sister-Book (Grubmüller 1969, 175, 181).

Bibliography

PRIMARY SOURCES

The Sister-Books

Quotations from the Sister-Books cited throughout this study take into account all the manuscripts listed in the Appendix (pp. 286–289). References are, however, given to the printed texts, the only readily available sources.

[Adelhausen Sister-Book.] 1880. "Die Chronik der Anna von Munzingen. Nach der ältesten Abschrift mit Einleitung und Beilagen." Ed. J. König. *Freiburger Diözesan Archiv* 13:129–236.

[Diessenhofen Sister-Book.] 1995. *Das St. Katharinentaler Schwesternbuch: Untersuchung, Edition, Kommentar.* (Münchener Texte und Untersuchungen 104.) Ed. Ruth Meyer. Tübingen: Niemeyer.

[Engeltal Sister-Book.] 1871. *Der Nonne von Engeltal Büchlein von der Genaden Uberlast.* Litterarischer Verein in Stuttgart. Ed. Karl Schröder. Tübingen.

[Gotteszell Sister-Book.] 1893. "Aufzeichnungen über das mystische Leben der Nonnen von Kirchberg bei Sulz Predigerordens während des XIV. und XV. Jahrhunderts." Ed. F.W.E. Roth. *Alemannia* 21:123–148 [the second half of Roth's edition of the Kirchberg text].

[Kirchberg Sister-Book.] 1893. "Aufzeichnungen über das mystische Leben der Nonnen von Kirchberg bei Sulz Predigerordens während des XIV. und XV. Jahrhunderts." Ed. F.W.E.Roth. *Alemannia* 21:103–123.

[Oetenbach Sister-Book.] 1889. "Die Stiftung des Klosters Oetenbach und das Leben der seligen Schwestern daselbst, aus der Nürnberger Handschrift." Ed. H. Zeller-Werdmüller and Jakob Bächtold. *Zürcher Taschenbuch* n.s. 12: 213–276.

[Töss Sister-Book.] 1906. *Das Leben der Schwestern zu Töss beschrieben von Elsbet Stagel, samt der Vorrede des Johannes Meyer und dem Leben der Prinzessin Elisabet von Ungarn.* Ed. Ferdinand Vetter. Deutsche Texte des Mittelalters 6. Berlin: Weidmann.

[Unterlinden Sister-Book.] 1930. "Les *vitae sororum d'Unterlinden*. Edition critique du manuscrit 508 de la Bibliothèque de Colmar." Ed. Jeanne Ancelet-Hustache. *Archives d'Histoire Doctrinale et Littéraire du Moyen Age* 5:317–517.

[Weiler Sister-Book.] 1916. "Mystisches Leben in dem Dominikanerinnenkloster Weiler bei Eßlingen im 13. und 14. Jahrhundert." Ed. Karl Bihlmeyer. *Württembergische Vierteljahreshefte für Landesgeschichte,* n.s. 25:61–93.

[Sister-Books – Selections.] 1985. "From the German Sister-Books (Thirteenth and Fourteenth Centuries)." In *Ecstatic Confessions,* collected and edited by Martin Buber; trans. Esther Cameron and ed. Paul Mendes-Flohr, pp. 77–90. San Francisco: Harper & Row. [1st German ed. 1909.]

Other Medieval Sources

Aelred of Rievaulx. 1977. *Spiritual Friendship*. (CF 5.) Trans. Mary Eugenia Laker, introd. Douglass Roby. Kalamazoo: Cistercian Publications.

Albertus Magnus. 1651–. *Opera*. Vol. 16. Ed. Petrus Jammy. Lyon: Prost & Rigaud.

Augustine. 1912. *Confessions*. Trans. William Watts 1631. Loeb Classical Library. London and New York: Heinemann.

—. *Epistola CCXI. PL* 33 [1841]: 958–965.

Book of Constitutions of the Nuns of the Order of Preachers. 1987. Ed. Damian Byrne (Master of the Order). USA: LCM.

Caesarius of Arles. 1988. *Regula ad virgines*. In *Oeuvres monastiques*, 1:170–273. SC 345. Paris: Cerf.

Caesarius of Heisterbach. 1929. *The Dialogue on Miracles*. Trans. H. von E. Scott and C.C. Swinton Bland. Introd. G.G. Couton. 2 vols. London: Routledge.

Codex Iuliacensis: Christine von Stommeln und Petrus von Dacien. 1975. Bischöfliches Diözesanarchiv Aachen 34. Ed. Peter Nieveler. Mönchengladbach: Kühlen.

Dante. 1981. *The Divine Comedy of Dante Alighieri*. Trans. Allen Mandelbaum. 3 vols. Toronto: Bantam Books.

Early Documents of the Dominican Sisters. 1969. Summit, NJ: Monastery of Our Lady of the Rosary.

Meister Eckhart. 1977. *Deutsche Predigten und Traktate*. Ed. and trans. Josef Quint. 4th ed. München: Hanser.

Elisabeth von Schönau. 1884. *Visionen nach den Originalhandschriften*. Ed. F.W.E. Roth. Brünn: Verlag der "Studien aus dem Benedictiner- und Cisterciensen-Order."

Gertrud von Helfta. 1968–1986. *Legatus divinae pietatis*. SC 139, 143, 255, 331. Paris: Cerf.

—. 1989. *Spiritual Exercises*. CF 49. Trans. Gertrud Jaron Lewis and Jack Lewis. Kalamazoo: Cistercian Publications.

Hadewijch. 1980. *The Complete Works*. Ed. and trans. Columba Hart. New York, Ramsey, Toronto: Paulist Press.

Hermann von Minden. 1925. "Drei Briefe Hermanns von Minden O.P. über die Seelsorge und die Leitung der deutschen Dominikanerinnenklöster." Ed. Gabriel Löhr. *Römische Quartalschrift für christliche Altertumskunde und Kirchengeschichte* 33:159–167.

Humbert of Romans. (1259) 1969. *Constitutions of the Sisters of the Order of Friars Preachers*. Trans. Dominican Sisters of Summit. Early Documents of the Dominican Sisters 2. Summit, NJ: Monastery of Our Lady of the Rosary.

—. 1955. *Treatise on Preaching*. Trans. by Dominican Students. Ed. Walter M. Conlon. London: Blackfriars Publications.

Jacques de Vitry. 1914. *Die Exemplas aus den Sermones feriales et communes des Jakob von Vitry.* Ed. Joseph Greven. Sammlung mittellateinischer Texte 9. Heidelberg: Winter.

Julian of Norwich. 1989. *A Revelation of Love.* Ed. Marion Glasscoe. Exeter: Exeter University Press.

Mechthild von Magdeburg. 1990–1993. *"Das fließende Licht der Gottheit." Nach der Einsiedler Handschrift in kritischem Vergleich mit der gesamten Überlieferung.* Ed. Hans Neumann; arr. Gisela Vollmann-Profe. MTU 100. 2 vols. München and Zürich: Artemis.

Johannes Meyer. 1880. In König [see Primary Sources, Adelhausen], "Beilagen," pp. 194–228.

The Primitive Constitution of the Monastery of San Sisto. 1969. Printed in French by J.J. Berthier. Trans. Dominicans of Summit Early Documents of the Dominican Sisters 1. Summit, NJ: Monastery of Our Lady of the Rosary.

Raymond of Capua. 1960. *The Life of St. Catherine of Siena.* Trans. George Lamb. London: Harvill.

Thomas Aquinas. 1945. *Basic Writings of Saint Thomas Aquinas.* Ed. Anton C. Pegis. New York: Random House.

S. Thomae de Aqvino, Svmma Theologiae. 1953. Ed. Institute of Medieval Studies, Ottawa. Ottawa: Commissio Piana. 5 vols.

[*Vitae fratrum* of Gerard de Frachete.] 1924. *Lives of the Brethren of the Order of Preachers 1206–1259.* Trans. Placid Conway. Ed. Bede Jarrett. London: Burns, Oates & Washbourne.

[*Vitas patrum*]. 1903. *Eine mhd. Übersetzung des Lebens der Väter.* Ed. Reinhold Nebert. *ZfdPh* 35:371–396.

SECONDARY WORKS

Works referred to only once are cited in full in the footnotes and do not appear in this bibliography.

Abendländische Mystik im Mittelalter. 1986. Ed. Kurt Ruh. Germanistische Symposien 4. Stuttgart: Metzler.

Acklin Zimmermann, Béatrice W. 1993. *Gott im Denken berühren. Die theologischen Implikationen der Nonnenviten.* Freiburg (Switzerland): Universitätsverlag.

Albert, Peter. 1898. "Johannes Meyer, ein oberdeutscher Chronist des fünfzehnten Jahrhunderts." *Zeitschrift für Geschichte des Oberrheins* n.s. 13:255–262.

Amschwand, Rupert. 1987. *Bruder Klaus.* Ergänzungsband zum Quellenwerk von Robert Durrer. Sarnen: von Ah.

Ancelet-Hustache, Jeanne. 1928. *La Vie mystique d'un monastère de Dominicaines au moyen-âge d'après la Chronique de Töss.* Paris: Perrin.

—, ed. 1930. See Primary Sources: Unterlinden.

—. 1960. "Ascétique et mystique féminine du haut moyen-âge." *Etudes germaniques* 15:152–160.

Altman, Charles F. 1975. "Two Types of Opposition and the Structure of Latin Saints' Lives." *Medievalia et Humanistica* 6:1–11.

Arnold, Klaus. 1980. *Kind und Gesellschaft in Mittelalter und Renaissance.* Sammlung Zebra B 2. München: Schöningh.

Atkinson, Clarissa W. 1983. "'Precious Balsam in a Fragile Glass': The Ideology of Virginity in the later Middle Ages." *Journal of Family History* 8:131–143.

—. 1991. *The Oldest Vocation: Christian Motherhood in the Middle Ages.* Ithaca and London: Cornell University Press.

Auerbach, Erich. 1953. *Typologische Motive in der mittelalterlichen Literatur.* Schriften und Vorträge des Petrarca-Instituts Köln 2. Krefeld: Scherpe.

Auf der Suche nach der Frau im Mittelalter. 1991. Ed. Bea Lundt. München: Fink.

Baring-Gould, Sabine. 1978. *Curious Myths of the Middle Ages.* Ed. and introd. Edward Hardy. New York: Oxford University Press.

Barthelmé, Annette. 1931. *La Réforme dominicaine au XVe siècle en Alsace et dans l'ensemble de la province de Teutonie.* Collection d'Etudes sur l'Histoire du Droit et des Institutions de l'Alsace 7. Strasbourg: Heitz.

Bauer, Dieter R. 1985. "Diskussionsüberblick." In *Frauenmystik im Mittelalter,* pp. 366–393.

Beard, Mary R. 1946. *Woman as Force in History. A Study in Traditions and Realities.* London: Collier-Macmillan. Repr. 1971.

Bell, Rudolph M. 1985. *Holy Anorexia.* Chicago: Chicago University Press.

Bell, Susan Groag. 1989. "Medieval Women Book Owners, Arbiters of Lay Piety and Ambassadors of Culture." In *Sisters and Workers in the Middle Ages,* ed. Judith M. Bennett, Elizabeth A. Clark, Jean F. O'Barr, B. Anne Vilen, and Sarah Westphal-Wihl, pp. 135–161. Chicago: Chicago University Press.

Belting, Hans. 1990. *The Image and Its Public in the Middle Ages: Form and Function of Early Paintings of the Passion* [1st German ed. 1981]. Trans. Mark Bartusis and Raymond Meyer. New Rochelle, NY: Caratzas.

Bennett, Ralph Francis. 1937. *The Early Dominicans. Studies in Thirteenth-Century Dominican History.* Cambridge Studies in Medieval Life and Thought. Cambridge: Cambridge University Press.

Benz, Ernst. 1934. "Christliche Mystik und christliche Kunst. Zur theologischen Interpretation mittelalterlicher Kunst." *DVJS* 12:22–48.

—. 1969. *Die Vision. Erfahrungsformen und Bilderwelt.* Stuttgart: Klett.

Bernards, Matthäus. 1982. *Speculum virginum. Geistigkeit und Seelenleben der Frau im Hochmittelalter.* Forschungen zur Volkskunde 36–38. Köln and Graz: Böhlau. [1st ed. 1955.]

Bernhart, Joseph. 1950. "Heiligkeit und Krankheit." *Geist und Leben* 23:172–195. [Repr. in: Joseph Bernhart, *Gestalten und Gewalten. Aufsätze, Vorträge*, ed. Max Rößler, pp. 257–293. Würzburg: Echter, 1962.]

Berthold, Luise. 1932. "Die Kindelwiegenspiele." *Beiträge zur Geschichte der deutschen Sprache und Literatur* 56:208–224.

Beyer, Rolf. 1989. "Vom Kindlein – Mystik der Dominikanerinnen." In *Die andere Offenbarung: Mystikerinnen des Mittelalters*, pp. 189–216. Bergisch Gladbach: Lübke Verlag.

Bihlmeyer, Karl, ed. 1916. See Primary Sources: Weiler.

Biller, Peter. 1990. "The Common Woman in the Western Church in the Thirteenth and Fourteenth Centuries." In *Women in the Church*, ed. W.J. Sheils and Diana Wood, pp. 127–157. Ecclesiastical History Society. Oxford: Blackwell.

Blank, Walter. 1962. *Die Nonnenviten des 14. Jahrhunderts. Eine Studie zur hagiographischen Literatur des Mittelalters unter besonderer Berücksichtigung der Visionen und ihrer Lichtphänomene*. Diss. Freiburg i.B.

—. 1964/65. "Dominikanische Frauenmystik und die Entstehung des Andachtsbildes um 1300." *Alemannisches Jahrbuch*: 57–86.

—. 1978a. "Umsetzung der Mystik in den Frauenklöstern." In *Mystik am Oberrhein und in den benachbarten Gebieten*, ed. Hans H. Hofstätter, pp. 25–36. Freiburg i.B.: Augustinermuseum.

—. 1978b. "Anna von Munzingen." *Verflex* 1:365–366.

Boehm, Laetitia. 1982. "Das mittelalterliche Erziehungs- und Bildungswesen." In *Propyläen. Geschichte der Literatur: Literatur und Gesellschaft der westlichen Welt*, vol. II: *Die mittelalterliche Welt 600–1400*, pp. 143–181. Berlin: Propyläen Verlag.

Bolton, Brenda. 1976. "Mulieres sanctae." In *Women in Medieval Society*, ed. Susan Mosher Stuard, pp. 141–158. Philadelphia: Pennsylvania University Press.

—. 1978. "*Vitae Matrum*: A Further Aspect of the *Frauenfrage*." In *Medieval Women*, dedicated to Rosalind M.T. Hill, ed. Derek Baker, pp. 253–273. Ecclesiastical History Society. Oxford: Blackwell.

Bornstein, Diane. 1982. "Antifeminism." *LexMA* 1:322–325.

Børresen, Kari Elisabeth. 1990. "Women's Studies of the Christian Tradition." In *Philosophy and Science in the Middle Ages*, ed. Raymond Klibansky, pp. 901–1001. *Contemporary Philosophy* 6, ed. Guttorm Fløistad. Dordrecht, Boston, London: Kluwer.

Borst, Arno. 1978. "Die ungenannte Dominikanerin in St. Katharinental." In A. Borst, *Mönche am Bodensee*, pp. 284–301. Sigmaringen: Thorbecke.

Bremond, Claude; Jacques LeGoff; and Jean-Claude Schmitt. 1982. *L'Exemplum*. Typologie des sources du Moyen-Age occidental 40. Turnhout: Brepols.

Brennan, Margaret. 1985. "Enclosure: Institutionalising the Invisibility of Women in Ecclesiastical Communities." In *Women: Invisible in Theology and Church* pp. 38–48.

Brett, Edward T. 1980. "The Dominican Library in the Thirteenth Century." *Journal of Library History* 15:303–308.

—. 1984. *Humbert of Romans. His Life and Views of Thirteenth-Century Society.* Studies and Texts 67. Toronto: Pontifical Institute of Mediaeval Studies.

Brincken, Anna-Dorothee van den. 1988. "Geschichtsschreibung." In *Deutsche Literatur. Eine Sozialgeschichte.* Ed. Horst Albert Glaser. Vol. I: *750–1320*, ed. Ursula Liebertz-Grün, pp. 304–313. Reinbek: Rowohlt.

Brody, Saul Nathaniel. 1974. *The Disease of the Soul: Leprosy in Medieval Literature.* Ithaca, NY: Cornell University Press.

Brooke, Christopher N.L. 1989. *The Medieval Idea of Marriage.* Oxford: Oxford University Press.

Browe, Peter. 1929. "Die öftere Kommunion der Laien im Mittelalter." *Bonner Zeitschrift für Theologie und Seelsorge* [offprint] 1–28.

—. 1933. *Die Verehrung der Eucharistie im Mittelalter.* München: Hueber.

—. 1938. *Die eucharistischen Wunder des Mittelalters.* Breslauer Studien zur historischen Theologie 4. Breslau: Müller & Seifert.

Bruckner, Albert. 1957. "Zum Problem der Frauenhandschrift im Mittelalter." In *Aus Mittelalter und Neuzeit. Gerhard Kallen zum 70. Geburtstag,* ed. Josef Engel, pp. 171–183. Bonn: Hanstein.

—. 1971. "Weibliche Schreibtätigkeit im schweizerischen Spätmittelalter." In *Festschrift Bernhard Bischoff,* pp. 441–448. Stuttgart: Hiersemann.

Brundage, James A. 1990. "Sexual Equality in Medieval Canon Law." In *Medieval Women,* pp. 66–79.

Bugge, John. 1975. *Virginitas: An Essay in the History of a Medieval Ideal.* International Archives of the History of Ideas 17. The Hague: Nijhoff.

Bynum, Caroline Walker. 1984a. *Jesus as Mother. Studies in the Spirituality of the High Middle Ages.* [1st ed. 1982] Berkeley and Los Angeles: University of California Press.

—. 1984b. "Women Mystics and Eucharistic Devotion in the Thirteenth Century." *Women's Studies* 11:179–214. [Repr. in: Bynum, *Fragmentation,* pp. 119–150.]

—. 1986a. "Body of Christ in the Later Middle Ages." *Renaissance Quarterly* 39: 399–439. [Repr. in: Bynum, *Fragmentation,* pp. 79–117.]

—. 1986b. "'... And Woman His Humanity': Female Imagery in the Religious Writing of the Later Middle Ages." In *Gender and Religion: On the Complexity of Symbols,* ed. Caroline Walker Bynum, Stevan Harrell, and Paula Richman, pp. 257–288. Boston: Beacon Press. [Repr. in: Bynum, *Fragmentation,* pp. 151–179.]

—. 1987a. *Holy Feast and Holy Fast. The Religious Significance of Food to Medieval Women.* Berkeley and Los Angeles: University of California Press.

—. 1987b. "Religious Women in the Later Middle Ages." In *Christian Spirituality*, Raitt ed., pp. 121–139.

—. 1989. "The Female Body and Religious Practice in the Later Middle Ages." In *Fragments for a History of the Human Body,* ed. Michel Feher, Ramona Naddaff, Nadia Tazi, 1:161–219. 3 vols. New York: Zone. [Repr. in: Bynum, *Fragmentation,* pp. 181–238.]

—. 1991a. *Fragmentation and Redemption: Essays on Gender and the Human Body in Medieval Religion.* New York: Zone Books.

—. 1991b. "Bodily Miracles and the Resurrection of the Body in the High Middle Ages." In *Belief in History: Innovative Approaches to European and American Religion,* ed. Thomas Kselman, pp. 68–106. Notre Dame and London: Notre Dame University Press.

Cabassut, André. 1986. "A Medieval Devotion to 'Jesus Our Mother.'" *Cistercian Studies* 21:345–355. [A translation of "Une Dévotion médiévale peu connue – la dévotion à Jésus notre mère." *Revue d'ascétique et de mystique* 25 (1949) 234–245.]

Carlé, Birte. 1980. "Structural Patterns in the Legends of the Holy Women of Christianity." In *Aspects of Female Existence,* ed. Birte Carlé et al., pp. 79–86. Proceedings Copenhagen 1978. Copenhagen: Nordisk Forlag.

Christ, Karl. 1942. "Mittelalterliche Bibliotheksordnungen für Frauenklöster." *Zentralblatt für Bibliothekswesen* 59:1–29.

Christian Spirituality: High Middle Ages and Reformation. 1987. Ed. Jill Raitt, with Bernard McGinn, John Meyendorff. World Spirituality: An Encyclopedic History of the Religious Quest 17. New York: Crossroad.

Chuzeville, Jean. 1935. *Les Mystiques allemands du XIIIe au XIX siècle.* Paris: Grasset.

Clark, James Matthew. 1970. *The Great German Mystics Eckhart, Tauler, and Suso* [1st ed. 1949]. Repr. New York: Russell & Russell.

Coakley, John. 1991. "Friars as Confidants of Holy Women in Medieval Dominican Hagiography." In *Images of Sainthood,* pp. 222–246.

Coldwell, Maria V. 1986. "*Jongleresses* and *Trobairitz*: Secular Musicians in Medieval France." In *Women Making Music,* pp. 39–61.

Constable, Giles. 1982. *Attitudes Toward Self-Inflicted Suffering in the Middle Ages.* The Ninth Stephen J. Brademas Sr. Lecture. Brookline, Mass.: Hellenic College Press.

The Continuing Quest for God: Monastic Spirituality in Tradition and Transition. 1982. Ed. William Skudlarek. Collegeville, MN: Liturgical Press.

Corbin, Solange. 1960. *La Déposition liturgique du Christ au Vendredi Saint. Sa place dans l'histoire des rites et du théâtre religieux.* Analyse de documents portugais; Collection Portugaise. Paris and Lisbon: Belles Lettres.

Creytens, Raymond. 1949. "Les Convers des moniales dominicaines au moyen âge." *Archivum Fratrum Praedicatorum* 19:5–48.

Cummings, Charles. 1986. *Monastic Practices.* Kalamazoo: Cistercian Publications.

Curtius, Ernst Robert. 1938. "Zur Literaturästhetik des Mittelalters I." *Zeitschrift für Romanische Philologie* 58:1–50.

—. 1963. *European Literature and the Latin Middle Ages* [1st German ed. 1948.] Trans. Willard R. Trask. New York and Evanston: Harper & Row.

Däniker-Gysin, Marie-Claire. 1958. *Geschichte des Dominikanerinnenklosters Töß 1233–1525.* 289. Neujahrsblatt. Winterthur: Stadtbibliothek.

Decker, Otmar. 1935. *Die Stellung des Predigerordens zu den Dominikanerinnen (1207–1267).* QFGD 31. Vechta: Albertus Magnus Verlag.

Degler-Spengler, Brigitte. 1969/70. "Die Beginen in Basel." *Basler Zeitschrift für Geschichte und Altertumskunde* 69/70:5–83.

—. 1984. "Die religiöse Frauenbewegung des Mittelalters: Konversen-Nonnen-Beginen." *Rottenburger Jahrbuch für Kirchengeschichte* 3:75–88.

—. 1985. "'Zahlreich wie die Sterne des Himmels.' Zisterzienser, Dominikaner und Franziskaner vor dem Problem der Inkorporation von Frauenklöstern." *Rottenburger Jahrbuch für Kirchengeschichte* 4:37–50.

Delehaye, Hippolyte. 1962. *The Legends of the Saints* [1st French ed. 1905]. Trans. Donald Attwater. New York: Fordham University Press.

Denifle, Heinrich Seuse. 1886a. "Über die Anfänge der Predigtweise der deutschen Mystiker." *Archiv für Litteratur- und Kirchengeschichte des Mittelalters* 2: 641–652.

—. 1886b. "Quellen zur Gelehrtengeschichte des Predigerordens im 13. und 14. Jahrhundert." *Archiv für Litteratur- und Kirchengeschichte des Mittelalters* 2: 165–248.

Descoeudres, Georges. 1989. "Mittelalterliche Dominikanerinnenkirchen in der Zentral- und Nordostschweiz." *Mitteilungen des Historischen Vereins des Kantons Schwyz* 81:39–77.

Deutsche Chroniken. 1936. Deutsche Literatur in Entwicklungsreihen: Realistik des Spätmittelalters 5. Ed. Hermann Maschek. Leipzig: Reclam.

Deutsche Literatur: Eine Sozialgeschichte. 1988. Vol. 1: 750–1320. Ed. Ursula Liebertz-Grün. Reinbek bei Hamburg: Rowohlt.

Die deutsche Literatur des Mittelalters. 1964. Ed. Wolfgang Stammler and Karl Langosch. Berlin: de Gruyter.

Die deutsche Literatur des Mittelalters–Verfasserlexikon. 1978– . 2nd completely rev. ed. by Kurt Ruh with Gundolf Keil, Werner Schröder, Burghart Wachinger, Franz Josef Worstbrock. Berlin and New York: de Gruyter.

Die deutsche Literatur im späten Mittelalter 1250–1370. 1987. Ed. Ingeborg Glier. Geschichte der deutschen Literatur von den Anfängen bis zur Gegenwart, ed. Helmut de Boor and Richard Newald, III 2. München: Beck.

Dictionary of Theology. 1985. Ed. Karl Rahner and Herbert Vorgrimler. 2nd ed. New York: Crossroad.

Dictionnaire de spiritualité ascétique et mystique, doctrine et histoire. 1937–1994. Ed. Marcel Viller, F.Cavallera, J. de Guibert, et al. Paris: Beauchesne.

Dictionnaire de théologie catholique. 1930–1972. [1st ed. 1902.] 3rd ed. by Bernard Loth and Albert Michel. 15 vols. Paris: Le Touzey et Ane.

Dinzelbacher, Peter. 1979a. "Klassen und Hierarchien im Jenseits." In *Soziale Ordnungen im Selbstverständnis des Mittelalters,* ed. Albert Zimmermann, pp. 20–40. Miscellanea Mediaevalia 12.1. Berlin and New York: de Gruyter.

—. 1979b. "Reflexionen irdischer Sozialstrukturen in mittelalterlichen Jenseitsschilderungen." *Archiv für Kulturgeschichte* 61:16–34.

—. 1979c. Review of Walter Blank, *Mystik am Oberrhein. OGE* 53: 118–121.

—. 1981. *Vision und Visionsliteratur im Mittelalter.* Monographien zur Geschichte des Mittelalters 23. Stuttgart: Hiersemann.

—. 1982a. "Das Christusbild der hl. Lutgard von Tongeren im Rahmen der Frauenmystik und Bildkunst des 12. und 13. Jahrhunderts." *OGE* 56: 217–277.

—. 1982b. Review of Ringler: *Viten- und Offenbarungsliteratur. ZfdA* 111:63–71.

—. 1983. "Katharina von Gebersweiler (Gueberschwihr)." *Verflex* 4:1073–1075.

—. 1985a. "Europäische Frauenmystik des Mittelalters. Ein Überblick" and "Kleiner Exkurs zur feministischen Diskussion." In *Frauenmystik,* pp. 11–23 and 391–393.

—. 1985b. "Körperliche und seelische Vorbedingungen religiöser Träume und Visionen." In *I Sogni nel medioevo,* ed. Tullio Gregory, pp. 57–86. Rome: Edizione dell' Ateneo.

—. 1985c. "Mittelalterliche Vision und moderne Sterbeforschung." In *Psychologie in der Mediävistik (Steinheimer Symposion),* ed. Jürgen Kühnel et al., pp. 9–49. GAG 431. Göppingen: Kümmerle

—. 1986. "Engelt(h)al." *LexMA* 3:1922f.

—. 1987. "Pour une histoire de l'amour au moyen âge." *Le Moyen-Age* 93:223–240.

—. 1988a. "Zur Interpretation erlebnismystischer Texte des Mittelalters." *ZfdA* 117:1–23.

—. 1988b. "Rollenverweigerung, religiöser Aufbruch und mystisches Erleben mittelalterlicher Frauen." In *Religiöse Frauenbewegung,* pp. 1–58.

—. 1989a. "Einführung." In *Mittelalterliche Visionsliteratur. Eine Anthologie.* Selected, trans., introd. and commentary by Peter Dinzelbacher, pp. 1–32. Darmstadt: Wissenschaftliche Buchgesellschaft.

—. 1989b. "Ötenbacher Schwesternbuch." *Verflex* 7:170–172.

—. 1990. "Mittelalterliche Religiosität." *Zeitschrift für Literaturwissenschaft und Linguistik* 80:14–34.

—. 1993. *Mittelalterliche Frauenmystik.* Paderborn: Schöningh.

Dumoutet, Edouard. 1926. *Le Désir de voir l'hostie et les origines de la dévotion au Saint-Sacrement.* Paris: Beauchesne.

Dupriez, Bernard. 1991. *A Dictionary of Literary Devices: Gradus, A-Z.* Trans. Albert W. Halsale. Toronto and Buffalo: Toronto University Press.

Elm, Kaspar. 1980a. "Ketzer oder fromme Frauen? Das Beginentum im europäischen Mittelalter." *Journal für Geschichte* 2:42–46.

—. 1980b. "Verfall und Erneuerung des Ordenswesens im Spätmittelalter. Forschungen und Forschungsaufgaben." In *Untersuchungen zu Kloster und Stift,* pp. 188–238. Veröffentlichungen des Max Planck-Instituts für Geschichte 68.14. Göttingen: Vandenhoeck & Ruprecht.

—. 1981. "Die Stellung der Frau in Ordenswesen, Semireligiosentum und Häresie zur Zeit der heiligen Elisabeth." In *Sankt Elisabeth–Fürstin Dienerin Heilige,* pp. 7–28. Sigmaringen: Thorbecke. [See also *Communio* 11 (1982) 360–379.]

Encyclopedic Dictionary of Religion. 1979. Ed. Paul Kevin Meagher et al. Washington DC: Corpus Publications.

Engelsing, Rolf. 1973. *Analphabetentum und Lektüre. Zur Sozialgeschichte des Lesens in Deutschland zwischen feudaler und industrieller Gesellschaft.* Stuttgart: Metzler.

Ennen, Edith. 1985. *Frauen im Mittelalter.* [1st ed. 1984]. München: Beck.

Erzberger, Matthias. 1902. *Die Säkularisation in Württemberg von 1802–1810. Ihr Verlauf und ihre Nachwirkungen.* Stuttgart: Deutsches Volksblatt.

Escherich, Mela. 1916. "Das Visionenwesen in den mittelalterlichen Frauenklöstern." *Deutsche Psychologie* 1:153–166.

Farmer, Sharon. 1985. "Personal Perceptions, Collective Behavior: Twelfth Century Suffrages for the Dead." In *Persons in Groups: Social Behavior as Identity Formation in Medieval and Renaissance Europe,* ed. Richard C. Trexler, pp. 231–239. Medieval and Renaissance Texts and Studies 36. Binghamton, NY: SUNY Press.

Fechter, Werner. 1983. "Meyer, Johannes OP." *Verflex* 6:474–489.

La Femme au moyen-âge. 1990. Ed. Michel Rouche and Jean Heuclin. Maubeuge: Touzot.

Ferrante, Joan M. 1980. "The Education of Women in the Middle Ages in Theory, Fact, and Fantasy." In *Beyond Their Sex: Learned Women of the European Past,* ed. Patricia H. Labalme, pp. 9–42. New York and London: New York University Press.

Fontette, Micheline de. 1967. "Les Dominicaines." In Micheline de Fontette, *Les Religieuses à l'âge classique du droit canon,* pp. 89–127. Bibliothèque de la Société d'Histoire Ecclésiastique de la France. Paris: Vrin.

Fox-Genovese, Elizabeth. 1987. "Culture and Consciousness in the Intellectual History of European Women." *Signs* 12:529–547.

Frank, Isnard Wilhelm. 1984. *Kirchengeschichte des Mittelalters.* Leitfaden Theologie 14. Düsseldorf: Patmos.

Frauenmystik im Mittelalter. 1985. Ed. Peter Dinzelbacher and Dieter R. Bauer. Ostfildern bei Stuttgart: Schwabenverlag.

Freed, John B. 1972. "Urban Development and the *cura monialium* in 13th Century Germany." *Viator* 3:311–327.

—. 1977. *The Friars and German Society in the Thirteenth Century.* Cambridge, Mass.: Medieval Academy of America.

Frei-Kundert, K. 1929. "Zur Baugeschichte des Klosters Katharinental." *Thurgauische Beiträge zur vaterländischen Geschichte* 66:1–150.

Fromm, Hans. 1989. "Die mittelalterliche Handschrift und die Wissenschaften vom Mittelalter." In Hans Fromm, *Arbeiten zur deutschen Literatur des Mittelalters,* pp. 349–366. Tübingen: Niemeyer. [Repr. from *Mitteilungen der Staatsbibliothek Preussischer Kulturbesitz* 8.2 (1976) 35–62.]

Galbraith, Georgina R. 1925. *The Constitution of the Dominican Order 1216 to 1360.* Manchester: Manchester University Press.

Gardini, Walter. 1987. "The Feminine Aspect of God in Christianity." In *Women in the World's Religions, Past and Present,* ed. Ursula King, pp. 56–67. New York: Paragon House.

Gehring, Hester [McNeal] Reed. 1957. *The Language of Mysticism in South German Dominican Convent Chronicles of the Fourteenth Century.* Diss., University of Michigan.

Geith, Karl-Ernst. 1980/81. "Elisabeth Kempf (1415–1485), Priorin und Uebersetzerin in Unterlinden zu Colmar." *Annuaire de la Société d'Histoire de Colmar* 29: 47–73.

—. 1983. "Kempf, Elisabeth." *Verflex* 4:1115–1117.

—. 1984. "Elisabeth Kempfs Uebersetzung und Fortsetzung der *Vitae Sororum* der Katharina von Gueberschwihr." *Annuaire de la Société d'Histoire de Colmar* 32:27–42.

—. 1986. "Zur Textgeschichte der *Vitae Sororum* (Unterlindener Schwesternbuch) der Katharina von Gueberschwihr." *Mittellateinisches Jahrbuch* 21: 230–238.

Gérold, Théodore. 1931. *Les Pères de l'Eglise et la Musique* [1st ed. Strasbourg]. Geneva: Minkoff 1973.

Gieraths, Gundolf Maria. 1956. *Reichtum des Lebens. Die deutsche Dominikanermystik des 14. Jahrhunderts.* Für Glauben und Leben 6. Düsseldorf: Albertus Magnus Verlag. English ed.: *Life in Abundance. Meister Eckhart and the German Dominican Mystics of the 14th Century. Spirituality Today* 38 (1986) Supplement [Repr. of "Spiritual Riches," trans. Edward Schuster and Sr. Mary of the Immaculate Heart, *Cross and Crown* 14 (1962) and 15 (1963)].

Glasser, Marc. 1981. "Marriage in Medieval Hagiography." *Studies in Medieval and Renaissance History* n.s. 4:1–34.

Glente, Karen. 1988a. "Katherina von Unterlinden." In *Mein Herz schmilzt,* pp. 176–190.

—. 1988b. "Mystikerinnenviten aus männlicher und weiblicher Sicht: Ein Vergleich zwischen Thomas von Cantimpré und Katherina von Unterlinden." In *Religiöse Frauenbewegung,* pp. 251–264.

Göpfert, Dieter. 1978. *Orden und Klöster im Schwarzwald.* Freiburg: Rombach.

Gössmann, Elisabeth. 1979. "Anthropologie und soziale Stellung der Frau nach Summen und Sentenzenkommentaren des 13. Jahrhunderts." In *Soziale Ordnungen im Selbstverständnis des Mittelalters,* ed. Albert Zimmermann, pp. 281–297. Miscellanea Mediaevalia 12.1. Berlin: de Gruyter.

—. 1987. "Wie könnte Frauenforschung im Rahmen der Katholischen Kirche aussehen?" *Eichstätter Hochschulreden* 57:3–25.

—. 1988a. "Himmel ohne Frauen? Zur Eschatologie des weiblichen Menschseins in östlicher und westlicher Religion." In *Das Gold im Wachs.* ed. Elisabeth Gössmann and Günter Zobel, pp. 397–426. München: Iudicium.

—. 1988b. "The Image of the Human Being according to Scholastic Theology and the Reaction of Contemporary Women." *Ultimate Reality and Meaning* 11:183–195.

—. 1989a. "Glanz und Last der Tradition. Ein theologiegeschichtlicher Durchblick." In *Mann und Frau: Grundproblem theologischer Anthropologie,* ed. Elisabeth Gössmann, Karl Lehmann, et al., pp. 25–52. Freiburg: Herder.

—. 1989b. "Mariologische Entwicklungen im Mittelalter. Frauenfreundliche und frauenfeindliche Aspekte." In *Maria: für alle Frauen oder über allen Frauen,* ed. Elisabeth Gössmann and Dieter R. Bauer, pp. 63–85. Freiburg: Herder.

—. 1990. "Reflexionen zur mariologischen Dogmengeschichte." In *Maria–Abbild oder Vorbild?* pp. 19–36.

—. 1991. "The Construction of Women's Difference in the Christian Theological Tradition." *Concilium* 188:50–59.

Goodich, Michael. 1981. "The Contours of Female Piety in Later Medieval Hagiography." *Church History* 50:20–33.

—. 1982. *Vita perfecta:The Ideal of Sainthood in the Thirteenth Century.* Monographien zur Geschichte des Mittelalters 25. Stuttgart: Hiersemann.

—. 1989. *From Birth to Old Age. The Human Life Cycle in Medieval Thought, 1250–1350.* Lanham, New York and London: University Press of America.

Gorce, M.-M. 1937. "Rosaire." *DThC* 13.2:2902–2911.

Graber, Rudolf. 1957. "Christina Ebner von Engeltal." *Historische Blätter für Stadt- und Landkreis Eichstätt* 6:1–3.

Grabmann, Martin. 1910/11. "Deutsche Mystik im Kloster Engelthal." *Sammelblatt des Historischen Vereins Eichstätt* 25/26:33–34.

—. 1923. *Kulturwerte der deutschen Mystik des Mittelalters.* Augsburg: Filser.

—. 1926. *Mittelalterliches Geistesleben. Abhandlungen zur Geschichte der Scholastik und Mystik.* München: Hueber.

Graf, Klaus. 1984. "Nonnenviten aus Kloster Gotteszell bei Schwäbisch-Gmünd. Zum Entstehungsort des sogenannten 'Ulmer Schwesternbuchs'." *Rottenburger Jahrbuch für Kirchengeschichte* 3:191–195.

Greenhill, Eleanor S. 1971. "The Group of Christ and St. John as Author Portrait: Literary Sources, Pictorial Parallels." In *Festschrift Bernhard Bischoff*, ed. Johanne Autenrieth and Franz Brunhölzl, pp. 406–416. Stuttgart: Hiersemann.

Greith, Carl Johann. 1860. "Heinrich Suso und seine Schule unter den Ordensschwestern von Töß bei Winterthur im vierzehnten Jahrhundert." *Katholische Schweizer Blätter* 2:65–77, 137–151, 399–416.

—. 1861. *Die deutsche Mystik im Prediger-Orden (von 1250–1350) nach ihren Grundlehren, Liedern und Lebensbildern aus handschriftlichen Quellen.* [1st ed. Freiburg i.B.] Amsterdam: Rodopi 1965.

Greven, Joseph. 1912. *Die Anfänge der Beginen. Ein Beitrag zur Geschichte der Volksfrömmigkeit und des Ordenswesens im Hochmittelalter.* Vorreformationsgeschichtliche Forschungen 8. Münster: Aschendorff.

Gropper, A. 1983. "Brauchtum in unserem Kloster." In *750 Jahre Dominikanerinnenkloster*, pp. 83–90.

Grubmüller, Klaus. 1969. "Die Viten der Schwestern zu Töss und Elsbeth Stagel (Überlieferung und Einheit)." *ZfdA* 98:171–204.

—. 1980. "Dießenhofener Schwesternbuch." *Verflex* 2:93–95.

—. 1986. "Einführung: Frauenmystik im Mittelalter." In *Abendländische Mystik*, pp. 347–353.

Grundmann, Herbert. 1931. "Zur Geschichte der Beginen im 13. Jahrhundert." *Archiv für Kulturgeschichte* 21:296–320.

—. 1934. "Die geschichtlichen Grundlagen der Deutschen Mystik." *DVJS* 12: 400–429.

—. 1935. *Religiöse Bewegungen im Mittelalter. Untersuchungen über die geschichtlichen Zusammenhänge zwischen der Ketzerei, den Bettelorden und der religiösen Frauenbewegung im 12. und 13. Jahrhundert und über die geschichtlichen Grundlagen der Mystik.* Historische Studien 267. Berlin: Ebering. (Rev. ed. repr. Hildesheim: Olms, 1961, 1977).

—. 1936. "Die Frauen und die Literatur im Mittelalter. Ein Beitrag zur Frage nach der Entstehung des Schrifttums in der Volkssprache." *Archiv für Kulturgeschichte* 26:129–161.

—. 1978. *Ausgewählte Aufsätze.* Schriften der Monumenta Germaniae Historica 25.3. Stuttgart: Hiersemann. See esp. "Jubel" [1954], pp. 130–162; and "*Litteratus–illiteratus*" [1958], pp. 1–66.

Günter, Heinrich. 1906. *Legenden-Studien.* Köln: Bachem.

—. 1910. *Die christliche Legende des Abendlandes.* Religionswissenschaftliche Bibliothek 2. Heidelberg: Winter.

Gurevich, Aron. 1990. *Medieval Popular Culture. Problems of Belief and Perception*. [1st Russian ed. 1987] Trans. Janos M.Bak and Paul A. Hollingsworth. Cambridge Studies in Oral and Literary Culture 14. Cambridge and New York: Cambridge University Press.

Haas, Alois Maria. 1983. "Traum und Traumvision in der deutschen Mystik." In *Spätmittelalterliche geistliche Literatur in der Nationalsprache*, Analecta Cartusiana 106, pp. 22–55. Salzburg: Institut für Anglistik.

—. 1984a. *Geistliches Mittelalter* (Dokimion). Fribourg, Switzerland: Universitätsverlag.

—. 1984b. "Die deutsche Mystik im Spannungsbereich von Theologie und Spiritualität." In *Literatur und Laienbildung im Spätmittelalter und in der Reformationszeit*, ed. Ludger Grenzmann and Karl Stackmann (Symposion Wolfenbüttel 1981), pp. 604–642. Stuttgart: Metzler.

—. 1986. "Was ist Mystik?" In *Abendländische Mystik*, pp. 319-341.

—. 1987a. "Deutsche Mystik." In *Die deutsche Literatur im späten Mittelalter*, pp. 234–305 and 485–496.

—. 1987b. "Schools of Late Medieval Mysticism." In *Christian Spirituality*, pp. 140–175.

—. 1988. "Schreibweisen der Frauenmystik." In *Deutsche Literatur: Eine Sozialgeschichte*, pp. 357–366.

—. 1989a. "Die Beurteilung der Vita contemplativa und activa in der Dominikanermystik des 14. Jahrhunderts." In Alois Maria Haas, *Gottleiden–Gottlieben: Zur volkssprachlichen Mystik im Mittelalter*, pp. 97–108. Frankfurt/Main: Insel.

—. 1989b. *Todesbilder im Mittelalter. Fakten und Hinweise in der deutschen Literatur*. Darmstadt: Wissenschaftliche Buchgesellschaft.

Hafner, A. 1879. "Das ehemalige Kloster des Dominikaner Ordens an der Tössbrücke. Eine kunsthistorische Studie." *Neujahrsblatt von der Stadtbibliothek Winterthur*. [Sonderdruck.]

Hale, Rosemary Drage. 1989. "For Counsel and Comfort: The Depiction of Friendship in 14th Century German Convent Literature." *Word and Spirit: A Monastic Review* 11:93–103.

—. 1992. "*Imitatio Mariae*: Motherhood Motifs in Late Medieval German Spirituality." Diss. Harvard. [Typescript.]

Halter, Annemarie. 1956. *Geschichte des Dominikanerinnenklosters Oetenbach in Zürich 1234–1525*. Winterthur: Keller.

Hamburger, Jeffrey F. 1990. *The Rothschild Canticles: Art and Mysticism in Flanders and the Rhineland circa 1300*. New Haven and London: Yale University Press.

Hammerstein, Reinhold. 1962. *Die Musik der Engel. Untersuchungen zur Musikanschauung des Mittelalters*. Bern and München: Francke.

Hartung, Wolfgang. 1982. *Die Spielleute. Eine Randgruppe in der Gesellschaft des Mittelalters*. Vierteljahrheft für Sozial- und Wirtschaftsgeschichte, Beihefte 72. Wiesbaden: Steiner.

Hauber, A. 1914. "Deutsche Handschriften in Frauenklöstern des späteren Mittelalters." *Zentralblatt für Bibliothekswesen* 31:341–373.

Hauck, Albert. 1911. *Kirchengeschichte Deutschlands*. [1st ed. 1887.] Leipzig: Hinrichs. Vol. 5.1.

Haussherr, Reiner. 1975. "Über die Christus-Johannes-Gruppen. Zum Problem 'Andachtsbilder' und deutsche Mystik." In *Beiträge zur Kunst des Mittelalters: Festschrift für Hans Wentzel*, pp. 79–103. Berlin: Gebr. Mann.

Heer, Gottlieb Heinrich. 1947. *Das Kloster Töß*. Beilage zur Jubiläumsschrift, Maschinenfabrik Winterthur-Töß 1795–1845. Winterthur.

—. 1961. *Das Kloster Töß*. Winterthur-Töß: Rieter.

Hefele, Friedrich. 1934. "Die Stifter des Adelhauser Klosters. Ein Beitrag zu seiner Geschichte anläßlich der 700-Jahrfeier." *Schau-ins-Land*: 21–29.

Heiler, Anne Marie. 1929. *Mystik deutscher Frauen im Mittelalter*. Berlin: Hochweg.

Henggeler, Rudolf. 1934. "Das Dominikanerinnenkloster Töss: 1233–19. Dezember 1933." *Diaspora-Kalender* 34:29–35.

Herlihy, David. 1990. *Opera muliebria: Women and Work in Medieval Europe*. New York and Toronto: McGraw-Hill.

Heusinger, Christian v. 1959. "Spätmittelalterliche Buchmalerei in oberrheinischen Frauenklöstern." *Zeitschrift für die Geschichte des Oberrheins* 107: 136–160.

Hinnebusch, William A. 1966/1973. *The History of the Dominican Order. I: Origins and Growth to 1500; II: Intellectual and Cultural Life to 1500*. 2 vols. Staten Island, NY: Alba House.

—. 1967. "Rosary." *NCE* 12:667–670.

Honemann, Volker. 1983. "Klostergründungsgeschichten." *Verflex* 2:1239–1247.

Illmer, Detlef. 1971. *Formen der Erziehung und Wissensvermittlung im frühen Mittelalter*. Münchner Beiträge zur Mediävistik und Renaissance-Forschung 7. München: Arbeo.

Images of Sainthood in Medieval Europe. 1991. Ed. Renate Blumenfeld-Kosinski and Thea Szell. Ithaca and London: Cornell University Press.

Jarrett, Bede. 1921. *The English Dominicans*. London: Burns, Oates & Washbourne.

—, ed. 1924. See Primary Sources: *Vitae fratrum*.

Johnson, Penelope D. 1989. "*Mulier et Monialis*: The Medieval Nun's Self-Image." *Thought* 64:242–253.

Jones, Rufus Matthew. 1939. *The Flowering of Mysticism. The Friends of God in the Fourteenth Century*. New York: Macmillan. Repr. New York: Hafner 1971.

Jostes, Franz. 1895. "Einleitung." In *Meister Eckhart und seine Jünger. Ungedruckte Texte zur Geschichte der deutschen Mystik*, ed. Franz Jostes, pp. xvi–xxvi. Collectanea Friburgensia 4. Freiburg (Switzerland): Commissionsverlag.

Jung, Carl Gustav. 1958. *Psychology and Religion. East and West.* Trans. R.F.C. Hull. London: Routledge & Kegan Paul.

—. 1980. *The Symbolic Life: Miscellaneous Writings* [1st ed. 1950]. Trans. R.F.C. Hull. Bollingen Series 20. Princeton: Princeton University Press.

Kieckhefer, Richard. 1984. *Unquiet Souls: Fourteenth Century Saints and Their Religious Milieu.* Chicago: Chicago University Press.

—. 1987. "Major Currents in Late Medieval Devotion." In *Christian Spirituality,* pp. 75–108.

—. 1990. *Magic in the Middle Ages.* (Cambridge Medieval Textbooks.) New York and Cambridge: Cambridge University Press.

Kirchberger, Claire. 1930. "A Forgotten Dominican Convent: Oetenbach, Zürich." *Dublin Review* 187:251–269.

Kirchhoff, Albrecht. 1853. *Die Handschriftenhändler des Mittelalters.* Leipzig: Teubner. Repr. New York: Franklin 1971.

Knapp, Fritz Peter. 1987. "Die Literatur von der Mitte des 13. bis zur Mitte des 14. Jahrhunderts (ca. 1250–ca.1350)." In *Handbuch der Literatur in Bayern vom Frühmittelalter bis zur Gegenwart: Geschichte und Interpretationen,* ed. Albrecht Weber, pp. 41–45. Regensburg: Pustet.

Knoepfli, Albert. 1989. *Die Kunstdenkmäler des Kantons Thurgau. Vol.IV: Das Kloster Katharinenthal.* Ed. Gesellschaft für Schweizerische Kulturge-schichte, Bern. Basel: Wiesel.

Koch, Gottfried. 1962. *Frauenfrage und Ketzertum im Mittelalter. Die Frauen-bewegung im Rahmen des Katharismus und des Waldensertums und ihre so-zialen Wurzeln (12.–14. Jahrhundert).* Forschungen zur mittelalterlichen Ge-schichte 9. Berlin: Akademieverlag.

Köhler, Oskar. 1982. *Kleine Glaubensgeschichte. Christsein im Wandel der Welt-zeit.* Herderbücherei 987. Freiburg: Herder.

König, J. 1878. "Zur Geschichte der Freiburger Klöster." *FDA* 12:291–303.

—, ed. 1880. See Primary Sources: Adelhausen.

Kolb, Gerhard M. 1977. "Das Dominikanerinnenkloster Gotteszell, eine Grün-dung der Stauferzeit." In *Die Staufer und Schwäbisch Gmünd,* ed. Stadt-archiv Schwäbisch Gmünd, pp. 95–128. Schwäbisch Gmünd: Einhorn.

Kramer, Dewey Weiss. 1991. "'Arise and Give the Convent Bread': Christine Ebner, the Convent Chronicle of Engelthal, and the Call to Ministry among Fourteenth Century Religious Women." In *Women as Protagonists,* pp. 187–207.

Krauss, R. 1894. "Geschichte des Dominikanerinnenklosters Kirchberg." *Würt-tembergische Vierteljahreshefte für Landesgeschichte* n.s. 3:291–332.

Krebs, Engelbert. 1904. "Die Mystik in Adelhausen. Eine vergleichende Studie über die Chronik der Anna von Munzingen und die thaumatographische Liter-atur des 13. und 14. Jahrhunderts als Beitrag zur Geschichte der Mystik im Predigerorden." In *Festgabe Heinrich Finke,* pp. 41–105. Münster: Aschendorff.

—. 1953. "Stagelin, Elsbeth." In *Die deutsche Literatur des Mittelalters – Verfasser-lexikon.* [1st ed.], ed. Wolfgang Stammler and Karl Langosch, 4: 256–258. Berlin: de Gruyter.

Kunze, Georg. 1952. "Studien zu den Nonnenviten des deutschen Mittelalters. Ein Beitrag zur religiösen Literatur im Mittelalter." Diss. Hamburg.

Kurras, Lotte. 1974. *Kataloge des Germanischen Nationalmuseums Nürnberg: Die deutschen mittelalterlichen Handschriften. I: Die literarischen und religiösen Handschriften.* Wiesbaden: Harrassowitz.

Langer, Otto. 1982. "Enteignete Existenz und mystische Erfahrung. Zu Meister Eckharts Auseinandersetzung mit der Frauenmystik seiner Zeit." In *So predigent etelîche. Beiträge zur deutschen und niederländischen Predigt im Mittelalter,* ed. Kurt Otto Seidel, pp. 49–96. GAG 378. Göppingen: Kümmerle.

—. 1985a. "Zur dominikanischen Frauenmystik im spätmittelalterlichen Deutschland." In *Frauenmystik,* pp. 341-346.

—. 1985b. "'We ist ein gut wort, we ist ein gnadenrichez wort.' Zur Spirituali-tät der Dominikanerinnen im Spätmittelalter." In *Lerne leiden,* pp. 21–34.

—. 1987. *Mystische Erfahrung und spirituelle Theologie. Zu Meister Eckharts Auseinandersetzung mit der Frauenfrömmigkeit seiner Zeit.* München and Zürich: Artemis.

Lechner, Gregor Martin. 1981. *Maria gravida: Zum Schwangerschaftsmotiv in der bildenden Kunst.* Zürich: Schnell & Steiner.

Leclercq, Jean. 1961. *The Love of Learning and the Desire for God.* [1st French ed. 1957.] Trans. Catherine Misrahi. New York: Fordham University Press.

—. 1981a. "Medieval Feminine Monasticism: Reality Versus Romantic Images." In *Benedictus,* ed. E. Rozanne Elder, pp. 53–70. CS 67. Kalamazoo, MI: Cistercian Publications.

—. 1981b. "La Clôture." *Collectanea Cisterciensia* 43:366–376.

—. 1981c. "L'Amour et le Mariage vus par des clercs et des religieux, spéciale-ment au XIIe siècle." In *Love and Marriage,* pp. 102–115.

—. 1982a. "Feminine Monasticism in the Twelfth and Thirteenth Centuries." In *The Continuing Quest for God,* pp. 114–126.

—. 1982b. "The Spirituality of Medieval Feminine Monasticism." In *The Continuing Quest for God,* pp. 127–138.

—. 1989. "Friendship and Friends in the Monastic Life." *Cistercian Studies* 24:293–300.

—. 1990. "Rôle et Pouvoir des épouses au moyen-âge." In *La Femme au moyen-âge,* pp. 87–97.

Lecouteux, Claude. 1981. "Introduction à l'étude du merveilleux médiévale." *Etudes Germaniques* 36:274–290.

Leff, Gordon. 1967. *Heresy in the Later Middle Ages: The Relation of Heterodoxy to Dissent c. 1250-1450.* Manchester: Manchester University Press; New York: Barnes & Noble.

—. 1976. *The Dissolution of the Medieval Outlook: An Essay on Intellectual and Spiritual Change in the Fourteenth Century*. New York: New York University Press.

Le Goff, Jacques. 1984. *The Birth of Purgatory* [1st French ed. 1981]. Trans. Arthur Goldhammer. Chicago: Chicago University Press.

Lerne leiden. Leidensbewältigung in der Mystik. 1985. Ed. Wolfgang Böhme. Herrenalber Texte 67. Karlsruhe: Tron.

Lerner, Robert E. 1972. *The Heresy of the Free Spirit in the Later Middle Ages*. Berkeley and Los Angeles: University of California Press.

Leroy, Olivier. 1928. *Levitation: An Examination of the Evidence and Explanations*. London: Oates & Washbourne.

Lewis, Gertrud Jaron. 1984-88. "The Mystical *Jubilus*." *Vox Benedictina* 1:237-247; 3:327-337; 5:164-174.

—. 1989. "Mystisches Leben in den Frauenklöstern." In Gertrud Jaron Lewis, *Bibliographie zur deutschen Frauenmystik des Mittelalters*. Berlin: Erich Schmidt, pp. 290-324.

—. 1990. "Eine Einsiedelner Handschrift des 'Adelhausener Schwesternbuchs.'" *ZfdA* 119:332-336.

Lexikon des Mittelalters. 1977- . Ed. Gloria Avella-Widhalm, Liselotte Lutz, Roswith Mattejiet, Ulrich Mattejiet et al. München and Zürich: Artemis.

Lexikon für Theologie und Kirche. 1957-1968. [1st ed. 1930-1938.] 2nd rev. ed. by Josef Höfer, Karl Rahner et al. 14 vols. Freiburg i.B.: Herder. Repr. 1986.

Loë, Paulus v. 1918. "Einleitung." In *Johannes Meyer, Liber de viris illustribus Ordinis Praedicatorum*, ed. Paulus v. Loë, pp. 1-15. QFGD 12. Leipzig: Harrassowitz.

Löhr, Gabriel M. 1924. *Die Teutonia im 15. Jahrhundert. Studien und Texte vornehmlich zur Geschichte ihrer Reform*. QFGD 19. Leipzig: Harrassowitz.

—. 1930. "Die Gewohnheiten eines mitteldeutschen Dominikanerklosters aus der ersten Hälfte des 14. Jahrhunderts." *Archivum Fratrum Praedicatorum* 1:87-105.

Loomis, C. Grant. 1948. *White Magic. An Introduction to the Folklore of Christian Legend*. Cambridge, Mass.: The Mediaeval Academy of America.

Lotter, Friedrich. 1979. "Methodisches zur Gewinnung historiographischer Erkenntnisse aus hagiographischen Quellen." *Historische Zeitschrift* 229: 298-356.

Love and Marriage in the Twelfth Century. 1981. Ed. Willy van Hoecke and Andries Welkenhuzsen. Medievalia Lovaniensis 1.8. Leuven: Leuven University Press.

Lucas, Angela M. 1983. *Women in the Middle Ages: Religion, Marriage and Letters*. Brighton: Sussex.

Lüers, Grete. 1926. *Die Sprache der deutschen Mystik des Mittelalters im Werke der Mechthild von Magdeburg.* München: Reinhardt. Repr. Darmstadt: Wissenschaftliche Buchgemeinschaft 1966.

Lutz, Eckart Conrad. 1984. *Rhetorica divina. Mittelhochdeutsche Prologgebete und die rhetorische Kultur des Mittelalters.* Quellen und Forschungen zur Sprach- und Kulturgeschichte der Germanischen Völker 82, 206. Berlin and New York: de Gruyter.

Mandonnet, Pierre. 1944. *St. Dominic and His Work* [1st French ed. 1943]. Trans. Mary Benedicta Larkin. St.Louis and London: Herder.

Maria–Abbild oder Vorbild? Zur Sozialgeschichte mittelalterlicher Marienverehrung. 1990. Ed. Hedwig Röckelein, Claudia Opitz, and Dieter R. Bauer. Tübingen: Ed. diskord.

Mazal, Otto. 1983. "Review of *Graduale.*" *Codices manuscripti* 9:175-177.

McDonnell, Ernest W. 1969. *The Beguines and Beghards in Medieval Culture with Special Emphasis on the Belgian Scene.* [1st ed. 1954.] Repr. New York: Octagon Books.

McGuire, Brian Patrick. 1989a. "Holy Women and Monks in the Thirteenth Century: Friendship or Exploitation?" *Vox Benedictina* 6:343-373.

—. 1989b. "Purgatory, the Communion of Saints, and Medieval Change." *Viator* 20:61-84.

McLaughlin, Eleanor Commo. 1974. "Equality of Souls, Inequality of Sexes: Women in Medieval Theology." In *Religion and Sexism,* ed. Rosemary Radford Ruether, pp. 213-266. New York: Simon & Schuster.

—. 1975. "Christ My Mother: Feminine Naming and Metaphor in Medieval Spirituality." *St. Luke's Journal of Theology* 18:366-388.

—. 1976. "Les Femmes et l'Hérésie médiévale. Un problème dans l'histoire de la spiritualité." *Concilium* 111:73-90.

McNamara, Jo Ann. 1991. "The Need to Give: Suffering and Female Sanctity in the Middle Ages." In *Images of Sainthood,* pp. 199-221.

Medieval Women and the Sources of Medieval History. 1990. Ed. Joel T. Rosenthal. Athens and London: Georgia University Press.

Mein Herz schmilzt wie Eis am Feuer. Die religiöse Frauenbewegung des Mittelalters in Porträts. 1988. Ed. Johannes Thiele. Stuttgart: Kreuz Verlag.

Metz, René. 1954. *La Consécration des vierges dans l'église romaine: Etude d'histoire de la liturgie.* Paris: Université de Paris.

Meyer, Ruth, ed. 1995. See Primary Sources: Diessenhofen.

Michael, Emil. 1903. *Geschichte des deutschen Volkes.* Vol. 3: 156-211. Freiburg i.B.: Herder.

Möckershoff, Barbara. 1983. "Religiöses Brauchtum im Kloster." In *750 Jahre Dominikanerinnenkloster Heilig Kreuz Regensburg,* ed. Paul Mai, pp. 48-54 [with illustrations]. Kunstsammlungen des Bistums Regensburg 1. München and Zürich: Schnell & Steiner.

Monssen, Maria Magna. 1964. *Die Dominikanerinnen.* Orden der Kirche 7. Freiburg (Switzerland): Paulusverlag.

Morse, Ruth. 1991, *Truth and Convention in the Middle Ages: Rhetoric, Representation, and Reality.* Cambridge: Cambridge University Press.

Müller, Anneliese. 1971. "Studien zur Besitz- und Sozialgeschichte des Dominikanerinnenklosters St. Katharinental bei Dießenhofen". Diss. Tübingen.

Müller, Daniela. 1991. "Beginenmystik als ketzerische Frauentheologie?" In *Auf der Suche,* pp. 213-232.

Müller, Hans Peter. 1977/78. "Das Schwesternbuch von Kloster Kirchberg (1237-1305)." *Der Sülchgau* 21/22:42-56.

Münzel, Karl. 1933. "Mittelhochdeutsche Klostergründungsgeschichten des 14. Jahrhunderts." Diss. Berlin 1933. *Zeitschrift für bayrische Kirchengeschichte* 8 [special offprint].

Murphy, James J. 1971. "Introduction." In *Three Medieval Rhetorical Arts,* ed. J.J. Murphy, pp. vii-xxiii. Berkeley and Los Angeles: University of California Press.

—. 1974. *Rhetoric in the Middle Ages: A History of Rhetorical Theories from Saint Augustine to the Renaissance.* Berkeley and Los Angeles: University of California Press.

Muschg, Walter. 1935. *Die Mystik in der Schweiz 1200–1500.* Frauenfeld and Leipzig: Huber.

—. 1943. *Mystische Texte aus dem Mittelalter.* Klosterberg and Basel: Schwabe.

Neumann, Eva Gertrud. 1960. *Rheinisches Beginen- und Beghardenwesen. Ein Mainzer Beitrag zur religiösen Bewegung am Rhein.* Mainzer Abhandlungen zur mittleren und neueren Geschichte 4. Meisenheim am Glan: Hain.

Neunheuser, Burkhard. 1963. *Eucharistie in Mittelalter und Neuzeit.* Handbuch der Dogmengeschichte IV, 4b. Freiburg i.B.: Herder.

New Catholic Encyclopedia. 1967. Washington, DC.: The Catholic University of America; New York, etc.: McGraw-Hill.

Newman, Barbara. 1990. "Some Mediaeval Theologians and the Sophia Tradition.": *The Downside Review* 108 (no. 371):111-130.

—. 1992. "The Pilgrimage of Christ-Sophia." *Vox Benedictina* 9:9-37.

Noffke, Suzanne. 1990. "The Evolution of Dominican Life for Women." In *Common Life: In the Spirit of St. Dominic,* pp. 53-64. River Forest, IL: Parable.

Noonan, John T., Jr. 1973. "Marriage in the Middle Ages." *Viator* 4:419-434.

Ochsenbein, Peter. 1988a. "Leidensmystik in dominikanischen Frauenklöstern des 14. Jahrhunderts am Beispiel der Elsbeth von Oye." In *Religiöse Frauenbewegung,* pp. 353-372.

—. 1988b. "Deutschsprachige Privatgebetbücher vor 1400." In *Deutsche Handschriften 1100–1400,* ed. Volker Honemann and Nigel F. Palmer, pp. 379-398. Oxforder Kolloquium 1985. Tübingen: Niemeyer.

Oediger, Friedrich Wilhelm. 1953. *Über die Bildung der Geistlichen im späten Mittelalter*. Studien und Texte zur Geistesgeschichte des Mittelalters 2. Leiden and Köln: Brill.

Oehl, Wilhelm. 1924. "Einführung." In *Das Büchlein von der Gnaden Überlast von Christine Ebner*, ed. and trans. Wilhelm Oehl, pp. 5–18. Dokumente der Religion 11. Paderborn: Schöningh.

—. ed. 1931. *Deutsche Mystikerbriefe des Mittelalters 1100–1550*. Mystiker des Abendlandes 1. München: Georg Müller. Repr. Darmstadt: Wissenschaftliche Buchgesellschaft 1972.

Ohlenroth, Derk. 1992. "Darbietungsmuster in dominikanischen Schwesternbüchern aus der Mitte des 14. Jahrhunderts." In *Festschrift Walter Haug und Burghart Wachinger*, pp. 423–456. Tübingen: Niemeyer.

Ott, Norbert H. 1984. "Chronistik, Geschichtsepik, historische Dichtung." In *Epische Stoffe des Mittelalters*, ed. Volker Mertens and Ulrich Müller, pp. 182–204. Kröner Tb. 483. Stuttgart: Kröner.

Panofsky, Erwin. 1927. "Imago Dei." In *Festschrift für Max Friedländer*, pp. 261–308. Leipzig: Seemann.

Parisse, Michel. 1983. *Les Nonnes au moyen-âge*. Le Puy: Bonneton.

Patze, Hans. 1977. "Klostergründung und Klosterchronik." *Blätter für deutsche Landesgeschichte* 113:89–121.

Peters, Ursula. 1988a. "Frauenliteratur im Mittelalter? Überlegungen zur Trobairitzpoesie, zur Frauenmystik und zur feministischen Literaturbertachtung." *Germanisch-Romanische Monatsschrift* 38:35–56.

—. 1988b. *Religiöse Erfahrung als literarisches Faktum. Zur Vorgeschichte und Genese frauenmystischer Texte des 13. und 14. Jahrhunderts*. Tübingen: Niemeyer.

—. 1988c. "Nonnenbuch und Gnaden-Vita: mystische Vitenliteratur süddeutscher Dominikanerinnen im 14. Jahrhundert." In *Deutsche Literatur von Frauen*, ed. Gisela Brinker-Gabler, 1:99–105. München: Beck.

Petroff, Elizabeth Alvilda. 1979. *Consolation of the Blessed*. New York: Alta Gaia Society.

—. 1986. *Medieval Women's Visionary Literature*. New York and Oxford: Oxford University Press.

—. 1994. "Male Confessors and Female Penitents: Possibilities for Dialogue." In E.A. Petroff, *Body and Soul: Essays on Medieval Women and Mysticism*, pp. 139–160. New York and Oxford: Oxford University Press.

Pfister, Oskar. 1911. "Hysterie und Mystik bei Margaretha Ebner (1291–1351)." *Zentralblatt für Psychoanalyse* 1:468–485.

Pfister, Rudolf. 1964. "Die Klöster der Dominikanerinnen." In Rudolf Pfister, *Kirchengeschichte der Schweiz*, 1:279–300. Zürich: Zwingli Verlag.

Pfleger, Luzian. 1937. "Die Mystik im Kloster Unterlinden." *Annuaire de Colmar* 3:35–45.

Phillips, Dayton. 1941. *Beguines in Medieval Strasbourg: A Study of the Social Aspects of Beguine Life.* Stanford: Stanford University Press.

Pickering, Frederick P. 1980. "The Gothic Image of Christ: The Sources of Medieval Representations of the Crucifixion." In Frederick P. Pickering, *Essays on Medieval German Literature and Iconography,* pp. 3–30. Cambridge: Cambridge University Press. [Originally in: *Euphorion* 47 (1953).]

Power, Eileen. 1975. *Medieval Women.* Ed. M.M. Postan. Cambridge: Cambridge University Press.

Preger, Wilhelm. 1874–1893. *Geschichte der deutschen Mystik im Mittelalter nach den Quellen untersucht und dargestellt.* 3 parts, esp. 1:133–141 and 2: 247–306. Leipzig: Dörffling & Franke. Repr. Aalen: Zeller 1962.

Quint, Josef. 1958. "Mystik." In *Reallexikon der deutschen Literaturgeschichte,* ed. Paul Merker and Wolfgang Stammler, 2:544–568. Berlin: de Gruyter.

Rahner, Karl. 1948. "Über Visionen und verwandte Erscheinungen." *Geist und Leben* 21:179–213.

Rapp, Francis. 1985. "Zur Spiritualität in elsässischen Frauenklöstern am Ende des Mittelalters." In *Frauenmystik,* pp. 347–365.

Religiöse Frauenbewegung und mystische Frömmigkeit im Mittelalter. 1988. Ed. Peter Dinzelbacher and Dieter R. Bauer. Köln and Wien: Böhlau.

Richstätter, Carl. 1919. "Aus den Lebensbildern von Dominikanerinnen." In C. Richstätter, *Die Herz-Jesu-Verehrung des deutschen Mittelalters,* 2:170–174. Paderborn: Verlag Bonifacius-Druckerei.

Richter, Michael. 1976. "Kommunikationsprobleme im lateinischen Mittelalter." *Historische Zeitschrift* 222:43–80.

Ringbom, Sixten. 1969. "Devotional Images and Imaginative Devotions: Notes on the Place of Art in Late Medieval Piety." *Gazette des Beaux-Arts,* 6th series, 73:159–170.

—. 1980. "Some Pictorial Conventions for the Recounting of Thoughts and Experiences in Late Medieval Art." In *Medieval Iconography and Narrative: A Symposium,* ed. Flemming G. Andersen et al., pp. 38–69. Odense: Odense University Press.

Ringler, Siegfried. 1975. "Zur Gattung Legende. Versuch einer Strukturbestimmung der christlichen Heiligenlegende des Mittelalters." In *Würzburger Prosastudien II,* pp. 255–270.

—. 1980a. *Viten- und Offenbarungsliteratur in Frauenklöstern des Mittelalters. Quellen und Studien.* Münchener Texte und Untersuchungen 72. München and Zürich: Artemis.

—. 1980b. "Ebin (Eybin), Anna." *Verflex* 2:295–297.

—. 1980c. "Ebner, Christine." *Verflex* 2:297–302.

—. 1980d. "Elisabeth von Kirchberg." *Verflex* 2:479–482.

—. 1988. "Christine Ebner." In *Mein Herz schmilzt,* pp. 146–159.

—. 1990. "Gnadenviten aus süddeutschen Frauenklöstern des 14. Jahrhunderts. Vitenschreibung als mystische Lehre." In *"Minnichlichiu gotes erkennusse"*: *Studien zur frühen abendländischen Mystikinterpretation* (Symposium 1989), ed. Dietrich Schmidtke, pp. 89–104. Mystik in Geschichte und Gegenwart 1.7. Stuttgart-Bad Cannstatt: Frommann-holzboog.

Rode, Rosemarie. 1957. "Studien zu den mittelalterlichen Kind-Jesu- Visionen." Diss. Frankfurt/Main.

Rokseth, Yvonne. 1935. "Les Femmes Musiciennces du XIIe au XIVe siècle." *Romania* 61:464–480.

Roth, F.W.E. 1892. "Mittheilungen aus mittelhochdeutschen Handschriften und alten Drucken." *Germania* 37:191–201.

—, ed. 1893. See Primary Sources: Gotteszell and Kirchberg.

Rubin, Miri. 1991. *Corpus Christi. The Eucharist in Late Medieval Culture.* Cambridge: Cambridge University Press.

Ruh, Kurt. 1953. "Die trinitarische Spekulation in deutscher Mystik und Scholastik." *ZfdPh* 72:24–53.

—. 1956. *Bonaventura deutsch.* Bern: Francke.

—. 1957. "Altdeutsche Mystik. Ein Forschungsbericht." *Wirkendes Wort* 7:135–231.

—. 1978. "Geistliche Prosa." In *Europäisches Spätmittelalter (Neues Handbuch der Literaturgeschichte)*, ed. Willi Erzgräber, pp. 565–605. Wiesbaden: Athenaion.

—. 1981. "Deutsche Literatur im Benediktinerinnenkloster St. Andreas in Engelberg." *Titlis Grüße* 67:47–55 and 77–88.

—. 1982. *Vorbemerkungen zu einer neuen Geschichte der abendländischen Mystik im Mittelalter.* BAW 7. München: Bayerische Akademie der Wissenschaften.

—. 1985. "Überlieferungsgeschichte mittelalterlicher Texte als methodischer Ansatz zu einer erweiterten Konzeption von Literaturgeschichte." In *Überlieferungsgeschichtliche Prosaforschung*, ed. Kurt Ruh, pp. 262–272. Tübingen: Niemeyer.

The Rule of St. Benedict 1980. 1981. In Latin and English with notes. Ed. Timothy Fry. Collegeville, MN: Liturgical Press.

Salisbury, Joyce E. 1990. *Medieval Sexuality: A Research Guide.* New York and London: Garland.

—. 1991. *Church Fathers. Independent Virgins.* London and New York: Verso.

Sauer, Josef. 1928. "Mystik und Kunst unter besonderer Berücksichtigung des Oberrheins." *Jahrbuch der Görres-Gesellschaft* 1:3–28.

Scheeben, Heribert Christian. 1964. "Über die Predigtweise der deutschen Mystiker" [1st printed as "Zur Biographie Johannes Taulers" in 1961]. In *Altdeutsche und altniederländische Mystik*, ed. Kurt Ruh, pp. 100-112. Wege der Forschung 23. Darmstadt: Wissenschaftliche Buchgesellschaft.

Scheibelreiter, Georg. 1988. "Die Verfälschung der Wirklichkeit. Hagiographie und Historizität." In *Fälschungen im Mittelalter* [Internationaler Kongress der *Monumenta Germaniae Historica,* Proceedings 1986], pp. 283–319. Monumenta Germaniae Historica 33.5. Hannover: Hahn.

Schillebeeckx, Edward. 1983. "Dominican Spirituality." In Edward Schillebeeckx, *God Among Us, the Gospel Proclaimed,* pp. 232–248. New York: Crossroad.

Schipperges, Heinrich. 1990. *Die Kranken im Mittelalter.* 2nd ed. München: Beck.

Schleusener-Eichholz, Gudrun. 1985. "Äußere und innere Augen." In Gudrun Schleusener-Eichholz, *Das Auge im Mittelalter,* pp. 931–958. Münstersche Mittelalter-Schriften. München: Fink.

Schmaus, Michael. 1957–1962. *Katholische Dogmatik.* Rev. ed. Vols. 2.1; 4.1, 4.2. München: Hueber.

Schmid, Josefine. 1963. "Studien zu Wesen und Technik der Gegenwarts-Chronistik in der süddeutschen Historiographie des ausgehenden 13. und des 14. Jahrhunderts." Diss. Heidelberg.

Schmidt, Josef. 1985. "Introduction." In *Johannes Tauler. Sermons,* pp. 1–34. Trans. Maria Shrady. Pref. Alois M. Haas. New York/ Mahwah /Toronto: Paulist Press.

Schmidt, Wieland. 1930. "Ein Bücherverzeichnis des St. Katharinenklosters zu Nürnberg." *Zentralblatt für Bibliothekswesen* 47:161–168.

Schneider, Heinrich. 1941. "Die Adelhauser Handschriften des Erzb. Diözesanmuseums zu Freiburg i.B." *FDA* 69:132–148.

Schneider, Karin. 1965. *Die deutschen mittelalterlichen Handschriften.* Beschreibung des Buchschmucks Heinz Zirnbauer. In *Die Handschriften der Stadtbibliothek Nürnberg.* Vol. 1. Wiesbaden: Harrassowitz.

—. 1975. "Beziehungen zwischen den Dominikanerinnenklöstern Nürnberg und Altenhohenau im ausgehenden Mittelalter. Neue Handschriftenfunde." In *Würzburger Prosastudien II,* pp. 211–218.

—. 1983. "Die Bibliothek des Katharinenklosters in Nürnberg und die städtische Gesellschaft." In *Studien zum städtischen Bildungswesen des späten Mittelalters und der frühen Neuzeit* (Kolloquium 1978–81), ed. Bernd Moeller et al., pp. 70–82. Göttingen: Vandenhoeck & Ruprecht.

Schrade, Hubert. 1958. "Die Bilder und die Ungebildeten." In H. Schrade, *Vor- und frühromanische Malerei. Die karolingische, ottonische und frühsalische Zeit,* pp. 105–111. Köln: DuMont.

Schraut, Elisabeth. 1991. "Überlegungen zu den Möglichkeiten der Frauen im mittelalterlichen Kunstbetrieb am Beispiel Nürnberg." In *Auf der Suche,* pp. 81–114.

Schröder, Karl, ed. 1871. See Primary Sources: Engeltal.

Schulenburg, Jane Tibbetts. 1986. "The Heroics of Virginity. Brides of Christ and Sacrificial Mutilation." In *Women in the Middle Ages and the Renaissance. A Historical Perspective,* ed. Mary Beth Rose, pp. 29–72. Syracuse: Syracuse University Press.

—. 1990. "Saints' Lives as a Source for the History of Women, 500–1100." In *Medieval Women*, pp. 285–320.

Schwietering, Julius. 1954. "The Origins of the Medieval Humility Formula." *PMLA* 69:1279–1291.

Seifert, Petra. 1985. "Der Einfluß der 'Vitas Fratrum' auf das Tösser Schwesternbuch." MA-Thesis, München.

Shahar, Shulamith. 1981. *Die Frau im Mittelalter*. Trans. Ruth Achlama. Königstein i.T.: Athenäum.

750 Jahre Dominikanerinnenkloster Heilig Kreuz Regensburg 1233–1983. 1983. Ed. Dominikanerinnen Regensburg. Abensberg: Kral.

Söll, Georg. 1984. "Maria in der Geschichte von Theologie und Frömmigkeit." In *Handbuch der Marienkunde*, pp. 93–231. Regensburg: Pustet.

Southern, Richard William. 1970. *Western Society and the Church in the Middle Ages*. Harmondsworth: Penguin.

Spamer, Adolf. 1910. *Ueber die Zersetzung und Vererbung in den deutschen Mystikertexten*. Diss. Gießen.

Spiess, Emil. 1935. *Ein Zeuge mittelalterlicher Mystik in der Schweiz*. Rorschach: Weder.

Steer, Georg. 1987. "Geistliche Prosa." In *Die deutsche Literatur im späten Mittelalter*, ed. Glier, pp. 306–370 and 496–500.

Stoudt, Debra L. 1991. "'ich súndig wip muos schriben': Religious Women and Literary Tradition." In *Women as Protagonists*, pp. 147–168.

Strauch, Philipp. 1881. Review of J. König ed., Adelhausen. *Afda* 7:96.

Sulzer, Heinrich. 1903. "Bilder aus der Geschichte des Klosters Töß." *NeujahrsBlatt der Hülfsgesellschaft in Winterthur* 41 [Sonderdruck].

Sutter, Ludwig. 1893. *Die Dominikaner-Klöster auf dem Gebiete der heutigen Schweiz im dreizehnten Jahrhundert*. Diss. München. Luzern: Räber.

Tanz, Sabine and Ernst Werner. 1993. *Spätmittelalterliche Laienmentalitäten im Spiegel von Visionen, Offenbarungen und Prophezeiungen*, Beiträge zur Mentalitätsgeschichte 1. Frankfurt/Main, Berlin, Bern, New York: Peter Lang.

Taubert, Gesine and Johannes Taubert. 1969. "Mittelalterliche Kruzifixe mit schwenkbaren Armen: Ein Beitrag zur Verwendung von Bildwerken in der Liturgie." *Zeitschrift des Deutschen Vereins für Kunstwissenschaft* 223:79–121.

Thiele, Johannes. 1988. "Die religiöse Frauenbewegung des Mittelalters." In *Mein Herz schmilzt*, pp. 9–34.

Thompson, James Westfall. 1960. *The Literacy of the Laity in the Middle Ages*. New York: Franklin.

Thurston, Herbert. 1952. *The Physical Phenomena of Mysticism*. Ed. J.H. Crehan. London: Burns Oates.

Tipka, Ernst. 1989. "Subjekt und Text. Nonnenviten und Offenbarungsliteratur in Frauenklöstern des 14. Jahrhunderts." *Mediaevistik* 2:225–253.

Tobin, Rosemary Barton. 1974. "Vincent of Beauvais on the Education of Women." *Journal of the History of Ideas* 35:485–489.

Tuchman, Barbara W. 1978. *A Distant Mirror: The Calamitous Fourteenth Century.* New York: Ballantine Books.

Tugwell, Simon. 1982. *Early Dominicans. Selected Writings.* Ed. S. Tugwell. Pref. Vincent de Couesnongle. New York, Ramsey, Toronto: Paulist Press.

—. 1987. "The Mendicants: The Spirituality of the Dominicans." In *Christian Spirituality*, pp. 15–31.

Uhland, Robert. 1961. "Das Dominikanerinnenkloster zu Weil." in: "Die Esslinger Klöster im Mittelalter." *Eszlinger Studien* 8:13–16.

Uhrle, Susanne. 1968. *Das Dominikanerinnenkloster Weiler bei Esslingen (1230–1571/92).* Veröffentlichung der Kommission für geschichtliche Landeskunde in Baden-Württemberg B 49. Stuttgart: Kohlhammer.

Underhill, Evelyn. 1955. *Mysticism. A Study in the Nature and Development of Man's Spiritual Consciousness* [1st ed. 1910] New York: Noonday Press.

Unger, Helga. 1986. *Text und Bild im Mittelalter.* Schriften der Universitätsbibliothek Bamberg 2. Graz: Akademische Druck- und Verlagsanstalt.

Vagaggini, Cipriano. 1976. *Theological Dimensions of the Liturgy.* Collegeville, MN: Liturgical Press.

Vauchez, André. 1987. *Les Laïcs au moyen-âge. Pratiques et expériences religieuses.* Paris: du Cerf.

—. 1988. *La Sainteté en occident aux derniers siècles du moyen-âge d'après les procès de canonisation et les documents hagiographiques.* Bibliothèque des Ecoles Françaises d'Athènes et de Rome 241 [1st ed. 1981]. Rev. ed. Rome: Ecole Française.

Vavra, Elisabeth. 1985. "Bildmotiv und Frauenmystik—Funktion und Rezeption." In *Frauenmystik*, pp. 201–230.

Vernet, Felix. 1930. *Mediaeval Spirituality.* Trans. by the Benedictines of Talacre. Catholic Library of Religious Knowledge 13. London: Sands; St. Louis, MO: Herder.

Vetter, Ewald M. 1978. "Das Christus-Johannes-Bild der Mystik." In *Mystik am Oberrhein und in den benachbarten Gebieten*, pp. 37–50. Freiburg i.B.: Augustinermuseum.

Vetter, Ferdinand. 1882. "Ein Mystikerpaar des vierzehnten Jahrhunderts, Schwester Elsbeth Stagel in Töss und Vater Amandus (Suso) in Konstanz" [Vortrag]. *Öffentliche Vorträge gehalten in der Schweiz* 6. Basel: Schweighauser.

—, ed. 1906. See Primary Sources: Töss.

Vicaire, M.-H. 1964. *Saint Dominic and His Times* [1st ed. 1961]. Trans. Kathleen Pond. Green Bay, WI: Alt.

Völker, Paul-Gerhard. 1963. "Die Überlieferungsformen mittelalterlicher deutscher Predigten." *ZfdA* 92:212–227.

Vogt, Kari. 1985. "'Becoming Male': One Aspect of an Early Christian Anthropology." In *Women: Invisible in Theology and Church*, pp. 72–83.

Vogüé, Adalbert de. 1980. "The Evangelical Counsels in the Master and St. Benedict." *Cistercian Studies* 15:3–16.

Voit, Gustav. 1958. "Geschichte des Klosters Engelthal." Diss. Erlangen [Typescript].

—. 1977. *Engelthal. Geschichte eines Dominikanerinnenklosters im Nürnberger Raum*. Nürnberg: Korn & Berg.

Volksreligion im hohen und späten Mittelalter. 1990. Ed. Peter Dinzelbacher and Dieter R. Bauer. Quellen und Forschungen aus dem Gebiet der Geschichte 13. Paderborn, München, Wien, Zürich: Schöningh.

Volpert, Anneliese. 1971. "Christina Ebner 1277–1356." In *Fränkische Klassiker. Eine Literaturgeschichte in Einzeldarstellungen*, ed. Wolfgang Buhl, pp. 149–159. Nürnberg: Verlag Nürnberger Presse.

Wachtel, Hildegard. 1938. "Die liturgische Musikpflege im Kloster Adelhausen seit der Gründung des Klosters 1234 bis um 1500." *FDA* 66, n.s. 39:1–91.

Wallach-Faller, Marianne. 1986. "Ein mittelhochdeutsches Dominikanerinnen-Legendar." In *Abendländische Mystik*, pp. 388–401 and 470f.

Walz, Angelus. 1967. *Dominikaner und Dominikanerinnen in Süddeutschland (1225–1966)*. Meitingen: Kyrios.

Wattenbach, Wilhelm. 1958. *Das Schriftwesen im Mittelalter* [1st ed. 1871]. 4th ed. Graz: Akademische Druck-und Verlagsanstalt.

Weakland, R. G. 1967. "Music, Sacred, History of." *NCE* 10:105–109.

Wehofer, Thomas M. 1897. "Die Schrift des Gérard de Frachet, *Vitas fratrum OP*, eine noch unbenutzte Quelle zur Philosophiegeschichte des 13. Jahrhunderts." *Jahrbuch für Philosophie und spekulative Theologie* 11:17–41.

Wehrli, Max. 1980. "Schwesternleben." In M. Wehrli, *Geschichte der deutschen Literatur vom frühen Mittelalter bis zum Ende des 16. Jahrhunderts*, pp. 657–661. Stuttgart: reclam.

Wehrli-Johns, Martina. 1980. *Geschichte des Zürcher Predigerkonvents (1230–1524). Mendikantentum zwischen Kirche, Adel und Stadt*. Zürich: Rohr.

—. 1985. "Aktion und Kontemplation in der Mystik." In *Lerne leiden*, pp. 9–20.

—. 1986. "Maria und Martha in der religiösen Frauenbewegung." In *Abendländische Mystik*, pp. 354–367.

—. 1990. "Haushälterin Gottes. Zur Mariennachfolge der Beginen." In *Maria–Abbild oder Vorbild?*, pp. 147–167.

Weigand, Rudolf. 1981. "Liebe und Ehe bei den Dekretisten des 12. Jahrhunderts." In *Love and Marriage*, pp. 41–58.

Weinhandl, Margarete. 1921. "Einleitung." In M. Weinhandl, *Deutsches Nonnenleben: Das Leben der Schwestern zu Töss und der Nonne von Engeltal Büchlein von der Gnaden Überlast*, pp. 1–109. Katholikon 2. München: Recht.

Weinstein, Donald and Rudolph M. Bell. 1982. *Saints and Society: The Two Worlds of Western Christendom, 1000–1700.* Chicago: Chicago University Press.

Wentzel, Hans. 1947. *Die Christus-Johannes-Gruppen des 14. Jahrhunderts.* Berlin: Gebr. Mann (2nd ed. Stuttgart: reclam 1960).

—. 1954. "Christus-Johannes-Gruppe." In *Reallexikon zur deutschen Kunstgeschichte,* ed. Otto Schmitt et al., 3:658–669. Stuttgart: Druckenmüller.

—. 1959. "Unbekannte Christus-Johannes-Gruppen." *Zeitschrift für Kunstwissenschaft,* n.s. 13:155–176.

—. 1960. "*Ad infantiam Christi*–zu der Kindheit unseres Herrn." In *Das Werk des Künstlers, Hubert Schrade Festschrift,* pp. 134–160. Stuttgart: Kohlhammer.

Wentzlaff-Eggebert, Friedrich-Wilhelm. 1969. *Deutsche Mystik zwischen Mittelalter und Neuzeit. Einheit und Wandlung ihrer Erscheinungsformen* [1st ed. 1943]. 3rd rev. ed. Berlin: de Gruyter.

Williams-Krapp, Werner. 1986a. "Die monastische Rezeption." In W. Williams-Krapp, *Deutsche und niederländische Legendare des Mittelalters,* pp. 356–365. Tübingen: Niemeyer.

—. 1986b. "Ordensreform und Literatur im 15. Jahrhundert." *Jahrbuch der Oswald von Wolkenstein Gesellschaft* 4:41–51.

—. "Frauenmystik und Ordensreform." In *Literarische Interessenbildung im Mittelalter,* ed. Joachim Heinzle, pp. 301–313. Stuttgart and Weimar: Metzler.

Wilms, Hieronymus. 1920. *Geschichte der deutschen Dominikanerinnen 1206–1916.* Dülmen i.W.: Laumann.

—. 1923. *Das Beten der Mystikerinnen, dargestellt nach den Chroniken der Dominikanerinnenklöster zu Adelhausen, Dießenhofen, Engeltal, Kirchberg, Ötenbach, Töß, Unterlinden und Weiler.* 2nd.rev. ed. Freiburg i.B.: Herder.

—. 1928. *Das älteste Verzeichnis der deutschen Dominikanerinnenklöster* (QFGD 24.) Leipzig: Harrassowitz.

Winter, Irene. 1951. "Eucharistische Frömmigkeit mittelalterlicher Nonnen (ca. 1250–ca. 1350)." Diss. Marburg [Typescript].

Wittmer, Charles. 1946. *L'obituaire des Dominicaines d'Unterlinden: Edition critique du manuscrit 576 de la Bibliothèque de la Ville de Colmar.* Strasbourg and Zürich: Heitz.

Wörterbuch der Mystik. 1989. (Kröners Taschenausgabe 456.) Ed. Peter Dinzelbacher. Stuttgart: Kröner.

Women as Protagonists and Poets in the German Middle Ages: An Anthology of Feminist Approaches to Middle High German Literature. 1991. Ed. Albrecht Classen. GAG 528. Göppingen: Kümmerle.

Women: Invisible in Theology and Church. 1985. Ed. Elisabeth Schüssler Fiorenza and Mary Collins. Edinburgh: Clark.

Women Making Music. The Western Art Tradition, 1150–1950. 1986. Ed. Jane Bowers and Judith Tick. Urbana and Chicago: Illinois University Press.

Wuellner, Wilhelm. 1987. "Where is Rhetorical Criticism Taking Us?" *Catholic Biblical Quarterly* 49:448–463.

Würzburger Prosastudien II. Untersuchungen zur Literatur und Sprache des Mittelalters. 1975. (Medium Aevum 31.) Ed. Peter Kesting. München: Fink.

Wyschogrod, Edith. 1990. *Saints and Postmodernism. Revisioning Moral Philosophy.* Chicago and London: Chicago University Press.

Yardley, Anne Bagnall. 1986. "'*Ful weel she soong the service dyvyne*': The Cloistered Musician in the Middle Ages." In *Women Making Music*, pp. 15–38.

Zeller-Werdmüller, H., and Jakob Bächtold, ed. 1889. See Primary Sources: Oetenbach.

Zimmermann, Gerd. 1973. *Ordensleben und Lebensstandard. Die cura corporis in den Ordensvorschriften des abendländischen Hochmittelalters.* (Beiträge zur Geschichte des alten Mönchtums und des Benediktinerordens 32.) Münster: Aschendorff.

Zittard, Conrad. 1596. *Kurtze Chronica, Das ist Historische beschreibung (neben andern mercklichen Puncten) der General Maister Prediger Ordens vnd was zu eines jeden zeit für Fürnehme, Hochgelehrte, auch Heylige Bruder vnd Schwestern im Prediger Ordern gelebt haben.* Dillingen.

Zoepf, Ludwig. 1914. *Die Mystikerin Margaretha Ebner (c.1291–1351).* Beiträge zur Kulturgeschichte des Mittelalters und der Renaissance 16. Leipzig and Berlin: Teubner.

Index